2

*Assessment of Individual
Mental Ability*

Assessment of Individual Mental Ability

GEORGE P. ROBB
North Texas State University

The Late
L. C. BERNARDONI
The University of New Mexico

RAY W. JOHNSON
North Texas State University

INTEXT EDUCATIONAL PUBLISHERS
New York • *London*

The **Intext** Series in
Psychological Assessment

Consulting Editor
Harold J. Vetter
Loyola University, New Orleans

U-QN-RI

ISBN 0 • 7002 • 2357 • 6

Copyright © 1972, International Textbook Company

Library of Congress Catalog Card Number: 73 • 177298

TO

The parents of three testy professors

Preface

This textbook was written in order to meet the long-existing need for a book designed specifically for courses in *mental ability testing*. While a number of psychological measurement textbooks currently are available, they have two major shortcomings as far as courses in intelligence testing are concerned. First, these books include material that is extraneous, and secondly, they lack some material that should be provided for the student. In writing this textbook we have striven to overcome these two limitations.

We believe that every chapter in this book presents an important topic for the mental testing course, but for the sake of brevity we shall mention only the most salient features here. Chapter 2, for example, is designed to help the student acquire an understanding of the basic statistical concepts utilized in mental testing. The explanations and examples have been written with the assumption that the student may not have had a course in statistics. For the student who already has a good background in statistics, Chapter 2 may provide a useful review.

Chapter 8 provides useful suggestions for the administration and scoring of intelligence tests. It also presents some important ethical and professional considerations in testing.

Chapters 9 and 10 cover another important area of mental testing, the interpretation of test data. Chapter 9 discusses the interpretation of *normative data* from tests, while Chapter 10 discusses *clinical uses* of the Stanford-Binet and Wechsler scales. By following the procedures explained in Chapter 10 the student can extract a considerable amount of useful information from a subject's performance in a testing session.

The importance of psychological reports in mental testing cannot be overemphasized, and in order to help the student develop the ability to write a useful report, we have included this topic in Chapter 10. In addition to discussing the various aspects of report writing, the chapter provides some sample reports written by experienced psychologists.

The final chapter is unique because it discusses various aspects of research in the behavioral sciences. The major purpose of the chapter is to emphasize the necessity for reading research reports critically. The test user, whether a producer or consumer of research, should be able to evaluate the research reports from which he seeks information.

The emphasis in this textbook is on individual mental ability testing, but we have presented some material on group testing, too. We feel that the book will be useful in courses that are of the lecture type as well as courses that are of the laboratory type where students are expected to learn to administer tests. If used in the latter course, the instructor may be able to rely extensively on the book for the presentation of essential information. This could permit him to spend more time in the supervision of student practice testing.

We are hopeful that this textbook will prove to be an interesting and useful source of information for students in courses pertaining to mental ability testing, and we shall welcome any suggestions that readers may be able to offer for the improvement of the book.

We gratefully acknowledge the assistance of Dr. Lillian Solomon, child psychologist, and Richard Naylor, Coordinator of Diagnostic Services, Texas Department of Mental Health and Mental Retardation, for their assistance in the preparation of the manuscript. We also wish to express our appreciation to the many authors and publishers who have permitted us to use their materials. We are indebted to the Literary Executor of the late Sir Ronald A. Fisher, F. R. S., and to Oliver and Boyd, Edinburgh, for their permission to reprint Table V-A from their book *Statistical Methods for Research Workers*.

G. P. R.
L. C. B.
R. W. J.

Denton, Texas
January, 1972

Contents

13. RESEARCH AND MEASUREMENT . . . 309

Historical Background

CHAPTER

1

No one actually knows just when man first became interested in human intelligence and its measurement, but Itard's study of the "Wild Boy of Aveyron" may have been the initial *scientific* investigation in this area. At any rate, this intriguing experiment stimulated psychologists to explore the problems of mental deficiency and mental measurement, and thus it suggests a starting point in our survey of the major events in the history of intelligence testing.

In 1798 a naked boy was found wandering alone in a forest at Aveyron, France. The boy, who was judged to be about twelve years old, exhibited behavior which was characteristic of wild animals. He ate and drank like an animal, ran on his hands and feet, fought with his teeth and nails, and made only animallike sounds. Shortly after his discovery the "wild boy" came to the attention of Jean Marc Itard, who was a medical officer in the National Institution for the Deaf and Dumb in Paris (Humphrey and Humphrey, 1932).

Itard believed that the boy's condition was the result of isolation from people rather than mental deficiency. He also believed that through teaching and training the boy would soon progress to normal human behavior. Much to Itard's dismay the progress was slight and slow, so the experiment was given up after about five years. The boy then was placed under the supervision of a caretaker with whom he stayed until his death in 1828. In spite of the outcome, Itard's study of the "wild boy" was significant because it was a serious attempt to understand mental ability, and it stimulated others to study the problem of mental deficiency.

In 1838 the French physician Jean Étienne Esquirol, who was intensely interested in the study of mental disorders, published a book on this subject. In it he made an important distinction between mental deficiency and mental illness. He stated that "idiocy" is not a disease, but a condition in which the

1

intellectual faculties are never manifested, or have never been developed sufficiently to enable the retarded person to acquire as much knowledge as persons of his own age reared in similar circumstances are capable of acquiring (Esquirol, 1838).

Esquirol applied the term "idiocy" to all degrees of mental deficiency, but he realized that there was a need to discover objective methods of distinguishing between levels of retardation as well as between normal and subnormal mentality. Still, as was true of the efforts of others interested in the problem of identifying and classifying the mentally retarded, Esquirol's efforts were not very fruitful. The chief reason for the lack of success was that Esquirol attempted to assess mental ability by means of the measurement of physical characteristics, such as skull size and proportions. Eventually he concluded that speech was the best criterion to use in attempting to gauge an individual's intelligence. Esquirol's choice of a verbal criterion appears to have been sound, for today's mental ability tests and scales generally are heavily weighted with verbal items.

Edward Seguin, an eminent French physician who had studied with Itard and Esquirol, was a pioneer in the area of educating and training the mentally deficient. Unlike other psychologists of his day, he strongly believed that mental retardation was not an incurable disease. Seguin felt that the retarded could be brought closer to normality by the utilization of special training procedures and techniques. He published a book on the care and treatment of the mentally deficient in 1846 (Seguin, 1907).

After several years of work devoted to the education of mentally deficient children, Seguin emigrated to the United States. Following his arrival in America in 1848 he found that his ideas for educating the mentally handicapped were much better accepted than they had been in France. His methods, which were designed to develop greater sensory sensitivity and improved motor control, soon were put to use in institutions for the mentally deficient. Many of the sense-training and muscle-training techniques presently in use in institutions for the retarded were originated by Seguin (Anastasi, 1968 p. 6.). Some of Seguin's training materials, such as the Seguin Form Board (which requires the insertion of solid pieces into recessed areas of corresponding shape), have been utilized in various performance tests.

Another famous pioneer in the field of psychological testing was Sir Francis Galton, an English biologist. Galton's strong interest in the relationship between heredity and intelligence led him into the study of individual differences and the development of techniques for measuring them. His keen interest in heredity is revealed in his publications: *Hereditary Genius* (1869), *English Men of Science: Their Nature and Nurture* (1874), and *Natural Inheritance* (1889).

Galton believed that by measuring such characteristics as vision, hearing, reaction time, and physical strength, it would be possible to get an estimate of an individual's mental ability. In 1882 he opened a laboratory in London where visitors could be given physical measurements and a series of sensory and motor tests for a small fee. In this and other laboratories he collected a wealth of data on individual differences. This brilliant scientist devised a number of tools and techniques of measurement, among them being the Galton whistle for measuring sensitivity to sounds of high frequency, a test for weight discrimination, a bar for visual discrimination and an apparatus for measuring reaction time.

Another very significant contribution made by Galton lies in the area of the application of statistical procedures to the analysis of data obtained from tests and measurements. His ideas and efforts led to the development of numerous statistical methods and techniques by such great statisticians as Karl Pearson and Charles Spearman.

The understanding of individual differences was greatly enhanced by the work of James McKeen Cattell, an American psychologist who had studied under the eminent German psychologist Wilhelm Wundt. By emphasizing the importance of individual differences, Cattell broke away from the traditional Wundtian approach to the study of intelligence.

Cattell seems to have been the first person to use the term "mental test" (Cattell, 1890). His tests, which were given individually to children, college students, and adults, provided measures of visual acuity, hearing ability, color vision, color preference, rote memory, reaction time, sensitivity to pain, weight discrimination, and muscular strength. Cattell probably hoped that the measurements obtained through the use of these tests would show a strong relationship to intelligence, but no significant correlations were found in studies such as Wissler's (1901).

In the 1890's several other psychologists were engaged in testing and related research to find devices or techniques which would provide accurate estimates of mental ability. Among the noteworthy names were Kraepelin, Oehrn, and Ebbinghaus in Germany; and Jastrow, Munsterberg, Bolton, Gilbert, and Sharp in the United States (Peterson, 1926). Generally speaking, their efforts to find valid measures of intelligence were unsuccessful, for as we know now intellectual ability is not highly correlated with simple sensory or motor functions or physical measurements.

In order to keep the coverage of the historical developments of the mental ability tests reasonably brief, it is necessary to limit discussion to those instruments which we consider to be noteworthy. Thus we shall confine our comments to certain instruments which are classified as individual scales, performance scales, infant and preschool scales, and group tests. The reader who finds that his appetite for knowledge of the historical development of mental tests has not been satisfied is encouraged to turn to references which treat this aspect of testing more comprehensively.

INDIVIDUAL SCALES

A test or scale which is administered to only one person at a time is referred to as an *individual* test or scale, while one that can be given to several persons at a time is called a *group* instrument. Individual mental ability scales of the type that we use today had their origin in the work of Alfred Binet, a French physician. In 1895 Binet and Henri published an article in which they criticized the previously constructed tests and proposed a variety of new tests to measure a number of mental functions. Among these functions were memory, imagination, attention, mental imagery, comprehension, suggestibility, aesthetic appreciation, and motor skill. The tests which Binet and Henri developed were tried out on school children to determine how the results correlated with academic performance in school. Some of the measures showed little correlation with estimated mental ability, but others gave promising results.

Binet, after years of trying to find valid tests of intelligence, became convinced that it was not possible to measure intellectual ability by means of simple sensory or motor tests or tests of simple mental abilities. He believed that the complexity of mental ability necessitated the use of a more direct approach. It was his belief that general intelligence was a composite of abilities rather than a simple ability, and that performance on a number of carefully chosen mental tasks could be used as an estimate of a person's level of intelligence.

In 1904 Binet was given an opportunity to put his ideas on mental testing to practical use. At this time the Minister of Public Instruction in France appointed a commission to study methods of educating defective children in Paris schools, and since a part of the problem was to identify those children who were truly retarded, the commission turned to Binet for assistance. Binet, in collaboration with Theodore Simon, constructed the first Binet-Simon scale in 1905.

THE BINET SCALES

The 1905 Binet-Simon scale, *The Measuring Scale of Intelligence*, contained thirty mental tasks which were arranged according to estimated level of difficulty. A few examples of the tests follow:

1. Visual coordination—degree of coordination of movements of head and eyes while following a lighted match.
4. Recognition of food—a piece of chocolate and a piece of wood are presented to determine whether the child recognizes the food.
6. Execution of simple orders and imitations of simple gestures.
9. Naming the objects shown in pictures.
11. Repeating three digits immediately after hearing them.
15. Repetition of a sentence of fifteen words after hearing them read once.
18. Drawing two different geometric designs from memory.
20. Stating the similarities of common objects.
25. Sentence completion—providing the correct words to complete sentences.
30. Distinguishing between paired abstract words.

In this scale, item 6 was said to mark the upper limit for idiots (adult) and item 15 the upper limit for imbeciles (adult). Variations of many of these tests were used subsequently in other scales of mental ability and some are in use today. Thus the 1905 scale became the forerunner of modern individual intelligence scales which use an interview situation to gather qualitative as well as quantitative test data.

Binet and Simon published a revision of their 1905 scale in 1908. They were well aware of many of the shortcomings in the first scale, such as the inadequate sampling of children at different age levels, the insufficient norms, and the lack of precision in the scale.

The 1908 Binet-Simon scale contained fifty-nine items, some of which came from the 1905 scale. The tests were grouped according to the age at which they were commonly passed. For example, at age 8, the following tests were given:

1. Reads a passage and recalls two items.
2. Totals the values of five coins.
3. Names the four colors: red, yellow, blue, green.
4. Counts backward from twenty to zero.
5. Writes short sentences from dictation.
6. States differences between objects.

The ages covered by the 1908 scale were 3 through 13. The number of items used at the various age levels varied from only three items at age 13 to eight items at age 7.

The standardization of the 1908 scale was made on the basis of test administrations for 203 Paris school children, and though this was a relatively small group, Binet and Simon had taken a big step toward better standardization for mental-ability tests. The chief criterion used to place an item at the appropriate level was the percent passing the item at each age level. That is, a test item generally was placed at the level where it was passed by two-thirds to three-fourths of a group of children of that age.

The term *mental age* was brought into use for the first time with the development of the 1908 scale, although Binet had discussed the concept as early as 1905. The term refers to the age level at which an individual tends to function mentally. It was found by first assigning a "basic" mental age corresponding to the highest age level where all the items were passed and then adding to this basal age another year for each five tests passed at higher levels. The total figure represented the subject's mental age. Since the number of items at the different levels varied from three to eight, and because no credit was given for a fraction of a year, the results were not very precise. Still, this was a major step in the development of mental-testing procedures.

Although the 1908 scale brought several noteworthy improvements in the realm of intelligence testing, such as grouping test items at appropriate age levels, providing better norms, and a mental age, there were some serious shortcomings in the scale. For example, psychologists who used the scale criticized its standardization. They felt that some of the items were not properly placed, and thus were too easy or difficult. They also questioned the validity and appropriateness of some of the items. Making use of the suggestions as well as his own research, Binet modified the scale and produced the 1911 revision.

The major changes effected in the 1911 revision of the Binet-Simon scale included the elimination of some of the previously used items, the relocation of some items, the addition of some new items, and a change in the method of determining mental age. The 1911 scale had items grouped at ages 3, 4, 5, 6, 7, 8, 9, 10, and 15. There were no tests at ages 11, 12, 13, and 14, and this was a major limitation in the scale.

The method of determining the mental age of a subject by means of the 1911 scales was altered to permit the use of fractions of a year. That is, above the basal age, .2 years of credit was given for each item passed.

The Binet-Simon scales became known throughout the world and were translated by psychologists in many countries. One of the first psychologists to translate the 1908 scale into English was Henry Goddard. As director of the Training School at Vineland, New Jersey, Goddard was in need of a diagnostic scale that could be used to identify subnormal children and indicate their level of mental retardation. He and his assistants administered his translated 1908 Binet-Simon scale to approximately 2,000 children in the Vineland public schools in 1910 and they were heartened by the results (Goddard, 1911). They felt that the Binet-Simon scale would provide an objective means of identifying the mentally deficient, who could then be taught in special classes to the benefit of all concerned.

There are three early revisions of the Binet-Simon scales which seem worthy of mention here. These are the *Point Scale* by Yerkes, Bridges, and Hardwick (1915), the *Stanford Revision* of the Binet-Simon Scales by L. M. Terman (1916), and the *Herring Revision* (1922).

Yerkes, though acknowledging the value of the mental-age concept, criticized two aspects of Binet's scoring procedures. He pointed out that the use of the basal age with the assumption that an individual would pass all of the items below that level was a questionable procedure. Perhaps, he argued, some children would *not* be able to pass *some* of the tests below the basal year, so they could be given too much assumed credit. A similar criticism was made of the ceiling-age concept. That is, in some cases a subject might be able to pass certain items which are found above the age where all of the tests were failed. In this instance he would not receive enough credit because the test administration would have been terminated too soon.

The other major criticism that Yerkes expressed concerned the matter of success or failure on certain tests. Some of the Binet items were made up of parts, and such an item could be passed only if a minimum number of parts were passed—say two out of four. If the child responded correctly on only one part, he did not receive any credit for the item. On the other hand, if he passed on all of the four parts, he received no extra credit for scoring beyond the minimum. Yerkes felt that because of this scoring feature the Binet-Simon scale did not measure as precisely as it might have. He and his co-workers devised their point scale in order to provide what they considered to be a more precise scoring system for the scale. Nineteen of the twenty tests in Yerkes' scale were from the Binet scale, but the tests were not arranged according to age. Scores were interpreted by comparing them with data in a table of age standards or norms. The point scale had these advantages:

1. The norms could be revised relatively easily.
2. Norms could easily be obtained for different groups, such as cultural groups.
3. The flexible organization of the point scale permitted relatively easy change or reorganization.
4. The point scale was relatively easy to administer.

Their scale, however, did not receive the acceptance accorded the *Stanford Revision of the Binet-Simon Intelligence Scale*.

The Stanford Revision, which was published at Stanford University by L. M. Terman and associates in 1916, was a major revision of the Binet-Simon scales. The previous revisions of the scales were mainly translations with minor modifications, but the 1916 revision included changes in the number and location of items as well as changes in the methods of administration and scoring procedures for certain items in the scale (Terman, 1916).

The 1916 scale contained 90 test items, of which 54 came from the 1911 scale. Many of the original Binet tests were modified to make them more suitable for the revised scale. The items were arranged according to age levels which extended from age 3 to "superior-adult." The test items which were included in the 1916 scale were selected after extensive testing. A group of about 1,000 California school children who were within two months of a birthday and were of "average" social status were used to standardize the tests for age 14 and below. For the ages above 14, small groups of adolescents and adults were used.

In general, the items for the 1916 scale were selected on the basis of the percent passing each item at successive age levels and the observations of the persons who administered the test items. An attempt was made to choose and group items so that a median intelligence quotient (IQ) of 100 would be found for unselected groups of children at each age level from 4 to 14. Terman reported that the final revision of the 1916 scales met this criterion, since it yielded a median intelligence quotient closely approximating 100 for the 4 to 14 age group. (Terman, 1916).

The term *intelligence quotient* appeared in the literature as early as 1912 when Stern and Kuhlmann suggested it as an index of brightness, but it was Terman who put it to practical use. "The simplicity of the measure, the ease with which it could be computed, together with the fact that it supplemented but did not displace the mental age concept which had proved so valuable, as an aid to understanding the mental capacities of children, appealed at once to those who had been groping for a quantitative measure that would have equivalent meaning for all." (Goodenough, 1949, p. 63)

The formula used for finding an IQ is:

$$IQ = \frac{MA}{CA} \times 100$$

where:

MA = Mental age in years or months as determined by a mental test
CA = Chronological age or age in years or months since birth

Terman enhanced the meaning and usefulness of the intelligence quotient by providing data relative to the percent of children who had scored at different levels of IQ, and by providing a classification chart to describe in qualitative terms the levels of mental ability for successive ranges of IQ.

The 1916 scale consisted of six subtests (or items) at ages 3 through 10, with alternate items at each level. There were eight items at year 12, six at year 4, six at the Average Adult level, six at the Superior Adult level and alternate items for levels 14 and Average Adult. The alternate test items were to be used if the examiner spoiled a test or felt that the alternate was more appropriate than one of the regular items of the series. There were no tests provided at ages 11 and 13.

During the administration of this scale the examiner established a *basal year* which was a level at which all the tests were passed. He then proceeded to test upward at higher and higher age levels until a level was reached where all the tests were failed. The latter level was the *terminal year*. When the terminal level was reached the testing was discontinued. The mental age was determined on the basis of the basal age plus the months of credit earned at higher levels.

The development of the 1916 scales was a very important milestone in the history of mental testing for a number of reasons. The use of the IQ is one of the reasons. Another is the improved technique for selecting valid items. The standardization of the scale, while not ideal, was an improvement over previous endeavors, as Terman attempted to secure sizable representative groups for most of his scale. He provided standardized procedures for administering and scoring the scale, and emphasized the importance of following those procedures.

The 1916 scale, however, was not a completely satisfactory instrument for testing mental ability. One of the serious limitations of the scale concerns the lack of objectivity for certain subtests in the scale resulting from shortcomings in the procedures for administering and scoring the subtests. Another limitation relates to the standardization of the scale. Specifically, while Terman used a relatively large sample of native-born school children in California, there was the question of whether the test results could be valid for the entire population of children in the United States. At the highest levels of the scale the standardizing sample was relatively small, so the validity of the adult section of the scale was even more in question that the validity for the tests below age 14. Finally, since the scale included relatively few nonverbal items, its validity for children who had verbal handicaps probably was quite low. To a great extent these major limitations were overcome when Terman and his associates published the 1937 scale. This scale and the 1960 revision will be discussed in a later chapter.

The *Herring Revision of the Binet Scale* (1922) was a point scale which was comprised of 38 subtests taken mainly from the Binet scale. The chief novelty of the scale was its method of organization (Freeman, 1926, p. 135). Instead of being arranged in a single series the tests were placed in five groups. The first group could be used alone as a very brief mental test, or the additional tests could be used for a larger scale. The subject was given a certain number of points for each test passed, and his mental age was determined by comparing the total number of points earned with age standards or norms.

THE WECHSLER SCALES

In 1939 David Wechsler, who at that time was Chief Psychologist at the Bellevue Psychiatric Hospital in New York City, published the first of his intelligence scales. This scale, the *Wechsler-Bellevue Intelligence Scale* was standardized on 670 white children whose ages ranged from 7 to 16 and 1,081 white adults whose ages ranged from 17 to 70. The sample was made up of residents of New York City and surrounding areas, with attention given to representativeness with regard to education and occupation.

The Wechsler-Bellevue scale consisted of ten subtests—five in a verbal scale and five in a performance scale. A vocabulary test which could be used as an alternate for a verbal test also was included in the scale. The subtests which comprised the Verbal Scale were entitled Information, Comprehension, Arithmetic, Similarities, and Memory Span for Digits. The Performance Scale subtests were Object Assembly, Picture Arrangement, Block Design, Digit Symbol, and Completion. These tests are described in Chapter 6.

The Wechsler-Bellevue differed from the Binet scale significantly in a number of ways. The W-B had the verbal and performance items separated into the two scales instead of mixed throughout the scale. The W-B provided three scores—the Verbal, Performance and Full Scale IQs—rather than one IQ. The IQs were determined on the basis of points earned on the subtests instead of mental age achieved by the subjects as on the Binet scale. Also, the W-B scores of adults who were administered the scale were compared with scores made by other adults of about the same age, so special adult norms were available. This scale became very popular among psychologists and it was widely used.

Wechsler published the *Wechsler Intelligence Scale for Children* (WISC) in 1949, the *Wechsler Adult Intelligence Scale* (WAIS) in 1955, and the *Wechsler Preschool and Primary Scale of Intelligence* (WPPSI) in 1967. These scales are discussed in Chapter 6.

PERFORMANCE SCALES

In 1911 Healy and Fernald developed a series of 23 tests, many of which were performance tests (which require the manipulation of nonverbal materials). This was the beginning of psychologists' efforts to produce a scale which could be used successfully to test individuals who, because of verbal handicaps, could not be tested adequately with verbal instruments.

The performance tests included memory for a picture, puzzle construction, and picture completion. The Healy completion tests were new and unique tests which required that the subject be able to place cutout squares of a picture (such as a rural scene) into the appropriate spaces in the scene. The Healy-Fernald series of tests did not provide a single score, such as a mental age or IQ. The performance on each test had to be evaluated separately to determine strengths and limitations, and since there were no norms (scores indicating typical performance) the interpretation of test results depended greatly upon the examiner's judgment.

Another series of performance tests was developed by Knox (1914) for the purpose of testing immigrants to the United States who could not speak English. Perhaps the most interesting test in this group is the *Knox Cube Test*, which is still being used in intelligence scales today. When the *Knox Cube Test* is administered, the examiner taps each of four cubes in a set order and then indicates that the subject should go through the same procedure. The test is repeated to provide a series of performances in which the tapping pattern becomes increasingly difficult.

The *Pintner-Paterson Performance Scale* (1917) represented the first major attempt to develop a standardized series of performance tests with general norms. (Anastasi, 1961, p. 244) This scale contained 15 tests, some of which had been developed by Seguin, Healy, Knox and other psychologists. While the scale was an improvement over the previously used series of performance tests, its results did not correlate highly with the more verbal scales, such as the Stanford-Binet. This meant that the results of the scale were very difficult to evaluate. Many of the Pintner-Paterson tests were used later in other scales.

Brief descriptions of the Pintner-Paterson subtests follow:

1. Mare and Foal Form Board

   This is a picture-completion test which requires that the subject place cutout pieces into proper recessed areas in a picture board which shows a mare, foal, other animals and scenery. The score depends upon the time required and errors made.

2. Seguin Form Board

   The examiner removes ten pieces of various shapes from a board and stacks them in a predetermined way. The subject is told to put them back as quickly as he can. The scoring is based upon the fastest performance in three trials.

3. Five-Figure Form Board

This form board has five geometric figures, each of which is divided into two or three parts. The pieces must be placed in the proper recessed areas. Scoring is based upon errors made and time required.

4. Two-Figure Form Board

This test utilizes a board which has two geometric figures. One figure is cut into two pieces, the other into five. Scoring depends upon speed and number of moves.

5. Casuist Form Board

This is a more difficult form board which requires fine discriminations between shapes of pieces. Twelve pieces must be placed correctly in four spaces. The score is based upon number of errors and time required.

6. Triangle Test

In this test, four triangular sections must be fitted into the board. Scoring is based on the time required and the number of errors.

7. Diagonal Test

This requires that five pieces of various shapes be placed in a rectangular form board. The score depends upon the time required and number of errors.

8. Healy Puzzle

This test requires that five rectangular pieces be fitted into a rectangular board. Scores are based on the number of moves made and time required.

9. Manikin Test

Arms, legs, head, and trunk are assembled to construct a wooden man. Scoring is based on the quality of the subjects' performance.

10. Feature Profile Test

This test requires that wooden pieces be put together to form a profile of a head. The score is based on time required and quality of performance.

11. Ship Test

The pieces of a cut-up picture of a ship must be properly placed in a rectangular frame. The scoring is based upon quality of performance.

12. Healy Picture-Completion Test I

Ten small squares have been cut out of a picture of a rural scene. The missing squares must be selected from a set of 48 squares and inserted in the correct places. The score depends upon the quality of performance within a ten-minute time period.

13. Substitution Test

Rows of geometric figures are to be marked with appropriate digits to match a key at the top of a page. The score is based upon number of errors and the time required.

14. Adaptation Board
    This is another form-board test. It requires the placing of a circular block in the correct hole as the board is moved into different positions.
15. Knox Cube Test (Previously described)

Several of the tests of the Pintner-Paterson scale were used in constructing the *Army-Performance Scale*, which was used to test World War I recruits who made low scores on the Alpha and Beta scales (discussed later). Brief descriptions of each of the subtests of this scale follow:

Test 1. Knox Ship Test
    The subject is required to assemble the pieces of a cut-up picture of a ship.
Test 2. Manikin and Feature Profile
    The subject must put together the pieces of two picture puzzles—one of a man and the other of a face.
Test 3. Knox Cube Test
    The subject must imitate the performance of the examiner who taps four cubes in a predetermined manner, using another cube.
Test 4. Cube Construction
    This test requires that small colored cubes be put together to form a larger pattern.
Test 5. Dearborn Form Board
    Pieces of various shapes must be fitted into spaces in a board.
Test 6. Designs
    The subject is shown a series of designs which he must copy from memory.
Test 7. Digit-Symbol Test
    This is a test which requires the substitution of symbols for digits according to a key which is provided.
Test 8. Porteus Maze
    Requires that the subject draw a path through a maze from entrance to exit. A series of mazes of increasing difficulty is used.
Test 9. Picture Arrangement
    In this test a set of pictures displayed in a mixed-up order must be arranged in a proper sequence. A series of picture-arrangement tests is used.
Test 10. Healy Picture Completion
    The subject must replace cut-out pieces in a picture board.

The *Arthur Point Scale of Performance* (*Form I*) was designed for testing children whose ages ranged from 5 to 16 years. This scale of nonverbal tests was constructed as a substitute for the highly verbal Binet scale. Form I (1928) contained eight subtests from the Pintner-Paterson scale plus the *Kohs Block-Design Test* (1923) and the *Porteus Maze Test* (1924).

In 1947 the Revised Form II of the Arthur scale was published. Form II, which often is used as a supplement or substitute for verbal instruments, will be discussed in Chapter 7.

The *Cornell-Coxe Performance Abiility Scale* (1934) utilized tests which were taken from various sources, such as the *Army Performance Scale* and the Pintner-Paterson. There are seven tests in the Cornell-Coxe scale: Manikin, Block Design, Digit Symbol, Picture Arrangement, Memory for Designs, Cube Construction, and Picture Completion.

The performance scales which have been mentioned briefly have been replaced by more modern instruments, some of which are discussed in Chapter 7.

INFANT AND PRESCHOOL SCALES

In the 1920's when Terman's Stanford-Binet was being used extensively for testing children and adults, psychologists realized that there was a real need for an instrument which could be used to test infants and very young children. The Stanford-Binet was not suitable for testing at the very low age levels. In an attempt to meet this need, Kuhlmann revised the Binet scale and extended it downward to the three-month level (Kuhlmann, 1922). The next major effort to develop an instrument for testing infants and preschool children was made at the Yale University Clinic of Child Development, where Arnold Gesell and his fellow workers developed a series of tests for evaluating the development and behavior of very young children from four weeks through five years of age. This work, which extended from 1925 to 1949, culminated in the publication of the *Gesell Developmental Schedules*.

In 1927, Gesell and his colleagues started a longitudinal study of infant and child behavior (Gesell et al., 1938). They gathered behavior data based on observations of 107 "normal" infants whose parents were middle class, native born, and of north-European descent. The subjects in the sample were examined when they were four, six and eight weeks old and then after every four weeks until they reached the age of 56 weeks. Later examinations were made at 1½, 2, 3, 4, 5, and 6 years of age, though only some of the children were tested at each age level. In addition, some children were reexamined after age 6. The *Gesell Schedules* were developed on the basis of the data obtained from this sample. The schedules, discussed in Chapter 7, are used to assess developmental behavior in four areas—motor, adaptive, language and personal-social behavior.

Another early preschool scale was the *Merrill-Palmer Scale of Mental Tests* (Stutsman, 1931), designed for use with young children (24–63 months). It was constructed from 38 subtests which were chosen from 78 tests on the basis of a number of criteria, such as the ease of administration, childrens' interests, and apparent effectiveness in differentiating bright and dull children. The 38 tests were administered to a sample of 631 children, ages 18 to 77 months, in Detroit, Michigan in order to establish norms. The scale, which stresses motor skills and speed in performance, has been a popular instrument with children and examiners.

The *Minnesota Preschool Scale* (Goodenough, Maurer, and Van Wagenen 1932–1940), was constructed from items taken from a Kuhlmann revision of the Binet scale, some additional items from other scales, and some new subtests. Two equivalent forms of 26 subtests each were constructed, each form yielding a verbal and a nonverbal score. The test was standardized on a sample of 900 children who were selected according to father's occupation. The children in the standardization sample came from clinics, settlement houses, nursery schools, and public and private schools. Their ages ranged from 1½ to 6.

Psyche Cattell, the daughter of James McKeen Cattell, published the *Infant Intelligence Scale* in 1940. This scale, which included items from the 1937 Stanford-Binet, as well as tasks from the *Gesell Developmental Schedules*, was designed for use with infants between two and thirty months of age. It was standardized on a sample of 274 children of middle-class parents of north-European descent. This scale is further discussed in Chapter 7.

GROUP TESTS

Although the individual tests of mental ability had gained widespread acceptance by psychologists, it became evident that there was a need for an instrument that could be used to test large numbers of individuals in a relatively short period of time. This need became very evident when the United States entered World War I in 1917. At this time a group of Army psychologists led by R. M. Yerkes undertook the difficult task of developing tests which would be useful in assessing mental ability in order to facilitate the selection, placement, and classification of recruits.

Following the ideas and previous work of psychologist Arthur Otis, the Army psychologists constructed the *Army Scale Alpha* and the *Army Scale Beta*. Both of these instruments could be administered to large groups, but the Beta was a nonlanguage test designed to be used in testing individuals who could not understand English because they were of foreign origin, or illiterate, or mentally retarded.

The Army Alpha consisted of eight tests which were timed. The subject earned one point for each item answered correctly, and since there were 212 items, the highest possible score was 212. Brief descriptions of the eight tests follow:

Test 1. Direction Test
         The subjects were required to mark the items according to directions
         given by the examiner. For example: "Make a cross in the second circle
         and a figure in the third circle."

Test 2. Arithmetic Test
> This test consisted of a set of arithmetic problems to be solved by the examinees.

Test 3. Common-Sense Test
> Sixteen items were used in this test. Each item presented a question or statement with three answers from which the subject was to choose the best.

Test 4. Same-Opposite Test
> The subject had to decide whether each pair of words presented were the same or opposite in meaning.

Test 5. Disarranged Sentence Test
> The examinees were required to rearrange mentally the words in a mixed-up sentence and then mark the statement true or false.

Test 6. Number Comparisons Test
> In this test the examinees were required to examine each of several series of numbers and determine what the two missing numbers at the end of a series should be. Example: 2   4   6   8   10   12   ___   ___

Test 7. Analogies Test
> The examinees were given a series of analogy-type items to test their ability to see verbal relationships. Example: day–night::white–red black   clear   pure

Test 8. Information Test
> In this test the subjects were asked to draw a line under one of four words which made a statement true. For example: People hear with the eyes ears nose mouth. The series of statements provided a test of information.

A brief discussion of the Army Beta will be provided later in the section concerning nonlanguage group tests.

The Army Alpha and Beta proved useful during the war, and following the war several revisions of the Alpha were used extensively with civilians. During the period between World War I and World War II a great deal of research was conducted in which the Alpha tests and other group tests were used. Most of the other tests of mental ability were based upon the design of the Alpha, which had become a model.

The original Otis test was renamed the *Otis Group Intelligence Scale, Advanced Examination*, when the first edition was published for school use by the World Book Company in 1918. This Otis test, which was designed for use in grades 5–13, was extensively used, but in the early 1920's it was displaced by other tests which did not require as much time and were easier to administer (Linden and Linden, 1968, p. 55).

S. L. and L. M. Pressey (1918) published the first group intelligence test designed specifically for use in high schools. It was called the *Group Point Scale for Measuring General Intelligence.* This instrument was widely used during the 1920's, particularly the short form which was employed in surveys of Indiana secondary schools (Linden and Linden, 1968, p. 55).

Another early group test which received considerable attention was the *National Intelligence Test* (1920). It was developed by the National Research Committee which consisted of M. E. Haggerty, L. M. Terman, E. L. Thorndike, G. M. Whipple, and R. M. Yerkes, all outstanding psychologists and test experts. Each of the two scales (A and B) of the test had two parallel forms which could be used in grades 3–8. While the subtests resembled the Army Alpha, the *National Intelligence Test* was notable because of the use of practice exercises which preceded the subtests, and because of the scale's extensive norms.

Thurstone's *Psychological Examination for College Freshman*(1919) contained a variety of test activities arranged in cycles, which was a departure from the usual practice of providing a series of graded tests with all similar tasks segregated from dissimilar tasks (Linden and Linden, 1968, p. 57). Thurstone used examples of appropriate difficulty to introduce new varieties of test activity. He also provided brief directions for each set of items. This feature made it possible to give general directions at the beginning of a testing session and then time the whole test as a unit instead of in parts. Later Thurstone's innovations were utilized in other tests.

The *Terman Group Test of Mental Ability* (1920) was designed for use in grades 7–12. This highly regarded test offered several advantages over other instruments. It was easy to administer and score, it required only about half an hour of testing time, it was well constructed, and it sampled both verbal and quantitative ability. The test was revised by Terman and Quinn McNemar and published in 1942 as the *Terman-McNemar Test of Mental Ability*.

Frederick Kuhlmann and Rose Anderson collaborated to publish the *Kuhlmann-Anderson Tests of Intelligence* in 1927. A distinctive feature of this test was that it provided mental ages based upon the scores earned by the subjects tested.

COLLEGE-ADMISSION TESTS

E. L. Thorndike has been credited with being the first psychologist to advocate the use of mental ability tests as aids in selecting students for college admission (Linden and Linden, 1968, p. 58). His *Intelligence Examination* (1918) was used by Columbia University and other institutions of higher learning as a selection device for students applying for entrance. This test differed from others at this time by being an especially long test, requiring a three-hour testing period. It also was unique because it included subject-matter material along with the usual general-intelligence content. This feature was included by Thorndike in order that students who were bright but who had poor preparation in high school would not make an unduly high grade (Freeman, 1926, p. 171). Still another unusual characteristic of the test was that it had several parallel forms.

Thurstone's second examination for college freshmen, which was published as the *American Council on Education Psychological Examination for College Freshmen* (1925) was unique because it provided both a linguistic (verbal) score and a quantitative (nonverbal) score. Thurstone and his wife Thelma also published the *A C E Psychological Examination for High School Students* in 1933. The Thurstones published forms of each of these instruments for several years, and the tests were extensively used.

The *Miller Analogies Test* was constructed by W. S. Miller and published in 1926. It was the first group mental ability test to be used extensively for the purpose of selecting students for admission to graduate schools. It is still widely used for this purpose. As the test's title indicates, it is made up of a series of analogy-type items.

Recently such tests as the *Ohio State University Psychological Test*, the *Graduate Record Examination* (GRE), and the *Concept Mastery Test* have been used extensively to test high-ability students. The *Ohio State Psychological* is a strictly verbal test with a very ample time limit. The GRE was developed through the efforts of the Carnegie Foundation for the Advancement of Teaching in cooperation with four universities. It has a scholastic-aptitude section which yields both a verbal and quantitative score, and it has two sets of achievement tests. The *Concept Mastery Test* was developed in connection with Terman's famous longitudinal study of gifted children. It contains a combination of two kinds of items which can be classified as same-opposite and analogies items.

PROFILE TESTS

Thorndike and his co-workers in the Institute of Educational Research (IER) at Teachers College, Columbia University, produced a mental-ability test which provided a set of scores, or profile. The *IER Intelligence Scale* (Thorndike et al., 1927) was referred to as the CAVD because it consisted of four sections: Completion, Arithmetic, Vocabulary and Directions. The CAVD provided three types of scores: (1) level of achievement, found by determining the level at which the examinee was successful in answering half or more of the items; (2) breadth of a level, found by determining the percent of items an individual passed at that level; and (3) area of achievement, found by summing the number of successes at all levels. This instrument was the forerunner of the test batteries which are used to provide a number of scores representing the extent to which an individual possesses specific aptitudes or abilities.

Four new forms of the CAVD were published in 1935. They were designed for use at the college level.

In 1941 psychologist L. L. Thurstone published his *Primary Mental Abilities* test battery (Thurstone and Thurstone, 1941). This experimental battery consisted of 17 tests in six booklets, each representing one of the primary factors: memory, verbal comprehension, reasoning, word fluency, number and space. The tests were administered to Chicago school children in grades 5 through 12 for standardization. The experimental test battery was developed out of Thurstone's research to identify and measure the primary mental abilities which he believed constituted intelligence. Revisions of the PMA tests were published in 1946 and later years.

The *Army General Classification Test* (AGCT) was developed during the World War II period (1942–45) for use with millions of inductees much in the manner in which the Army Alpha was employed. The test consists of a composite of arithmetic, vocabulary, and block-counting items to provide a sampling of quantitative, verbal, and spatial abilities. The results of the scale have been found to correlate well with other tests of mental ability.

Using factor-analysis procedures, J. P. Guilford identified a number of mental-ability factors, several of which were similar to or identical with those that Thurstone reported. In 1959 Guilford published the results of his research which culminated in the development of a three-dimensional model of intelligence. According to this model, which is discussed in Chapter 4, the human intellect involves at least 120 different abilities.

In addition to the PMA, a few of the currently popular profile tests are the *Differential Aptitude Tests* (DAT), *General Aptitude Test Battery* (GATB), *Multiple Aptitude Tests* (MAT) and the *Academic Promise Tests* (APT).

NONLANGUAGE GROUP TESTS

The *Army Examination Beta* (1918) was the first of the nonlanguage group tests developed for use with individuals who cannot be tested adequately with a verbal instrument. The Army Beta was a paper-and-pencil test which could be administered by the use of pantomime, gestures, and blackboard demonstrations. The Beta was made up of seven subtests (Mursell, 1947, p. 141): (1) Five mazes, (2) sixteen pictures of piles of cubes, (3) nonverbal completions consisting of patterns of the letters X and O to be completed in series as begun, (4) association of symbols with numbers according a code, (5) a series of pairs in numbers to be compared, (6) drawing the missing parts of a picture, and (7) ten paper form-board problems.

Because the subtests of the Beta were timed, speed of performance was emphasized. The scale, which was patterned closely after Army Alpha, correlated .80 with Alpha and .73 with the Stanford-Binet (Anastasi, 1961, p. 250).

The Beta, like the Alpha, underwent a number of revisions. The 1946 version of the Revised Beta (Kellogg et al., 1946–57) contains six subtests: (1) mazes, (2) digit-symbol, (3) pictorial absurdities, (4) paper form board, (5) picture completion, and (6) perceptual speed. In this revision the administration and scoring were simplified. The Revised Beta has been used extensively in penal institutions and in mass industries which employ many persons who have foreign backgrounds or who lack education (Anastasi, 1961, p. 251).

M. E. Haggerty, who had worked in psychological services in the Army during World War I and who had become familiar with the Army tests, published the *Haggerty Intelligence Examinations*: Delta I and Delta II (1919 and 1920). Delta I was a nonlanguage test which closely resembled the Army Beta. It was designed for use in the primary grades.

In 1920 W. F. Dearborn published his *Dearborn Group Tests of Intelligence*, Series I and II. Series I was designed for use in grades 1-3 and Series II for use in grades 4-9. Dearborn used some of the subtests of the Army Beta and added some new subtests of his own in constructing his tests. His tests were distinctive because he selected subtests on the basis of their appeal to childrens' interests, and because he used a great variety of subtests to make up each series (Freeman, 1926, p. 169).

The *Primary Mental Test*, published by Rudolph Pintner and Bess Cunningham in 1923, was similar to the Dearborn tests in terms of its content. The Pintner-Cunningham test contained seven subtests based on pictorial materials. It was the forerunner of other Pintner tests such as the currently used *Pintner General Ability Tests: Non-Language Series*.

The *Pintner Non-Language Test* which is now used extensively to test elementary school children who have verbal handicaps, was originally designed for use with deaf children. Pintner discovered the need for nonverbal instruments when his studies of deaf children revealed that these individuals tend to be so retarded in language development that they cannot be tested adequately with verbal tests. The test, which contains six timed subtests, has norms based on over 6,000 school children.

The *Chicago Non-Verbal Examination* (1940) was designed for use with the age range 7 years to adult. It contains 10 subtests which involve a wide variety of mental tasks. Its norms were based on over 1,800 hearing children.

The Goodenough *Draw-A Man-Test* (1926), designed for use with individuals in the 3 1/2-to-13 1/2-year age range, is a novel nonlanguage instrument which makes use of a drawing in the assessment of mental ability. Florence Goodenough based her belief that this method of testing would be valid upon her observation of children and the research of other psychologists. The instructions used in this test are:

> "On these papers I want you to make a picture of a man. Make the very best picture that you can. Take your time and work very carefully. I want to see whether the boys and girls in_____ school can do as well as those in other schools. Try very hard and see what good pictures you can make."

Goodenough chose a man as the subject to be drawn because it is one with which all children are familiar and because it has broad appeal. A man was chosen rather than a woman because a man's clothing varies less than that of a woman.

In the scoring of the test, points are given for the presence of a line representing part of a man as well as for correct proportion and perspective. A total of 51 points can be earned and the points of credit can be converted to mental age.

The test has been used extensively as a supplement for verbal scales. Although it once was regarded as a possible "culture-fair" test which would be free from cultural influences, this notion has had to be abandoned because of lack of supporting research data. Perhaps, as Goodenough and Harris have concluded, the search for a culture-free test is illusory (1950).

CURRENT ISSUES

During the early 1920's educational and psychological measurement experienced widespread acceptance and rather unrestricted use. No doubt the enthusiasm for tests was related to the hope that these tools could be used to improve education and psychological services. Then late in the decade the literature began to reflect a concern about the shortcomings of measurement. The new emphasis on the limitations of testing involved both the instruments and the persons who administered and used them.

During the 1930's a considerable amount of research was conducted in the field of measurement in order to improve the quality of tests and the interpretation of test data. This kind of research is going on today, but there has been noticeable evidence of opposition to the use of tests. As Treible (1969, p. 74) views the situation,

> Psychological testing is a concept whose mention is analogous to the Loch Ness Monster. At a mere utterance of the term adherents and opponents gather afresh in their respective camps and attempt either to substantiate or disprove that psychological testing, like the famed monster, is really worth attention.

Evidence of strong opposition to educational and psychological testing is found in speeches, legislative hearings, test-burning incidents (Eron and Walder, 1961), numerous articles, and such books as *The Brain Watchers* (Gross, 1962), *The Tyranny of Testing* (Hoffman, 1962) and *They Shall Not Pass* (Black, 1963).

While some of the critics of measurement may have been irrational in their criticism, the public rightfully asks such questions as:

1. Are tests fair and accurate?
2. What types of tests, if any, should be used?
3. Are tests being overused?
4. Should more testing be done?
5. Who should administer tests?
6. Who should interpret test results?
7. Who should have access to test results?

These questions seem to suggest that there are three major issues confronting those who use tests today. We shall refer to these issues as "Invasion of Privacy," "Fairness to Minorities," and "Use of Test Data." In the discussion of these topics it will become apparent that the three issues are interrelated.

INVASION OF PRIVACY

A major criticism of psychological measurement is that it amounts to an invasion of the privacy of those who are tested. This is a growing concern to many individuals because test results are a key part of the new concept of the career record which will accompany a person throughout his life (Brim, 1965, p. 126).

Psychologists like to believe that the data collected from psychological tests and inventories will always be treated as confidential information to be used only by strictly professional individuals. It is, however, extremely difficult to protect confidential information. Test information can be subpoenaed by any group with proper authority and thus become a matter of record (Brim, 1965, p.126).

When should it be permissible for persons employed by state or federal institutions to require that an individual provide information about himself which he may consider to be strictly personal? When should it be alright to invade a person's privacy? In the past it has been considered legal and appropriate to collect various kinds of test data from military inductees, inmates in penal institutions, and students in schools. Still, the question of whether psychological testing constitutes an invasion of privacy remains.

It is likely to remain as long as there are known incidents of the revealing of confidential test data, such as the reporting of a person's IQ in a newspaper or magazine.

The public has a right to know who will have access to test data and how the data will be used. *The Ethical Standards of the American Psychological Association* state that a psychologist should be sure that his subject is "fully aware of the ways in which the information may be used" before he requests the individual to reveal information (American Psychological Association, 1963, pp. 56-60).

After a person has been tested he is entitled to useful information concerning the results. With young children in school, the parents will be the ones who are apt to want to obtain this information. If tests are given but no opportunity is provided to obtain any information concerning the test performance, tests will be regarded as "snooping around" and strongly rejected (Yamamoto, 1966, p. 368).

This does not mean, however, that all confidential data, including test results, should be made available to the public. Such a policy could be extremely unwise, for most people are not sufficiently knowledgeable to be able to make good use of psychological data. In fact, the indiscriminate release of information can lead to anxiety, misunderstanding, and misconceptions. What really should be provided is an opportunity for the examinee (or parent) to have psychological data interpreted in such a way that they can be accepted and understood. This would be helpful to those concerned, and it would serve to reduce the fear of invasion of privacy.

FAIRNESS TO MINORITIES

Are psychological tests unfair to the members of minority groups? Many critics of testing will answer this question with an emphatic "Yes!", for they feel that psychological tests discriminate against many minority subjects.

The major criticism is that "tests of ability screen out from opportunities for advancement those individuals from a background of cultural deprivation, who because of deprivation give an inferior performance on the tests" (Brim, 1965, p. 127). There is perhaps complete agreement among psychologists, educators, and sociologists that some minority groups are culturally deprived. Most would also agree that a culturally impoverished environment is detrimental to performance on mental-ability tests. Mays (1966, p. 319) asserts that one of the reasons why African natives are not very successful in nonverbal tests, such as Raven's Matrices, is that as children they do not play with clear-cut geometrical shapes, as do children in European and American cultures.

While there is considerable agreement that environment is an important contributing factor with respect to test performance, psychologists express differing points of view concerning the *extent* to which a person's environmental background influences test results. The "nature versus nurture" controversy has been around for a long time, but recently it has received additional attention with the publication of an article by psychologist Arthur Jensen. Jensen (1969) maintains that IQ tests measure only one important portion of the whole spectrum of human abilities. He suggests that efforts be made to study the other aspects of mental ability to determine how they might be used to enhance educational achievement. Jensen, basing his views on a review of research, intelligence, testing, and psychology, concludes that individual differences in IQ are largely determined by heredity. He suggests that most of the individual difference variance in IQ can be attributed to genetic factors and that there are genetic differences in mental ability between races.

Although Jensen's points of view are supported by some psychologists, his ideas have met with a great amount of criticism. Anastasiow (1969) and others feel that Jensen underestimates the effect which early experiences and socialization have upon the young child, and his mental development. In general, Jensen's critics feel that the influence of environment on mental development is extremely important and that cultural differences can easily account for racial differences in mental ability.

While the question concerning the extent to which heredity and environment influence test scores has not yet been resolved, it is obvious that some culturally deprived minority groups have done less well on IQ tests than the groups on which the tests have been standardized. In a sense, then, the tests tend to discriminate or differentiate between whites and some minority groups. Whether this differentiation is unfair depends upon what use is made of the data which the tests yield. We shall explore this point and other aspects of the use of tests in the next section.

USE OF TESTS

If mental ability test scores are useful in schools for predicting achievement, for placing students in special classes, or for counseling, then the fact that the tests show *group* as well as individual differences is immaterial. The important point here is that test data can be used to assist individuals regardless of race or cultural background. If, however, test data are used to label people or to discriminate against them, then the critics who claim that tests are unfair to minorities have a genuine grievance. Some of the people who are opposed to the use of psychological tests express the belief that reporting data from tests on which some minority groups do not do as well as whites will tend to reinforce attitudes of bias against those who belong to minorities.

It is unfortunate as well as unethical for culturally deprived children to be labeled as slow learners and not be given adequate opportunity and encouragement to learn as a result of low test scores. This of course is an instance of the *misuse* of test data. The tests themselves are not unfair because they discriminate—they are supposed to do this. If they are used when they are not appropriate for a person or a group, or if the test results are not correctly interpreted, there will be a kind of unfairness which results from the misuse of the instruments. "Many tests are used today for selection, employment, and classification purposes in such a way that they actually lead to and encourage discriminatory practices. In many cases these tests are misused because psychologists have failed to take into account the differences in validity, and perhaps reliability, that tests have for different populations." (Berdie, 1965, p. 146)

Some critics of psychological testing oppose the use of tests because they feel that certain items of the instruments are objectionable. Ashbrook (1962), in his article on "brainpicking," expresses the belief that those items which probe at attitudes toward the Bible, parents, and patriotism plant seeds of doubt in the minds of examinees. He also perceives testing as a possible attempt by some people to undermine American democracy. Naturally, psychologists and test publishers reject this notion. The concern about the nature of test items generally involves personality inventories (which may contain items that relate to sex, morals, attitudes, and religious beliefs) rather than tests of aptitude, intelligence, or achievement. The status of mental testing could be adversely affected, however, if an antitesting movement led to the abolition of all psychological testing.

Another criticism related to the use of tests is that some of the instruments deny opportunity to persons with different and possibly very valuable talents (Brim, 1965, p. 127). The critics who feel this way believe that mental ability tests measure only one narrow aspect of intelligence, failing to sample such human qualities as creativity, ambition, altruism, and foresight. The concern is, of course, that those individuals who are highly endowed with these characteristics may be missed by the presently used intelligence tests and thus not be given their rightful chance for special education or employment opportunities.

Personality inventories, interest inventories, and other psychological instruments also have been criticized for being limited in what they can measure. To a certain extent this charge has validity, and it behooves psychologists and test publishers to strive for the development of instruments which will sample a greater spectrum of human traits and abilities.

Finally, there has been criticism that psychological tests sometimes are being used, or misused, by persons who are not competent or sufficiently qualified for testing. There is some evidence to support this charge. For example, Garfield and Affleck (1960) in their unique study found that a number of persons were incorrectly diagnosed as mentally deficient and committed to an institution for the retarded. A major reason for this unfortunate situation was that those who examined the subjects were not sufficiently adept at conducting psychological examinations. For other examples of incidents related to the use of psychological tests by unqualified persons the reader may refer to the APA *Ethical Standards of Psychologists* (1953).

Those who use tests have the ethical responsibility to be qualified to administer, score, and interpret them properly. It is unfortunate that many test users do not assume this responsibility (Mehrens and Lehman, 1969, p. 281).

CONCLUDING REMARKS ABOUT ISSUES

The advocates of psychological testing argue that without the benefit of tests educators, counselors, psychologists, personnel workers, and others would be much less effective in their work than they presently are. They maintain that tests are tools which are necessary for the understanding of the student, client, or worker. On the other hand, the critics of testing point to the shortcomings of tests, testing procedures, and the users of tests when they voice their opposition.

Since tests are likely to be employed extensively in the future, it seems to be extremely important that test publishers and test users work diligently to bring about improvements in test quality and in the use of the instruments. Test publishers can and should follow the guidelines in the publication *Standards for Educational and Psychological Tests and Manuals* (APA, 1966) to improve tests and testing, while test users should adhere to the ethical standards referred to in the previously mentioned *Ethical Standards of Psychologists*. It would be helpful, too, if the public were kept informed about the nature and purposes of testing programs.

Ideally, all tests should be adequate for their intended purposes; they should be properly used by well-qualified personnel, and a well-informed public should support sound testing practices and programs.

REFERENCES

Anastasi, Anne, *Psychological Testing*. 2nd ed. New York: Macmillan, 1961.

————, *Psychological Testing*. 3rd ed. New York: Macmillan, 1968.

Anastasiow, Nicholas, "Educational Relevance and Jensen's Conclusions," *Phi Delta Kappan* 51 (1969), 32–35.

American Personnel and Guidance Association, "Ethical Standards," *Personnel and Guidance Journal* 40 (1961), 206-209.

American Psychological Association, *Ethical Standards of Psychologists.* Washington, D.C.: The Association, 1953.

American Psychological Association, "Ethical Standards of Psychologists," *American Psychologist* 18 (1963), 56-60.

American Psychological Association, *Standards for Educational and Psychological Tests and Manuals.* Washington, D.C.: The Association, 1966.

Arthur, Grace, "The Restandardization of a Point-Performance Scale," *Journal of Applied Psychology* 12 (1928), 278-303.

Ashbrook, John, "Brainpicking in the School," *Human Events*, Sec. 4, 1962.

Barclay, James R., "The Attack on Testing and Counseling," *Personnel and Guidance Journal* 43 (1964), 6-16

Berdie, Ralph, "The Ad Hoc Committee on Social Impact of Psychological Assessment," *American Psychologist* 202 (1965), 143-146.

Binet, Alfred, and V. Henri, "La Psychologie Individuelle," *L'Année Psychologique* 2 (1895), 411-463.

———, and T. Simon, "Methodes Nouvelles pour le Diagnostic du Niveau Intellectuel des Anormaux," *L'Année Psychologique* 11 (1905), 191-224.

———, "Le Development de L' Intelligence Chez les Enfants," *L'Année Psychologique* 14 (1908), 1-90.

Black, Hillel, *They Shall Not Pass.* New York: Morrow, 1963.

Boring, Edward G., *A History of Experimental Psychology.* New York: Appleton-Century, 1929.

———, *A History of Experimental Psychology.* New York: Appleton-Century, 1950.

Brim, Orville, Jr., "American Attitudes Toward Intelligence Tests," *American Psychologist* 20 (1965), 125-130.

Brown, Andrew W., "The Development and Standardization of the Chicago Non-Verbal Examination," *Journal of Applied Psychology* 24 (1940), 36-47, 122-129.

Cattell, J. M., "Mental Tests and Measurements," *Mind*, 15 (1890), 373-380.

Cattell, Psyche, *The Measurement of Infants and Young Children.* New York. Psychological Corporation, 1947.

Cornell, Ethel, and W. W. Coxe, *A Performance Ability Scale: Examination Manual.* Tarrytown-on-Hudson, New York: World Book, 1934.

Eron, Leonard D., and Leopold Walder, "Test-Burning II," *American Psychologist*, 16 (1961), 237-244.

Esquirol, J. E. D., *Des Maladies Mentales Considéréés sous les Rapports Médical, Hygienique, et Médico Légal.* Paris: J. B. Ballière, 1838.

Freeman, Frank, *Mental Tests: Their History, Principles and Applications.* Boston: Houghton Mifflin, 1926.

Galton, Francis, *Hereditary Genius.* London: Macmillan, 1869.

———, *English Men of Science: Their Nature and Nurture.* London: Macmillan, 1874.

———, "Psychometric Experiments," *Brain* 2 (1879), 149-162.

_____, *Inquiries into Human Faculty and Its Development*. London, Macmillan, 1883.

_____, *Natural Inheritance*. London: Macmillan, 1889.

Garfield, S. L., and D. C. Affleck, "A Study of Individuals Committed to a State Home for the Retarded Who Were Later Released as not Mentally Defective," *American Journal of Mental Deficiency* 64 (1960), 907–915.

Gesell, A., Helen Thompson, and Catherine Amatruda, *The Psychology of Early Growth*. New York: Macmillan, 1938.

Gilbert, J. A., "Researches on the Mental and Physical Development of Children," *Studies from the Yale Psychological Laboratory* 2 (1894), 40–100.

_____, "Researches upon School Children and College Students," *Studies in Psychology*, University of Iowa, I (1897), 1–39.

Goddard, H. H., "A Revision of the Binet Scale," *The Training School Bulletin* 8 (1911), 56–62.

Goodenough, Florence L., *Measurement of Intelligence by Drawings*. New York World Book, 1926.

_____, *Mental Testing: Its History, Principles and Applications*. New York: Holt, 1949.

_____, R. M. Maurer, and M. J. Van Wagenen, *Minnesota Preschool Scales: Manual*. Minneapolis: Educational Test Bureau, 1940.

_____, and D. B. Harris, "Studies in the Psychology of Children's Drawings: II, 1928–1949," *Psychological Bulletin* 47 (1950), 369–433.

Gross, M. J., *The Brain Watchers*. New York: Random House, 1962.

Haggerty, M.E., et al. (National Research Committee), *National Intelligence Tests, Scales A and B*. New York: World Book, 1920.

Healy, W., and Grace Fernald, *Tests for Practical Mental Classification*. Psychological Monograph 13, 2 (1911).

Herring, John B., *Herring Revision of the Binet-Simon Test: Examination Manual, Form A*. New York: World Book, 1922.

Hoffman, Banesh, *The Tyranny of Testing*. New York: Crowell-Collier, 1962.

Humphrey, George, and Muriel Humphrey, *The Wild Boy of Aveyron*. New York. Appleton-Century, 1932.

Jastrow, J., "Some Anthropometric and Psychologic Tests on College Students: A Preliminary Survey," *American Journal of Psychology* 4, (1891–92), 420–428.

Jensen, Arthur, "How Much Can We Boost I.Q. and Scholastic Achievement?," *Harvard Educational Review* 39 (1969), 1–123.

Kellogg, C. E., N. W. Morton, R. M. Lindner, and M. Gurvitz, *Revised Beta Examination*. New York: Psychological Corporation, 1946–57.

Kohs, S. C., Intelligence Measurement: *A Psychological and Statistical Study Based Upon the Block-Design Tests*. New York: Macmillan, 1923.

Knox, H. A., "A Scale Based on the Work on Ellis Island for Estimating Mental Defect," Journal of American Medical Association 62 (1914), 741–747.

Kuhlmann, F. A., *A Handbook of Mental Tests*. Baltimore. Warwick and York, 1922.

——, and R. G. Anderson, *Kuhlman-Anderson Intelligence Test.* Princeton, N.J.: Personnel Press, 1927–63.

Linden, Kathryn W., and James Linden, *Modern Mental Measurement: A Historical Perspective.* Guidance Monograph Series. Boston: Houghton Mifflin, 1968.

Lutey, Carol, *Individual Intelligence Testing: A Manual.* Greeley, Colo.: Execuitary, Inc., 1966.

Mays, Wolfe, "A Philosophic Critique of Intelligence Tests," *Educational Theory* 16 (1966), 318–332.

Mehrens, William, and Irving Lehmann, *Standardized Tests in Education.* New York: Holt, 1969.

Miller, W. S., *Miller Analogies Test.* New York: World Book, 1926.

Murphy, G., *A Historical Introduction to Modern Psychology.* Rev ed. New York: Harcourt, 1949.

Mursell, James L. *Psychological Testing.* New York: Longmans, 1947.

Peterson, J., *Early Conceptions and Tests of Intelligence.* New York: Harcourt, 1926.

Pintner, R., *Pintner General Ability Tests, Non-Language Series: Intermediate Tests.* New York: World Book, 1945.

——, and Bess V. Cunningham, *Pintner-Cunningham Primary Mental Test.* New York: World Book, 1923.

——, and D. G. Paterson, *A Scale of Performance Tests.* New York: Appleton-Century, 1917.

Porteus, S. D., *Guide to Porteus Maze Test.* Vineland, N.J.: The Training School, 1924.

Pressey, S. L., and L. M. Pressey, "A Group Point Scale for Measuring General Intelligence, With Results from 1100 School Children," *Journal of Applied Psychology* 2 (1918), 250–269.

Seguin, E., *Idiocy: Its Treatment by the Psychologie Method.* New York: Bureau of Publications, Teachers College, Columbia University, 1907.

Stutsman, R., *Mental Measurement of Preschool Children.* New York: World Book 1931.

Terman, L. M. and Maud Merrill, *Measuring Intelligence.* Boston: Houghton-Mifflin, 1916.

——, *Terman Group Test of Mental Ability.* New York: World Book, 1920.

Thorndike, E. L., *Intelligence Examination.* New York: T. C. Burroughs, 1918.

——, Ella Woodyard, and I. Lorge, "Four New Forms of The I. E. R. Intelligence Scale for use on the College and Higher Levels," *School and Society* 42 (1935), 271–272.

——, et al., *The Measurement of Intelligence.* New York: Bureau of Publications, Teachers College, Columbia University, 1927.

Thurstone, E. L., *Intelligence Examination.* New York: T. C. Burroughs, 1918.

Thurstone, L. L., and T. G. Thurstone, *American Council on Education Psychological Examination for College Freshmen.* Washington D.C.: American Council on Education, 1925–47. Princeton, N.J.: Educational Testing Service, 1947–54.

———, *The Chicago Tests of Primary Mental Abilities*, Chicago, Science Research Associates, 1941.

Treible, Reed R., "On the Firing Line—Psychological Testing," *Journal of College Placement* 29 (1969), 74-80.

Wechsler, David, *The Measurement of Adult Intelligence*. Baltimore: Williams & Wilkins, 1939.

———, *Manual for the Wechsler Intelligence Scale for Children*. New York: Psychological Corporation, 1949.

———, *Manual for the Wechsler Adult Intelligence Scale*. New York: Psychological Corporation, 1955.

———, *The Measurement and Appraisal of Adult Intelligence*. 4th ed. Baltimore: Williams & Wilkins, 1958.

Wissler, C. "The Correlation of Mental and Physical Traits," *Psychological Monographs* 3, 16 (1901).

Yamamoto, Kaoru, "Psychological Testing: Invasion of Privacy?" *Educational Leadership* 23, 5 (1966), 363–368.

Yerkes, R. M. (ed.), "Psychological Examining in the United States Army," *Memoirs of the National Academy of Sciences* 15 (1921).

———, J. U. Bridges, and R. S. Hardwick, *A Point Scale for Measuring Mental Ability*. Baltimore: Warwick and York, 1915.

Yoakum, C. S., and R. M. Yerkes, *Army Mental Tests*. New York: Holt, 1920.

Yourman, Julius, "The Case Against Group I.Q. Testing," *Phi Delta Kappan* 46 (1964), 108-110.

Basic Statistical Background

Whether an individual is actively engaged in test administration and interpretation or reading the literature, it is essential that he have an adequate understanding of certain statistical concepts and procedures. Without sufficient statistical background, the person's ability to comprehend either test data or professional literature simply will not be what it could or should be.

The purpose of this chapter is to discuss statistical concepts that are commonly used to describe test data in such ways as to make them more meaningful and useful. A set of *raw* scores from a test may have little meaning, even to the sophisticated psychologist, but the same test data when organized and treated statistically can be of considerable value.

Beginning with the organization of test data, we shall discuss those elementary statistical concepts and procedures which are most likely to be encountered by the person who is studying in the field of tests and measurements.

ORGANIZATION OF DATA

When several test scores have been obtained for a group of individuals it is usually necessary to organize the scores in a systematic way which facilitates the use of them. The arrangement of scores which appears in Table 2-1 is referred to as a *frequency distribution*.

FREQUENCY DISTRIBUTION

The scores presented in Table 2-1 have been obtained from a group of 65 senior-class high school students who were given a mental ability test. By examining the table we can see that the raw scores are headed by the column X

TABLE 2-1 Frequency Distribution of Sixty-Five Mental-Ability Scores

Score, X	Frequency, f	Score, X	Frequency, f
79	1	55	3
76	1	54	4
73	1	53	3
71	2	52	2
69	1	51	2
67	1	50	3
66	2	49	2
65	2	48	1
64	1	47	1
63	2	46	2
62	1	45	1
61	2	44	2
60	2	42	2
59	2	41	1
58	3	39	1
57	3	37	1
56	6	34	1

(symbol for a raw score) and that the scores have been arranged from highest to lowest. The column headed by f indicates the frequency of scores. Thus it can be seen that one person made a score of 79, two individuals made a score of 71, etc. The frequency distribution, then, shows the number of times each score appears in the whole distribution.

Often it is useful to group the scores into class intervals, or classes, as is shown in Table 2-2. The data which appear in Table 2-2 have been grouped into class intervals of five score points. That is, the highest ranking interval (75–79) has five possible score values—75, 76, 77, 78, and 79, the next highest class has scores which range from 70 to 74, the next highest from 65 to 69, and so on. The interval size was found by dividing the *range* of scores for the whole distribution by 10 to get an approximate figure for interval size and then rounding the resulting value. Thus the range (highest minus lowest score), which is 45 (79 – 34), divided by 10 gave the value 4.5. This was rounded to 5. Five was chosen rather than 4 because 5 gives a whole-number midpoint for the intervals,

TABLE 2-2 Grouped Frequency Distribution

Class Interval	f
75–79	2
70–74	3
65–69	6
60–64	8
55–59	17
50–54	14
45–49	7
40–44	5
35–39	2
30–34	1

which is sometimes desirable. By inspection one can see that 10 classes, or groups of scores, have been organized from the original distribution of raw scores.

An important point to make here is that the *apparent limits* of the single scores and classes are not the same as the *real limits*. For example, a score of 34 has *real* limits of 33.5 and 34.5. This is so because we assume that each score represents a continuum, and that the scores need not be integers, or whole numbers. The class interval 60–64 has apparent limits of 60 and 64, but real limits of 59.5 and 64.5.

GRAPHICAL REPRESENTATION OF DATA

Three kinds of graphs are frequently used to produce clearer pictures of distributions of test scores—the *frequency polygon*, the *histogram*, and the *ogive*. Figure 2-1 shows a frequency polygon based upon the test scores in Table 2-2, while Fig. 2-2 shows a histogram based upon the same data.

The graphs in Figs. 2-1 and 2-2 show score values along the horizontal axis, or abscissa, and the frequency of the scores along the vertical axis, or ordinate. The frequency polygon was constructed by plotting points to indicate the frequency of scores for each class interval and then connecting these points by straight lines. The points are located over the midpoints of the class intervals. The histogram was constructed by using columns to indicate the frequency of

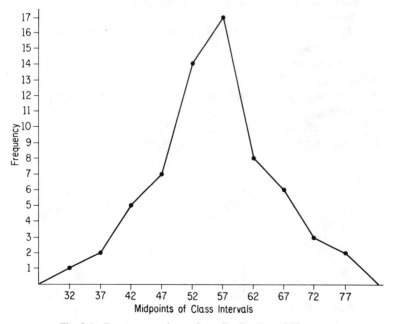

Fig. 2-1. Frequency polygon for a distribution of 65 scores.

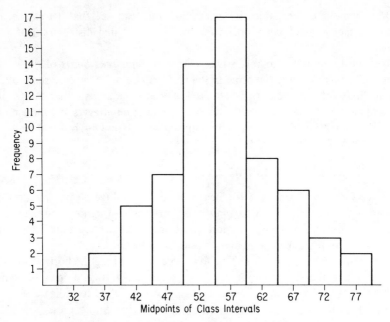

Fig. 2-2. Histogram for a distribution of 65 scores.

scores of each class interval, the columns being centered over the midpoints of the class intervals.

Generally speaking, either the histogram or the frequency polygon can be used to show a distribution of test scores, but the latter graph would be more satisfactory if two distributions were to be placed on one graph, because overlapping histograms would obscure some data.

Table 2-3 shows the cumulative frequencies and cumulative percents for the test data presented in Table 2-1. The cumulative frequencies in Table 2-3 were found by adding the next highest frequency of a class interval to the total frequency below, starting with the lowest class interval (30–34). Class interval

TABLE 2-3 Cumulative Frequencies and Cumulative Percents for a Distribution of Sixty-Five Scores

Class Interval	f	Cumulative f	Cumulative Percents
75–79	2	65	100
70–74	3	63	97
65–69	6	60	92
60–64	8	54	83
55–59	17	46	71
50–54	14	29	45
45–49	7	15	23
40–44	5	8	12
35–39	2	3	4.5
30–34	1	1	1.5

30-34 has a frequency of 1, and when this is added to the frequency (2) of the next interval (35-39), the cumulative frequency for the two intervals becomes 3. The cumulative percents were determined by dividing each cumulative frequency by the total number of scores in the distribution. For instance, the class interval 65-69 has a cumulative percent of 92 (60/65 = .92 or 92 percent).

Using the data from Table 2-3, an *ogive*, or cumulative percentage graph, has been constructed and is shown in Fig. 2-3. The points shown in this graph are

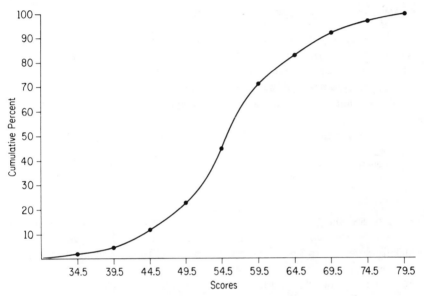

Fig. 2-3. Cumulative percentage curve for 65 scores.

plotted above the upper real limit of each class interval to show the cumulative percent of scores at each interval. An ogive is useful for finding the percent of scores which fall below given score values. More will be said about this procedure a little later when percentile ranks are discussed.

POPULATIONS AND SAMPLES

Psychologists, researchers, and others who conduct studies involving test scores generally make use of *samples* or groups of subjects selected from *populations* instead of using the entire population. It is often either impossible or impractical to use an entire population of individuals (or scores for them) in a study, so a sampling method is employed to select the desired number of cases. Inferences then are made on the basis of the sample.

While samples can be drawn from parent populations in many ways, it is generally desirable to select a *random sample*—a sample that has been drawn in such a way that every individual or case in the population has had an equal chance of being selected. There are several ways of assuring randomness in choosing cases for a sample, including the use of a table of random numbers. The random-numbers procedure is explained in many of the statistics textbooks listed at the end of this chapter.

DESCRIPTIVE STATISTICS

PARAMETERS AND STATISTICS

When distributions of test scores or similar data are described, it is generally necessary to make reference to certain characteristics of the distributions, such as the mean, median, or standard deviation. Such characteristics of populations are classified as *parameters*, and those of samples are called *statistics*.

Some commonly used symbols for statistics and corresponding parameters are:

Characteristic	Statistic	Parameter
Mean	$\overline{X}$	μ (mu)
Variance	s^2	σ^2 (sigma)
Product-moment correlation coefficient	r	ρ (rho)
Standard deviation	s	σ

Statistics and parameters enable us to achieve a certain degree of exactitude in the description of test data, and this is essential. For example, it is generally necessary to know where the scores tend to be concentrated in a distribution; and while inspection of a graph or a frequency distribution will give a general indication of this point, a measure of *central tendency* will provide much greater precision.

MEASURES OF CENTRAL TENDENCY

The *mode* is a measure of central tendency that is found simply by inspection, for it is the most frequent score in a distribution. In Table 2-1 a score of 56 appears more often than any other score, so it is designated as the mode. This measure can vary considerably from sample to sample, so it lacks stability and is therefore less useful than the mean or median. Furthermore, some distributions have two or more modes.

The *mean* or "average" score for a distribution of scores is found by the formula:

$$\overline{X} = \frac{\Sigma X}{N}$$

where $\overline{X}$ = mean of the test
  ΣX = sum of the scores in the distribution
  N = number of scores in the distribution

Thus the mean is simply the total or sum of the scores divided by the number of scores.

When the correct values are substituted in this formula, the mean for the data in Table 2-1 is found to be 3610/65 = 55.54.

The mean ordinarily is the most useful measure of central tendency, because it tends to be stable and it is useful for finding other statistical measures. If, however, a distribution has a few extreme scores near one end of a distribution (either high or low), the mean is pulled toward the extreme scores, and does not portray central tendency as well as does the *median*.

The *median* is the middle-score value in a distribution, or the point that divides a distribution in two; and there are therefore as many scores above it as below it. The median is also properly referred to as the 50th percentile because 50 percent of the scores in the distribution fall below it (a percentile being a point below which a stated percent of the cases in a distribution fall). The formula which follows can be used to find the median or any other percentile:

$$\text{Percentile} = (\text{LRL of class}) + i \left[\frac{(n\text{th case}) - (\text{cum.} f \text{ of the interval below})}{f \text{ of class}} \right]$$

where LRL = lower real limit of a class interval
                   i = interval size
                   n = number of cases or scores being considered

cum. f of

interval below = total number of scores below the interval in which nth case is found

f of class = frequency of the interval in which nth case is found

COMPUTING PERCENTILES AND PERCENTILE RANKS

Let us use the formula which appears above to find the median score value for the data in Table 2-1. Fifty percent of the scores fall below the median, so we are looking for a point below which there are 32.5 scores. Thus the nth case = 32.5. Going up from the bottom of the distribution and counting scores we find that the 32nd and 33rd scores are in the class interval 55–59. The frequency of this interval is 17 and the cumulative frequency below the interval is 29. The total number of cases is 65 and the interval size is 5. Using these figures, we can determine the value of the median, or 50th percentile, by substituting in the formula:

$$\text{50th percentile} = 54.5 + 5 \left(\frac{32.5 - 29}{17} \right)$$

$$= 54.5 + 5 \left(\frac{3.5}{17} \right)$$

$$= 54.5 + 1.03$$

$$= 55.53$$

Thus the median score is 55.53—or rounded, 56.

Other percentiles can be found in the same manner. For example, suppose that we wanted to find the 25th percentile for the data in Table 2-2. Since the problem is to find the point below which there are 25 percent of the scores, it will be necessary to determine first how many scores are being considered. Twenty-five percent of 65 scores equals .25 × 65 or 16.25 scores (for precision we will not drop the decimal). By using the formula, the point below which there are 16.25 scores in the distribution can be found as follows:

$$25\text{th percentile} = (\text{LRL of class}) + i\left[\frac{(n\text{th case}) - (\text{cum.}f \text{ of the interval below})}{f \text{ of class}}\right]$$

$$= 49.5 + 5\left(\frac{16.25 - 15}{14}\right)$$

$$= 49.5 + 5\left(\frac{1.25}{14}\right)$$

$$= 49.5 + .45$$

$$= 49.95 \text{ or } 50$$

Below a score of 50, then, we expect to find 25 percent of the scores in this distribution.

Sometimes it is necessary to know the *percentile rank* of a score in a distribution, or to know what percent of the scores rank below a given score. To find a percentile rank one can use the formula:

$$PR = 100\left[\frac{(\text{Raw score} - \text{LRL of class})}{i} \times (f \text{ of the class}) + (\text{cum.}f \text{ of the interval below})\right] \div N$$

As an example, suppose that we wished to determine the percentile rank of a score of 62 in the distribution shown in Table 2-2. The computation is as follows:

$$\text{Raw score} = 62$$

$$\text{LRL of class} = 59.5$$

$$i = 5$$

$$f = 8$$

$$\text{cum.}f \text{ of interval below} = 46$$

$$N = 65$$

$$PR = \frac{100 \left[\left(\frac{62 - 59.5}{5} \times 8\right) + 46\right]}{65}$$

$$= \frac{100 \left[\left(\frac{2.5}{5} \times 8\right) + 46\right]}{65}$$

$$= \frac{100 \, (4 + 46)}{65}$$

$$= \frac{5000}{65}$$

$$= 76.9 \text{ or } 77$$

Thus in the distribution shown in Tables 2-1 and 2-2, the raw score of 62 has a percentile rank of 76.9. This means that nearly 77 percent of the scores fall below a score of 62.

As was mentioned previously, an ogive, or cumulative frequency curve, can be used to determine percentile ranks. The procedure is as follows.

First, locate the raw score along the horizontal axis, then extend a vertical line upward to the curve, and finally sight straight across to the left to the vertical scale where the percentile rank can be read. Suppose, for example, that we wanted to find the percentile rank of a score of 49 for the distribution from which the ogive in Fig. 2-3 was made. By following the steps indicated we can see that a raw score of 49 has a percentile rank of 23. The values read from an ogive are generally less accurate than those found by means of a formula, so it would be best to regard them as close approximations. It should also be pointed out that a particular ogive is valid only for the distribution upon which it is based.

The two formulas for finding percentiles and percentile ranks presented in this chapter can be used with *ungrouped* data as well as with *grouped* data. If the data are not grouped, the size of the class interval will be 1 and each different score value will be considered a class or class interval.

MEASURES OF VARIABILITY

As has been explained, central tendency is an important characteristic with respect to the analysis of a score distribution. Another useful characteristic is *variability*, or dispersion. Specifically, it is essential to know the extent to which scores are dispersed or scattered in a distribution. Two distributions may have the same mean but quite different score-spread patterns. Consider, for example, these two groups of scores:

    Group A: 20, 30, 36, 40, 41, 42, 43, 44, 46, 48, 54, 60
    Group B: 34, 36, 37, 38, 39, 40, 42, 43, 45, 47, 49, 54

Both groups have a mean of 42, but the scores of Group B show much less variability. That is, they tend to be less spread out.

Several measures of variability can be used to indicate score variability, but only the most frequently used measures will be considered in this chapter. One of the commonly used measures of dispersion is the *range*.

The range is a statistic which gives a rough indication of variability. It is found simply by subtracting the lowest score in the distribution from the highest. For the data in Table 2-1, the range is 79 – 34, or 45. The range, while easy to calculate, is not a very stable measure of variability. It is based upon only two scores in the whole distribution (which are likely to vary from sample to sample), so it is not a dependable statistic.

The *semi-interquartile range* is a measure of variability which is defined as half of the interquartile range (the middle 50 percent of the scores of a distribution). The formula for finding the semi-interquartile range is

$$\frac{Q_3 - Q_1}{2}$$

where Q_3 = third quartile, or 75th percentile
               Q_1 = first quartile, or 25th percentile

This measure of score dispersion does not reflect the value of individual scores, nor does it include the scores beyond the first and third quartiles, so its usefulness is quite limited.

The *Variance* and *Standard Deviation* are the two most often used measures of variability. These statistics, which consider all of the scores in a distribution, are quite stable and can be used in the computation of other useful statistics. Since the variance generally is calculated prior to finding the standard deviation of a score distribution, we shall consider it first.

The *variance* may be defined as the mean of the squares of the deviations of scores from the mean. The formula for finding the variance is:

$$s^2 = \frac{\Sigma x^2}{N-1}$$

where s^2 = variance
            Σx^2 = sum of squared deviations
            N = number of scores

In order to find the standard deviation, which is defined as the square root of the mean of the squared deviations from the mean, it is merely necessary to calculate the variance and find the square root of it. Thus the formula for the standard deviation is

$$s = \sqrt{\frac{\Sigma x^2}{N-1}}$$

By using the following set of test scores, the computation of the variance and standard deviation can be demonstrated.

Test Score, (X)	$X - X(x)$	x^2
30	10	100
27	7	49
25	5	25
23	3	9
21	1	1
20	0	0
19	−1	1
18	−2	4
16	−4	16
11	−9	81
10	−10	100
$\Sigma X = 220$		$\Sigma x^2 = 386$

$$\text{Mean } (\overline{X}) = \frac{\Sigma X}{N} = \frac{220}{11} = 20$$

$$s = \sqrt{\frac{\Sigma x^2}{N-1}} = \sqrt{\frac{386}{10}} = \sqrt{38.60} = 6.21$$

An examination of the work shown above, will reveal that the following steps were taken to find s, the standard deviation.

Step 1. The test scores were added to get ΣX.

Step 2. The mean was found by dividing ΣX by the number of scores, N.

Step 3. The mean $(\overline{X})$, which was found to be 11, was subtracted from each score, to get the deviations (x).

Step 4. Each deviation was squared to get x^2.

Step 5. The squared deviations were added to get Σx^2.

Step 6. Σx^2 was divided by $N - 1$ to get the variance.

Step 7. The square root of the variance $\dfrac{\Sigma x^2}{N-1}$ was calculated to get the standard deviation.

One can avoid the necessity of having to compute deviations in order to find a standard deviation by using the "raw-score" formula

$$s = \sqrt{\frac{N\Sigma X^2 - (\Sigma X)^2}{N(N-1)}}$$

where X = raw score
X^2 = squared raw score
N = number of scores
Σ = sum of

Using the data from the previous page, we shall demonstrate the use of this formula.

Test Score, X	X^2
30	900
27	729
25	625
23	529
21	441
20	400
19	361
18	324
16	256
11	121
10	100
$\Sigma X = \overline{220}$	$\Sigma X^2 = \overline{4786}$

$$s = \sqrt{\frac{N\Sigma X^2 - (\Sigma X^2)}{N(N-1)}}$$

$$= \sqrt{\frac{11(4786) - (220)^2}{11(10)}}$$

$$= \sqrt{38.60}$$

$$= 6.21$$

Generally speaking, when a calculator is available and many scores are to be dealt with, this raw-score formula is more convenient to use than the "deviation" formula.

Students sometimes wonder what value the standard deviation has other than that of showing relative degree of dispersion of scores, or indicating whether one set of scores is more variable than another. As has previously been mentioned, the standard deviation is necessary for finding other statistical measures, and a case in point is the standard score. Standard scores are useful because they make raw scores considerably more meaningful, as we shall explain.

STANDARD SCORES

One of the standard scores that will be considered in this chapter is the z-score, which is found by the formula

$$z = \frac{X - \overline{X}}{s} = \frac{x}{s}$$

where z = standard score
X = raw score
$\overline{X}$ = mean
x = deviation of a raw score from the mean
s = standard deviation

In order to explain the computation and meaning of z-scores, let's turn to an example. Suppose for instance that it seemed desirable to convert raw-score data to z-scores. By using the data shown below and following a few steps the z-scores can be determined without difficulty.

Raw Score, X	Deviation, x	x/s	z-score
30	10	$\dfrac{10}{6.21}$	1.61
27	7	$\dfrac{7}{6.21}$	1.13
25	5	$\dfrac{5}{6.21}$	.80
23	3	$\dfrac{3}{6.21}$	.48
21	1	$\dfrac{1}{6.21}$	.16
20	0	$\dfrac{0}{6.21}$	0
19	−1	$\dfrac{-1}{6.21}$	−.16
18	−2	$\dfrac{-2}{6.21}$	−.32
16	−4	$\dfrac{-4}{6.21}$	−.64
11	−9	$\dfrac{-9}{6.21}$	−1.45
10	−10	$\dfrac{-10}{6.21}$	−1.61

The steps followed in computing the z-score values which are shown above are:

Step 1. Calculate the deviation of each raw score from the mean of the distribution.

Step 2. Divide each deviation by the standard deviation for the distribution.

Since the mean and standard deviation for the data were found to be 20 and 6.21 respectively, we can use these values in the formula to find the z-scores. For example, a raw score of 30 in this distribution yields a z-score of 1.61:

$$z = \frac{X - \overline{X}}{s} \text{ or } \frac{x}{s}$$

$$z = \frac{30 - 20}{6.21} = \frac{10}{6.21} = 1.61$$

Thus a raw score of 30 is 1.61 standard deviations above the mean of 20. A raw score of 11 yields a z-score of -1.45:

$$z = \frac{11 - 20}{6.21} = \frac{-9}{6.21} = -1.45$$

The z-score of -1.45 tells us that a raw score of 11 is 1.45 standard deviations *below* the mean in *this distribution*.

Because z-scores can be negative (when the raw scores are below the mean) and extremely small (such as .01), it is often desirable to convert z-scores to Z-scores and overcome these two disadvantages. The Z-score formula is as follows:

$$Z = 10z + 50,$$

or

$$10 \left(\frac{X - \overline{X}}{s} \right) + 50$$

In order to illustrate the calculation of a Z-score, let's start with a raw score of 30. It has already been determined that a raw score of 30 has an equivalent z-score of 1.61. If this z-score is substituted into the Z-score formula, the resulting standard score is 66.1. That is, $Z = 10(1.61) + 50 = 66.1$. The Z-score for a raw score of 11 is 35.5, because $Z = 10(-1.45) + 50 = 35.5$. Notice that the z-score of -1.45 yields a positive Z-score value. By now it should be apparent that both z-scores and Z-scores make raw scores more meaningful. A z-score of 2.5 (or a Z-score of 75) should tell us that the original score was two and a half standard deviations above the mean for a particular distribution. A z-score of -1.5 (or Z-score of 35) should tell us that the raw score was one and a half standard deviations *below* the mean.

If z-scores or Z-scores were plotted on a graph, they would show the same shape of curve as the original data. If the original data were not "normally" distributed, neither would the standard scores be so distributed. If one wanted the standard scores to show a "normal" distribution he could compute another kind of standard score known as the T-score. T-scores are normally distributed standard scores. They can be computed by "normalizing" a set of raw scores as follows:

Step 1.   Convert each raw score to a percentile.
Step 2.   Use a normal-curve table to find the z-scores which correspond to each percentile.
Step 3.   Use the Z-score formula to change the z-scores to corresponding T-scores. (In the formula T is substituted for Z).

NORMAL FREQUENCY-DISTRIBUTION CURVE

The normal-curve concept is of great value in describing test data and in making statistical inferences concerning such data. The normal curve is a sym-

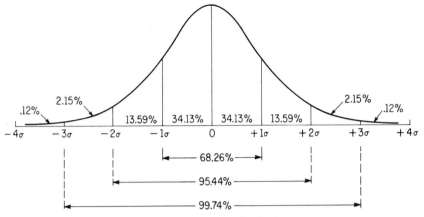

Fig. 2-4. Normal frequency-distribution curve.

metrical, bell-shaped curve which is based upon a mathematical formula. It represents a theoretical frequency distribution which is derived from the laws of chance. Such a curve is shown in Fig. 2-4.

Let's look at the unit normal curve in this figure. It has a mean of zero and a standard deviation of one. The base line, or abscissa, is marked off in standard deviation units (σ). The vertical axis, or ordinate, shows the frequency for different points along the curve. It can be seen that the greatest frequency occurs at the mean, which is zero, and that the lowest frequencies occur at the extremes of the curve. The percents shown in the marked-off sections of the curve indicate the percent of area under the different portions of the curve, as well as the proportions of the cases that one can expect to find between the reference points indicated along the base of the curve (σ units). For example, in a normal distribution we can expect 34.13 percent of all the scores in the distribution to have values which range from the mean to one standard deviation above the mean. Likewise, 13.59 percent of the cases will be between $+1\sigma$ and $+2\sigma$ above the mean, and 2.15 percent of all the scores will range between $+2\sigma$ and $+3\sigma$ above the mean. Since the curve is symmetrical, the same percents will be found for areas below the mean. If we consider scores or values which range from -1σ to $+1\sigma$ about the mean, it is apparent that there will be 68.26 percent of the total number of scores in this range. Also, there will be approximately 95 percent of the total number of scores or values ranging from -2σ to $+2\sigma$ around the mean.

It should be emphasized that the normal curve percents which have just been discussed do not apply to nonnormal distributions. The curve drawn for the data in Table 2-1, for example, is not normal, but is an approximation of the normal curve (see Fig. 2-1). The farther from a normal distribution a distribution of scores is, the more difficult it becomes to apply the characteristics of the normal curve to the distribution in question.

From a normal-curve table it is possible to read the z-scores and corresponding curve areas. The z-scores are, of course, standard deviation units along the baseline of the curve. Table B of the Appendix is a normal-curve table. It can be used for such purposes as finding percentile ranks or for locating z-scores for given percentiles. If we wished to find the percentile rank for a raw score which had a z-score value 1.83, we would first locate 1.8 in the z-column and then read across to the column headed by .03. The value we find is .4664. Since all of the values found in Table B represent the proportion of the total area under the curve between the mean and the z-score, and because a z-score of 1.83 lies to the right of the mean, we must add .50 to .4664. That is, we add the percent of the lower half of the curve to the table value just found. The sum of .50 and .4664 is .9664 or 96.64 percent. Therefore, the percentile rank for a z-score of 1.83 is 96.64 or 97. This means that approximately 97 percent of the scores in a *normal distribution* will lie below a z-score of 1.83, or below a point which is 1.83 standard deviations above the mean.

One can find a z-score from a percentile rank by first locating the percentile rank in the table and then reading the corresponding z-score. For example, let's find a z-score for a percentile rank of 33. A percentile rank of 33 means that there will be 33 percent of the total frequency, or the area under the curve, below this point. Since the table values are for areas *from the mean*, it is necessary to subtract .33 from .50, which gives .17. By locating .17 and reading both upward and across from this point in the table, we find that the z-score value must be .44 (.4 + .04). Actually, since the 33rd percentile is below the mean, the z-score must be written – .44.

Earlier in this chapter reference was made to the use of a normal-curve table to locate z-scores when it was necessary to normalize standard scores (form them into a normal distribution). In case this procedure is not yet sufficiently clear, the reader may wish to review the essential steps. To normalize standard scores in order to obtain T-scores proceed as follows:

1. Convert the raw scores to percentile ranks.
2. Using a normal-curve table, find the z-scores which correspond to the percentile ranks assigned to the raw scores.
3. Substitute the z-score values into the formula

$$T = 10z + 50$$

Various applications of the normal curve to psychological problems can be made, but let's use just one as our example: Suppose that we assume that the intelligence quotients (IQs) obtained from the Wechsler Intelligence Scale for Children (WISC) are normally distributed and that the mean IQ is 100 while the standard deviation is 15. If the "normal" range of mental ability is 90 to 110, in terms of IQs, what percent of the children for which the WISC is suitable can be expected to have measured IQs which are in the normal range?

The first step in solving this problem is to find z-scores for 90 and 110.

z-score for 90 z-score for 110

$$z = \frac{X - \mu}{\sigma} \qquad\qquad z = \frac{X - \mu}{\sigma}$$

$$= \frac{90 - 100}{15} \qquad\qquad = \frac{110 - 100}{15}$$

$$= -.67 \qquad\qquad\qquad = .67$$

The next step is to find the percentage of scores lying between the mean and each of the z-scores. In Table B of the Appendix we can see that the area under the curve which is between the mean and a z-score of .67 is .2486. Because the area we are considering lies on both sides of the mean, we must double .2486, which gives .4972. In terms of percent, then, the result is 49.72. That is, 49.72 percent of the children can be expected to have IQs that lie between 90 and 110. In other words, about half of the population should have scores in the "normal" range.

Apparently most physical and mental measures that can be obtained through the use of tests or other measurement devices are normally distributed if we consider whole populations or large random samples. That is, whether we measure height, weight, speed, strength, spelling ability, reading ability, academic aptitude, or word fluency the scores or measures are likely to show a normal frequency distribution curve, provided that many measures have been obtained at random. Small samples, however, can deviate considerably from the normal with respect to score distribution.

SKEWNESS

Frequency-distribution curves that are asymmetrical because of a preponderance of scores near one end of a distribution and a few extreme scores near the other end are said to be *skewed*. Two examples of skewness are shown in Figs. 2-5 and 2-6.

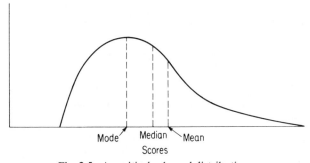

Fig. 2-5. A positively skewed distribution.

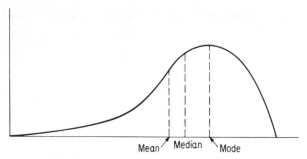

Mean / Median \ Mode

Fig. 2-6. A negatively skewed distribution.

A positively skewed distribution such as the one shown in Fig. 2-5 has relatively few extreme scores at the right-hand side of the curve. That is, the "tail" (which determines the direction of skewness) is at the high-value side of the curve. Fig. 2-6 shows a negatively skewed curve, with the extreme values at the left. In each case the mean and median are found closer to the tail of the curve than is the mode, and the mean is affected more by the extreme scores than the median. (In a normal distribution the mean, mode and median are the same.)

A positively skewed distribution will result if a test, in general, is too difficult for the group tested, and a negatively skewed distribution will occur when a test is too easy for the group.

MEASURES OF RELATIONSHIP

Up to this point our discussion has been related principally to the distribution of a single variable, such as the scores on a particular psychological test. There are times, however, when it is essential to know how two or more variables compare. For example, one might want to know the extent to which the scores for two different mental-ability tests go together or are correlated. Or it may be necessary to determine the degree of relationship between mental-ability scores and grade-point averages for, say, college freshmen.

A rather general estimate of the amount of correlation that exists between two sets of psychological measures can be made on the basis of an inspection of the data, but precise measures of relationship can come only from the application of certain statistical procedures. Before we get into statistical measures of relationships, however, it may be desirable to discuss briefly the concept of *rectilinear correlation* or "straight-line" relationships, which is generally the kind of correlation that is involved when one works with sets of test scores.

Let's consider the two sets of test data which appear in Table 2-4. These are the raw scores earned by a hypothetical group of high-school seniors on two standardized tests of mental ability.

Table 2-4 shows two scores, one for Test X and one for Test Y, for each of the persons listed in the table. These pairs of scores have been plotted in the scattergram shown in Fig. 2-7. That is, a point was placed on the graph to show the corresponding scores (X and Y) for each person. An examination of Table

TABLE 2-4   Raw Scores Earned by Sixteen High School Seniors on
Two Mental Ability Tests

Student	Test X	Test Y
Muir, Dee	50	53
Voyant, Claire	47	46
O'Shea, Rick	43	49
Bund, Morrie	40	48
Shores, Sandy	39	45
Burger, Lim	36	41
Combes, Honey	36	40
Mander, Jerry	36	38
Wood, Holly	35	37
Garkey, Ollie	33	35
Mossity, Annie	30	35
Byrd, Jay	30	36
Mattick, Otto	29	33
Kadellic, Cy	28	34
Glott, Polly	26	30
Able, Hardley	22	25

2-4 and Fig. 2-7 will reveal that the scores on the tests tend to rise and fall together. That is, there is a *tendency* for high scores on the first test to be accompanied by high scores on the second. This means that there is a *positive* correlation between the two variables, X and Y. Notice that the pattern of scores is

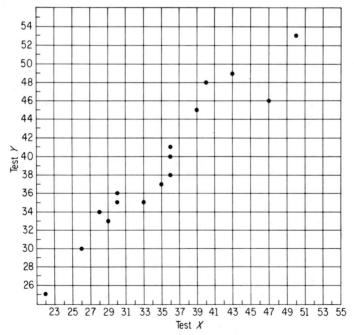

Fig. 2-7. Scattergram showing relationships of scores on Text X and
Test Y.

elliptical and shows a rectilinear relationship, which is the kind of relationship that is being considered in this chapter.

Had the correlation been perfect for the data in Table 2-4, rather than just very high, the subjects would have ranked exactly the same on both tests. That is to say, Dee Muir would have ranked at the top on both tests, Claire Voyant would have been second on both, Rick O'Shea third on both, etc.

The scattergrams which appear in Figs. 2-8, 2-9, and 2-10, show positive, negative, and zero correlations for pairs of variables. Notice that in Fig. 2-9, the pattern runs from the upper end of the Y axis to the upper end of the X axis, just opposite of the pattern in Fig. 2-8. This means that there is a tendency for the scores on variable Y to decrease as the scores on variable X increase. Thus there is a *negative* correlation between variables X and Y. When there is no correlation we find a pattern like the one in Fig. 2-10.

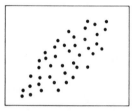

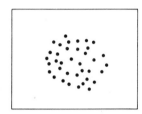

Fig. 2-8. Scattergram for a positive correlation. Fig. 2-9. Scattergram for a negative correlation. Fig. 2-10. Scattergram for a zero correlation.

PRODUCT-MOMENT CORRELATION COEFFICIENT

The most frequently used procedure for obtaining a statistical measure of the amount of correlation between sets of test scores involves the use of a formula for finding a product-moment coefficient of correlation. The formula was developed by the famous British statistician, Karl Pearson. The basic formula is:

$$r = \frac{\Sigma xy}{N s_x s_y}$$

where r = zero-order product-moment correlation coefficient
        $x = X - \overline{X}$ (raw score minus the mean of the X variable)
        $y = Y - \overline{Y}$ (raw score minus the mean of the Y variable)
        N = number of pairs of scores
        s_x = standard deviation of variable X
        s_y = standard deviation of variable Y

While this basic formula can be used quite satisfactorily to find the correlation coefficient for the data in Table 2-4, let's use a variation of it, which may be called the raw-score formula, for convenience of computation. The variation is as follows.

$$r = \frac{N\Sigma XY - \Sigma X \Sigma Y}{\sqrt{[N\Sigma X^2 - (\Sigma X)^2][N\Sigma Y^2 - (\Sigma Y)^2]}}$$

where N = Number of pairs of scores

ΣXY = Sum of the products obtained by multiplying each X-score by the corresponding Y-score.

ΣX = sum of the X-scores.

ΣY = sum of the Y-scores

ΣX^2 = sum of the squared X-scores

ΣY^2 = sum of the squared Y-scores

$(\Sigma X)^2$ = square of sum of the X-scores

$(\Sigma Y)^2$ = square of sum of the Y-scores

Using a worksheet, one can obtain the necessary values and then substitute into the formula.

X	Y	X^2	Y^2	XY
50	53	2,500	2,809	2,650
47	46	2,209	2,116	2,162
43	49	1,849	2,401	2,107
40	48	1,600	2,304	1,920
39	45	1,521	2,025	1,755
36	41	1,296	1,681	1,476
36	40	1,296	1,600	1,440
36	38	1,296	1,444	1,368
35	37	1,225	1,369	1,295
33	35	1,089	1,225	1,155
30	35	900	1,225	1,050
30	36	900	1,296	1,080
29	33	841	1,089	957
28	34	784	1,156	952
26	30	676	900	780
22	25	484	625	550
$\Sigma X = 560$	$\Sigma Y = 625$	$\Sigma X^2 = 20,466$	$\Sigma Y^2 = 25,265$	$\Sigma XY = 22,697$

$$r = \frac{N\Sigma XY - \Sigma X\Sigma Y}{\sqrt{[N\Sigma X^2 - (\Sigma X)^2]\,[N\Sigma Y^2 - (\Sigma Y)^2]}}$$

$$= \frac{(16 \times 22,697) - (560 \times 625)}{\sqrt{[16 \times 20,466 - (560)^2]\,[16 \times 25,265 - (625)^2]}}$$

$$= \frac{13,152}{\sqrt{13,856 \times 13,615}}$$

$$= \frac{13,152}{\sqrt{188,649,440}}$$

$$= \frac{13,152}{13,731.33}$$

$$= .958$$

$$= .96$$

INTERPRETATION OF A CORRELATION COEFFICIENT

In order to be able to make use of a coefficient of correlation such as the one just found for the data in Table 2-4, it is necessary to have a good understanding of what the statistic means. In other words, it is necessary to know the *amount* and the *kind* of relationship indicated by this measure of correlation.

Correlation coefficients can vary in size from +1.00 to -1.00, with the former figure representing perfect positive correlation between two variables and the latter indicating perfect negative correlation. Rarely if ever will we expect to find perfect correlation between sets of test scores. As was explained earlier, to get a perfect positive correlation (+1.00) the ranks of the two sets of data would have to be exactly the same. For a perfect negative correlation (-1.00) the ranks of scores on the one set of data would have to be exactly opposite of the ranks on the second set. Put another way, a coefficient of -1.00 would mean that the highest scoring individual on variable X would be the lowest scoring individual on variable Y, the second highest on variable X would be the next to the lowest person on variable Y, etc. A coefficient of correlation of .00 would indicate no correlation whatsoever, or that the two sets of data were not related.

When we consider coefficients of correlation, then, we are interested in the size of r which indicates the magnitude or amount of relationship, and the sign (+ or -) of r which indicates the direction of the correlation. The classification system which follows may be useful for providing a qualitative description of co-efficients of correlation:

.80 to 1.00—very high correlation
.60 to .79—substantial correlation
.40 to .59—moderate correlation
.20 to .39—little correlation
.01 to .19—practically no correlation

It should be emphasized that correlation coefficients must not be thought of as percents in the usual sense. That is, a correlation of .50 does not mean that 50 percent of the variation of variable X is the result of variation in variable Y. Actually, such a correlation (.50) indicates that only 25 percent of the variation of X is directly associated with variation in Y, a result which can be obtained by squaring .50 ($.50 \times .50 = .25$). It would be incorrect to assume that a correlation coefficient of .40 indicates half as much correlation between the variables as an r of .80, because an r of .40 really indicates much less than half the relationship of an r of .80. Again, squaring each r will bear this out ($.40^2 = .16$ and $.80^2 = .64$). Certainly, as the r's approach 1.00, whether positive or negative, they indicate much greater correlation between the variables.

One should keep in mind that a correlation between two variables does not necessarily imply a cause-effect relationship. If X and Y are found to be correlated, we cannot tell from the coefficient of correlation whether X is the cause of Y or Y is the cause of X. In fact, X and Y may be correlated because each is correlated with a third variable, Z.

SIGNIFICANCE OF A CORRELATION COEFFICIENT

One should not accept a coefficient of correlation as valid unless it has been subjected to a statistical test of significance. Such a test takes into consideration the size of the correlation coefficient as well as the number of cases used to obtain the correlation. It is necessary to apply such a test because small samples of data often will yield correlation coefficients which are not typical or true. That is, the computed correlation for a small sample is more likely to be a matter of chance than the computed correlation for a large sample.

While correlation coefficients can be tested by means of a mathematical formula, it is much simpler and faster to make use of a table such as Table C in the Appendix. Table C shows how large a correlation coefficient must be (for a certain sample size) in order to be considered statistically significant at either the 5 percent or 1 percent level of confidence. Our data on page 49 showed a correlation of .96. Since this r is based upon sixteen pairs of scores, there will be fourteen degrees of freedom ($N - 2$). To test the significance of the coefficient .96, it is necessary to locate 14 in the degrees-of-freedom column and then read across to the 5 percent column and the 1 percent column. In the 5 percent column a coefficient of .497 is found and in the 1 percent column a coefficient of .623 appears. Thus it can be seen that a coefficient of at least .497 is needed for significance at the 5 percent level and a coefficient of at least .623 is needed for significance at the one percent level of confidence. In other words, the chances of getting a correlation coefficient as large as .497 *by chance* are only five out of a hundred, and the chances of getting one as large as .623 by chance are only one out of a hundred. Since the computed coefficient of .96 is much higher than .497 and .623, it is evident that it is statistically significant at both levels of confidence and very likely did not occur by chance. Table C can be used to test coefficients of correlations of various magnitudes for various sample sizes. Of course, both negative and positive r's can be checked by means of the table.

OTHER MEASURES OF CORRELATION

While the Pearson zero-order product moment correlation coefficient generally is used to show a relationship between test scores, there are special instances in which other measures of correlation are needed. For example, a researcher might wonder whether a high positive correlation coefficient found between reading-test scores and general academic achievement (as measured by an achievement test) might be greatly influenced by mental ability (as measured by a test). By using the following formula for finding a *partial r*, he could rule out the effect of the third variable, mental ability, on the other variables:

$$12.3 = \frac{r_{12} - r_{13}\, r_{23}}{\sqrt{1 - r_{13}^2}\ \sqrt{1 - r_{23}^2}}$$

where   12.3 = correlation between Test 1 and Test 2 (Reading and Achievement) with the effect of Test 3 (Mental Ability) partialed out

r_{12} = correlation between Tests 1 and 2

r_{13} = correlation between Tests 1 and 3

r_{23} = correlation between Tests 2 and 3

The *point-biserial r* is often used during the construction and development of a test because the author of the test wants to know whether each item being considered for the test discriminates well between the high-scoring and low-scoring individuals who are given the test. That is, the point-biserial *r* formula will tell him what degree of correlation there is between performance on a single test question and performance on the entire test. The formula follows:

$$r_{bp} = \frac{(\overline{X}_2 - \overline{X}_1)\,\sqrt{P_1 P_2}}{s_t}$$

where r_{bp} = point-biserial correlation coefficient

$\overline{X}_2$ = mean of group who passed item

$\overline{X}_1$ = mean of group who failed item

P_1 = percent of persons who failed the item

P_2 = percent of persons who passed the item

s_t = standard deviation of whole distribution of scores

There are still other measures of correlation which can be used to find relationships between test scores for special situations or problems, such as the multiple *R*, the phi coefficient, and Spearman's rho, but these will not be covered in this textbook. The reader who wishes to know more about other correlation techniques is encouraged to consult the suggested references at the end of the chapter.

SAMPLING STATISTICS

In testing, it is often necessary to know how much confidence one can place in the descriptive statistics he is using. Sampling statistics, or *inferential statistics* as they are often called, tell us something about the probability that an obtained statistic is a close approximation of the parameter for the population from which the sample was drawn. We are of course assuming randomness for the sample when we use sampling statistics.

Inferential statistics, then, give us a means of judging the accuracy or dependability of the statistics which have been computed from test data. Without going deeply into the theory underlying inferential statistics, we shall discuss the concepts most likely to be encountered by the person who works with test results.

STANDARD ERRORS

The mean, standard deviation, correlation coefficient, and the other statistics which have been discussed all have their own standard errors. The standard error of a statistic is an estimate of the standard deviation of a distribution of like statistics. It is useful because it is an indicator of how much variation a person might expect if he were to compute the same statistic, say the mean, for several samples like the sample with which he is working.

Standard errors tend to become smaller as the number of cases or scores in the sample increases and the variability of the scores decreases. Of course, the smaller the standard error of a statistic the better, for with a small standard error one can be more confident about a statistic than with a large standard error. At this point we shall discuss a few of the most often used standard errors.

The *standard error of the mean* is useful because it tells us how much variability we could expect if we were to calculate the means for many randomly drawn samples from a parent population. We could of course find the standard deviation for the distribution of sample means in the usual way, but we can save a great deal of time and effort by using a formula which *estimates* the standard deviation of the sampling distribution of means. The formula for the standard error of the mean is as follows:

$$\sigma_{\overline{x}} = \frac{\sigma}{\sqrt{N}}$$

where $\quad \sigma_{\overline{x}}$ = standard error of the mean

σ = an unbiased estimate of the population standard deviation

$\sqrt{N}$ = square root of the sample size

Let's consider an example of how $\sigma_{\overline{x}}$ would be computed with this formula: Suppose that we had drawn a random sample of 100 scores on a mental ability test which had been given to thousands of students. Also, assume that the mean score for the sample was 62 and the standard deviation was 12.5. The standard error of the mean would be computed as follows:

$$\sigma_{\overline{x}} = \frac{12.5}{\sqrt{100}} = \frac{12.5}{10} = 1.25$$

The figure 1.25 tells us that we can expect approximately 68 percent of our sample means to be within plus or minus 1.25 score points of the true mean (population mean). This expectation is based on the normal frequency distribution curve, which the sampling distribution is known to follow. Thus we can also say that approximately 95 percent of the sample means would be expected to lie within $\pm 2\sigma_{\overline{x}}$, or within 2.5 points of the true mean. Stated differently, the population mean μ is likely to be within the range of the sample mean $\overline{X}$ plus or minus the standard error of the mean. In this case that would be 62 ± 1.25, or from 60.75 to 63.25. It is even more likely that the true mean will be within $\pm 2\sigma_{\overline{x}}$ of the sample mean (95 % probability).

The *standard error of measurement* is another useful standard error. It helps us determine how much we could expect a person's score to vary if he were tested frequently, so it is a measure of reliability. The formula used to compute this statistic is:

$$SE_m = s\sqrt{1 - r_{xx}}$$

where SE_m = standard error of measurement
           s = standard deviation
        r_{xx} = reliability coefficient for the test

An example should serve to show how the standard error of measurement can be used in estimating the reliability of a test in terms of test-score units.

Suppose that a student had a score of 63 on an aptitude test. How near is the student's score to his true score? (We are assuming that, if he had taken the test a number of times, his scores would vary because of the usual measurement error, or sampling error.) For this problem we shall assume that the test's reliability coefficient (a term to be discussed later) is .91, and that the standard deviation is 10. Using the formula we can compute SE_m:

$$SE_m = 10\sqrt{1 - .91} = 10\sqrt{.09} = 10 \times .3 = 3$$

Because this statistic applies to the student's *true* score, which is unknown, we cannot be certain about where the true score lies. However, it is customary to assume that it probably lies within a range of ± 1 SE_m. In this case that would be 63 ± 3, or 60 to 66.

The *standard error of a product-moment correlation coefficient* S_r enables us to estimate the amount of variation expected in correlation coefficients for samples of various sizes. If N exceeds 30 and r exceeds .50, we can safely use the following formula for this statistic:

$$S_r = \frac{1}{\sqrt{N - 1}}$$

where S_r = standard error of a product-moment correlation coefficient
       N = number of pairs of scores in the sample

When small r's and small samples are used it is best to turn to advanced statistics texts for the appropriate procedures.

Let's consider a problem. Suppose that we had found an r of .55 for a sample which had 50 pairs of scores. How certain can we be that this r represents a true correlation and is not likely to have occurred just by chance? Using the formula,

$$S_r = \frac{1}{\sqrt{50-1}} = \frac{1}{\sqrt{49}} = \frac{1}{7} = .14$$

If $S_r = .14$, then 68 percent of the sample coefficients that we might obtain for the data used should lie between $+.14$ and $-.14$. In other words, only 32 percent of the coefficients are expected to exceed those limits by chance. If we use $2S_r$, we can say that approximately 95 percent of the chance correlation coefficients will lie within the range $-.28$ to $+.28$. Our coefficient of .55 exceeds these limits easily, so we can feel rather confident that we have evidence of a true correlation for the data.

As was mentioned earlier in the chapter, however, it is generally assumed that a person will use a table (see Appendix, Table C) for determining whether correlation coefficients are statistically significant.

Unless a correlation coefficient has the value of either $+1.00$ or -1.00, errors are likely to be made if one tries to predict a second set of score values from the first set. That is, when the correlation is not perfect, our estimates of variable Y from variable X are not likely to be perfect, and the farther that the r is from ± 1.00 the less accurate our estimates will be. When we make such estimates, the difference between an observed value and a predicted value is referred to as the *error of estimate*.

The *standard error of estimate*, which is the standard deviation of the "estimate errors," is a useful measure of the accuracy of estimates. The formula for this statistic is:

$$SE_{xy} = s_y \sqrt{1 - r_{xy}^2}$$

where s_y = standard deviation of variable Y

r_{xy} = correlation coefficient between variables X and Y

In order to show how SE_{xy} can be useful with respect to test-score prediction, let's turn to an example. Suppose, for instance, that we had found a correlation of .80 between Test X and Test Y, and that the standard deviation of Test Y was known to be 4.5. By substituting these values in the formula we obtain the figure 2.7 for SE_{xy}. We should now expect that approximately 68 percent of the "errors" made in predicting Test Y scores from Test X scores will be within 2.7 score points of the predicted score. Of course, we can also say that approximately 95 percent of the "errors" in prediction will be within 5.4 points of the predicted values. We are assuming, now, that the scores which were obtained for the two tests were normally distributed.

The authors are aware of the fact that some of the readers may desire more statistical information than has been provided in this chapter. For those whose needs have not been met sufficiently, we suggest the use of an appropriate statistics textbook.

REFERENCES

Adkins, Dorothy C., *Statistics: An Introduction for Students in the Behavioral Sciences*. Columbus: Merrill, 1964.

Downie, N. M., and R. W. Heath, *Basic Statistical Methods*. New York: Harper, 1959.

Edwards, Allen L., *Statistical Analysis for Students in Psychology and Education*. New York: Holt, 1953.

Fergusen, George A., *Statistical Analysis in Psychology and Education*. New York: McGraw-Hill, 1959.

Fisher, R. A., *Statistical Methods for Research Workers*. 13th ed., Edinburgh: Oliver and Boyd, 1963.

Garrett, Henry E., *Statistics in Psychology and Education*. 5th ed. New York: Longmans, 1958.

Guilford, J. P., *Fundamental Statistics in Psychology and Education*. 4th ed. New York: McGraw-Hill, 1965.

Hays, W., *Statistics for Psychologists*. New York: Holt, 1963.

Lacey, Oliver L., *Statistical Methods in Experimentation: An Introduction*. Boston: Houghton Mifflin, 1953.

Lindquist, E. F., *Statistical Analysis in Educational Research*. Boston: Houghton Mifflin, 1940.

McNemar, Quinn, *Psychological Statistics*. New York: Wiley, 1949.

Popham, W. James, *Educational Statistics: Use and Interpretation*. New York: Harper, 1967.

Roscoe, John T., *Fundamental Research Statistics for the Behavioral Sciences*. New York: Holt, 1969.

Turney, B. L. and G. P. Robb, *Simplified Statistics for Education and Psychology*. Scranton, Pa., International Textbook, 1968.

_____ , Statistical Methods for the Behavioral Sciences. Scranton, Pa., Intext Educational Publishers, 1972.

Walker, Helen, and Joseph Lev, *Elementary Statistical Methods*. New York: Holt, 1958.

Wert, James E., Charles O. Neidt, and J. Stanley Ahmann, *Statistical Methods in Educational and Psychological Research*. New York: Appleton-Century, 1954.

Basic Characteristics of Mental Ability Tests and Scales

Before proceeding with a discussion of the fundamental characteristics of those standardized instruments which are currently being used to assess mental ability, it may be advantageous to comment briefly on some of the terms that will be used frequently in this and subsequent chapters. First, it should be understood that the terms *intelligence* and *mental ability* will be used interchangeably for convenience. Secondly, the term *scale*, as used in this textbook, refers to an instrument which consists of a composite or series of test items or subtests. What is said about tests in this chapter will pertain to scales as well.

Many of the characteristics of standardized tests of intelligence are common, to a considerable extent, to standardized tests of all types. In this chapter we shall describe both general and specific characteristics and relate them directly to the measurement of intelligence.

GENERAL CHARACTERISTICS

One of the important inherent characteristics of an intelligence test is that the measurement obtained from the instrument is *indirect* rather than *direct*. Nothing tangible within the skull of the subject is measured. What is measured is the subject's performance on a series of tasks, and from this performance we infer the amount of intelligence that he possesses. The difficulty of making this kind of inference is aggravated by the lack of consensus relative to the definition of this characteristic called intelligence (definitions are covered in more detail in Chapter 4). Although the word intelligence is often used by people in all walks of life as though it were a tangible attribute that can be directly measured, users of intelligence tests should constantly be aware that they are measuring a somewhat nebulous concept indirectly.

Another general characteristic of intelligence tests is that they are *relative* rather than *absolute*. No unit in intelligence testing has a specific meaning as do physical units used in measuring temperature, velocity, or weight. In the measurement of temperature, each unit denotes a specific amount of heat and there are rather definite reference points such as absolute zero or the point at which a liquid boils. In measuring intelligence, however, the size of the units varies among tests and the only reference point that we have is the performance on a specific test by other persons. Thus the units used in intelligence testing are meaningful only as they relate to the size of a particular unit and how this compares to the performance of others on the test. We can speak of deviation from average performance, but cannot relate a subject's performance to such reference points as zero intelligence or the absolute maximum in intelligence.

A third general characteristic of tests of intelligence is that they do not yield a comprehensive measure of all aspects of intelligence. The concept of intelligence is so complex that any test attempting to measure all of the theorized aspects of intelligence would be too lengthy to be practical. While most mental tests measure from one to ten facets of intelligence, Guilford and Hoepfner (1963) have included 120 factors in a three-dimensional model of intelligence. Thus intelligence test results should be thought of as limited samples of mental ability.

Thus far intelligence tests have been characterized as inexact, indirect, relative, and limited samplers of an abstract concept called intelligence. One could also add that tests do not clearly reveal why the person achieved a certain score. Factors such as motivation, energy, cultural background, perceptive ability, anxiety, and reading ability may contribute to a particular score, but the relative contributions of these factors are not specifically identified. At this point one might wonder whether administering intelligence tests is worthwhile.

Despite their undesirable characteristics, intelligence tests have the following desirable attributes:

1. Intelligence tests can provide an assessment of a person's general ability more quickly and economically than other procedures. Through prolonged observation of a person working at a job, or performing in a learning situation, it is possible to gain an impression of a person's ability, but this process is very time-consuming. Frequently, personnel workers, school administrators, and others need to make judgments about an individual's mental ability without having the opportunity for prolonged observation or the collection of data which would provide evidence of ability. An intelligence test that can be administered in a relatively short period of time can be used as an aid in determining whether an individual should be considered for a job, what academic courses he should take, or his level of academic potential. Although intelligence tests do not insure that our decisions will be perfectly accurate, they are much more dependable than initial impressions of individuals.

2. Intelligence tests give an objective appraisal of ability that is usually more accurate than subjective methods, and therefore they frequently challenge other assessments. Most informal appraisals of intelligence are influenced by the personal characteristics of the subject and the social context within which the assessment is made. People who are friendly, verbal, personable, attractive, or who are encountered in social situations that are pleasing are likely to be rated as more intelligent than those whose who are hostile, unkempt, withdrawn, or encountered in adverse social situations. Intelligence tests are administered in a structured testing situation that attempts to minimize the personal or social impact of the subject. Thus the shy, unattractive, or offensive student who may have been regarded as dull, has the opportunity to exhibit his actual ability on an objective intelligence test. Conversely, the personable subject in the same situation may achieve a lower score than anticipated.
3. Scores on intelligence tests are more meaningful and exact than verbal descriptions. Although IQs are not exact scores, it is more meaningful to say that a person has a measured IQ of 115 than to say that he is somewhat above average.

SPECIFIC CHARACTERISTICS

We have been discussing some general characteristics of mental ability tests and scales. These instruments also have *specific* qualities that must be considered in their selection and use. The most important of these qualities are reliability, validity, objectivity, and norming.

RELIABILITY AND VALIDITY

Reliability, as we shall use the term, refers to the consistency of the instrument, while validity refers to the accuracy with which it measures what it is purported to measure. At this point it should be stressed that no intelligence test has intrinsic reliability or validity. Reliability and validity refer to the test scores that subjects have achieved on the test. Hence, measures of reliability and validity refer to a particular group, not to individual performance or intrinsic attributes of the test.

While validity will be discussed in detail a little later, it seems appropriate at this point to discuss briefly the relationship between reliability and validity. The validity of a test is limited by its reliability. Stated another way, the accuracy of a test depends upon the test's consistency. That is, a test which is erratic with respect to the scores it yields will lose some of its validity. High reliability will not, however, insure validity. A test may be highly reliable yet not measure what it is designed to measure.

Reliability. In discussing the reliability of measures of individual intelligence tests, we are concerned with *error variance*, or the variation of scores that is not due to variations of intelligence. Even when tests are given under standardized procedures, the score that an individual obtains may be influenced by irrelevant factors. Thus it is customary to label an IQ score as an *obtained* score rather than a *true* score, indicating that this IQ is only one of many that might be achieved by the subject—depending on the error variance present. Establishing the reliability of a test is the first step in identifying the error variance that may be present in an obtained score, so at this point we shall discuss the common methods of determining test reliability.

The *test-retest method* of establishing test reliability simply involves administering the test to a group of subjects, then readministering the test to the same group at a later date. The coefficient of correlation between the two sets of scores then becomes the coefficient of reliability. If the subjects are able to maintain their positions within the group (rank about the same way each time), the reliability coefficient will be high. If the subjects radically alter their positions within the group, the coefficient will be low. When this method is used, the "practice effect" may raise the scores of the subjects. This effect will not lower the correlation coefficient if the effect is uniform for all subjects, but if some individuals gain more than others the coefficient will be decreased somewhat.

In using the test-retest method to determine reliability, two crucial factors to consider are (1) the amount of time between the first and second administrations, and (2) the nature of the tasks performed. If the second administration follows the first administration immediately, the subjects may remember their answers to questions and respond in exactly the same way the second time, which will tend to result in a spuriously high coefficient of reliability. If the second administration is delayed too long, accrued learnings or changes in the subjects' lives will result in a decreased coefficient. Related to the problem of timing the retest is a consideration of the nature of the task. Those tasks which result in unequal gains by examinees upon repetition should not be subjected to the retest method. Anastasi (1961) would limit the retest method to tests of sensory discrimination and motor skills.

Cronbach (1960) calls the retest correlation a "coefficient of stability" because it indicates how stable a test performance is over a period of time. As the time between mental-test administrations is lengthened, it is common to refer to this stability as the "constancy of the IQ." Thus it is possible to have a large number of coefficients of stability, depending on the time lapse between administrations of the test. The purpose of testing will indicate which duration of stability is desirable. If short-range predictions are to be made, the immediate retest procedure is adequate, but if long-range predictions are needed, the long-range stability of the test should be investigated. In this connection it is interesting to note that the results of a study by Bayley (1949) indicated that for seven-year-olds taking the Stanford-Binet Intelligence Scale the immediate retest correlation was about .90, but it declined to .74 after four years, and was only .68 after eleven years.

One way of reducing the objections to the test-retest procedure in establishing reliability is to administer equivalent forms of the test in question to a group of students and then compute the correlation for the two forms. This method is referred to as the *equivalent-forms method*. The coefficient of correlation between the two equivalent forms is a reliability coefficient. Actually, this type of reliability establishes the stability and equivalency or comparability of the test forms, and these are important considerations in testing. In addition to providing reliability data, alternate forms offer a satisfactory means for retesting individuals. For example, if a subject's score on Form A is questioned, it can be checked by the administration of Form B.

One of the major problems faced in obtaining this type of reliability is the difficulty in constructing two tests that are comparable in all important ways, including the number of items, level of difficulty, content measured, and the various aspects involved in the administration of the forms. If the forms are not truly comparable, the error variance may reflect this lack of equivalence even though the tests are stable. Another danger in using this method of establishing reliability is that, if the forms are truly comparable, there may be differential practice effect among students, which would result in a lower coefficient of reliability. Few researchers utilize this method of determining reliability because of the practical problems involved in constructing comparable forms of a test.

When a test is to be given only once in order to establish its reliability, it is likely that the investigator will use either the *split-halves method* or one of a number of appropriate statistical formulas. These are *internal-consistency methods* of determining test reliability. The split-halves method consists of dividing the test into two comparable halves and correlating the scores made by a group of subjects on the two halves. This provides a measure of equivalence between the halves and is a measure of the adequacy of item sampling. Since the test, when split into halves, is only half as long as it was originally, and because reliability is in part a function of the length of a test, the obtained reliability coefficient must be corrected for the test's full length. This correction frequently is accomplished by using the Spearman-Brown formula, which in this case is

$$r_{tt} = \frac{2r'_{tt}}{1 + r'_{tt}}$$

where r_{tt} = estimated reliability coefficient for the full-length test
              r'_{tt} = coefficient obtained between the two halves

A shortcoming of the Spearman-Brown formula is that it assumes that the variabilities of scores in each half are equal when, in practice, this may not be true. Guttman (1945) has devised a formula which is superior in that it accounts for the variabilities of the half scores:

$$r_{tt} = 2\left(1 - \frac{\sigma_a^2 + \sigma_b^2}{\sigma_t^2}\right)$$

where r_{tt} = estimated reliability coefficient of the total test

σ_t^2 = square of the standard deviation of the total test

$\sigma_a^2 + \sigma_b^2$ = squares of the standard deviations of the half tests

The major problem involved in using the split-halves method is dividing the test so that the halves are comparable. If the test items are arranged in ascending order of difficulty, it is usually possible to split the test into odd and even-numbered items to obtain comparable halves.

The most commonly used formulas for estimating reliability are the Kuder-Richardson formulas 20 and 21. These formulas were developed as an attempt to overcome the problem of obtaining different split-half reliability estimates as a result of splitting a test different ways. The Kuder-Richardson formulas are in effect measures of interitem consistency and represent the mean of coefficients obtained from dividing a test in different ways. These formulas should, therefore, only be used when the test items are similar in level of difficulty and intercorrelation. The Kuder-Richardson formulas follow.

KR 20 $$r_{tt} = \left(\frac{n}{n-1}\right) \frac{\sigma_t^2 - \Sigma\, pq}{\sigma_t^2}$$

KR 21 $$r_{tt} = \left(\frac{n}{n-1}\right) \frac{\sigma_t^2 - n\,\bar{p}\,\bar{q}}{\sigma_t^2}$$

where n = number of test items

p = proportion passing an item

$q = 1 - p$

$\bar{p}$ = average proportion passing an item

$\bar{q}$ = average proportion failing an item

σ_t^2 = squared standard deviation of the test

KR20 generally will provide a close approximation of an equivalent-forms correlation coefficient. KR21, while less accurate, is easy to compute and can be used to get quick estimates of the coefficient of equivalence if the test is scored by the "number right" formula (Cronbach, 1960, p. 141).

Since the prerequisites of equal levels of difficulty and intercorrelation of items are seldom fully attained in tests, it is generally assumed that the Kuder-Richardson formulas will yield estimates of reliability that are too low. This may not be true, however, if speed is an important factor in test performance. A study by Wesman and Kernan (1952) indicates that, on speeded tests, the Kuder-Richardson formulas may produce spuriously high reliabilities.

FACTORS THAT INFLUENCE RELIABILITY

The factors that may influence reliability appreciably can be categorized as either situational factors or test factors. Situational factors include the testing environment as well as the psychological condition of the persons being tested.

In individual mental testing, the competent examiner is careful to control as many situational factors as possible so that test performances will not be erratic. This topic is discussed rather extensively in a later chapter.

The major factors within the test itself that affect reliability are the ambiguity of the questions, the length of the test, the range of individual differences within the group tested, and the level of difficulty of the test.

Ambiguity of the test items poses a problem for most authors of mental ability tests. Items that can be interpreted in only one way elicit more consistent responses from subjects, and hence are more reliable than those which are open to different interpretations. However, many test authors feel that only by preparing some ambiguous questions is it possible to discriminate among various levels of intellectual functioning. One method of maintaining reliability for ambiguous questions is to construct an elaborate scoring system that will reflect the level of intellectual functioning for different responses. An example of this procedure is found in the scoring system for the Comprehension subtest of the *Wechsler Intelligence Scale for Children*. This subtest is briefly discussed in Chapter 6.

The second test factor affecting reliability, the length of the test, is a reflection of how adequately a test samples a particular type of behavior. The longer a test is, the more likely that it will reflect the true ability of the subject and hence be a more consistent measure of that ability. This results from the fact that a longer test samples an ability better than a shorter one, all other things being equal. Since extremely long tests are likely to fatigue the subject, test authors try to construct tests that are long enough to have high reliability yet short enough to be economical of time. When using portions of intelligence tests for diagnostic purposes, the examiner should be cognizant of the fact that a subtest or portion of a test will be less reliable than the total test. If subtest reliability is not available, the examiner should use great caution because the reliability may be low enough to make his interpretations inaccurate.

The third test factor affecting reliability is the range of individual differences of the members of the group upon which the reliability has been calculated. If the reliability of an intelligence test were calculated for a group that ranged from institutionalized mental defectives to doctoral-level professionals, a computed reliability coefficient would be quite high because minor inconsistencies in performance would not grossly affect examinees' positions in the total group. If this same test were given to a group of college juniors, the reliability coefficient would be lowered because small variations in performance might markedly alter the ranks of individuals in the group. This factor should be considered in evaluating the reliability of a test. A test may be quite reliable if a subject is being compared to a diverse group, yet relatively unreliable when a homogeneous group is the comparison group.

The level of difficulty of a test is the fourth test factor affecting reliability. If a test is constructed to examine subjects with a wide range of intelligence or age, the reliability may fluctuate at different levels of ability or age. The test may be so difficult for the youngest or less adept subjects that their scores will be influenced unduly by guessing. In this case, reliability will be lowered. Conversely, a test may be so easy for the gifted that their scores may fluctuate unduly because of one item that is passed or failed. If the publisher of an intelligence test gives only one reliability coefficient in the test manual and if it is based upon a diverse group, the examiner should seek evidence that the test is equally reliable for groups of particular ability or age levels.

USE OF RELIABILITY DATA

The reliability data listed in the manuals of most intelligence tests were obtained in most cases by administering the test to a selected group and by using a particular method to obtain a reliability coefficient. Thus the listed reliability is not inherent in the test, but rather is the estimate of reliability obtained at a particular time for a particular group. The test user faces the problem of determining whether the test will be equally reliable for the subjects he plans to test. If the subjects are comparable in every way to the group upon which the test reliability was established, the test user may assume that the reported reliability is the same for his group. This may be a dangerous assumption, however, because rarely are sufficient data available to verify that the subjects to be tested will be comparable in every way to the group upon which reliability has been established. The logical solution to this problem is to establish reliability of the test locally.

A more difficult problem is encountered when one attempts to assess the reliability of a test for a particular individual. Even if the reliability of the test has been established locally, the resultant reliability coefficient is a *group statistic*. The individual in question may be more erratic or less erratic than the group. Although we cannot unequivocally establish the reliability of one particular test score, it is possible to obtain some evidence to evaluate its reliability. This evidence may include the results of previous testing and observation of test behavior or behavior exhibited in other situations. Frequently, if the test is discussed with the subject after it has been completed, he will be able to give some clues concerning elements that affect reliability, such as his physical and emotional state and his attitude toward the test.

When assessing the reliability of a test, one should keep in mind the fact that reliability should be related to the purpose of testing. For example, if long-range predictions are to be made, the stability of the test over a period of time is important. Or, if one is attempting to assess a subject's status within a group, the within-group reliability becomes important.

VALIDITY

While the reliability of a test is important, the most crucial characteristic of intelligence tests is their validity. As previously defined, validity refers to how well a test measures what it is supposed to measure. Related to this definition is the assumption that a test will be given to serve a specific purpose, and the extent to which it serves this purpose is a measure of its validity. Further expansion of this concept of validity would reveal, however, that since intelligence tests are given for many purposes, it becomes impossible to arrive at a particular quantitative datum which indicates the validity of the test. Rather, intelligence tests may have as many validities as there are purposes for which they will be used.

Many naive test users have assumed that because a test is called an intelligence test it therefore measures some innate, stable, well-defined variable. Since there is no consensus concerning how intelligence manifests itself in behavior, test users are now seeking evidence of how well intelligence tests serve their various purposes. Three types of validity—content validity, criterion-related validity, and construct validity—serve most of our purposes and will be discussed. These validities follow the format contained in the revised edition of *Standards for Educational and Psychological Tests and Manuals* (1966) prepared by a joint committee of the American Psychological Association, the American Educational Research Association and the National Council on Measurements in Education.

Content Validity. Content validity may be described as the adequacy with which a test samples the content of a particular situation or subject matter. This type of validity is of prime importance in achievement tests, but it also has some importance with respect to intelligence tests. An analysis of the items on an intelligence test frequently gives us a subjective impression of the definition of intelligence upon which the test is based. Thus an intelligence test based solely upon the ability to manipulate geometric designs may imply a narrow definition of intelligence. Probably the most important use of content validity in intelligence tests is to attempt to discover whether the content of the test might adversely affect the attitude of the subject, resulting in an atypical performance.

Criterion-Related Validity. Criterion-related validity is obtained by relating the results of an intelligence test to an external variable that is another measure of the ability or behavior being investigated. For example, if an intelligence test is to be used to predict academic success, the external variable used as a criterion might be the grade-point average attained by students who have varying test scores. This validity could be shown by means of a coefficient of correlation or in the form of experience charts.

Two important types of criterion-related validity are *predictive validity* and *concurrent validity*. Both of these validities are concerned with the relationship of test scores to the external criterion, but they differ in one important respect. Predictive validity is concerned with predicting or understanding *future* behavior, while concurrent validity, is concerned with relationships between test scores and *present* behavior.

Predictive validity is crucial for intelligence tests because almost invariably after an intelligence test is administered the results are used to predict future performance. The statement that John obtained an IQ score of 125 is frequently followed by the comment or assumption that John should be able to achieve well in school. Because intelligence tests are used so often for prediction, validity studies indicating how well the tests predict certain behaviors should be available as guides for these predictions.

Concurrent validity is estimated when test scores are correlated with an external criterion determined at essentially the same time. The Binet scale was originally accepted because scores on the scale agreed with teachers' assessments of intelligence. After the Binet became established, it was often used as the external criterion to validate group tests of intelligence. If a new test correlated highly with the Binet, it was assumed to be measuring the same quality as the Binet and was considered to be valid. The tendency of the Stanford-Binet to correlate positively with school achievement has been so well established in a multitude of studies that now it is frequently used to contradict teachers' judgments—a principal criterion that initially was used in the scale's validation.

The use of the Stanford-Binet to challenge teachers' judgments points to a weakness in criterion-related validity: that the validity of the outside criterion may be in doubt. The original validation of the Stanford-Binet used age differentiation as a major criterion for validation. The Stanford-Binet was originally validated upon the assumption that scores on an intelligence test should increase with age. While this is generally true up to certain ages, the deviations from this assumption lower the validity correlations.

Other criteria frequently used in the validation of intelligence tests include grade-point averages, results of achievement tests, promotion or graduation, teachers' ratings, amount of education achieved, and success in specialized training or on a job. Since the validity coefficients obtained from all of these criteria are suspect to a degree, their use in validating intelligence tests is somewhat limited. Nevertheless, they allow us to define operationally what intelligence tests measure.

Construct Validity. Construct validity may be defined, in general terms, as being an ongoing process involving formulating, evaluating, and modifying the theory underlying a test in order to account for test performance. In intelligence testing, the process of determining construct validity might involve developing a theory of intelligence, identifying the facets of intelligence crucial to the theory, and predicting how these facets of intelligence might logically interact. Next, one might construct a test selecting content that appears to sample these facets of intelligence. After standardization of the test, obtained scores could be subjected to factor analysis to observe whether the facets of intelligence that were theorized actually emerged as factors. The test would also be correlated with a wide variety of outside criteria to see whether the results postulated by the theory were actually obtained. If the obtained results could not be explained by the original theory, the theory would be modified to incorporate the results. The theory might then be used to generate new hypotheses that could be tested at some future time.

The establishment of construct validity may involve the consideration of both content and criterion-related validity. However, all of the empirical data obtained should be continually related to an underlying theory in the attempt to explain *why* different scores are related to other criteria. For instance, when individual intelligence tests are used in a clinical manner, such as hypothesizing that a particular pattern of scores on the *Wechsler Intelligence Scale for Children* is related to brain damage, it is vitally important that the test user be familiar with the construct validity that might warrant such a hypothesis.

The importance of construct validity to the users of intelligence tests will vary according to the applications that will be made of the test results. If prediction is the only purpose for giving an intelligence test, predictive validity may be the most appropriate type of validity to use. However, many of the more widely used individual scales of intelligence such as the Stanford-Binet and the Wechsler scales have been used in such a wide variety of research studies that the enormous amounts of data allow the formulation of constructs which enable us to go beyond simple prediction. These constructs allow us to describe, tentatively, the etiology and causal factors influencing performances on the scales. Some of these constructs are described in more detail in Chapter 10.

USE OF VALIDITY DATA

As is the case with respect to reliability data, the criterion-related validity data printed in test manuals were obtained for a particular group at a particular time, using a particular outside criterion. Unless the group used in the standardization process is very similar to the group being tested, the coefficients cited in the validity studies should be used cautiously. It is usually a good procedure to assess the predictive ability of a test locally before assuming that the test is a useful predictor.

Even after the local validity of a test has been established, the test user is faced with the task of interpreting the meaning of the obtained validity coefficient for individual prediction. For example, if an intelligence test correlates .60 with the grade-point average attained by students, one might wonder how accurate a predictor this test is for an individual. A useful measure in this regard is k, the coefficient of alienation, which is found by the formula: $k = \sqrt{1 - r_{xy}^2}$. Table 3-1 contains various coefficients of correlation, the resultant coefficients of alienation, and the increase of prediction over chance.

As can be seen by reference to Table 3-1, the coefficient of .60, obtained locally, is 20 percent better than chance, but it still leaves an error 80 percent as great as chance error (mere guessing). The data in Table 3-1 show that many of the validity coefficients commonly used will permit a high degree of error in prediction.

Table 3-1 Coefficients of Alienation and Percentage Increase in
Predictive Efficiency for Various Coefficients of Correlation

Correlation Coefficient	Coefficient of Alienation	Percentage Increase in Predictive Efficiency
0.00	1.00	0.0
0.10	.99	1.0
0.20	.98	2.0
0.30	.95	5.0
0.40	.92	8.0
0.50	.87	13.0
0.60	.80	20.0
0.70	.71	29.0
0.80	.60	40.0
0.90	.44	56.0
0.95	.31	69.0
1.00	.00	100.0

Another way of portraying validity data is through the use of *experience charts* (sometimes referred to as *expectancy tables*). This method has the advantage of accentuating the variability in performance that may exist even though a positive correlation is obtained with test data. Table 3-2 is an experience chart illustrating the relationship between intelligence test scores and grades in a mathematics course.

Table 3-2 Experience Chart Showing the Relationship Between IQ
Scores and Grades in Mathematics

IQ Score	Number of Students	Percent Receiving Each Grade				
		F	D	C	B	A
130–139	3				20	80
120–129	5				33	67
110–119	31		3	16	62	19
100–109	65		6	65	18	11
90–99	51	2	10	66	20	2
80–89	28	10	57	29	4	
70–79	4	75	25			
60–69	1	100				

When interpreting this experience chart, it is quite clear that, based upon past student performance, one may expect in the future that a student with an IQ of 115 would stand a 3 percent chance of getting a D, 16 percent chance of getting a C, 62 percent chance of getting a B, and a 19 percent chance of getting an A, providing conditions remain comparable to the past year. When interpreting experience charts, one should be cautious in predicting from cells containing few numbers, since the sampling may be less than adequate.

As previously mentioned, the reliability of a test is affected by the nature of the group on which it is used. This is true also of validity. Groups containing a wide range of abilities are more likely to achieve high validity correlations than groups with a restricted range. It is likely that a predictive validity coefficient for an intelligence test given to students who had measured IQs between 95 and 100 would be less than the coefficient obtained from students whose measured IQs ranged from 60 to 139.

It should be noted that the validity discussed in this section is based upon group data. When one uses an individual IQ one is still faced with the problem of establishing whether this individual score is more or less valid than the group data. The usual method of evaluating the validity of an individual score is to observe carefully the subject during test administration. These observations, coupled with other data about the subject, will frequently give the test administrator a basis for deciding whether the score obtained is likely to serve the desired testing purpose. It is generally assumed that the test administrator will include in the test report his assessment of the validity of that particular test administration. Let us now turn to the test characteristic referred to as objectivity.

OBJECTIVITY

Objectivity, which concerns scoring in this discussion, is important because it relates to validity and reliability. Objectivity is generally assumed to have been achieved when trained, competent people can administer and score a test and achieve the same results. In other words, the values, biases, and judgments of the test administrator are minimized for the sake of good testing, and the responses of the subject are elicited and scored in a standardized manner.

Many *group* tests are very objective because their instructions are clear and well stated, the questions are specific, the possible answers are precise, and the tests may be scored by a key or a machine. Many *individual* intelligence tests pose a greater problem than group tests with respect to objectivity because greater latitude is given the test administrator in establishing a relationship with the subject and in coping with the wide variety of behaviors a subject might exhibit. Secondly, many individual intelligence tests involve tasks or ask questions to which the subject may respond in a wide variety of ways.

In an attempt to objectify individual test of intelligence, the test author usually describes in detail the types of examiner behavior which should be used in eliciting responses, and carefully describes the scoring procedures that are to be used. To insure that students who are learning to give these tests follow standardized procedures, it is common practice to observe the student during a number of test administrations and to check his scoring of the responses until it is apparent that the student can be objective in his administration and scoring of tests.

While proper instruction and training may minimize the amount of subjectivity in the administration of individual intelligence tests, it is commonly acknowledged that a small amount of subjectivity is likely to be present. An interesting study by Masling (1959) showed that when test subjects (who were actually accomplices) acted in a warm manner toward examiners, the scoring of responses became more lenient and the number of reinforcing responses increased. On the other hand, cold behavior on the part of the subjects produced less leniency and fewer reinforcing responses. After reviewing 65 studies involving the modification of standardized procedures, Sattler and Theye (1967) concluded that groups such as the elderly, retarded, or disturbed are more likely to be affected by departures from standardized procedures than normal subjects. The researchers also concluded that children are more susceptible to modifications of standardized procedures than are older examinees.

NORMS AND NORM GROUPS

As previously stated, intelligence test scores are not absolute measures, and they become meaningful only when compared to the performance of a particular group. Intelligence test results usually are reported in terms of *age norms*—that is, a subject's score is compared to scores achieved by a group of children the same age. The scores generally are reported as intelligence quotients, deviation IQs, percentiles, or standard scores. Each of these methods of reporting age norms allows the examiner to compare the subject's performance to the performance of others of his same age.

This comparison becomes meaningful only when the test user becomes aware of the characteristics of the group with which the subject is being compared (the *norm* group). Most intelligence tests have norm groups that are carefully selected to be representative of the general population of the country.

If "subjects in general" (national) norms are to be meaningful, the norm groups should be carefully described so that the user can verify that the sample is adequate in size and is representative of population in general with respect to such factors as geographic location, socioeconomic level, and education. These national norms are appropriate only when one wishes to compare the examinee with subjects in general. If one wishes to compare the subject with a selected group, norms for this group should be available. For example, if a researcher wishes to determine how the subject compares with freshmen at a particular college, he should have norms for this selected group.

Of course, norms for a particular group are not always available to the examiner, so he will frequently need to compile these data. If it is not feasible to do so, he should be especially careful in predicting from his test scores. One frequent problem that involves the use of norms is the problem of interpreting a test score for a member of a particular ethnic group when this ethnic group is not adequately represented in the norm group. Many examiners in such cases simply state that the norms are not appropriate for members of this ethnic group and discount the results. This generalization is not always appropriate, for if the purpose of testing is to predict how a member of an ethnic group will perform when competing with subjects in general, and if the predictive validity is high, then the established norms may suffice. Conversely, a person may be a member of the norm group and yet deviate from it sufficiently so that his norm group is not an appropriate group for him.

In summary, test users should use norms carefully and should consider the composition of the norm group as well as the purposes of testing before norms are accepted as appropriate for a particular examinee.

REFERENCES

American Psychological Association, *Standards for Educational and Psychological Tests and Manuals*. Washington, D.C.: The Association, 1966.

Anastasi, Anne, *Psychological Testing*. 2nd ed. New York: Macmillan, 1961.

Bayley, Nancy, "Consistency and Variability in the Growth of Intelligence from Birth to Eighteen Years," *Journal of Genetic Psychology* 75 (1949), 165-196.

Chase, C. I., and Ludlow, H. G., *Readings in Educational and Psychological Measurement*. Boston: Houghton Mifflin, 1966.

Cronbach, Lee J., *Essentials of Psychological Testing*. 2nd ed. New York: Harper, 1960.

Guilford, J. P., *Fundamental Statistics in Psychology and Education*. New York: McGraw-Hill, 1956.

———, and R. Hoepfner, "Current Summary of Structure-of-Intellect Factors and Suggested Tests," *Rep. Psychol. Lab.*, No. 30, University of Southern California, Los Angeles (1963).

Guttman, L., "A Basis for Analyzing Test-Retest Reliability," *Psychometrika* 10 (1945), 255-282.

Krugman, J. L., et al., "Pupil Functioning on the Stanford-Binet and the Wechsler Intelligence Scale for Children," *Journal of Consulting Psychology* 15, (1951), 475-483.

Masling, Joseph, "The Effects of Warm and Cold Interaction on the Administration and Scoring of an Intelligence Test," *Journal of Consulting Psychology* 23 (1959), 336-341.

Noll, Victor, *Introduction to Educational Measurement*. 2nd ed. Boston: Houghton Mifflin, 1965.

Sattler, J. M., and F. Theye, "Procedural, Situational and Interpersonal Variables in Individual Intelligence Testing," *Psychological Bulletin* 68, (1967), 347-360.

Thorndike, R. L., and E. Hagen, *Measurement and Evaluation in Psychology and Education*. 2nd ed. New York: Wiley, 1961.

Warters, Jane, *Techniques of Counseling*. New York: McGraw-Hill, 1964.

Wesman, A. G., and J. P. Kernan, "An Experimental Comparison of Test-Retest and Internal Consistency Estimates of Reliability with Speeded Tests," *Journal of Educational Psychology* 53 (1952), 292-298.

The Nature
of Intelligence

CHAPTER

4

The logical approach to measuring intelligence would be to define carefully what is meant by intelligence, then construct a test that would accurately measure this concept. Yet it is very disconcerting for students to discover that there is no consensus concerning the definition of intelligence. Their natural reaction is to ask, "How can you measure something that is not specifically defined?" When they become aware that many tests with the term intelligence in their titles measure seemingly entirely different abilities, they are prone to come to the conclusion that intelligence is whatever the authors of the tests had in mind when they constructed these highly divergent instruments.

The student is further disillusioned when he discovers that many of the same test items appear on tests with different labels. Typically he may ask, "Why do these same items appear in tests that are called tests of scholastic ability, scholastic aptitude, general intelligence, mental ability, academic aptitude, achievement, or aptitude?" One of the explanations for this state of affairs is that, historically, many tests of intelligence were constructed before a comprehensive definition of intelligence had been attempted. Many of these early instruments measured quite different abilities. Psychologists are still struggling with the problem of evolving a definition or theory of intelligence that will adequately incorporate what has been learned through the use of these tests.

Some very general or *global* definitions have been advanced that stress the ability to adjust to the environment or to profit from experience. While these general definitions are appropriate for many tests of intelligence, they are too general to give much direction. The question likely to be raised is, "What type of adjustment to what aspects of the environment: what types of learning from what experience in the environment?" Garrett's (1946) definition of intelligence as "the abilities demanded in the solution of problems which require the comprehension and use of symbols" is a rather specific definition, but it still raises the question of "what symbols, what problems?"

In the past, many definitions of intelligence have implied that the ability to learn is synonomous with intelligence. A number of studies have been conducted which relate the results of intelligence tests to gain-scores on a variety of tasks. The conclusions reached on the basis of these studies is that while there is some overlap between the ability to learn and what is commonly measured by intelligence tests, there is not an extremely high correlation, so intelligence involves more than a simple ability to learn. An individual may acquire a vast amount of learned material and yet not act any more intelligently in a new situation than someone who has not accumulated as large a store of knowledge. A review of Binet's first scale and his writing reveals that much of his concept of intelligence is appropos today. His scale stresses the ability to perform abstract thinking, it goes beyond the measurement of rote learning, it implies adaptation to circumstances, it incorporates novel or creative thinking, and it includes autocriticism.

Nonintellectual factors also are implied. When Binet talks about a goal or direction, he is including drive and motivation in his concept of intelligence. Tests which are loaded with numerical and verbal problems similar to those learned in schools are criticized because they are too dependent upon the educational history of the person. On the other hand, tests which ignore these aspects of intelligence and measure some type of performance devoid of verbal and numerical symbols are criticized because they do not predict ability to function in a school situation.

While it is not possible at this time to offer a concise, accurate definition of intelligence and a universally accepted theory of intelligence, it may be helpful to discuss briefly a number of definitions and theoretical concepts which have received considerable attention to date.

DEFINITIONS OF INTELLIGENCE

Binet recognized that intelligence is very complex and he did not attempt a comprehensive definition. Throughout his writings, however, is the major premise that judgment, or what might be called practical common sense in adapting to circumstances, is essential to intelligence. He characterized intelligent behavior as behavior having a goal or direction and felt that, in attempting to achieve this goal, a person must have the ability to produce tentative solutions that would help him adapt to a given problem situation. According to Binet's concept, in order to behave intelligently a person must have the ability to select, to make judgments, and to criticize any solution that he may have to a problem. Involved in this process is the ability to comprehend well. Binet's concept of intelligence may be summarized as having four important characteristics: direction, comprehension, invention, and criticism (critique).

According to Wechsler's (1958, p. 7) succinct definition, intelligence is "the aggregate or global capacity of the individual to act purposefully, to think rationally, and to deal effectively with his environment." Wechsler asserts that intelligence cannot simply be the sum of abilities or elements that are measured because (1) intelligent behavior also involves the way in which these elements are combined, (2) factors such as drive and incentive are involved, and (3) a great amount of one ability contributes little to the effectiveness of behavior as a whole. He concludes that the only way intelligence can be measured quantitatively is by the measurement of various elements. From these elements an index of global capacity can be obtained. This global capacity is what Wechsler has attempted to measure with his scales (discussed in Chapter 6). It is ironic that although Wechsler stressed a global capacity in the measurement of intelligence, his scales are probably used more than any other scales to examine differential abilities among the elements of intelligence that are measured. His definition is too brief to give any inclination of which methods should be used to assess purposeful action, rational thinking, or effectiveness in dealing with one's environment.

Earlier it was indicated that many definitions of intelligence involved the ability to adjust or adapt, and thus these definitions imply that intelligence consists of the ability to learn. Thorndike et al. (1927) stressed this ability and stated that truth, development with age, and ability to learn are criteria for intelligence. He thought that these elements could be tested by a series of "tasks" labeled CAVD. The four letters represent the following abilities: C—to supply words so as to make a statement true and sensible; A—to solve arithmetic problems; V—to understand single words; and D—to understand connected discourse as in oral direction or paragraph reading. This type of definition has great appeal for many individuals who want to use intelligence tests to predict achievement in school. An examination of Thorndike's CAVD reveals that these tasks are closely related to the tasks common to a classroom. Hence one would expect they would predict academic achievement well. Some test experts will point out that this is a very narrow type of test which does not measure nonacademic abilities that are also indices of intelligence. A more severe criticism of this type of definition would be to question whether these tests actually measure intelligence or whether they are actually measuring scholastic achievement.

Stoddard (1943, p. 4) has attempted to define intelligence by characterizing the activity involved in the tasks included in a test of mental ability. His definition states that "intelligence is the ability to undertake activities that are characterized by (1) difficulty, (2) complexity, (3) abstractness, (4) economy, (5) adaptiveness to a goal, (6) social value, and (7) the emergence of originals, and to maintain such activities under conditions that demand a concentration of energy and a resistance to emotional forces." Stoddard's attempt to evolve an explicit, comprehensive definition of intelligence points to an interesting problem—that one could continue to define operationally, or become more explicit on each facet of intelligence measured, until the definition itself would become too cumbersome to have general applicability. Stoddard's definition is comprehensive in that it incorporates most of the definitions discussed to date. His definition, however, has been criticized by those who argue that the notion that social value enters into intelligence involves a subjective element based on group acceptability. This concept would tend to penalize the inventive individual or "forward-thinking" individual who is not in line with the current group thinking. Both Stoddard and Wechsler have been criticized for considering nonintellective factors such as motivation in their definitions. Many test experts feel that nonintellective factors can invalidate efforts to measure intelligence. The argument over whether it is better to include or exclude nonintellective factors such as motivation in definitions of intelligence may be academic, because whichever position one takes these factors must be incorporated in the assessment of the results of intelligence tests.

There are some individuals such as Fromm and Hartman (1955) who contend that intelligence is a function of the total personality and cannot be dissected from the living organism in which it functions. They contend that intelligence is interrelated with emotions, feelings, moods, life experiences, physical illness, or well being, and leads no life of its own. In other words, it can be understood and tested only if it is conceived as a dynamic functioning part of the unit called personality. This attitude, based on gestalt and psychoanalytic thinking, eschews the viewing of intelligence as a discreet entity rather than part of a total personality. The position taken by Fromm and Hartman seems to suggest that intelligence testing should be incorporated with a thorough assessment of the total personality in every case. While this objective may be laudable, it is not very practical. Furthermore, experience shows that intelligence tests as now given can provide psychological information or predict limited aspects of behavior.

Probably the definition of intelligence least subject to criticism and with the most widespread implications is the very simple one advocated by Wesman (1968, p. 267) who says that "intelligence . . . is a summation of learning experiences." This simple definition implies that, when measuring intelligence, we are not measuring an entity but rather an attribute. It also clearly specifies that what we measure is a summation of *many* learning experiences. This definition allows us to measure diverse performances; it is compatible with many different theories of learning and motivation and it avoids the pitfalls involved in indicating the source of intelligent behavior. Wesman's definition, by implication, does away with artificial divisions between intelligence, aptitude, and achievement tests. He contends that all of these devices measure what the individual has learned. The difference in labeling merely signifies the different purposes for which the tests will be used. Thus if a test were to be used to predict learning over broad areas of environmental exposure, we would select previous learnings that would most likely predict future learnings and call this selection an intelligence test. We would not be measuring different abilities but merely using different criteria.

The relevance of the learnings we selected for testing would determine how we would classify our test as well as the degree of success achieved in testing.

USE OF DEFINITIONS

One way of solving the problem of defining intelligence would be to discard the word intelligence and evolve four or five other words—each of which would be more explicit. Another solution would be to define various types of intelligence very specifically and possibly call them Intelligence 1, Intelligence 2, etc. This resolution of the problem is not very feasible because, although it is a very ambiguous word, the word intelligence has become so well established in our vocabularies that it is almost impossible to discard. Hence, while it is unlikely that a simple definition of intelligence that will be acceptable to everyone can be developed, the attempt probably will not be abandoned. Definitions of intelligence can serve many useful purposes. One purpose is to delineate clearly what intelligence is not. Wesman's definition cited above is commendable in that it clearly dispels many erroneous concepts implied in the definition of intelligence used by the layman.

A second important function of definitions of intelligence is that operational definitions, while they may be restricted to a particular test and a particular purpose, often provide us with guidelines that allow us to predict behavior. A great deal of ambiguity involved in intelligence testing might be removed if the author of each test would clearly define the concept of intelligence incorporated in his test, and provide some evidence that this test does in fact provide the information attributed to it. The test user can obtain this kind of information only when he combines a critical review of the contents of a test with a wide variety of practical experiences in the use of the instrument and a review of studies that indicate how the results of this test are related to behavior. Cronbach (1970) has advocated the placing of tests on a spectrum ranging from those containing maximum educational loading to those containing minimum educational loading. This spectrum is reproduced in Fig. 4-1.

When this spectrum is used, it provides an operational frame of reference that indicates both the content of a test and, indirectly, the type of use that may be made of this test. Hence a test high in maximum educational loading could be used to predict success in school, while a test with minimum educational loading could be used to detect undeveloped potential that might be developed by novel treatment of the student. If the Stanford-Binet and Wechsler scales were placed on this spectrum, one would expect that both would range from the A to the D categories with the Wechsler scales being rather evenly distributed and the Stanford-Binet being concentrated toward the maximum educational loading.

Placing tests upon a spectrum incorporating educational loading illustrates but one dimension that should be considered in using tests. Other factors, including the importance of speed in test taking, the cultural loading of the test, the necessity for understanding verbal communication, and so forth, could be

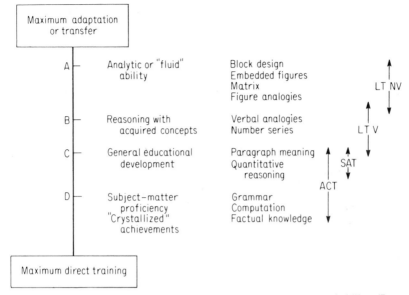

Fig. 4-1. Spectrum for comparing tests of scholastic aptitude or general ability. (Reproduced by permission of Harper & Row, Publishers, New York.)

used in organizing spectrums that would provide for more distinct operational definitions and specific uses of intelligence tests.

THEORIES OF INTELLIGENCE

While definitions of intelligence generally attempt to indicate how intelligence functions, many psychologists are quite concerned with the underlying factors or "structure" of intelligence. These psychologists feel that in order to adequately understand intelligence one must work out the theoretical structure of this complicated concept so that its complexities may be better described. Since *factor analysis* is basic to many of these theories, a brief description of this statistical method is indicated.

FACTOR ANALYSIS

Factor analysis is essentially a statistical technique which utilizes coefficients of correlation. With this technique the researcher attempts to find the psychological functions that are basic to test performance. If one were to correlate many of the intelligence tests in existence, he would find that many of them are correlated positively, which means that they measure some of the same psychological functions. On the other hand, there are some tests that do not correlate positively, which indicates that they measure unique functions. By a complicated process of correlating a great many tests with each other it is possible to isolate a number of elements that seem to be common in these tests, and from these elements to hypothesize about the structure of intelligence. To illustrate part of this process, a set of correlations between seven different tests and five different factors (A, B, C, D, E) is shown in Table 4-1, which shows the

Table 4-1 Correlations Between Seven Tests and Five Factors

| Test | Factor | | | | |
	A Numerical	B Induction	C Spatial	D Associative Memory	E Verbal Compre- hension
1. Addition of digits	.81	−.05	.12	−.11	.40
2. Completion of statements	.04	.25	−.02	.20	.73
3. Synonyms-antonyms	−.02	.16	.07	.21	.70
4. Word-number association	.09	−.03	.23	.53	−.07
5. Arithmetical reasoning .	.19	.38	.03	−.03	.22
6. Number series	.20	.15	.27	.08	.18
7. Mechanical arrangements	.19	.44	.25	−.21	.26

extent to which each test correlates with each of the five factors. These factors may be thought of as intellectual traits or abilities. The higher a correlation coefficient the greater the amount of agreement between the scores yielded by a test and the factor in question. In the language of factor-analysis research, the correlation coefficients are referred to as loadings. In Table 4-1 the addition test shows a high loading on Factor A (.81), so the test would be useful in measuring the numerical factor. Test 2 and Test 3 appear to be good indicators of Factor E, verbal comprehension.

Cohen (1959) performed a factor analysis on the *WISC* and found five primary factors which the scale seemed to be measuring. He referred to these factors as Verbal Comprehension I, Perceptual Organization, Freedom from Distractibility, Verbal Comprehension II, and a specific factor (measured by coding). A second-order factor that was found was referred to as *g*, or general mental ability. In essence what Cohen discovered through factor analysis was that the subtests of the *WISC* showed strong correlations with one or more of the factors mentioned. This same process has been used in attempts to develop a "structure" of intelligence, but in this instance it generally involves a much wider variety of tests. It is possible to correlate a large number of tests with each other and then identify the factors that seem to account for the basic functions that these tests measure. These functions can then be examined, and from them a "structure of intelligence" may be theorized.

While factor analysis is a useful tool in attempting to isolate some of the basic structures measured by intelligence tests, it has several inherent weaknesses. One of these is that the results of factor analysis are dependent upon the tests that are correlated initially; hence one selective input would result in a different set of factors than another selective input. One may be fairly well assured that this type of analysis does not include all possible types of intelligence but rather is dependent upon the tests commonly in existence. Another weakness of factor analysis is that the factors one obtains are frequently dependent upon the judgment of the investigator in organizing his results. Starting with the same basic tests, one investigator may find a different set of factors than another because of the type of manipulations he uses. A third criticism of the factor-analysis approach is that frequently the factors discovered are treated as entities in and of themselves rather than as descriptive categories. Despite these criticisms of factor analysis, however, this technique still remains a useful tool in organizing a vast amount of data collected from test results. A discussion of several theories of intelligence based upon factor analysis, as well as other procedures or systems, follows.

MULTIFACTOR THEORY

It was Thorndike's (1927) contention that intelligence is composed of a large number of very specific elements or factors. These factors were said to be relatively minute and could appear in combination with other minute factors to form what seem to be clusters of general intelligence. According to Thorndike, any mental activity consists of a great number of these minute elements operating together. It would thus be possible to have correlations of intelligence tests, but these would be explained on the basis of a *collection* of very minute factors that Thorndike hypothesized as the basic construct of intelligence. His theory appears to rule out the existence of "general intelligence," but his view of intelligence did not preclude the development of tests that were composed of a number of factors. As a matter of fact, Thorndike's CAVD test referred to earlier would be classified as a test of abstract intelligence. Thorndike contended, however, that each of these portions of this test was composed of very specific elements of intelligence. While it is difficult to prove this theory invalid, Thorndike himself recognized that for most practical purposes tests would be constructed of larger elements than the "specifics" that he talked about, and hence that it would be more practical to construct tests to measure abilities involving specifics rather than the minute elements themselves.

TWO-FACTOR THEORY

Spearman (1927) was one of the first to use factor analysis in psychology in an attempt to explain the nature of intelligence. The results of his factor-analysis studies led him to believe that intelligence is composed mainly of two factors— the "general factor" which he called g, and a large number of specific factors which he called s factors. According to the two-factor theory, intelligence is primarily dependent upon the *g* factor which is common to all kinds of mental ability. This *g* factor is believed to be possessed by everyone in varying degrees and is considered to be the most important aspect of intelligence measured by intelligence tests. Spearman theorized that the most important characteristic of the *g* factor is that it requires insight into relationships. The *g* factor is believed to account for the correlations that exist between many intelligence tests because all of them are measuring, to a degree, this same factor. Conversely, one could hypothesize that the tests that correlate highly are measuring the *g* factor to a greater degree than those that do not correlate highly.

In his research Spearman recognized that many intelligence tests did not correlate highly with each other. This fact was explained on the basis of the existence of specific factors, *s* factors, which are factors that are unique to a particular type of activity. According to the two-factor theory, these factors do not, in general, involve insight into relationships. Rote memory is an example of a specific factor.

Later in his work Spearman recognized that many mental tasks had in common a membership to a particular group. He did not consider this important in his theory of intelligence and did not pursue this finding very actively. In general, the two-factor theory maintains that all mental activities have a common *g* factor which is the most important characteristic, each activity has its own specific factor or factors, and some of the specific factors may be members of a group. The major implication of this theory is that when constructing tests of intelligence, one should attempt to evolve a test with a maximum amount of *g* loading (correlation) and variable *s* factors which tend to cancel out, leaving the *g* factor as the crucial measure of intelligence.

In his early research, Wechsler was very impressed with Spearman's findings and concurred with respect to the existence of a *g* factor. Wechsler, however, did not agree with Spearman that an ideal intelligence test would have a very high loading of the factor. It was Wechsler's contention that specific factors and non-intellective factors are essential in the measurement of intelligence because they frequently are the basis for effective behavior. Wechsler's scales reflect the acceptance of much of Spearman's theoretical structure but they stress the *s* factor and nonintellective factors.

GROUP-FACTOR THEORY

Other researchers who used factor analysis in the process of manipulating test results discovered that frequently group factors appear. That is, a selected number of tests seem to contain a limited number of factors but not a very large number of elementary factors or a universal *g*. Thurstone (1938) tends to discount the *g* factor and the independent factors as being crucial to the structure of intelligence. He contends that a "group-factor theory," which is based on the correlation of a limited group of tests, is the best theoretical base for discussing intelligence. Thurstone initially gave 56 different tests to students and reduced them to six tests that he thought measured basic factors. He labeled the factors V, Verbal, N, Number, S, Spatial, W, Word Fluency, M, Memory, and R, Reasoning. Thurstone thought that these were "primary abilities," suggesting that any complex intellectual performance was based upon a mixture of these group factors. Since he found no general intercorrelation among them, he argued that no general factor existed. Based upon these findings, he constructed the *Chicago Tests of Primary Mental Abilities*. Later work with these tests (PMA) indicated that the primary factors, in fact, did relate to each other. Thurstone has retained his concept of the primary group factors, and he explains the relationship by identifying a "second-order factor" which unites the primary group factors.

HIERARCHICAL THEORY

Several theorists have indicated that the best way to explain the results of factor analysis is with a hierarchical model that ranges from specific factors through group factors to a general factor. Vernon's model (Fig. 4-2) represents

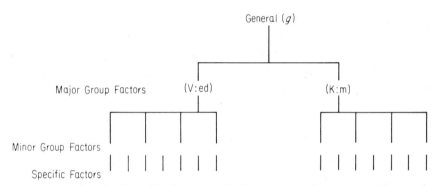

Fig. 4-2. Hierarchy of abilities (after Vernon, 1951, pp. 22-24).

one such attempt. Vernon's model is based upon factor analyses conducted with test data from British Army and Navy conscript recruits. Vernon postulates that the most important factor in the structure of the intellect is the *g* factor. He also maintains that there are major group factors (V:ed and K:m). The major group factor, V:ed, contains such minor group factors as verbal, numerical, and educational factors. The K:m factor contains such group factors as practical, mechanical, spatial and physical factors. In explaining the results of his factor-analysis studies, Vernon (1960) theorizes that intelligence corresponds to the general level of complexity and flexibility of a person's "schemata" which have been built up cumulatively in the course of his lifetime. He maintains that innate ability in humans limits the ability to acquire schemata, and that persons who have acquired a larger stock of perceptual schemata can build more complex and flexible schemata. As these schemata are built, the later ones that develop will be of higher order and will contain more of the *g* factor, while the earlier ones will be more specific. Vernon theorizes that if the environment is stimulating, the individual will increase the complexity and flexibility of schemata. He contends that the *g* factor is not constant throughout life and that children show a wide variation in this factor. He also maintains that adults become very specialized and that *g* is not a good measure of their abilities in later life.

As the number of factor analysis studies grows, the results become more difficult to evaluate because more and more factors are discovered. Factor analysis, however, will continue to be a very important tool in handling vast amounts of data, and in grouping the contents found in many tests.

PIAGET'S THEORY

Piaget's view of intelligence reflects his background both as a biologist and as a developmental psychologist (Flavell, 1963). His theory, which is based upon a careful description and analysis of successive ontogenic stages in a given culture, considers intelligence to be an extension of certain fundamental biological characteristics. Fundamental to Piaget's theory is the idea that we have two types of heredities—*specific* and *general*. Specific heredity is believed to be composed of the biological structures (such as our nervous and sensory systems) that limit what one perceives, and it is not thought to be as important as general heredity. General heredity is described as the inheritance of a "mode of intellectual functioning" that amounts to the manner of dealing with our environment. This mode of intellectual functioning remains constant throughout life and generates cognitive (knowing or perceiving) structures. The mode of intellectual functioning can also overcome limitations that are acquired through specific heredity.

According to Piaget's theory, two characteristics of intellectual functioning are *organization* and *adaptation*. Organization is defined as a system or structure underlying our acts that is motivated toward the goal of maintaining equilibrium. Adaptation is divided into assimilation and accommodation. *Assimilation* involves changing various elements of the environment so that they can be incorporated into the structure of the organism. *Accommodation*, on the other hand, involves accommodating the organism's functioning to the object it is trying to assimilate. In the process of attempting to maintain equilibrium, the organism develops cognitive structural units called "schema." These schema develop and form interlocking systems with each other, and are classes of similar action sequences. A child is not motivated solely by primary or secondary drives or needs, he also wants to nourish his cognitive schema. He wants to reach out into his environment and incorporate what he can.

Piaget distinguishes three different aspects of intelligence: *content, function*, and *structure*. Content involves the raw, uninterpreted behavioral data of the individual, and may be described as the observable behavior. Function involves broad characteristics of intelligent activity common to all ages. Structure refers to the cognitive structures that are developed and changed with age. They contain organizational properties created through functioning in any environment. There are hierarchical stages with each stage built upon the previous stage, and each higher stage necessarily preceded by the earlier stage.

In relationship to function, Piaget also uses two other concepts: concrete operations and formal operations. *Concrete* mental operations are characteristic of a child under eight and are closely related to sensory-motor perceptions. They tend to be concrete (dealing with real objects) and time-bound—that is, they are restricted to a certain time order. Concrete operations involve little abstraction and are not separated from objects and events of the real world. *Formal* operations are more typical of adults and adolescents than children. These operations are not time-bound and are not as closely related to sensory-motor or real-world experiences as concrete operations. Formal operations are likely to contain appreciable logic and to be based more on internalized concepts rather than the world outside the individual.

Because Piaget's theory stresses the developmental aspects of behavior, it appears to have a great deal to offer for the educator. Its concept of education schema gives the educator a place to start in remediation and in extending the abilities of children because it provides the goal (schema) toward which the educator can strive. His concepts of organization and adaptation give the educator a vehicle or means of dealing with the children in order to change behavior. The hierarchical concept of learning provides the educator with the orderly sequence of approaches that give direction to instruction.

Piaget's model has not been subjected to rigorous standardized testing procedures. Piaget has assessed the progress of children in his work, but he has done so mainly on the basis of very intense observation. His work has been of value, though, in pointing out the *process* aspect of intelligence that is quite different from the content of certain cross-sectional abilities stressed in most current intelligence tests.

WESMAN'S AMORPHOUS MODEL

Wesman (1968) stresses that, when dealing with intelligence, we are dealing with a response-capable organism that has reacted in a highly complex way to environmental stimuli. Intelligence, according to Wesman, is composed of tiny bits or modules of information or skill that may be in the form of either content or process. Furthermore, he indicates that they are multidimensional, and that some modules have more dimensions than others. Each module is subject to change and further learning experiences. Wesman contends that each act of learning creates new modules, changes existing ones, or both, and that modules are not independent—rather, they overlap with other modules. Hence he postulates a complex amorphous structure of intelligence with a large number of dimensions and interrelationships. This model is somewhat frustrating to psychologists in that the lack of stability of the structure of intelligence suggests an extremely difficult task in measuring intellect. Wesman's definition of intelligence as the summation of learned experiences is a natural outgrowth of his concept of intelligence as a somewhat amorphous mass. His theory holds that intelligence is highly unstructured and that the most that can be attempted in testing intelligence is to select samples of learning that have predictive ability and can provide useful information for the purposes desired.

GUILFORD'S STRUCTURE OF THE INTELLECT

Guilford (1967), after conducting extensive research in measurement, became disenchanted with hierarchal models evolved from factor analysis. He noted that research revealed that many different factors had been reported, that there was conflicting evidence concerning the existence of the g and group factors, and that many of the factors discovered had parallel properties rather than being discreet. Guilford concluded that a two-dimensional hierarchical model could not adequately reflect the structure of intellect, and he turned to what he calls a morphological model. This model is a cross-classification of phenomena with intersecting categories rather than categories within categories. Guilford's model, shown in Fig. 4-3, contains three major categories with subcategories in

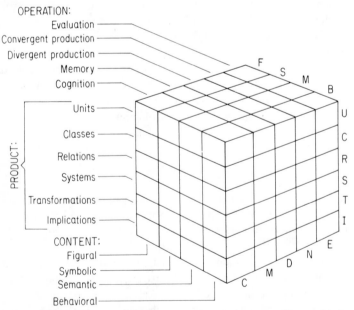

Fig. 4-3. The structure-of-intellect model, with three parameters (other parameters may need to be added). (From J. P. Guilford, *The Nature of Human Intelligence*, 1967, p. 53. Used with permission of McGraw-Hill Book Company.)

each of these, and it results in a total of 120 possible human abilities. While Guilford describes three major categories (referred to as parameters at the present time), he anticipates that other parameters may need to be added. An intellectual factor results when any one of the five operations combines with any one of the six products and any one of the four contents. Each of the content, operation and product categories is briefly described below.

CONTENT	Recognized sets of items of information grouped by virtue of their common properties. Emphasis is placed upon things that may be observed and perceived from units to types of classes, forms of relations, and systems. Emphasis is upon attributes or properties of units of information.
Figural	Information in concrete form as perceived or recalled in the form of images. This implies some degree of structuring, if only in the form of figure and ground. Different sense modalities such as visual, auditory and kinesthetic may be involved.
Symbolic	Information in the form of signs that have no significance in and of themselves. Examples of this would be letters, numbers, musical notations, and other types of coding.
Semantic	Information in the form of meanings to which words have become attached. This is usually in the form of verbal thinking and verbal communication, although semantic information may occasionally be nonverbalized.
Behavioral	Essentially nonverbal information involved in human interactions. Generally an awareness of the attitudes, needs, desires, moods, intentions, or perceptions of other people and ourselves, is important in this category.
PRODUCTS	Forms in which information occurs. Concerns how the individual conceives of information while attempting to know and understand it.
Units	Information conceived in the form of things, segregated wholes, figures on grounds, etc. Units are ordinarily described by nouns.
Classes	An abstraction derived from units that involve class membership by reason of common properties.
Relations	A connection between two things, a kind of bridge or connecting link which has its own character. Relation ideas are commonly expressed by prepositions.
Systems	Organized or structured items of information such as complexes, patterns, or organizations of interdependent or interacting parts. These are commonly stated as arithmetic problems, outlines, equations, or programs.
Transformations	Products of information are changed from one thing into another by revisions, redefinitions or modifications.
Implications	Going from information to something that is expected, anticipated or predicted from the information.
OPERATIONS	Intellectual activities or processes involved in the handling of material that the organism discriminates.

Cognition	Awareness, immediate discovery or rediscovery, or recognition of information in various forms; comprehension or understanding.
Memory	Retention or storage, with some degree of availability, of information in the same form in which it was committed to storage and connection with the same cues with which it was learned.
Divergent Production	Generation of information from given information, where the emphasis is on variety and quantity of output from the same source. This is likely to involve transfer.
Convergent Production	Generation of information from given information attempting to achieve better or unique outcomes. It is likely to involve cues from given information as well as transfers, and frequently produces a search model.
Evaluation	Deciding or judging the goodness or worth of information in terms of criteria such as identity, similarity, satisfaction of class membership and consistency.

Since the definitions given above are quite concise, it may be helpful to give examples of Content, Products, and Operations.

Figural content	If you look away from the book, everything that you feel, smell, hear, see, etc., that is not in the form of signs or words probably involves figural content.
Symbolic content	Information such as the letters A, B, C, or the numbers 1, 2, 3, or the sign + are all examples of symbolic content. These signs have meaning to us when in a particular context but, in and of themselves are meaningless.
Semantic Content	If you have obtained some meaning from the example of symbolic content listed above, this is a form of semantic content.
Behavioral Content	When reading this chapter, if you are aware of feeling bored, anxious, or confused, this feeling is an example of behavioral content. If you are sensitive at the present time to what someone else probably feels about you, this is another example of behavioral content.
Unit	A segregated whole or "thing" such as the word *book* is a unit. In this case it is a semantic unit.
Classes	Information grouped because of common properties, such as calling something a liquid, gas, or solid, is an example of class.
Relations	Saying that 32 is less than 35 is an example of a symbolic relation. Indicating that *amigo* is the Spanish equivalent to *friend* is expressing a semantic relation.
Systems	A discussion of the laws governing a patriarchal society would be an example of a semantic system. The laws governing the metric system would be an example of a symbolic system.
Transformations	Writing a book or changing a verbal statement to a numerical equation are examples of transformations.

Implications	If you attempt to predict what your instructor might use in this chapter on a forthcoming test, this is an example of implication.
Cognition	Remembering the definition of evaluation given above is an example of cognition.
Divergent Production	Listing as many words as you can that rhyme with *cat* in one minute is an example of divergent production.
Convergent Thinking	The picture arrangement test in the WISC which involves putting parts of a cartoon strip in correct sequence serves as an example of convergent thinking.
Evaluation	Looking at a series of pictures and identifying the one thing that is "wrong" with them is an example of evaluation.

THE USE OF THEORIES OF INTELLIGENCE

Attempts to evolve a theory of intelligence that would be acceptable to everyone have not been successful. The process involved in this task is closely related to that of construct validity previously discussed. Each theory of intelligence that has been proposed has generated a great deal of research aimed at verifying the elements of the theory. The research is then incorporated in the construction of other theories of intelligence, resulting in modification of theory to fit the empirical results that have been obtained. Constructing a theory of intelligence, then, may be looked upon as an ongoing process with the complex facets becoming more and more well defined. This long struggle in evolving theories of intelligence has resulted in a vast amount of data that provide more and more information to test administrators concerning what their tests actually measure. Factor analysis has been particularly effective in the identification of some of the basic factors measured by many tests with entirely different names. Guilford's model is extremely important in pointing out three dimensions to intellective factors without discounting the possibility of there being other dimensions.

The ultimate purpose in intelligence testing, of course, is to achieve certain purposes such as the prediction of behavior. A theory of intelligence can be useful in the development of a test that will measure what needs to be measured. For example, although Piaget's theory of intelligence has not been adequately tested, preliminary studies seem to provide some verification of his major hypothesis. A test constructed on Piaget's model should have a great deal to contribute to the understanding of the learning process, since it so closely relates to it. A test constructed to measure some very specific factor (such as the space factor S) probably will predict more effectively for a specific type of activity than a test constructed to measure the g factor.

The complexities of the theories briefly discussed in this chapter should indicate to the test user that any particular intelligence test that he employs probably is testing a very limited portion of what we call intelligence, and that caution must be exercised in predicting behavior with such an instrument.

STABILITY OF INTELLIGENCE

Knowledge concerning the stability of intelligence-test data is important because many of the decisions based upon the results of mental ability tests have implications for long-range educational and vocational plans. One index of stability, the standard error of measurement (discussed in Chapter 2), provides useful information relative to short-term test stability. In addition to this type of stability, test users must be concerned about the stability of test data over long periods of time.

In a comprehensive study of the consistency of mental ability by Bayley (1949), children were tested and retested from the age of one month to eighteen years. Although a variety of tests were used in this process, the results indicate the amount of stability that can be attributed to intelligence testing at various age levels (see Table 4-2). The low correlations obtained by Bayley indicate that during the first two years of life test results tend to be very inconsistent. From the age 2 to age 6 there is an increase in the predictive power of intelligence tests, and after age 6 the scores tend to become relatively stable for most individuals. The older the child is when tested, the more certain we can be that his test scores will remain stable over a period of time.

Although the correlations obtained in the Bayley study are fairly high after age 10, one must remember that these are group statistics and that there is considerable variation in individual cases. In a number of studies in which children were tested after a year's lapse of time, it has been found that the average change in IQ points tended to be about five. This type of information is not very helpful when dealing with an individual child, since occasionally children's IQs, on retesting, have been found to vary as much as 30 points or more from a previous testing. Because of these wide variations found in certain individuals, it is considered good practice to obtain at least two test results from at least two examinations when making important decisions, and to avoid the use of test scores that are several years old.

GROWTH AND DECLINE OF INTELLIGENCE

In some research studies tests of mental ability have been given to individuals of various ages and the changes in the scores have been plotted. While there is a considerable amount of variation in intelligence-test scores, in general it has been found that the scores tend to increase until young adulthood and then slowly decline as the age of the person increases. Shown in Fig. 4-4 are curves based on WAIS data which indicate a decline in test performance with age.

It should be remembered that these data are cross sectional and that the individuals represented by these curves are from different generations. Studies

Table 4-2   Correlation Coefficients Between Age-Level Standard Scores Of Intelligence*

Average of months	Years											
	4, 5, & 6	7, 8, & 9	10, 11, & 12	13, 14 & 15	18, 21, & 24	27, 30, & 36	42, 48 & 54	5, 6, & 7	8, 9, & 10	11, 12, & 13	14, 15, & 16	17, 18
1, 2 & 3	.57	.42	.28	.10	-.04	-.09	-.21	-.13	-.03	.02	-.01	.05
4, 5, & 6		.72	.52	.50	.23	.10	-.16	-.07	-.06	-.08	-.04	-.01
7, 8, & 9			.81	.67	.39	.22	.02	.02	.07	.16	.006	.20
10, 11, & 12				.81	.60	.45	.27	.20	.19	.30	.23	.41
13, 14, & 15					.70	.54	.35	.30	.19	.19	.09	.23
18, 21, & 24						.80	.49	.50	.37	.43	.45	.55
27, 30, & 36							.72	.70	.58	.53	.46	.54
42, 48, & 54								.82	.71	.64	.70	.62
Years												
5, 6, & 7									.92	.85	.87	.86
8, 9, & 10										.94	.92	.89
11, 12, & 13											.96	.96
14, 15, & 16												.96

*These scores are the means of standard scores for three consecutive test-ages, e.g., months 1, 2, and 3; 4, 5, and 6, etc., and years 5, 6, and 7. The last level is composed of only two test ages, 17 and 18 years. Each child's score is the average of all tests taken by him for the ages included in that level. (From Bayley, 1949, p. 181.)

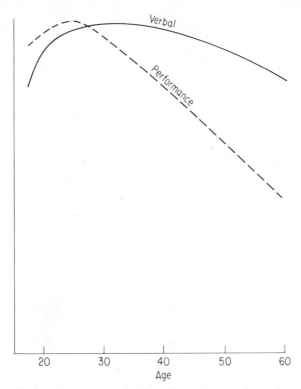

Fig. 4-4. Curves approximating changes in mental-test score with age, based on cross-sectional samples for the WAIS (Wechsler, 1955).

described by Bayley (1955) and Owens (1953) indicate that, in longitudinal studies, groups of individuals frequently increase their performance until age 50 or later. It might be hypothesized that these increases are due to cultural changes taking place in this country, but the hypothesis would be difficult to test.

Wechsler, after noting that there is a more rapid decline in some tests than in others, devised what he called a deterioration quotient (DQ). This quotient is a ratio between tests that tend to show a definite score decline ("don't hold" tests) and those tests that tend to show little score decline ("hold" tests). The tests indicated as "hold" tests are Vocabulary, Information, Object Assembly, and Picture Completion. The "don't hold" tests include Digit Span, Similarities, Digit Symbol, and Block Design. The formula for computing a deterioration quotient is as follows: DQ = Hold – Don't hold ÷ Hold. Wechsler's deterioration quotient has been criticized quite severely. It has been pointed out that many young individuals have lower scores on the "don't hold" items than on the "hold" items, and hence might be portraying a high deterioration quotient early in life when no deterioration should be expected.

ENVIRONMENT AND HEREDITY

Early in the history of mental testing, when it was assumed that intelligence tests measured innate ability, it was also natural to assume that the IQ remained constant and was largely determined by heredity. More recently a large number of studies dealing with children of various types of deprivation apparently have indirectly demonstrated that environment also influences intelligence. Since the studies lack rigid experimental controls (because it would be inhumane to subject children to deprivation intentionally to measure its effect upon intelligence) caution must be used in drawing inference from them.

Goldfarb (1943) compared children who had been in orphanages for the first three years of their lives to children who had been adopted immediately after birth. The two groups involved had nearly the same heredity backgrounds. Goldfarb found that 37.5 percent of the orphanage children were classified as mentally retarded, while only 7.5 percent of those in foster homes were so classified. He concluded that the greater incidence of retardation in the orphanage children was due to the lack of stimulation. Speer (1940) correlated the IQs of children arriving at a placement agency with the length of time the children had remained with their feeble-minded mothers. He obtained a negative correlation, which seems to indicate that the longer the children lived with their feeble-minded mothers, the lower their IQs tended to be when they arrived at the agency. Yarrow (1961) reviewed a great many studies involving deprivation and concluded that mental impairment was the greatest if deprivation came between the ages of three and twelve months. Bloom (1964) concurred that environmental deprivation or stimulation was most crucial during the younger years. Bloom suggests that a deprived child may score as much as ten IQ points lower than a child in an abundant environment by the age of four, and that, by age 17, the difference may be as high as 20 points. Bloom's opinion is based on the assumption that 50 percent of mature intelligence is obtained by age four and that 100 percent is obtained by age seventeen.

Some studies indicate that environmental enrichment tends to raise the IQ. Wellman (1940) summarized several studies and reported a mean gain of 6.6 IQ points by 652 children who had been exposed to nursery school. Skeels (1965) indicated that foster children whose real mothers were believed to be mentally retarded were generally in the normal range when followed up after intervals of 16 to 21 years.

Many of the studies relating to the effects of heredity have involved twins and parent-child relationships. Figure 4-5 shows a summary of the results of several such studies as reported by Erlenmeyer-Kimling and Jarvik (1963). An inspection of the reported correlations indicates that heredity contributes substantially to intelligence. For example, identical twins tend to have more similar IQs than fraternal twins and parent-child IQs tend to correlate higher than fosterparent-child IQs. The IQs of siblings reared together tend to be more alike

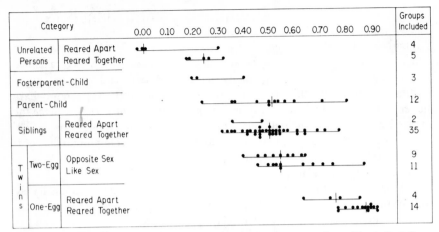

Category		0.00 0.10 0.20 0.30 0.40 0.50 0.60 0.70 0.80 0.90	Groups Included
Unrelated Persons	Reared Apart		4
	Reared Together		5
Fosterparent - Child			3
Parent - Child			12
Siblings	Reared Apart		2
	Reared Together		35
Twins Two-Egg	Opposite Sex		9
	Like Sex		11
Twins One-Egg	Reared Apart		4
	Reared Together		14

Fig. 4-5. Correlation coefficients for "intelligence" test scores from 52 studies. Some studies reported data for more than one relationship category; some included more than one sample per category, giving a total of 99 groups. Over two-thirds of the correlation coefficients were derived from IQs, the remainder from special tests (for example, Primary Mental Abilities). Midparent-child correlation was used when available, otherwise mother-child correlation. Correlation coefficients obtained in each study are indicated by dark circles; medians are shown by vertical lines intersecting the horizontal lines which represent the ranges. (From Erlenmeyer-Kimling and Jarvik, 1963, p. 1478.)

than the IQs of siblings reared apart, which suggests some environmental influence.

Burt (1958) used an analysis-of-variance procedure to attempt to identify the percentage of test-score variation that can be attributed to environment and the variation that results from heredity. He estimated that 23 percent of the variance can be attributed to environment and 77 percent to heredity. His conclusions, of course, may be limited strictly to his tests and his statistical procedures.

A cautious summary of the research findings discussed here seems to indicate that heredity tends to influence intelligence more than environment, but that environment has a greater potential than heredity for inhibiting intelligence during the early formative years. Both heredity and environment may limit the degree of intellectual attainment. However, it is believed by most psychologists that few people function mentally near the limit imposed by either heredity or environment; hence an enriched environment should result in greater intellectual attainment.

RACIAL AND CULTURAL DIFFERENCES

The use of tests of intelligence with any group other than the middle-class "Anglo" population has created problems that have not been satisfactorily solved to date. Early in the history of testing it seemed quite appropriate to administer intelligence tests to various racial or cultural groups, and simply report in studies that a particular group averaged so many IQ points lower than the population upon which the test was standardized. Later such studies were criticized because the tests in use at that time had not been standardized on divergent racial and cultural populations, and hence had doubtful validity. The answer to this criticism is to establish norms for various racial and cultural populations, but when this is attempted one generally finds that the validity of these tests for predictive purposes is frequently disappointing.

An abortive attempt to solve this problem was made with the construction and use of so-called culture-fair or culture-free intelligence tests. In the construction of these tests, nonverbal tasks such as geometric designs were frequently utilized to measure intelligence. The criticisms of this approach are that these types of tests (1) measure only a very limited aspect of intelligence; (2) are not "culturally fair" to more than a few isolated cultures; (3) when constructed, generally have very little practical use. The tests fail to predict well or to give much useful information about the person tested. Frequently the culturally biased tests, which are obviously unsuitable for a particular population in question, have given a better prediction of such criteria as achievement in school than the culture-free or culture-fair test. Several difficult problems face those who wish to construct culture-fair tests. (1) It is very difficult to obtain representative samples. (2) Factors such as socioeconomic class and educational background which tend to affect test performance are difficult to control. (3) Most of our present tests have been developed within the context of the middle-class Anglo culture and are dependent upon definitions of intelligence from that culture; to use the definition of intelligence for a culture under question might easily result in a test that rewarded behavior not considered indicative of intelligence by the dominant cultures. (4) Test-taking motivation with other racial or cultural groups cannot be assumed. (5) Language problems frequently invalidate the test.

In 1957, when the process of school desegregation was an issue, 18 social scientists met and reaffirmed a statement that had been made by several other social scientists. The summary statement of this conference (Special Comment on Race and Intelligence: a joint statement, 1957) was the conclusion that there was no basis for any innate racial difference in intelligence, that most differences of intelligence could be accounted for by environmental difference, that there is a great overlapping between Negroes and whites and that many Negroes are more intelligent that the average white. Recently, though, some scientists have challenged this statement. Shuey (1966) surveyed research covering a fifty-year period involving approximately 382 different studies in which 81 different tests were administered. She concluded that these studies ". . . all taken together, inevitably point to the presence of native differences between Negroes and whites as determined by intelligence tests." Shuey's study is open to criticism in that the racial samples were not selected by any set of genetic coordinates, but rather by the subjects' or investigators' subjective impressions.

Jensen (1969) expressed concern over the apparent failure of compensatory education to produce significant improvement in the measured intelligence or scholastic performance of disadvantaged children. To account for this failure, he has suggested a reevaluation of the assumptions, theories, and practices upon which compensatory education is based, and has developed a genetic model for educational intervention. He contends that intelligence is a nebulous thing measured by standard intelligence tests, and that it is characteristic of the mental abilities of European and North American middle-class populations. Jensen points out that this trait figures prominently in the nature of the traditional school curriculum, instruction, and resultant student academic or occupational behavior. He further maintains that intelligence, as measured by most standard IQ tests, is highly heritable, with genetic factors accounting for approximately 80 percent of the individual differences and environmental factors accounting for the remaining 20 percent. Environment is assumed to be most influential during the prenatal and early postnatal periods. Citing his own research and that of others, Jensen suggests that an explanation of differences in IQ and scholastic ability of different socioeconomic and ethnic groups must include genetic differences as well as environmental differences. He reports that when socioeconomic level is held constant the black population tests about 11 IQ points below the average for the white population.

Using studies involving traditional as well as newer, less culture-bound intelligence tests, Jensen divides intelligence into two kinds of abilities: associative learning ability, which he calls Level 1; and cognitive or conceptual learning and problem-solving ability, which he calls Level 2. He concludes that lower- and middle-class school children perform equally well on Level 1 tasks, but differ between 15 and 20 IQ points on Level 2 tasks. The Level 2 task is closely related to the generalized IQ or g factor. Jensen believes that much of the instruction in schools is based on the g factor and that this handicaps the disadvantaged children. He advocates a greater emphasis on Level 1 type learnings for disadvantaged children to improve compensatory education.

Jensen's views on racial differences and compensatory education in American schools have evoked a number of critical comments. The following points are most often emphasized by the critics.

1. Rather than say that compensatory education has failed, it would be more accurate to say that certain techniques or compensatory programs have failed.

2. It is impossible to filter out the contributions of heredity and environment to intelligence.

3. The concept of race which has been used is not genetically sound and different populations rather than different races are being sampled.

4. The behavior of blacks is looked upon as a type of pathological white behavior while, in essence, it is based upon a distinct culture of its own.
5. Environmental factors such as hunger, malnutrition, prenatal, and early childhood impairments may account for any differences in intelligence that exist.
6. Racial oppression may account for any obtained differences in test results.
7. The individual's identification with race is quite important and may distort the results of testing.
8. Intelligence tests may not measure intelligence reliably enough to permit Jensen's conclusions.
9. We have insufficient information concerning the administration of intelligence tests to white and black populations under comparable circumstances to conclude that the races differ mentally.

Jensen's research and the reaction to it indicate that the matter of racial and cultural differences is highly complex and that the problems in this area are going to be difficult to solve.

REFERENCES

American Journal of Orthopsychiatry, "Special Comment on Race and Intelligence: a Joint Statement," Vol. 27, No. 2 (1957).

Bayley, Nancy, "Consistency and Variability in the Growth of Intelligence from Birth to Eighteen Years," *Journal of Genetic Psychology* 75 (1949), 165–196.

———, "On the Growth of Intelligence," *American Psychologist* 10 (1955), 805–818.

Binet, Alfred, and T. Simon, *The Development of Intelligence in Children*. Trans. Elizabeth S. Kite. Baltimore: Waverly Press, 1944.

Bloom, B. S., *Stability and Change in Human Characteristics*. New York: Wiley, 1964.

Burt, Cyril, "The Inheritance of Mental Ability," *American Psychologist* 13 (1958), 1-15.

Cohen, Jacob, "The Factorial Structures of the WISC at Ages 7-6, 10-6, and 13-6," *Journal Consulting Psychology* 23 (1959), 285-299.

Cronbach, Lee J., *Essentials of Psychological Testing*. 3rd ed. New York: Harper, 1970.

Erlenmeyer-Kimling, L., and L. F. Jarvik, "Genetics and Intelligence: a Review," *Science* 142 (1963), 1477-1478.

Flavell, John J., *The Developmental Psychology of Jean Piaget*. Princeton, N. J.: Van Nostrand, 1963.

Fromm, Erika, and Lenore Dumas Hartman, *Intelligence: A Dynamic Approach*. Garden City, N.Y.: Doubleday, 1955.

Garrett, H. E., "A Developmental Theory of Intelligence," *American Psychologist* 1 (1946), 372.

Goldfarb, W., "Infant Rearing and Problem Behavior," *American Journal of Orthopsychiatry* 13 (1943) 249-265.

Guilford, J. P. *The Nature of Human Intelligence*. New York: McGraw-Hill, 1967.

Jensen, A. R., "How Much Can We Boost IQ and Scholastic Achievement?" *Harvard Education Review* 39 (1969), 1-123.

Owens, W. A., Jr., "Age and Mental Abilities: A Longitudinal Study," *Genetic Psychology Monograph* 48 (1953) 3-54.

Skeels, H. M., "Effects of Adoption of Children From Institutions," *Children* 12 (1965), 33-34.

Spearman, C., *The Abilities of Man*. New York: Macmillan, 1927.

Speer, G. S., "The Mental Development of Children of Feebleminded and Normal Mothers," *Yearbook National Society for the Study of Education* 39, Part II (1940), 309-314.

Stoddard, George D., *The Meaning of Intelligence*. New York: Macmillan, 1943.

Shuey, Audrey M., *The Testing of Negro Intelligence*. 2nd ed. New York: Social Service Press, 1966.

Thorndike, E. L., et al., *The Measurement of Intelligence*. New York: Teachers College Press, 1927.

Thurstone, L. L., "Primary Mental Abilities," *Psychometric Monograph*, No. 1 (1938).

Vernon, Philip E., *The Structure of Human Abilities*. New York: Wiley, 1951.

———, *Intelligence and Attainment Tests*. New York: Philosophical Library, 1960.

Wechsler, David, *The Measurement and Appraisal of Adult Intelligence*. 4th ed. Baltimore: Williams & Wilkins, 1958.

———, *Wechsler Adult Intelligence Scale Manual*. New York: Psychological Corporation, 1955.

———, *Measurement of Adult Intelligence*. 3rd ed. Baltimore: Waverly Press, 1944.

Wellman, B. L., "Iowa Studies of the Effects of Schooling," *Yearbook of the National Society for the Study of Education* 39, Part II (1940), 377-399.

Wesman, Alexander G., "Intelligence Testing," *American Psychologist* 23 (1968), 267-274.

Yarrow, L. J., "Maternal Deprivation: Toward an Empirical and Conceptual Reevaluation," *Psychological Bulletin* 58 (1961), 459-490.

The Stanford-Binet Scales

Although the 1960 revision of the *Stanford-Binet Intelligence Scale* is generally considered to be superior to the 1937 revision as a test of mental ability, the latter will be discussed at length in this chapter for a number of reasons. One of the reasons is that the test items of the 1960 scale were taken from two forms of the 1937 scale, and a better understanding of the more recent instrument is likely to result if one has knowledge of the older scale. Another important reason for discussing the 1937 scale is that the use of the forms L and M has provided a considerable amount of useful data for research and the interpretation of test results. A third major reason for giving attention to the forerunner of the 1960 revision is that forms L and M are still being used, though on a very limited scale, by some psychologists and researchers.

THE 1937 STANFORD-BINET INTELLIGENCE SCALE

The 1937 scale consists of two equivalent forms (L and M), each having 129 items or subtests. The forms are equivalent in the sense that they have similar content and difficulty. The items in the forms came chiefly from the 1916 scale. Both forms extend from age 2 through three superior-adult levels, I, II, and III.

A number of significant changes were made in the 1916 scale in order to produce the improved 1937 revision. One of the major changes, the construction of two equivalent forms, has already been mentioned. The availability of two comparable forms provided examiners with the opportunity to retest subjects without an appreciable influence on test results due to practice effect. Also, researchers had another means of measuring reliability of the scale; i.e., through comparing results for the two equivalent forms.

Another improvement found in the 1937 Stanford-Binet revision was effected by extending the scale downward and upward, which made the testing of younger and older individuals possible. The scale also was made more useful by better standardization at the lower and higher levels.

The scale was improved considerably by providing subtests at ages 11 and 13 where there were none in the previous scale, and by providing groups of test items at half-year levels from ages 2 to 5. The use of half-year groupings permitted greater accuracy of testing at the age levels where mental growth is quite rapid.

Further refinement in the Stanford-Binet scale was accomplished by improving the directions for administering and scoring the subtests, which probably improved the scale's reliability.

In the standardization of the 1937 scale, over three thousand American-born subjects were used. The authors of the scale carefully chose their standardization sample of subjects from homes which appeared to be representative of the general population. The subjects were from eleven states representing different areas of the country.

MENTAL AGE AND INTELLIGENCE QUOTIENT

The 1937 Stanford-Binet scale utilizes essentially the same procedures for finding mental ages and intelligence quotients as the 1916 scale. The 1937 revision, however, provides for a possible maximum mental age of 22 years and 10 months, as compared with a maximum of 19 years and 6 months for the 1916 scale. Another difference between the scales is that for the 1916 scale a maximum chronological age of 16 was used to determine the intelligence quotient of a subject who was 16 years of age or older, but for the 1937 scale the maximum CA is 15. By using the formula, $IQ = \dfrac{MA}{CA} \times 100$, we can see that the maximum attainable Form L or M quotient for a subject who is 15 or older is 152. That is, $\dfrac{22.8}{15} \times 100 = 152$.

As previously mentioned, in the original Stanford-Binet scale the authors chose 16 as the maximum CA which might be used in determining an IQ. If a maximum CA were not used, a subject would appear to become less and less intelligent as he became older because his MA would eventually reach its maximum, while his CA would continue to increase. So, without a terminal CA, every person regardless of mental age could eventually have a test score indicating mental deficiency.

For the 1916 scale, the mean adult *mental age* was placed at 16 and chronological ages above 16 were disregarded in calculating the IQs of older persons. The correct placement of the terminal CA should be based upon the age at which unselected subjects cease to improve in mean score (Terman and Merrill,

1937). It is, however, extremely difficult to determine precisely what the terminal age should be because it is quite difficult to obtain unselected test populations beyond the age of fourteen or so. That is, since the less intelligent high school students tend to drop out of school earlier than the brighter students, this test population is not truly unselected. Terman and Merrill attempted to make the distribution of IQs of the older subjects comparable to those of the younger individuals by making some adjustments in the denominator of the IQ formula, starting with age 13 years, two months.

From the test data, Terman and Merrill had found that gains in mental ability began to decrease after age 13, until at age 16 there was practically no further gain. They decided that, because age improvement gradually diminished, beginning at age 13 years they would disregard increasing fractions of successive CA increments. From CA 13 to CA 16 they cumulatively dropped one of every three additional months of chronological age. After age 16, additional CA was disregarded. Table 5-1 shows the corrected CA divisors for actual chronological ages.

Table 5-1. Correction Table for Higher Chronological Ages
(From Terman and Merrill, 1937, p. 31, by permission of Houghton Mifflin Company.)

Actual CA	Corrected CA Divisor	Actual CA	Corrected CA Divisor	Actual CA	Corrected CA Divisor
13-0	13-0	14-0	13-8	15-0	14-4
13-1	13-1	14-1	13-9	15-1	14-5
13-2	13-1	14-2	13-9	15-2	14-5
13-3	13-2	14-3	13-10	15-3	14-6
13-4	13-3	14-4	13-11	15-4	14-7
13-5	13-3	14-5	13-11	15-5	14-7
13-6	13-4	14-6	14-0	15-6	14-8
13-7	13-5	14-7	14-1	15-7	14-9
13-8	13-5	14-8	14-1	15-8	14-9
13-9	13-6	14-9	14-2	15-9	14-10
13-10	13-7	14-10	14-3	15-10	14-11
13-11	13-7	14-11	14-3	15-11	14-11
				16-0 and above	15-0

DISTRIBUTION AND VARIABILITY OF INTELLIGENCE QUOTIENTS

An examination of the data in Table 5-2 will reveal that the mean IQs for the standardization group are somewhat above 100. The fact that the mean IQs run above the theoretical mean of 100 is intentional on the part of the authors, who wanted to allow for somewhat inadequate sampling of subjects from the "lower" occupational groups. Terman and Merrill accomplished the adjustment in mean IQs by dividing the subjects into seven groups according to fathers' occupations, then computing the mean IQ for each group, and finally weighting each mean at each age level according to the occupational frequency of each

Table 5-2. Composite L-M IQ Means Adjusted for 1930
Census Frequencies of Occupational Groupings
(From Terman and Merrill, 1937, p. 31, by
permission of Houghton Mifflin Company)

Age	N	Raw	Smoothed
2	76	102.1	
2½	74	104.7	103.3
3	81	103.2	104.1
3½	77	104.3	102.2
4	83	99.2	101.6
4½	79	101.2	100.8
5	90	101.9	100.4
5½	110	98.3	100.0
6	203	100.0	99.8
7	202	101.2	100.8
8	203	101.1	102.0
9	204	103.6	102.7
10	201	103.5	103.0
11	204	101.9	102.2
12	202	101.2	101.6
13	204	101.8	101.0
14	202	100.0	101.3
15	107	102.0	101.3
16	102	101.8	103.3
17	109	103.2	103.8
18	101	106.3	

group. Table 5-2 shows the raw and smoothed values for the composite L-M
means after the adjustment.

Figure 5-1 shows graphically the adjusted L-M intelligence quotients for the
standardization group in terms of percent of the scores at ten-point IQ intervals.

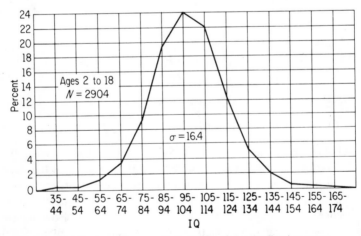

Fig. 5-1. Distribution of composite L–M IQs of standardization group
(From Terman and Merrill, 1937, p. 37, by permission of Houghton Mifflin
Company).

In mental testing it is desirable to have a scale provide a normal distribution of scores with a range broad enough to include all or nearly all of the population for which it is designed. It is readily apparent that the distribution of scores shown in Fig. 5-1 closely approximates a normal distribution. The highest percentages of IQs are found near the middle of the distribution and the lowest at the extremes. This graph rather vividly shows the variability in intellectual ability for the American-born white children who were included in the standardization group. The range is sufficiently broad for most testing purposes.

An examination of the data in Tables 5-3 and 5-4 will enable the reader to compare the means and standard deviations obtained for the standardization groups for Forms L and M. Such a comparison is essential to an understanding of the data which the forms yield.

Table 5-3.   IQ Means by Age for the Standardization Group
(From Terman and Merrill, 1937, p. 35, by permission
of Houghton Mifflin Company)

Age	N	Form L		Form M	
		Raw	Smoothed	Raw	Smoothed
2	76	107.5 ± 1.3		104.0 ± 1.2	
2½	74	109.9 ± 1.6	107.4	108.3 ± 1.6	105.7
3	81	104.8 ± 1.4	107.8	104.8 ± 1.4	107.1
3½	77	108.0 ± 1.3	105.1	108.2 ± 1.3	105.5
4	83	102.5 ± 1.3	104.7	103.5 ± 1.2	104.8
4½	79	103.7 ± 1.2	103.5	102.7 ± 1.2	103.4
5	90	104.3 ± 1.0	103.1	104.0 ± 1.0	103.0
5½	110	101.4 ± 0.9	102.2	102.2 ± 0.9	102.8
6	203	101.0 ± 0.6	101.4	102.1 ± 0.6	102.6
7	202	101.8 ± 0.8	101.7	103.5 ± 0.7	103.0
8	203	102.4 ± 0.7	102.8	103.3 ± 0.7	104.1
9	204	104.3 ± 0.8	103.7	105.4 ± 0.8	104.6
10	201	104.5 ± 0.8	104.4	105.0 ± 0.8	105.0
11	204	104.3 ± 0.9	104.1	104.7 ± 0.8	104.2
12	202	103.6 ± 0.9	104.0	102.9 ± 0.9	103.8
13	204	104.0 ± 0.8	102.8	103.7 ± 0.8	102.6
14	202	100.9 ± 0.8	102.6	101.2 ± 0.8	102.5
15	107	102.8 ± 1.2	101.7	102.6 ± 1.3	101.9
16	102	101.3 ± 1.1	103.0	101.9 ± 1.2	103.3
17	109	104.8 ± 0.9	104.4	105.4 ± 0.9	104.9
18	101	107.3 ± 1.2		107.3 ± 1.1	

Table 5-3 shows that the mean IQs for the two scales are very similar at most of the age levels. The average difference between the means, in terms of raw means, is only 0.8 point. There is only one difference that is greater than 1.7 points and that is found at age 2 (3.5 points). If age 2 is disregarded, the average difference between the means is only 0.67 IQ point. The smoothed means show even greater agreement, with a mean difference of only 0.56 point.

Table 5-4 shows interesting data relative to the variability of IQs from age to age for the two forms of the 1937 scale. It can be seen that the standard

Table 5-4. IQ Variability in Relation to Age (From Terman and Merrill, 1937, p. 40, by permission of Houghton Mifflin Company)

CA	N	σ_L IQ	σ_M IQ
2	102	16.7	15.5
2½	102	20.6	20.7
3	99	19.0	18.7
3½	103	17.3	16.3
4	105	16.9	15.6
4½	101	16.2	15.3
5	109	14.2	14.1
5½	110	14.3	14.0
6	203	12.5	13.2
7	202	16.2	15.6
8	203	15.8	15.5
9	204	16.4	16.7
10	201	16.5	15.9
11	204	18.0	17.3
12	202	20.0	19.5
13	204	17.9	17.8
14	202	16.1	16.7
15	107	19.0	19.3
16	102	16.5	17.4
17	109	14.5	14.3
18	101	17.2	16.6

deviations (σ_s) of the IQs average around 16 IQ points. It is also evident that there is close agreement between the two scales with respect to the σ_s at the different ages shown. Terman and Merrill state that "since inspection of the values reveals no marked relationship between IQ variability and CA over the age range as a whole, we may accept 16 points as approximately the representative value of the standard deviations of IQs for an unselected population." (Terman and Merrill, 1937, p. 40)

In Table 5-4, extremes in deviation fluctuations for Form L can be found at ages 6 (12.5), age 2½ (20.6) and age 12 (20.0). Form M shows extremes at age 6 (13.2) and age 2½ (20.7). The extremes of low and high deviations, at ages 6 and 12 respectively, are very likely not attributable to chance fluctuations (Terman and Merrill, 1937, p. 40). The authors were unable to explain the reason for these extreme fluctuations. The composite IQ distribution (Forms L and M) for the whole standardization group has a standard deviation of 16.4.

The similarities in the distributions of composite L-M intelligence quotients at three age levels can be seen in Fig. 5-2.

Using 16 IQ points as the standard deviation and assuming that IQs are comparable at various age levels, Terman and Merrill have provided a table which shows intelligence ratings in terms of standard scores. In Table 5-5 one can see that an IQ of 148, for example, would be the equivalent of a standard score of 3.00. An IQ of 60 would have a z-score of −2.50. Such standard scores might be useful in research and test interpretation.

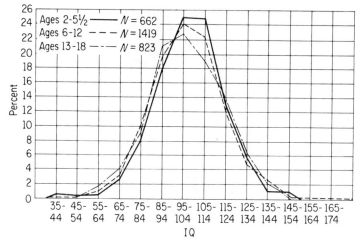

Fig. 5-2. Distributions of composite L–M IQs at three age levels (from Terman and Merrill, 1937, p. 41, by permission of Houghton Mifflin Company).

Table 5-5. IQ Equivalents of Standard Scores
(From Terman and Merrill, 1937, p. 42, by permission of Houghton Mifflin Company)

Standard Score	IQ	Standard Score	IQ
+5.00	180	− .25	96
+4.75	176	− .50	92
+4.50	172	− .75	88
+4.25	168	−1.00	84
+4.00	164	−1.25	80
+3.75	160	−1.50	76
+3.50	156	−1.75	72
+3.25	152	−2.00	68
+3.00	148	−2.25	64
+2.75	144	−2.50	60
+2.50	140	−2.75	56
+2.25	136	−3.00	52
+2.00	132	−3.25	48
+1.75	128	−3.50	44
+1.50	124	−3.75	40
+1.25	120	−4.00	36
+1.00	116	−4.25	32
+ .75	112	−4.50	28
+ .50	108	−4.75	24
+ .25	104	−5.00	20
.00	100		

CLASSIFICATION OF INTELLIGENCE QUOTIENTS

Terman and Merrill have provided a system for classifying intelligence quotients, which can be useful is one wishes to apply qualitative or descriptive terms to the quantified data from intelligence testing. The system is shown in Table 5-6.

Table 5-6. Distribution of the 1937 Standardization Group (From Terman and Merrill, 1960, p. 18, by permission of Houghton Mifflin Company)

IQ	Percent	Classification
160–169	0.03	
150–159	0.2	Very superior
140–149	1.1	
130–139	3.1	Superior
120–129	8.2	
110–119	18.1	High average
100–109	23.5	Normal or average
90–99	23.0	
80–89	14.5	Low average
70–79	5.6	Borderline defective
60–69	2.0	
50–59	0.4	Mentally defective
40–49	0.2	
30–39	0.03	

It is interesting to note that, according to this classification table, 1.33 percent of the group are classified as very superior, 2.63 as mentally defective, and 46.5 as normal or average. It should be emphasized, however, that a competent clinician often would not classify subjects solely on a single measure of intelligence. Our knowledge of the standard error of measurement should serve to remind us that chance errors might easily lead to the misclassification of individuals.

VALIDITY

The authors of the 1937 scale selected for inclusion in the scale those subtests or items which were most suitable in terms of validity, ease and objectivity of scoring, interest to subjects, time required for administration, and variety of tasks. As would be expected, validity was the criterion considered to be most essential.

Validity of the individual subtests was determined in part on the basis of the amount of increase in percentage of successful performance with an increase in age. This criterion involved two considerations: (1) increase in the percents passing from one age (or mental age) to the next, and (2) a weight based on the ratio of the difference to the standard error of the difference between the mean age (or mental age) of subjects passing the test and of subjects failing it (Terman and Merrill, 1937, p. 9).

Another criterion used to judge the validity of individual items involved the use of biserial correlation coefficients. In order for an item to be included in one of the forms it had to show a sizable positive correlation with the total scores of subjects at some age level. In other words, it had to contribute appreciably to the total test score.

The biserial coefficients which were calculated for the items in Form L ranged from .28 (for Memory for Designs, year 9), to .89 (Abstract Words, year 11; and Vocabulary, year 14). For Form M, the range of biserial r's was from .27 (Memory for Stories, year 13) to .91 (Abstract Words, year 13). The median biserial r for Form L was approximately .69, and the median value for Form L was approximately .64 (McNemar, 1942). Since none of the biserial coefficients fell below .27 and most were above .60, it can be assumed that the internal consistency of the scale is high, which should contribute substantially to the construct validity of the instrument.

Once the test items were selected for inclusion in the forms, it was necessary for the scale's authors to determine the proper age location for each of the items. In the process of accomplishing this objective, the authors arranged and rearranged the items until they would yield an IQ of 100 at each level. For Form L, six successive revisions were required to achieve this result. This task was accomplished for Form M by arranging subtests so that they matched Form L at each age level with respect to difficulty, validity, and shape of curves of percents by age. This standardization process was not limited to shifting items in a form. It also required shifting subtests from one form to another and modifying scoring standards to change the difficulty of some items. In making the necessary alterations the scale's authors also had to consider such factors as the variety of items in each form, correlation with the total score, sex differences, ease of scoring, appeal to the subjects, time requirements, etc. (Terman and Merrill, 1937, p. 23).

The foregoing discussion deals with *construct validity* for the 1937 Stanford-Binet. Another kind of validity that should be considered is *predictive validity*. Evidence of this kind of validity can be found in investigations involving Stanford-Binet scores and school achievement.

At the elementary and secondary school levels, correlation coefficients between Stanford-Binet scores and scholastic achievement have been determined in a number of studies. Freeman (1962, p. 215) reports the following summarization:

Elementary

Reading: a majority are .60 or higher, (modal interval .60–.69)
Arithmetic: a majority are .50 or higher (modal interval .45–.55)
Spelling: a majority are .45 or higher (modal interval .45–.55)

Secondary

(approximate medians)

Reading comprehension	.70
Knowledge of literature	.60
English usage	.60
History	.60
Algebra	.60
Biology	.55
Geometry	.50
Spelling	.45
Reading rate	.45

Evidence concerning *content validity* for the Stanford-Binet scales is provided by an examination of the tasks to be performed by the subject in the various tests. The tests include such varied activities as block building, naming objects, copying a circle, sorting buttons, and matching forms (all at the lower levels of the scale), as well as repeating digits, defining words, duplicating a bead pattern, solving problems, and explaining the meaning of proverbs (at the higher levels). At the upper age levels the verbal items greatly outnumber the performance items, but the scale's authors explain the emphasis on verbal content by stating

> At these levels the major intellectual differences between subjects reduce largely to differences in the ability to do conceptual thinking, and facility in dealing with concepts is most readily sampled by the use of verbal tests. Language essentially is the shorthand of the higher thought processes, and the level at which this shorthand functions is one of the most important determinants of the level of the processes themselves. (Terman and Merrill, 1937, p. 5)

RELIABILITY

Terman and Merrill (1937) compared test results for Form L with those for Form M and reported reliability coefficients ranging from .85 to .95 for several age groups. Figure 5-3 shows a scattergram of scores for Forms L and M at age 7. The r for this set of scores is .91.

A glance at the scattergram will reveal that the pattern of plotted points is fan-shaped—that is, there is greater scatter of the scores at the higher IQ levels than at the lower levels. This means of course that the reliability of the scale is higher at the lower levels of IQ than at the higher levels. This finding also holds true for the age levels other than CA 7. Terman and Merrill found the highest reliability coefficient (.98) for IQs below 70 and the lowest (.90) for IQs above 130 (McNemar, 1942).

The fact that the scale's reliability is greater at the lower IQ levels than at the higher levels probably is the result of differences in weighting of the subtests at the lower, intermediate, and higher levels. From level 2 to level 5 each subtest is given a weight of one month. From level 6 to the average-adult level, two months of credit are given for each test passed. At the remaining levels, four, five, and six months of credit are given for the passed items. Since passing or not passing a test at the higher levels can affect the total score of a subject more than at the lower levels, and because subjects who have higher IQs are tested at higher levels than those who have lower IQs (at given CAs), the measurement errors will tend to be larger and reliability lower for the higher levels (Pinneau, 1961).

The reliability of the 1937 scale was found to be higher for older individuals than for younger persons. McNemar (1942, pp. 62–63) reported reliability coefficients ranging from .83 to .92 for ages 2½ to 5½ for IQs in the 140–149 and

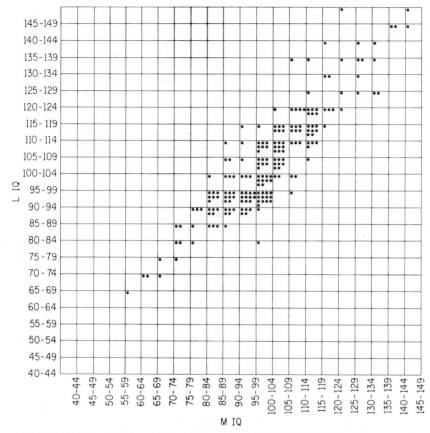

Fig. 5-3. Scatter plot of correlation between L and M IQs at CA 7 (From Terman and Merrill, 1937, p. 45, by permission of Houghton Mifflin Company).

70–79 ranges respectively. For ages 6 to 13 the reported coefficients range from .90 to .97 for IQs in the IQ ranges 120–129 and 60–69 respectively. For ages 14 to 18 and the same IQ ranges (120–129 and 60–69), the reported coefficients range from .93 to .98. These reliability coefficients were obtained by correlating IQs on Forms L and M administered to the standardization group within a one-week period.

The increase in reliability coefficients with age is typical of psychological tests. It probably is related to testing conditions, and differences in the behavior of younger subjects as compared with older ones. Any examiner who has tested young children knows that sometimes it is quite difficult to test them. Young children are more likely to be inattentive, reticent, uncooperative, or overactive than older children or adults, so it is generally more difficult to adhere to the standardized procedures when testing them. Deviations from the standardized procedures can adversely affect test reliability. Furthermore, older subjects are undergoing less change and are less likely to show random fluctuations in performance over short periods of time (Pinneau, 1961).

THE 1960 REVISION OF THE STANFORD-BINET SCALE

The most recent revision of the Stanford-Binet, the 1960 scale (Form L-M), was constructed from the best subtests of Form L and Form M of the 1937 scale. The authors explain that the construction of the single form in this way offers several advantages. First, the procedure avoids the duplication of subtests to obtain a sufficient number of satisfactory items at each level. Second, it provides enough good items to permit having an alternate subtest at each level, rather than at preschool levels only (as in the 1937 forms). Third, Form L-M is a better scale than Form L and Form M because the authors could be more selective in choosing only highly discriminative subtests.

Terman and Merrill (1960) chose the items for the 1960 scale on the basis of the results of tests administered to 4498 subjects, in an age range of 2½ to 18 years. These subjects had been given one or both forms (L and M) during the five-year period from 1950 to 1954. As can be seen in Table 5-7, the subjects in the assessment group resided in six states.

While the individuals in the assessment group did not comprise a representative sampling of American school children, the authors were careful to avoid the effect of special selective factors. For the purposes of evaluation and comparison of test results, the authors included in the assessment group two stratified

Table 5-7. Assessment Group Tabulated by Areas (From Terman and Merrill, 1960, p. 21, by permission of Houghton Mifflin Company.)

	Form L Item Analysis	Form M Item Analysis	L-M Stratified Samples	Pretesting Modified or Substitute Items	Total Number of Subjects
New Jersey	892				892
Minnesota	850	208			1058
Iowa[1]	102				(636)
New York and California				96 + 588	684
Massachusetts	91				91
California	1258	897	200		2355
Totals	3193	1105	200	684	5716

Main Sample 4498

[1] The Iowa total includes 336 cases, tested in 1940-44, for comparison with a similar sample similarly obtained tested ten years later in 1950-54. Both CA and MA breakdowns were made in an attempt to make a study of comparable populations, but the numbers of cases in each CA or MA class were too small to make comparisons meaningful. The number of cases that could actually be used is further reduced by the small numbers at the higher MA categories.

samples of California school children. These groups (100 six-year-olds and 100 fifteen-year-olds) were stratified on the basis of the father's occupation and the child's grade placement.

The use of the new test samples enabled the authors to check for changes in item difficulty and possible differences in subject performance because of regional or socioeconomic differences.

CHANGES IN THE 1960 SCALE

Terman and Merrill (1960) reported two kinds of changes in their 1960 scale—changes in content and structure. As far as changes in content are concerned, the changes consisted of the elimination of the least useful items, relocation of some subtests, and rescoring when a change in scoring was deemed necessary.

The authors focused much of their attention toward correcting recognized "structural inadequacies" of the 1937 scale. One of the corrections that they made provided an adjustment of intelligence quotients for atypical variability. It had long been known that the standard deviations of measured IQs varied considerably at different age levels. By utilizing deviation IQs (which take into account variability at different age levels) in the new IQ tables, Terman and Merrill have provided comparable intelligence quotients at all levels. The deviation IQs are actually standard scores derived from an assumed mean of 100 and standard deviation of 16. The deviation IQ is computed by means of the formula

$$DIQ = (IQ_x - IQ_m) K + 100$$

where

DIQ = deviation IQ

IQ_x = ratio IQ $\left(\dfrac{MA}{CA} \times 100 \right)$

IQ_m = 1937 scale mean IQ for age being considered

$K = \dfrac{16}{\sigma}$ (assumed $\sigma \div \sigma$ of 1937 scale for age in question)

The ratio IQ $\left(\dfrac{MA}{CA} \times 100 \right)$ may not agree with the deviation IQ in the manual tables at a given age level. For example, a subject who is 10 years old and has a mental age of 13 will have a ratio IQ of 130. In the table of the Stanford-Binet manual, however, the deviation IQ is 126. The latter figure is the one that should be used, since it can be compared more accurately with other DIQs. That is, a DIQ of 130 at age 10 is considered comparable to a deviation IQ of 130 at other ages.

Another correction effected by Terman and Merrill was to extend the IQ tables to include ages 17 and 18 on the assumption that mental growth continues beyond age 16. Bayley (1955), Bradway, Thompson, and Cravens (1958) and other investigators have provided findings to the effect that mental growth continues beyond the chronological age of 16 years.

VALIDITY AND RELIABILITY

To a great extent the 1960 scale has inherited its validity from the two forms of the 1937 scale. Since the 1960 scale's items were taken from the other scales, and because they are regarded as valid instruments for mental testing, it follows that the 1960 scale can be assumed to have validity. Estes et al. (1961) reported a correlation of .82 between the 1960 scale and the 1937 scale, which indicates a high level of agreement between the two scales. Evidence of validity for Form L-M also comes from the fact that an increase in mental age at successive age levels accompanied an increase in percent passing the items from level to level in forms L and M (Terman and Merrill, 1960).

Biserial correlation coefficients were computed to determine which items would be selected for Form L-M. Those subtests which did not correlate well enough with the total score were not used in the 1960 scale. The mean biserial correlation for the 1960 scale is .66 as compared with a mean of .61 for all tests in both forms in the 1937 scale (Terman and Merrill, 1960, p. 33). This higher mean coefficient probably can be taken as evidence of higher validity for the 1960 revision.

It seems reasonable to expect the reliability of the 1960 scale to be at least as high as that of the 1937 forms, since only the best items were chosen from those forms for use in the 1960 Stanford-Binet. Brittain (1968) reported a reliability coefficient of .94 for the 1960 scale based on results of a study of eight-year-old children. Share et al. (1964) reported a coefficient of .88 for IQs obtained from a group of young retarded children.

ADMINISTRATION OF THE 1960 SCALE

Figure 5-4 shows the test materials that are found in the Form L-M test kit. The materials include several small objects (such as autos, doll, flag), blocks, beads, scissors, two booklets containing printed cards and materials, and a test manual. A record booklet for recording examinee responses also is used during the administration of the scale. Since certain materials found in the kit are appropriate only for certain age levels, the examiner ordinarily will not use all of the test materials during a particular administration of the scale. At the highest levels, where the scale is highly verbal, the performance materials (such as beads and blocks) are not used. Figure 5-5 shows a testing scene in which one of the subtests is being administered.

The 1960 scale has the subtests arranged according to chronological age levels from age 2 (II) to Superior Adult III. From age II to age V the items (or

Fig. 5-4. Materials used in testing intelligence with the Stanford-Binet (By permission of Houghton Mifflin Company.)

subtests) are grouped according to half-year levels, such as II, II–6, III, III–6, etc. Between age V and age XIV the levels proceed on a yearly basis (V, VI, VII, etc.). Then beyond XIV the levels are referred to as AA (Average Adult), SAI (Superior Adult I), SAII (Superior Adult II) and SAIII (Superior Adult III). Each age level has six subtests except AA, which has eight.

In addition to the regularly given items, at each age level there is an extra subtest designated as an alternate item. The alternate may be substituted for another item at that age level when conditions call for a substitution. An alternate may be used when the examiner spoils an item (through poor administration) or when it is known that a particular item in the series is not appropriate for the subject being tested. Generally speaking, alternates are seldom used.

When the examiner finds it necessary to conserve time he can administer the *short form* of the Stanford-Binet. The short form consists of only four items at each age level, rather than the usual six. These items are designated in the record booklet by means of an asterisk. While it is recommended that the full scale be used whenever possible, there is evidence that the short-form results correlate

Fig. 5-5. The administration of a Stanford-Binet subtest.

highly with the full scale (Himmelstein, 1966; Silverstein, 1966; Terman and Merrill, 1960). The short form, however, tends to yield slightly lower IQs than the regular scale.

The administration of the Stanford-Binet usually is started at an age level which is at or slightly below the examinee's estimated mental-age level. If the examiner begins the testing at too low a level, the subject may become bored or tired before the testing is terminated. If the examiner starts at too high a level, however, S may become frustrated or discouraged because of repeated failure or difficulty. In either instance, the overall performance of the examinee may be adversely affected, and the scale may underestimate the subject's ability. If S seems to be about average in mental ability, his CA level or the level immediately below might be a good place to start. Wells and Pedrini (1967) suggest that one way to determine where to start is to administer the Picture Vocabulary (PV) and/or Verbal Vocabulary (VV) subtest first, and then use the subtest score(s) to obtain an approximation of the subject's overall performance. Since the vocabulary subtests occur at several levels in the scale, and because they correlate very well with total-scale scores, they can be used effectively for the purpose of deciding where to commence testing.

If an examinee passed all of the items at the level where the testing was started, age 10 for example, this age would be regarded as his *basal age* and the testing would continue at the next higher level. The examiner would continue to test upward in the scale until a level was reached where all of the subtests were failed. This level of total failure would be designated as the *ceiling age*. At this point the testing would be terminated. However, if S failed a test at age 10, the examiner would have to test at a lower level to establish the basal age (where all six items are passed). The assumption is made that a subject can pass all of the subtests below his basal age, because those subtests are easier than the passed items.

SCORING

The Stanford-Binet is scored as the items are administered. Typically, the examinee is given a question, the examiner awaits the response, and then records it in the record booklet. Responses are scored as + for passed and – for failed (although an examiner may prefer to use other symbols). Some of the items appear a single time in the scale and others are used at more than one level. Where the same item appears at different levels, passing at the higher levels requires a better performance than at the lower levels.

An examinee's mental age is determined by adding to the basal age the months of credit earned above the basal age. From age II to age V each item that

Table 5-8. Calculated Mental Ages and Intelligence Quotients Based on the Stanford-Binet Intelligence Scale

Year	Number of Items Passed	Months of Credit for each Item Passed	Total Credit
III (basal age)	6		3 Yrs 0 Mos
III-6	4	1	4 Mos
IV	2	1	2 Mos
IV-6	1	1	1 Mo
V (ceiling age)	0	1	0 Mos
			3 Yrs 7 Mos

CA = 3 years and 5 months (3-5).   MA = 3 years and 7 months (3-7).   Ratio IQ = 105
Deviation IQ = 100

Year	Number of Items Passed	Months of Credit for each Item Passed	Total Credit
VIII (basal age)	6	2	8 Yrs 0 Mos
IX	5	2	10 Mos
X	2	2	4 Mos
XI (ceiling age)	0	2	0 Mos
			8 Yrs 14 Mos

CA = 10-3   MA = 9-2   Ratio IQ = 89   DIQ = 88

Year	Number of Items Passed	Months of Credit for each Item Passed	Total Credit
XIV (basal age)	6	2	14 Yrs 0 Mos
AA	8	2	16 Mos
SA I	5	4	20 Mos
SA II	4	5	20 Mos
SA III	2	6	12 Mos
			14 Yrs 68 Mos

CA = 14-7   MA = 19-8   Ratio IQ = 135   DIQ = 135

is passed provides one month of credit toward the mental age. Between ages VI and AA each test passed is worth two months of credit. Superior Adult I provides four months of credit for each item passed, while the tests at levels SAII and SAIII are worth five and six months of credit respectively. Examples of calculated mental ages for hypothetical cases are presented in Table 5-8.

The first example in Table 5-8 shows how a child of 3 years and 5 months (CA = 3-5) might earn a mental age of 3 years and 7 months (MA = 3-7). Notice that 7 months of mental-age credit were earned above the basal age of 3. The ratio IQ is found to be 105, which is well within the "normal" range (90-110). The deviation IQ, however, is 100 (from the 1960 manual, p. 261). For the reasons mentioned earlier, we would generally prefer to use the DIQ rather than the ratio IQ. In the second example, the case of the individual whose mental age fell below his chronological age, the ratio IQ of 89 and the DIQ of 88 are slightly below the "normal" range. In the third example (the individual whose CA is 14-7 and MA is 19-8), both the ratio IQ and the deviation IQ are 135. This figure is within the "superior" range.

CONTENT OF THE SCALE

As an illustration of the content of the 1960 scale, we shall provide a brief description of the subtests which appear at selected year levels.

Year II

1. *Three-Hole Form Board.* (Subject must place three forms into their respective recessed areas in a form board in order to receive credit.)
2. *Delayed Response.* (S is asked to locate a toy kitten after it has been hidden under a small box and the box has been screened from view for 10 seconds.)
3. *Identifying Parts of the Body.* (S is asked to point to such parts of a paper doll as the hair, mouth, feet, etc.)
4. *Block Building: Tower.* (S must be able to build a simple four-block tower.)
5. *Picture Vocabulary.* (S is shown several cards having pictures of common objects and is asked, "What's this? What do you call it?"
6. *Word Combinations.* (S must use a combination of at least two words during the testing period in order to pass this item.)
Alternate
A. *Identifying Objects by Name.* (S is asked to point out such objects as a toy dog, ball, engine, etc., when these are presented on a card.)

Year VI

1. *Vocabulary.* (S is asked to give the meanings or definitions of words which range from a low level of difficulty to a very high level.)

2. *Differences.* (S must be able to state a difference between certain animals and objects, such as a bird and a dog, slipper and a boot, etc.)
3. *Mutilated Pictures.* (S looks at a card on which there are objects with parts missing and is asked to tell what part is missing in each object.)
4. *Number Concepts.* (S is provided with 12 blocks and is asked to count out a specified number of them. This is repeated for different numbers of blocks.)
5. *Opposite Analogies.* (S must complete statements which express analogies.)
6. *Maze Tracing.* (S is shown a diagram of a schoolhouse and a little boy. He is then asked to draw the shortest path between the boy and the schoolhouse.)
Alternate
A. *Response to Pictures Level II.* (S is asked to look at pictures and tell about them.)

Year XI

1. *Memory for Designs.* (S is shown a card, which has two designs on it, for ten seconds. The card is then taken away and S is asked to draw from memory what he has seen.)
2. *Verbal Absurdities.* (S is asked to tell what is foolish about certain absurd statements.)
3. *Abstract Words II.* (S must define words such as connection and compare).
4. *Memory for Sentences II.* (S must be able to repeat without error a sentence which the examiner states aloud.)
5. *Problem Situation II.* (S must give an explanation of a problem situation.)
6. *Similarities.* (S must tell how three things, such as a snake, cow, and sparrow are alike.)
Alternate
A. Finding Reasons II. (S must provide acceptable reasons for two statements read to him.)

Year SA II

1. *Vocabulary.* (Same as for Year VI).
2. *Finding Reasons.* (S must give three reasons for each of two statements read to him.)
3. *Proverbs II.* (S must be able to state the meaning of a proverb stated by the examiner.)
4. *Ingenuity.* (S must be able to devise a method of measuring out a specific quantity of water by using only two cans of specified capacities.)
5. *Essential Differences.* (S must be able to state the principal differences between such concepts as work and play.)

6. *Repeating Thought of Passage I*: Value of Life. (S is read a short passage and is asked to repeat as much of it as he can.)
Alternate
A. Codes (S must be able to write a word in code correctly after having been presented with an example.)

ABILITIES AND FUNCTIONS SAMPLED BY THE STANFORD-BINET SCALE

Terman and Merrill state that their 1960 scale undertakes to measure intelligence regarded as general mental adaptability (Terman and Merrill, 1960, p. 39). Even a cursory inspection of the scale will reveal that the authors used a variety of subtests measuring a considerable range of abilities in order to measure what is often referred to as general mental ability.

Factor analysis was employed by McNemar (1942) in a study of the mental functions which the subtests and scale measure. McNemar concluded that a common factor *g* was operative at all levels of the scale. His findings also seemed to suggest the possibility that group factors might be present at ages 2, 2½, 6, 7, 11, and 18.

Jones (1949, 1954) conducted factor analyses of the scale's subtests at four different levels 7, 9, 11, and 13 years. Jones found evidence of a number of group factors, such as reasoning, memory, and spatial, perceptual, and verbal factors.

Hofstaetter's study (1954) seems to indicate that after age 4, the items measure a general factor, "Manipulation of Symbols." He suggests that three factors can account for a child's performance on the Stanford-Binet. According to Hofstaetter, "Sensorimotor Alertness" is responsible for mental performance from birth to two years. Then, during the period from 2 years to 4 years, "Persistence" is important. Finally, after four years, "Manipulation of Symbols" can account for the variance in mental ability.

Psychologists and statisticians are much more likely to agree that the Stanford-Binet measures a general factor than they are to agree that it measures group or specific factors. That there is considerable agreement concerning the scale's measurement of a *g* factor is understandable, since items which showed high loadings (correlations) with the general factor were selected for the scale over the tests which showed low loadings (whenever possible). The items which were found to have relatively high or low loadings are presented below (McNemar, 1942).

Age Levels II to IV-6

High Loadings	Low Loadings
Picture vocabulary	Block building: tower
Identifying objects by name	Block building: bridge
Comparison of sticks	Three-hole form board—rotated
Comprehension	Copying a circle
Opposite analogies	Three commissions
Pictorial identification	Stringing beads

Age Levels V to XI

High Loadings	*Low Loadings*
Pictorial similarities and differences	Paper folding: triangle
Similarities: two things	Patience: rectangles
Vocabulary	Picture absurdities
Verbal absurdities	Word naming
Similarities and differences	Block counting
Naming the days of the week	Paper cutting
Dissected sentences	Memory for stories
Abstract words	

Age Level XII to SAIII

High Loadings	*Low Loadings*
Vocabulary	Problem of fact
Verbal absurdities	Copying a bead chain from memory
Abstract words	Enclosed box problem
Essential differences	Plan of search
Arithmetical reasoning	Repeating digits (Forward and backward)
Proverbs	
Sentence building	

Performance on the various subtests of the Stanford-Binet necessarily involves several different mental functions. Freeman, (1962, pp. 227–228) identifies these functions as follows:

Test Items	*Functions Involved*

Years 2–5

Form perception and manipulation (blocks, form boards, stringing wooden beads) Perception of differences in size and form	Visual perception and analysis
Visual-motor operations	Visual analysis plus motor development
Perception of relationships (in pictures)	Visual perception plus beginnings of concept formation
Rote memory (using digits and sentences)	Immediate recall
Use of words in combination Identifying objects by name or use Following directions	Language development and comprehension
Verbal comprehension and word knowledge Understanding of "opposites"	Reasoning with abstractions and concept formation

Years 6–12

Form perception	Visual analysis
Visual-motor operation	Visual analysis plus motor development
Rote memory (using digits and sentences)	Immediate recall
Word knowledge (concrete and abstract)	Language development and concept formation

Test Items	*Functions Involved*
Verbal comprehension	Reasoning with abstractions and concept formation
Number concepts Arithmetical reasoning	Number concept formation and reasoning with abstractions

Years 13–Superior Adult III

Visual analysis and imagery Perception of visual relationships Visual-motor operations	Visual perception and analysis plus reasoning with nonverbal materials
Rote memory (using digits, words, and sentences)	Immediate recall
Word knowledge	Language development and concept formation
Synthesis of verbal materials Problem solving, using verbal materials	Reasoning with abstractions
Verbal analysis Arithmetical problems Analysis and comprehension of symbols	Concept formation plus reasoning with abstractions

If one considers the loadings and the functions believed to be involved in performance on the tests, an interesting finding is apparent. With the exception of word naming and problems of fact, the subtests which have low loadings seem to involve only visualization, visual imagery, and rote memory. The high-loading items, on the other hand, involve such processes as use of vocabulary, verbal analysis, concept formation, analysis and synthesis of materials, and organization of materials.

There seems to be a strong indication that the items which have high loadings are measuring more complex abilities than the low-loading tests, and that the high-loading items require much greater use of symbols. "The mental activities required by these items have very much in common with Spearman's view that intelligence is essentially the ability to educe relations and correlates." (Freeman, 1962, p. 226)

Sattler (1965) has analyzed the functions of the 1960 scale according to a "classification schema" based somewhat arbitrarily on item-content groupings. The schema includes seven major categories and five subcategories, with the subcategories delineating the more specific functions. The descriptions of the major categories follow:

> *Language*. This category includes items which deal with maturity of vocabulary in regard to the prekindergarten level, extent of vocabulary referring to the number of words the S can define, quality of vocabulary measured by such tests as abstract words, rhymes, word naming, and definitions, and comprehension of verbal relations.
> *Memory*. This category is subclassified into meaningful, nonmeaningful, and visual memory. Other designations for this category include rote auditory memory, ideational memory, and attention span.
> *Conceptual Thinking*. This category while closely associated with

language ability is primarily concerned with abstract thinking. Such functions as generalization, assuming an "as if" attitude, conceptual thinking, and utilizing a categorical attitude are subsumed.

Reasoning. This category is subclassified into verbal and nonverbal reasoning. The verbal absurdity items are the prototype for the category. The pictorial and orientation problems represent a model for the nonverbal reasoning items. Reasoning includes the perception of logical relations, discrimination ability, and analysis and synthesis. A spatial reasoning factor is also included in the orientation items.

Numerical Reasoning. This category includes items specifically geared to numerical or arithmetical problems. The content is closely related to school learning. Numerical reasoning includes such factors as concentration and the ability to generalize from numerical data.

Visual-Motor. This category contains items concerned with manual dexterity, eye-hand coordination, and perception of spatial relations. Constructive visual imagery may be involved in such items as paper folding. Nonverbal reasoning ability is closely allied to this area.

Social Intelligence. This category strongly overlaps with the reasoning category so that consideration should be given to the test items classified in the latter as also reflecting social comprehension. The area of social intelligence includes aspects of social maturity and social judgment. The comprehension and finding reason items reflect social judgment, whereas the items concerning obeying simple commands, response to pictures, and comparison reflect social maturity.

Sattler's chart of the analysis of functions, which follows, has the Stanford-Binet items arranged according to the major and minor categories in which they fall. This information can be of value in making a qualitative analysis of test results. More will be said on this topic in Chapter 10.

Analysis of Functions Tested in the 1960 Stanford–Binet
Intelligence Scale, Form L–M*

Language (L)		
(1) II, 3:	Identifying parts of the body; (5) II-6, 2	
(2) II, 5:	Picture vocabulary; (7) II-6, 4; (8) III, 2; (9) IV, 1	
(3) II, 6:	Word combinations	
II, A:	Identifying objects by name	
(4) II-6, 1:	Identifying objects by use	
(6) II-6, 3:	Naming objects	
(10) IV, 4:	Pictorial identification; IV-6, A	
(11) V, 3:	Definitions	
(12) VI, 1:	Vocabulary; (13) VIII, 1; (15) X, 1; (19) XII, 1; (24) XIV, 1; (25) AA, 1; (28) SAI, 1; (31) SAII, 1; (32) SAIII, 1	
(14) IX, 4:	Rhymes: New form	
IX, A:	Rhymes: Old form	

(16) X, 3:	Abstract words I; (20) XII, 5	
(17) X, 5:	Word naming	
(18) XI, 3:	Abstract words II; (22) XIII, 2	
(21) XII, 6:	Minkus completion I	
(23) XIII, 5:	Dissected sentences	
(26) AA, 3:	Differences between abstract words	
(27) AA, 8:	Abstract words III	
(29) SAI, 3:	Minkus completion II	
(30) SAI, 5:	Sentence building	

Memory (M)

Meaningful Memory (mM)

(3) IV, 2:	Naming objects from memory	
IV, A:	Memory for sentences I	
(4) IV-6, 5:	Three commissions	

*From Sattler, 1965, pp. 174–175, by permission.

(6) VIII, 2:   Memory for stories:
              The Wet Fall
(11) XI, 4:   Memory for sentences II
(13) XIII, 3:   Memory for sentences III
(16) SAII, 6:   Repeating thought of passage
              I: Value of Life
(17) SAIII, 6:   Repeating thought of passage
              II: Tests

Nonmeaningful Memory (nmM)

(1) II-6, 5:   Repeating 2 digits
    III, A: Repeating 3 digits
(5) VII, 6:   Repeating 5 digits
    VII, A: Repeating 3 digits reversed
(8) IX, 6:   Repeating 4 digits reversed
(9) X, 6:   Repeating 6 digits
(12) XII, 4:   Repeating 5 digits reversed
(15) SAI, 4:   Repeating 6 digits reversed

Visual Memory (vM)

(2) III, 4:   Picture memories
(7) IX, 3:   Memory for designs I:
              (10) XI, 1
    XII, A: Memory for designs II
(14) XIII, 6:   Copying a bead chain from
              memory

Visual-Motor (VM)

(1) II, 1:   Three-hole form board
(2) II, 4:   Block building: Tower
    II-6, A: Three-hole form board:
              Rotated
(3) III, 1:   Stringing beads
(4) III, 3:   Block building: Bridge
(5) III, 5:   Copying a circle
(6) III, 6:   Drawing a vertical line
(7) V, 1:   Picture completion: Man
(8) V, 2:   Paper folding: Triangle
(9) V, 4:   Copying a square
    V, A: Knot
(10) VI, 6:   Maze tracing
(11) VII, 3:   Copying a diamond
(12) IX, 1:   Paper cutting; XIII, A
    AA, A: Binet paper cutting

Conceptual Thinking (CT)

(1) IV, 3:   Opposite analogies I;
              (2) IV-6, 2
(3) VI, 2:   Differences
(4) VI, 5:   Opposite analogies II
(5) VII, 2:   Similarities: Two things
(6) VII, 5:   Opposite analogies III
(7) VIII, 4:   Similarities and differences
(8) XI, 6:   Similarities: Three things
(9) XIV, 6:   Reconciliation of opposites;
              SAI, A

(10) AA, 5:   Proverbs I
(11) AA, 7:   Essential differences;
              (14) SAII, 5
(12) SAI, 6:   Essential similarities
(13) SAII, 3:   Proverbs II
(15) SAIII, 2:   Proverbs III
(16) SAIII, 3:   Opposite analogies IV
    SAIII, A: Opposite analogies V

Reasoning (R)

Nonverbal Reasoning (nvR)

(1) II, 2:   Delayed response
(2) III-6, 1:   Comparison of balls
(3) III-6, 2:   Patience: Pictures
(4) III-6, 3:   Discrimination of animal
              pictures
(5) III-6, 5:   Sorting buttons
    III-6, A: Comparison of sticks
(6) IV, 5:   Discrimination of forms
(7) IV-6, 3:   Pictorial similarities and
              differences I
(8) V, 5:   Pictorial similarities and
              differences II
(9) V, 6:   Patience: Rectangles
(10) VI, 3:   Mutilated pictures
(15) XIII, 1:   Plan of search
(18) XIV, 5:   Orientation: Direction I
(19) AA, 6:   Orientation: Direction II
(21) SAIII, 4:   Orientation: Direction III

Verbal Reasoning (vR)

(11) VIII, 3:   Verbal absurdities I
(12) IX, 2:   Verbal absurdities II;
              (14) XII, 2
    X, A: Verbal absurdities III
(13) XI, 2:   Verbal absurdities IV
(16) XIII, 4:   Problems of fact
(17) XIV, 3:   Reasoning I
(20) SAII, 2:   Finding reasons III
    SAII, A: Codes
(22) SAIII, 5:   Reasoning II

Numerical Reasoning (NR)

(1) VI, 4:   Number concepts
(2) IX, 5:   Making change
(3) X, 2:   Block counting
(4) XIV, 2:   Induction
(5) XIV, 4:   Ingenuity I; (6) AA, 2;
              (9) SAII, 4
    XIV, A: Ingenuity II
(7) AA, 4:   Arithmetical reasoning
(8) SAI, 2:   Enclosed box problem

Social Intelligence (SI)

(1) II-6, 6:   Obeying simple commands
(2) III-6, 4:   Response to pictures; VI, A

(3) III-6, 6:　Comprehension I
(4) IV, 6:　Comprehension II
(5) IV-6, 1:　Aesthetic comparison
(6) IV-6, 4:　Materials
(7) IV-6, 6:　Comprehension III
(8) VII, 1:　Picture absurdities I
(9) VII, 4:　Comprehension IV;
　　　　　　(10) VIII, 5

(11) VIII, 6:　Naming the days of the week
　　VIII, A:　Problem situations I
(12) X, 4:　Finding reasons I
(13) XI, 5:　Problem situation II
　　XI, A:　Finding reasons II
(14) XII, 3:　Picture absurdities II:
　　　　　　The Shadow

AN EVALUATION OF THE STANFORD-BINET SCALE

The Stanford-Binet scale has had widespread use in the United States and other countries for a number of years. Just how useful is this instrument? Is it as valuable as its extensive use in psychological testing would seem to indicate? In attempting to answer these questions we shall examine the scale's apparent strengths and limitations.

The Stanford-Binet, certainly, is a well-constructed scale. Years of thorough professional work involving the study of individual items, the analysis of test data, and the standardization of the scale, have been spent in the effort to develop a valid and reliable instrument. The scale's authors believe that they have a scale that measures general mental ability, and there is evidence to support their claim. The scale provides a valid measure of general mental ability for children and youths as well as a measure of academic aptitude past age 6 or so. The Stanford-Binet has been used successfully for such purposes as preadoption testing, school placement, psychological diagnosis, and counseling, so that its usefulness is quite evident. There are, however, certain major limitations associated with the scale which should be discussed briefly. The purpose of discussing these limitations is to emphasize the need for caution when interpreting the results provided by the instrument.

Those who use the results of the Stanford-Binet should realize that the scale does not completely sample an individual's intelligence, but only certain important aspects of it. Furthermore, it does not measure one's innate mental ability. What the scale really samples is present mental performance, which is influenced by inherited characteristics, experience, attitudes, and various psychological traits.

Another important limitation of the Stanford-Binet is that it does not provide measures of differential aptitude, but only a mental age and a single intelligence quotient. Since the items which measure in some degree various special aptitudes, skills, or abilities are not evenly distributed throughout the scale, and because the number of these items is relatively small, it is not possible to obtain a profile of aptitudes or abilities by using the scale. For the purpose of getting a profile of aptitudes one would have to turn to another instrument.

The Stanford-Binet is heavily weighted with verbal items, especially at the upper levels, and this may be considered to be a limitation. The individual who has high verbal ability is likely to do well on this scale and to perform well in school situations, so the instrument can be used to provide an estimate of scholastic aptitude. The person who has a language handicap, however, may have his general mental ability underestimated by the scale. Bilingual children, children who are hard of hearing, and poor readers may be at a disadvantage when they are tested with the Stanford-Binet.

It is essential that the person who utilizes Stanford-Binet results realize that certain personality variables of the subject being tested may have considerable influence on test performance. A child who is shy, reluctant to speak, overly anxious, or who has a poor self-concept may fail to respond to questions he can answer, and thus score too low. An individual who is indifferent about the scale's activities, or is uncooperative, likewise may not receive a valid score. Numerous other examples might be given in support of the contention that attitudinal and emotional aspects of the subject's personality may affect test results.

It is probable, too, that the Stanford-Binet may not be valid for certain purposes when used with children who have cultures quite different from the American white culture. In some cultures the previous experiences of the subjects and the subjects' attitudes toward tests may be so different from those of the standardization group that comparisons may be extremely difficult or impossible. This limitation is clearly perceived by Phillips and Bannon (1968), who emphasize the need for reliable English norms for "clinical decisions, epidemiological studies, and other research."

REFERENCES

Bayley, Nancy, "On the Growth of Intelligence." *American Psychologist* 10 (1955), 805-818.

Bradway, K. P., C. W. Thompson, and R. B. Cravens, "Preschool IQs After 25 Years," *Journal of Educational Psychology* 49 (1958), 278-281.

Brittain, Michael, "A Comparative Study of the Use of the Wechsler Scale for Children and the Stanford-Binet Intelligence Scale (Form L-M) With Eight-Year-Old Children," *British Journal of Educational Psychology* 38 (1968), 103-104.

Darcy, Natalie T., "The Effect of Bilingualism upon the Measurement of the Intelligence of Children of Preschool Age," *Journal of Educational Psychology* 37 (1946), 21-44.

Estes, Betty, et al., "Relationships Between the 1960 S-B, 1937 S-B, WISC, Raven, and Draw-a-Man," *Journal of Consulting Psychology* 25 (1961), 388-391.

Freeman, Frank S., *Theory and Practice of Psychological Testing* 3rd. ed. New York: Holt, 1962.

Himmelstein, Philip, "Research with the Stanford-Binet Form L-M: The First Five Years," *Psychological Bulletin* 65 (1966), 156-164.

Hofstaetter, P. R., "The Changing Composition of Intelligence: A Study of the *t*-Technique," *Journal of Genetic Psychology* 85 (1954), 159‑164.

Jones, L. V., "A Factor Analysis of the Stanford-Binet at Four Age Levels," *Psychometrika* 14 (1949), 299‑331.

———, "Primary Abilities in the Stanford-Binet, Age 13," *Journal of Genetic Psychology* 84 (1954), 125‑147.

McNemar, Quinn, *The Revision of the Stanford-Binet Scale*. Boston: Houghton Mifflin, 1942.

Phillips, C. J., and W. J. Bannon, "Stanford-Binet Form L-M Third Revision. A Local English Study of Norms, Concurrent Validity and Social Differences," *British Journal of Educational Psychology* 38 (1968), 148‑161.

Pinneau, Samuel, *Changes in Intelligence Quotient From Infancy to Maturity*. Boston: Houghton Mifflin, 1961.

Sattler, Jerome E., "Analysis of Functions of the 1960 Stanford-Binet Intelligence Scale, Form L-M," *Journal of Clinical Psychology* 21 (1965), 173‑179.

Share, J. B., et al., "The Longitudinal Development of Infants and Young Children with Down's Syndrome (Mongolism)," *American Journal of Mental Deficiency* 68 (1964), 685‑692.

Silverstein, A. B., "A Further Evaluation of the Stanford-Binet," *American Journal of Mental Deficiency* 70 (1966), 928‑929.

Terman, L. M., *The Measurement of Intelligence*. Boston: Houghton Mifflin, 1916.

———, and Maud Merrill, *Measuring Intelligence*. Boston: Houghton Mifflin, 1937.

———, *Stanford-Binet Intelligence Scale: Manual for the Third Revision: Form L-M*. Boston: Houghton Mifflin, 1960.

Wells, Donald, and Duilio Pedrini, "Where to Begin Testing in the Stanford-Binet L-M," *Journal of Clinical Psychology* 23 (1967), 182‑183.

The Wechsler Scales

The Wechsler Bellevue scale (1939), though a useful and popular instrument, has been supplanted by the *Wechsler Adult Intelligence Scale* (WAIS) published in 1955. The WAIS, while similar to the W-B, is superior to the older scale in terms of content, directions for administering and scoring, reliability of the subtests, and standardization. In revising the W-B to develop the WAIS, Wechsler (1955, p. 1) acknowledged some inadequacies in the older scale: "Restriction of range of item difficulty was the principal inadequacy. This restriction was largely responsible for less than the desired reliability for some of the single tests, though the reliability of the Scales (Verbal, Performance, and Full) has always been excellent. A few items in the tests were ambiguous; these required replacement."

THE WECHSLER ADULT INTELLIGENCE SCALE

The WAIS norms are based upon groups considered to be representative of American adults (Wechsler, 1955). The total standardization sample consisted of 850 males and 850 females who ranged in age from 16 to 64 years. A special standardization sample of 475 subjects was utilized in order to develop norms for persons who are beyond 64 years of age. Information concerning this sample can be found in the WAIS Manual.

In selecting subjects for the standardization sample, Wechsler proportioned them according to the 1950 United States census with regard to race (white vs. nonwhite), occupation, urban versus rural residence, geographic area, and education.

THE WAIS SUBTESTS

The WAIS has eleven subjects, six comprising the verbal scale and five the performance scale. A brief discussion of each of the subtests follows.

The Verbal Scale

1. *Information.* This consists of 29 questions which cover a broad area of information. Questions such as "What is the shape of a ball?" are asked in order to sample the subject's range of information. Certain assumptions are made in connection with the use of this kind of test. First, it must be assumed that the more intelligent person has more general information than the less intelligent individual. Second, the assumption is made that the questions used in the test cover a sufficiently wide range of information to provide adequate sampling of this variable. A third important assumption is that the adults who are being tested have had sufficient opportunity to acquire a broad range of information.

2. *Comprehension.* In this subtest there are 14 items in question form. Each item presents a problem situation to the examinee. For example, "Why should people pay taxes?" Passing these items, which measure the ability to understand a given situation, problem or saying, probably depends upon the subject's information, past experiences, and the ability to make use of these factors.

3. *Arithmetic.* There are 14 problems involving arithmetical reasoning in this test. The problems, which presumably do not require computational skills beyond the seventh grade, are presented orally to the subject who must provide the answer without the use of paper and pencil.

4. *Similarities.* This verbal subtest contains 13 pairs of words. For each pair the examinee is required to state how the two things are alike. Example: Orange . . . Banana.

5. *Digit Span.* Seven sets of digits are found in this test. The subject is required to listen to a series of digits given orally by the examiner and then repeat the digits without error. The easiest item has three digits and the most difficult has nine. After the subject has been given digits forward he is given other series of digits backward. The digits-backward sets range from only two digits to as high as eight. While this memory test does not contribute as much to the total score on the verbal scale as do some of the other tests, its inclusion in the WAIS can be justified on the basis of its diagnostic and clinical value. For instance, it is of value in identifying the mentally retarded, who are likely to have relatively short memory spans.

6. *Vocabulary.* A list of 40 words arranged in order of increasing difficulty is used in this test. The examiner asks for the meaning of each word as the subject views it on the word list. Vocabulary tests like this one are commonly found in instruments designed to measure general mental ability because they tend to correlate well with total scores.

The Performance Scale

1. *Digit Symbol.* In the administration of this subtest the examinee is required to substitute symbols for digits. After an explanation of the key which is used in the test performance, the subject is told to fill in correctly as many symbols as he can. The test has a time limit of 90 seconds. This is a variation of the code-substitution test found in many other performance scales.

2. *Picture Completion.* Twenty-one cards, each having a drawing on it which has an important part missing, are used in this test. The subject is shown the cards, one at a time, and is asked to indicate the missing part. The test has been found to discriminate better at the lower levels of mental ability than at the upper levels (where it is not sufficiently difficult).

3. *Block Design.* Nine blocks are used in this test which requires that the subject be able to reproduce designs of increasing difficulty. The cubes have red, white, and red-white sides. Four of the blocks are used to make the easier designs and all nine are needed for the more difficult ones. There is a time limit for the completion of each design. Fig. 6-1 shows the administration of the test.

4. *Picture Arrangement.* Eight sets of cards are used to form the items for this part of the performance scale. Each card in a set has a picture on it, and when the cards of a set are placed in proper order they tell a story. The subject is given one set of disarranged cards at a time and instructed to arrange the cards so that they tell the story. Each item is timed.

Fig. 6-1. The administration of the block-design test.

5. *Object Assembly.* Four cut-up objects which resemble a manikin, profile, hand, and an elephant are presented to the subject, one at a time, but in a disarranged pattern. The pieces must be arranged to form the whole object. Each item is timed.

FUNCTIONS OF THE SUBTESTS

To some extent the subtests are independent with respect to the functions they involve and the factor or factors which exert an effect upon the functions. A brief listing of the functions and their influencing factors follows.*

Subtest	Functions	Influencing Factors
Information	Range of information Old learning and memory Association and organization of experience	Interests Education Cultural background

Comprehension	Concept formation
	Organization and application of knowledge
	Reasoning with
	  abstractions
	Social judgment
		Social and cultural
		  background
		Moral code
		Emotional status

Arithmetic	Retention of arithmetical
	  processes
	Logical reasoning and
	  abstraction
	Alertness and concentration
		Education
		Occupational
		  pursuits

Similarities	Analysis of relationships Verbal concept formation Logical abstract thinking	Cultural opportunities
Vocabulary	Concept formation Language development Range of ideas, experiences or interests	Education Cultural opportunities
Digit Span	Retentiveness Auditory imagery Attention and concentration	Attention span Level of anxiety

Picture Completion	Visual imagery
	Visual perception
	Visual alertness and
	  memory
	Concentration and
	  appraisal of relationships
		Cultural experiences
		Visual acuity

*For reference, see Freeman, 1962; Wechsler, 1955; Kitzinger and Blumberg, 1951; Rapaport, et al., 1945.

Subtest	Functions	Influencing Factors
Picture Arrangement	Ability to comprehend a whole situation Anticipation and planning Ability to pick out essential cues	Visual acuity Cultural background
Block Design	Ability to perceive form Analysis and synthesis Visual-motor integration	Color vision Psychomotor speed
Object Assembly	Visual perception and synthesis Recognition of patterns Visual-motor integration	Psychomotor speed and precision
Digit Symbol	Rote recall Speed and accuracy in learning and writing symbols Visual imagery	Psychomotor speed

WAIS SCORES

The WAIS yields a raw score for each subtest administered to a subject. Each raw score must be converted to a scaled score by means of a table. The scaled scores for the Verbal Scale are added and the total score is used to find the Verbal IQ in an appropriate table in the WAIS manual. The same procedure is used with the scaled scores from the Performance Scale to determine the Performance IQ. A Full Scale IQ is obtained by adding the total of the scaled scores for the Verbal Scale to the total of the scaled scores of the Performance Scale and using the appropriate table. Thus, the WAIS provides scaled scores for the subtests plus the three IQs: Verbal, Performance, and Full Scale.

The mean of the scaled scores for each of the subtests is 10 and the standard deviation is 3 for all subject ages. Therefore, if a subject had a scaled score of 13 on Information, his performance *on this test* would be one standard deviation above the mean—definitely above average. If he had a scaled score of 4 on Arithmetic, his ability level for this test would be two standard deviations below the mean—quite low.

The mean IQ for the three scales (Verbal, Performance, and Full Scale) is considered to be 100 IQ points and the standard deviation 15. Thus a Verbal IQ of 130 would be two standard deviations above the mean, while a Verbal IQ of 85 would be one standard deviation below.

RELIABILITY

In Table 6-1 reliability coefficients and standard errors of measurement for the WAIS subtests and scales are presented. The age groups included in the table were selected as being representative of the age range included in the standardization sample (Wechsler, 1955, p. 12).

Odd and even items were correlated to determine the reliability coefficients

Table 6-1. Reliability Coefficients and Standard Errors of Measurement* of the WAIS Subtests (From Wechsler, 1955, p. 13, by permission of The Psychological Corporation).

Test	Age 18-19 $N = 200$		Age 25-34 $N = 300$		Age 45-54 $N = 300$	
	r_{11}	SE_m	r_{11}	SE_m	r_{11}	SE_m
Information	.91	.88	.91	.86	.92	.87
Comprehension	.79	1.36	.77	1.45	.79	1.47
Arithmetic	.79	1.38	.81	1.35	.86	1.23
Similarities	.87	1.11	.85	1.15	.85	1.32
Digit Span	.71	1.63	.66	1.75	.66	1.74
Vocabulary	.94	.69	.95	.67	.96	.67
Verbal IQ	.96	3.00	.96	3.00	.96	3.00
Digit Symbol	.92	.85	–	–	–	–
Picture Completion	.82	1.18	.85	1.14	.83	1.15
Block Design	.86	1.16	.83	1.29	.82	1.15
Picture Arrangement	.66	1.71	.60	1.73	.74	1.39
Object Assembly	.65	1.65	.68	1.66	.71	1.59
Performance IQ	.93	3.97	.93	3.97	.94	3.67
Full Scale IQ	.97	2.60	.97	2.60	.97	2.60

*The SE_m is in Scaled Score units for the tests and in IQ units for the Verbal, Performance, and Full Scale IQs.

for each of the subtests and the Spearman-Brown formula was used to correct for full length of each subtest, except for Digit Span and Digit Symbol.

The reliability coefficients for Digit Span were based on the correlation between Digits Forward and Digits Backward, with a correction for full length. Since Digit Symbol is a highly speeded test, the split-half technique was not appropriate for estimating its reliability. For this test, the reliability coefficient (.92) was estimated from the correlation of results on the WAIS Digit Symbol Test and Wechsler-Bellevue Digit Symbol Test for a group of nursery-school applicants (Wechsler, 1955).

The Verbal, Performance and Full-Scale coefficients were estimated from a formula for the correction between two sums of equally-weighted scores (Wechsler, 1955). As can be seen in Table 6-1, these coefficients tend to run higher than the subtest coefficients. For all three age groups the correlation coefficient for the full scale is .97, which indicates a very high level of internal consistency. The same can be said for the Verbal and Performance scales—they tend to be quite reliable. When using the subtest scores, however, one should be aware of the relatively low coefficients reported for some of the tests. Digit Span, Picture Arrangement, and Object Assembly, with coefficients ranging from .60 to .74, certainly are much less reliable than are such tests as Vocabulary and Information.

Table 6-1 also shows standard errors of measurement (SE_m) for each subtest (except Digit Symbol) and the three scales. These measures, which are based upon a test's standard deviation and reliability coefficient, provide estimate of each test's consistency or reliability. The smaller the SE_m is, the greater the probability that an obtained score is close to an individual's "true" score. Looking at the SE_m of .67 for the Vocabulary test for the age group 45-54 and the Digit Span SE_m of 1.74 for the same group, we can see that the former test has a much smaller standard error of measurement than the latter. For the Verbal Scale the reported SE_m is 3.00 for all age groups shown, while for the Performance Scale the SE_m's are 3.97, 3.97 and 3.67. The Full-Scale SE_m's are 2.60 for all three groups. The subtest SE_m's are for scaled scores, but the scale SE_m's (Verbal, Performance and Full Scale) are for IQ scores.

Perhaps it should be mentioned that the reliability coefficients reported in Table 6-1, while of great value, are from a single study. Another well-conducted study probably would yield somewhat different reliability data. Furthermore, the split-halves technique was used to get most of the reliability coefficients, providing estimates of *internal consistency*. It would be desirable to have extensive test-retest reliability data also.

VALIDITY

As is true of all other tests of mental ability, it is difficult to assess the validity of the WAIS. We shall, however, discuss a number of kinds of data which relate to the validity of the scale.

Content and Construct Validity. Evidence of content and construct validity for the WAIS can be found in an analysis of the relationships between the various subtests and the scales (Verbal, Performance, and Full Scale). As Wechsler says, "In selecting tests for a composite scale, common practice posits that the subtests should correlate highly with the total score (as criterion) and only modestly with each other. This is on the theory that a high correlation with total score indicates that the tests measure essentially the same thing while the lower intertest correlations imply that the tests measure different aspects of the criterion. The subtests of both the W-B and the WAIS are for the most part in accord with this expectation" (Wechsler, 1958, p. 98). Table 6-2 shows correlations between scores on the individual subtests of the WAIS and the Full Scale IQ at seven different age levels.

An examination of the coefficients in Table 6-2 will reveal that the highest correlations between the subtests and the Full Scale tend to be found for Information, Arithmetic, Similarities, and Vocabulary—all verbal subtests. It is also interesting to note that the verbal-test correlations tend to hold up better with age than do the performance-test correlations.

Judging from the magnitude of the correlations between the WAIS subtest scores and the Full Scale scores, there appears to be evidence in support of the assumption that the WAIS is measuring a general mental factor, *g*. Additional evidence along this line comes from research on the factorial composition of the WAIS. In a factorial study of the WAIS, Jacob Cohen (1957) identified four

Table 6-2. Correlations of the Individual Subtests of the WAIS with Full Scale Score at Different Age Levels (From Wechsler, 1958, p. 99 by permission of The Williams and Wilkins Company).

	Age Levels						
	18–19	25–34	45–54	60–64	65–69	70–74	75 +
Information	0.84	0.84	0.84	0.81	0.83	0.76	0.78
Comprehension	0.72	0.71	0.77	0.70	0.66	0.66	0.70
Arithmetic	0.70	0.66	0.75	0.75	0.77	0.73	0.73
Similarities	0.80	0.74	0.75	0.70	0.68	0.71	0.66
Digit Span	0.61	0.56	0.62	0.55	0.53	0.63	0.57
Vocabulary	0.83	0.82	0.83	0.79	0.83	0.82	0.73
Digit Symbol	0.68	0.63	0.69	0.74	0.73	0.72	0.70
Picture Completion	0.74	0.72	0.76	0.70	0.66	0.73	0.59
Block Design	0.72	0.69	0.67	0.77	0.68	0.56	0.65
Picture Arrangement	0.68	0.72	0.71	0.70	0.74	0.60	0.46
Object Assembly.	0.65	0.58	0.65	0.63	0.55	0.50	0.58

broad mental factors: a general factor, a verbal comprehension factor, a perceptual organization (nonverbal) factor, and a general or undifferentiated memory factor.

The general factor is considered to be the most important of the broad factors measured by the WAIS. This factor accounts for approximately 50 percent of the total variance contributed by all the tests and from 66 to 75 percent of the "communal" variance. That is, it accounts for about two-thirds to three-fourths of all the variance shared by two or more tests (Wechsler, 1958, pp. 120-121). The general factor appears to be similar to Spearman's *g*. It involves broad mental organization, it is independent of the modality or contextual structure from which it is elicited, and it cannot be exclusively identified with any single intellectual ability (Wechsler, 1958, p. 121). This factor is measured to some degree by all of the subtests of the WAIS.

The verbal factor, or verbal comprehension, appears to involve the ability to understand the meaning of individual words or combinations of words. It seems to be measured best by such tests as Vocabulary, Comprehension, Information, and Similarities.

The factor referred to as nonverbal organization seems to involve the capacity to organize discrete spatially perceived units into larger wholes or configurations (Wechsler, 1958, p. 125). This factor appears to be measured best by Object Assembly and Block Design. Picture Arrangement and Picture Completion contribute to the measurement of nonverbal organization, but to a lesser extent than the other two.

The general memory factor seems to be correlated best with Arithmetic and Digit Span. The undifferentiated-memory factor seems to be a kind of general retentiveness rather than any specific type of memory, such as rote, visual, auditory, recent, remote, etc. Perhaps it can be operationally identified as associative memory, where associative does not refer to a type, but an overall description (Wechsler, 1958, p. 125). If it is associative memory, this may account for the relatively high correlation with Arithmetic, which does not appear to be a memory test.

Shaw (1967), using test data from a sample of 100 college students, reported evidence of a factor similar to Cohen's verbal-comprehension factor and another similar to Cohen's nonverbal factor. As a result of his study, Shaw concluded that the collegiate population seems sufficiently different from the general adult population to "justify specific interpretive principles."

This brief discussion of the four broad mental factors which are sampled in the administration of the WAIS should not lead the reader to believe that the scale does not measure other important mental factors. On the contrary, other factors (both group and specific factors) probably are operant during a period of testing.

Concurrent Validity. Table 6-3 shows correlation coefficients found between WAIS scores and scores obtained from other scales in four different studies.

Table 6-3. Reported Correlations Between the WAIS and Other Mental Ability Tests

Researchers	Subjects	Tests or Scales	Correlation		
			V	P	FS
Wechsler (1958)	52 reformatory inmates, ages 16–26	Stanford-Binet (Form L)	.80	.69	.85
Brengelmann and Kenny (1961)	75 retardates	Leiter	.59	.75	
		Stanford-Binet	.79	.78	
Mc Leod and Rubin (1962)	55 males	Progressive	.78	.70	.72
	26 females	Matrices	.54	.44	.64
	Total (81)		.67	.58	.68
Giannell and Freeburne (1963)	109 College freshmen	Stanford-Binet			.897
		ACE			.882

In general, the correlation coefficients in Table 6-3 show a high degree of agreement between WAIS scores and scores for the other instruments.

Predictive Validity. Further evidence of the validity of the WAIS comes from its relationship with scholastic achievement. If the scale's results show a large enough correlation with grades or achievement-test scores, a claim can be made for predictive validity, for then it is possible to predict future achievement on the basis of WAIS scores with a fair amount of accuracy.

Giannell and Freeburne (1963) found a very high *r* of .841 between WAIS Full-Scale scores and grades for 109 college freshmen, but Olsen and Jordheim (1964) reported correlations of only .42 and .58 between WAIS Full Scale scores and grade-point averages for two groups of college freshmen (*N* = 109 and 120).

Conry and Plant (1965) reported predictor-criterion correlation coefficients for both high school and college samples. For the 335 college students they found correlations of .63, .44 and .62 for the Verbal, Performance, and Full Scale scores respectively. For the high school sample ($N = 98$), the corresponding correlations were .45, .23, and .43. The achievement criterion for the college group was grade-point average, but for the high-school students it was rank in the graduating class.

Knox, Grotelueschen and Sjogren (1968) reported a correlation of .78 between composite learning topic scores and WAIS Full Scale scores. They concluded that the WAIS is a very useful tool for research and evaluation related to adult learning.

Although the correlation coefficients vary considerably for the studies mentioned here, if one considers that grades often are not highly reliable and that motivation and other variables can have an appreciable effect upon scholastic achievement, then it would seem reasonable to accept these correlation coefficients as evidence of predictive validity for the WAIS. For the best results, however, those who are interested in the prediction of achievement should conduct their own prediction studies and use their own student samples rather than rely upon the data of other investigators.

DISTRIBUTION OF IQs

Two essential characteristics of mental ability tests and scales are (1) a relatively wide range of scores and (2) an approximation of a normal distribution of scores. These criteria appear to have been fairly well met, judging from the distribution of IQs shown in Fig. 6-2. Ideally, though, the distribution of scores

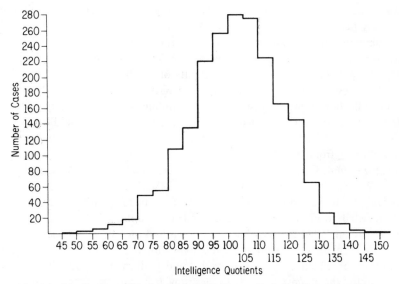

Fig. 6-2. Distribution of Wechsler Adult Intelligence Scale intelligence quotients. Ages 16–75 and over (2,052 cases). (From Wechsler, 1958, p. 107, by permission of The Williams & Wilkins Company.)

should show a few cases below IQ 45, a few cases above 155, and it should be smoother.

SHORT FORMS

Several studies related to the administration of short forms of the WAIS have been reported. A few have been chosen for discussion here to show the varied results for different abbreviated scales.

Using data from the national standardization sample, Doppelt (1956) selected the two best predictors of the Performance Scale score and the two best predictors of the Verbal Scale score of the WAIS to construct a short form of the complete scale. The short form thus included the Arithmetic and Vocabulary subtests from the Verbal Scale plus the Block Design and Picture Arrangement subtests from the Performance Scale. Doppelt reported correlation coefficients between the sum of the scaled scores on the four tests and the Full Scale score which varied between .95 and .96 for the seven age groups in the standardization sample. He concluded that the use of this abbreviated form permits an estimate of the Full Scale score after thirty to forty minutes of testing.

Monroe (1966) reported a correlation coefficient of .972 between results on the Doppelt short form and results on the WAIS in a study of 30 subjects at a state mental hospital.

Duke (1967) used two short forms of the WAIS and reported correlation coefficients above .90 between the short forms and the standard WAIS for all of the scales (V, P, and FS). The results were based upon a sample of 142 patients who had organic brain damage. Duke concluded that the short forms of the WAIS are valid for evaluating subjects with organic brain damage, when a time limit is necessary. One of Duke's short forms was comprised of Similarities, Vocabulary, Block Design, and Picture Arrangement. The other abbreviated form included the same subtests plus Information and Picture Completion.

Maxwell (1957) correlated the results of all the combinations of two or more subtests with results on the standard WAIS, using data from the national standardization group. The best duad was found to be Vocabulary and Block Design, $r = .924$. The best triad was Information, Vocabulary, and Block Design, $r = .952$. The tetrad which gave the highest correlation with the complete WAIS was formed from Information, Vocabulary, Block Design and Picture Arrangement, $r = .964$. Finally, two pentads gave the highest correlation with the standard WAIS, $r = .972$. The pentads were I, S, V, PA, OA; and I, S, V, BD, PA. Judging from the reported correlation coefficients, the predictive validity of the abbreviated forms increases as the number of subtests in the scale increases. Maxwell concluded that combinations comprised only of verbal tests or only of performance tests have lower correlations with the complete WAIS than the short forms which include both verbal and performance tests. She also concluded that the abbreviated verbal scales provide better estimates of full-scale results than the short performance scales.

Satz and Mogel (1962) devised an abbreviated form of the WAIS which included *selected items* from nine of the WAIS subtests and all of the items in Digit Span and Digit Symbol. This short form utilized 46 percent of the available WAIS items. The researchers reported that the calculated correlation coefficients between the original and abbreviated subtests and scales were consistently high. The advantage of this kind of short form over the Doppelt form is that the former represents the full variety of functions sampled by the WAIS while still providing a saving in time. Mogel and Satz (1963) used their short form of the WAIS with test data from the files of a large veteran's hospital and reported correlation coefficients between the short form and standard WAIS as follows: Verbal IQ, .99, Performance IQ, .97, and Full Scale IQ, .99.

Zytowski and Hudson (1965) used the Satz and Mogel short form with a sample of 100 students 16-19 years old. These researchers noted that in previous studies the reported correlation coefficients between part and whole WAIS scales are higher than the internal consistency coefficients which appear in the Wechsler manual. Zytowski and Hudson state that this effect is attributed to the contamination of the correlation by the presence of the abbreviated scale within the standard scale which is used as the criterion. They report that when the contamination of the short form is eliminated, the part-whole correlation coefficients are lower than the coefficients reported in other studies. The validity coefficients reported by Zytowski and Hudson for the short and long form, when corrected for contamination, range from .54 for Picture Arrangement to .95 for Vocabulary. For the scales, the reported coefficients are: Verbal IQ, .92, Performance IQ, .88, and Full Scale IQ, .88.

While the use of a short form offers the advantage of a saving in time, there are important reasons why this practice may be undesirable. One reason is that the reliability of the short form is less than that of the full scale, and any loss in reliability should be considered serious. Another important reason is that the short form provides less opportunity for observing the behavior of the examinee. A major advantage that an individual scale offers over a time-saving group test is the opportunity for observation, and this advantage is not so great with an abbreviated form.

WECHSLER INTELLIGENCE SCALE FOR CHILDREN

The *Wechsler Intelligence Scale for Children* (WISC), published in 1949, has been used extensively by psychologists in clinics, schools and various other institutions. It is designed for use with children whose chronological ages range from 5 through 15 years.

The WISC, like the WAIS, yields verbal, performance and full-scale scores, and the scoring procedure is very similar for the two scales. The mean scaled score for each subtest is 10 and the scaled-score standard deviation is 3. The IQ mean is 100 and the IQ standard deviation is 15.

Fig. 6-3. The Maze Test of the Wechsler Intelligence Scale for Children. (Courtesy of The Psychological Corporation.)

The subtests of the WISC are like those of the WAIS, with a few exceptions: a coding test is used instead of Digit Symbol; an optional maze test (Fig. 6-3) is included; and Digit Span is optional. In the usual administration of the WISC, five verbal and five performance tests are given, but some clinicians strongly recommend using all of the subtests. The verbal and performance subtests are listed below:

Verbal	Performance
1. General Information	1. Picture Completion
2. General Comprehension	2. Picture Arrangement
3. Arithmetic	3. Block Design
4. Similarities	4. Object Assembly
5. Vocabulary	5. Coding *or* Mazes
6. Digit Span	

Should an examiner wish to administer fewer or more than the ten subtests he would have to prorate the results because the figures in the IQ tables are based on the administration of ten tests. The two tests which were omitted in the construction of the IQ tables are Digit Span in the Verbal Scale and Mazes in the Performance Scale. These particular tests were omitted from the tables because of relatively low correlations with other tests in the WISC and, in the case of Mazes, the time required for administration (Wechsler, 1949, p. 6).

A test might be omitted during an administration of the WISC if, for some reason, the examiner considered the omission necessary. The reason might be lack of time, or some condition, such as a physical handicap, which would make a test unsuitable for a given subject. An additional test (more than the usual ten) might be given if the examiner wished to gather additional diagnostic or clinical information.

FUNCTIONS OF THE WISC SUBTESTS

Glasser and Zimmerman (1967, pp. 39–102) describe the functions of the WISC subtests as follows:

Information. This subtest is basically oriented to determine how much general information the subject has abstracted from his surrounding environment. The child is not asked to find relationships between facts but simply if he has obtained and stored them as general knowledge. This subtest calls into operation remote memory, ability to comprehend, capacity for associative thinking as well as the interests and reading background of the subject. Intellectual ambition as influenced by cultural background also is revealed by performance on these items.

Comprehension. This part of the WISC scale consists of an attempt to determine the level of a child's ability to use practical judgment in everyday social actions, the extent to which social acculturation has taken place, and the extent to which a maturing conscience or moral sense has developed. As seen by Wechsler, it requires use of so-called common sense judgment in a variety of situations. Success on this test probably depends a great deal on possession of practical information as well as the ability to evaluate and utilize past experience in socially acceptable ways. Success on this test also appears to be influenced by the child's ability to verbalize. Primarily this test is interested in determining if the child can use, in a socially accepted way, facts which he has gleaned from his surrounding environment.

Arithmetic. This subtest of the WISC requires meaningful manipulation of complex thought patterns. It is a measure of the child's ability to utilize abstract concepts of number and numerical operations, which are measures of cognitive development. Since concentration and attention are noncognitive functions in essence, and manipulation of number operations is cognitive, this test is of value in that it furnishes a demonstration of how the child relates cognitive and noncognitive factors in terms of thinking and performance.

Similarities. This part of the WISC is basically constructed to determine the qualitative aspects of relationships which the subject has abstracted from his environment. The subject has obtained facts and ideas from his surroundings and should be able to see basic, essential relationships between them. The test calls into operation remote memory, ability to comprehend, capacity for associative thinking, interests and reading patterns of the subject, as well as the ability to select and verbalize appropriate relationships between two ostensibly dissimilar objects or concepts.

Vocabulary. This subtest is probably the best single measure of general intellectual level. It gives an excellent picture of the child's learning ability, fund of information, richness of ideas, kind and quality of language, degree of abstract thinking, and character of thought processes. Vocabulary reflects a child's level of education and environment.

Picture Completion. Picture Completion calls for visual identification of familiar objects, forms, and living things and the further capacity to identify and isolate essential from non-essential characteristics. Attention and concentration are important elements in the test.

Picture Arrangement. Such factors as perception, visual comprehension, planning, involving sequential and causal events, and synthesis into intelligible wholes are involved in this test.

Block Design. Perception, analysis, synthesis, and reproduction of abstract designs are among the aspects measured by this subtest. Logic and reasoning must be applied to space relationships.

Object assembly. This test calls for adequate perception, visual-motor coordination, and simple assembly skills. For success there must be some visual anticipation of part-whole relationships, and flexibility in working toward a goal which may be unknown at first. A synthesis of concrete visual forms is required.

Object Assembly measures ability to assemble material drawn from life into a meaningful whole. It calls for the ability to see spatial relationships, as does Block Design, with one important difference: where the blocks must be assembled to match a pattern; the objects must be assembled with no clues beyond naming the "Boy" and the "Horse," and no leads at all for the "Face" and the "Car." Thus the child must look for the key to each object, figuring out in advance what he is constructing.

Coding. When used with children this test seems to be measuring visual-motor dexterity, particularly pencil manipulation, more than anything else. Ability to absorb new material presented in an associative context is called for. Speed and accuracy in making associations determines success.

Digit Span. This part of the scale is an attempt to determine the level of a child's ability to attend in a rather simple situation. It is an attempt to measure immediate auditory recall or immediate auditory memory (attention) span. If the child understands and masters methods of grouping operations, his success on this test probably is assured. In this sense then attention becomes an active as well as a passive process. Also of crucial importance for success on this test is the child's level of mental alertness. If he can suspend irrelevant thought processes while attending to this task his capacity for success on digits will be high. It might be noted, however, that a score on this test considerably above the subtest average can and often does indicate flattened affect or bland emotional life and a classical repression of feeling.

Mazes. Mazes call first for planning and foresight, for attention to instructions such as the request not to lift the pencil, for pencil control and hence visual-motor coordination, and for speed combined with accuracy.

STANDARDIZATION

The WISC was standardized on a sample of 2,200 white American children selected as representative of the population with regard to geographic area, father's occupational status, and rural-urban residence. The sample included 100 boys and 100 girls at each age from 5 through 15 years. With the exception of 55 mentally deficient children, the subjects in the sample were within 1½ months of their midyears (Wechsler, 1949, p. 7).

INTERCORRELATIONS OF THE TESTS

Wechsler has reported intercorrelations for the WISC subtests ranging from .10 to .75 for three different age groups: 7½, 10½, and 13½ (Wechsler, 1949, pp. 9–12). In general, higher intercorrelations are found among the verbal tests than among the performance tests.

As would be expected, the scores for the verbal tests tend to correlate better with the Verbal score than do the scores for the performance tests; the scores for the performance tests tend to correlate better with the Performance score than do the scores for the verbal tests.

The correlations between the Verbal Scale and the Performance Scale are reported to be .60, .68, and .56 for the ages 7½, 10½, and 13½ respectively. The correlations, though positive and substantial, are not large enough to permit the assumption that the verbal and performance scales can be regarded as comparable forms. The two scales are measuring somewhat different aspects of mental ability by means of different types of activities or tasks.

RELIABILITY

Reliability coefficients and standard errors of measurement for the WISC are shown in Table 6-4. With the exception of coefficients for Digit Span and Mazes, the reliability coefficients in Table 6-4 were computed by the split-halves technique and were corrected for full length of the test by the use of the Spearman-Brown formula. The split-halves technique could not be used to estimate the reliability of the Coding test because it is a speed test, so a reliability coefficient for it was obtained by correlating Coding A with Coding B, both forms having been administered to many of the children who were tested at ages 7½ and 8½. The reliability coefficients for Digit Span were obtained by correlating the scores on Digits Forward with the scores on Digits Backward and correcting with the Spearman-Brown formula (Wechsler, 1949).

The data in Table 6-4 show that the subtest reliability coefficients vary considerably and are not as high as the coefficients for the Verbal, Performance and Full Scale scores. The subtest reliability coefficients should be carefully considered when the scores earned on separate tests or the differences between scores on the tests are interpreted, for the smaller the reliability of a score, the less confidence one can place in the scores (Wechsler, 1949).

Table 6-4. Reliability and Standard Error of Measurement* of the WISC Tests (From Wechsler, 1949, p. 13, by permission of The Psychological Corporation).

N = 200 for each age level

	Age 7½		Age 10½		Age 13½	
	r	SE_m	r	SE_m	r	SE_m
Information	.66	1.75	.80	1.34	.82	1.27
Comprehension	.59	1.92	.73	1.56	.71	1.62
Arithmetic	.63	1.82	.84	1.20	.77	1.44
Comparison	.66	1.75	.81	1.31	.79	1.37
Vocabulary	.77	1.44	.91	.90	.90	.95
Digit Span	.60	1.90	.59	1.92	.50	2.12
Verbal Score	.88	5.19	.96	3.00	.96	3.00
(without Digit Span)						
Picture Completion	.59	1.92	.66	1.75	.68	1.70
Picture Arrangement	.72	1.59	.71	1.62	.72	1.59
Block Design	.84	1.20	.87	1.08	.88	1.04
Object Assembly	.63	1.82	.63	1.82	.71	1.62
Coding†	.60	1.90	–	–	–	–
Mazes	.79	1.37	.81	1.31	.75	1.50
Performance Score	.86	5.61	.89	4.98	.90	4.74
(without Coding and Mazes)						
Full Scale Score	.92	4.25	.95	3.36	.94	3.68
(without Digit Span, Coding and Mazes)						

*The SE_m is in Scaled Score units for the tests and in IQ units for the Verbal, Performance and Full Scale Scores.
†Based on correlating Coding A and Coding B, 115 cases.

Gehman and Matyas (1956) have reported stability coefficients of .77, .74, and .77 for the Verbal Scale, Performance Scale, and Full Scale respectively. These coefficients are based upon scores earned by 60 children who were tested with the WISC in the fifth grade and then again in the ninth grade. The coefficients suggest that a number of the children tested showed appreciable changes in their scores over the four-year period.

Davis (1966) investigated the internal consistency of the WISC when it was administered to 142 mental retardates. He obtained split-half reliability coefficients, for the essentially nonspeed tests, ranging from .54 for Picture Arrangement to .89 for Vocabulary and Block Design. Reliability coefficients of .83, .84, and .83 were reported for the Performance Scale and coefficients of .90, .91, and .97 for the Full Scale for three groups of retardates in the study.

Quereshi (1968) studied the internal consistency of the WISC by using test data from a sample of 392 urban school children, ages 5–16. He reported split-half reliability coefficients for the subtests ranging from .01 for Arithmetic (ages 6½ to 7½) to .92 for Block Design (ages 14½–15½). For the Verbal Scale, Quereshi reported reliability coefficients ranging from .83 (ages 14½–15½) to .92 (ages 12½–13½). For the Performance Scale the correlations ranged from .81 (ages 6½–7½) to .90 (ages 10½–11½), and for the Full Scale the range was .89 (ages 5–6 and 14–15½) to .96 (ages 8½–9½).

Test-retest reliability coefficients for the WISC were obtained in a study by Turner, Mathews, and Rachman (1967). These researchers used a sample of 26 boys, ranging in ages from 7-7 to 15 years, who were receiving psychiatric care. The reported considerable variation in the subtest results for their sample. The reported reliabilities ranged from .11 for Picture Arrangement to .82 for Vocabulary. The retest reliability coefficients for the three scales were .81 for Verbal, .73 for Performance, and .80 for Full Scale. Although this retest took place after two years, the researchers noticed evidence of practice effect, especially for the Performance Scale. They concluded that the results in this study are quite consistent with earlier findings based on non-psychiatric groups.

VALIDITY

Numerous studies have been conducted in which measures of the WISC have been correlated with the results of other tests of intelligence or achievement. Since investigations provide evidence of validity for the WISC, a number of them will be discussed briefly.

Concurrent Validity. In Table 6-5 are the correlation coefficients which have been reported for several studies in which WISC results were correlated with the scores of other scales or tests of mental ability. In some of the studies individual instruments were used, while in others group tests were administered.

Table 6-5. Reported Correlations Between the WISC and Other Mental Ability Tests

Researchers	Subjects	Tests or Scales	Correlation		
			V	P	FS
Martin and Wiechers (1954)	100 nine-year-old school children	Colored Progressive Matrices	.84	.83	.91
Smith and Fillmore (1954)	91 children with reading difficulties	Ammons Full Picture Vocabulary Test	.73	.54	.75
Stacey and Carleton (1955)	150 possibly mentally retarded children ages 7-5 to 15-9	Colored Progressive Matrices	.54	.52	.55
Altus (1955)	100 children referred to a guidance department	California Test of Mental Maturity			
		Language	.71	.57	.70
		Nonlanguage	.65	.67	.68
		Total	.76	.68	.77
Barratt (1956)	70 fourth-grade children	Progressive Matrices	.692	.699	.754
		Columbia Mental Maturity Scale	.559	.478	.606

Table 6-5. (continued)

Researchers	Subjects	Tests or Scales	Correlation V	P	FS
Cooper (1958)	51 fifth-grade children on Guam	Leiter International Performance Scale	.73	.78	.83
		Columbia Mental Maturity Scale	.66	.68	.74
Himmelstein and Herdon (1962)	48 emotionally disturbed children ages 62 to 14-8	Peabody Picture Vocabulary Test	.642	.522	.629
Rohrs and Haworth (1962)	46 mentally retarded children ages 9-1 to 15-6	Stanford-Binet, Form L-M	.72	.50	.69
Estes (1965)	85 children in grades 4 through 10	Stanford-Binet			.76
		Otis			.67
Gage and Naumann (1965)	31 children referred to a psychological service center- ages 5-6 to 15-11	Peabody Picture Vocabulary Test	.69	.56	.68
Barclay and Carolan (1966)	104 children ages 7-12	Stanford-Binet, Form L-M	.85	.68	.83
Shaw, Mathews, and Klove (1966)	83 maladjusted children	Peabody Picture Vocabulary Test	.71	.53	.66
Ross and Morledge (1967)	30 students ages 15-11 to 16	Wechsler Adult Intelligence Scale	.95	.92	.96
Brittain (1968)	41 eight-year-old British children	Stanford-Binet, Form L-M	.81	.82	.89
Anderson and Flax (1968)	406 children, ages 6-13, with academic and emotional problems	Peabody Picture Vocabulary Test	.66	.46	.58

In general, there appears to be a substantial degree of relationship between WISC scores and the scores of other mental-ability tests, and this can be considered evidence of concurrent validity. However, because the correlations frequently are not high, one should be extremely cautious in attempting to equate WISC scores with the results of other mental ability tests or scales.

Further evidence of concurrent validity for the WISC is found in data in Table 6-6. The table shows the correlation coefficients reported by a number of

Table 6-6. Reported Correlations Between the WISC and Achievement
Tests

Researchers	Subjects	Test	Correlation		
			V	P	FS
Frandsen and Higginson (1951)	54 fourth-grade children ages 9-1 to 10-3	Stanford Achievement, Total Score	.62	.65	.76
Mussen, et al. (1952)	39 "highly selected" children ages 6-0 to 13-10	Metropolitan Arithmetic	.74	.74	.81
		Metropolitan Reading	.62	.76	.75
		Stanford Arithmetic	.47	.29	.69
		Stanford Reading	.73	.57	.65
Richardson and Surko (1956)	165 delinquent children	Gray Oral Reading	.59		.58
		Stanford Reading			.59
		Stanford Arithmetic			.64
Barratt and Baumgarten (1957)	30 achievers in grades 4–6	California Reading	.61	.29	.56
		California Arithmetic	.09	.14	.14
	30 nonachievers in grades 4–6	California Reading	.51	.30	.61
		California Arithmetic	.73	.33	.79
Stroud et al. (1957)	621 pupils referred to psychological study center	Iowa Basic Skills Reading	.58	.63	.66
		Iowa Basic Skills Arithmetic	.67	.52	.66
		Iowa Basic Skills Spelling	.62	.60	.67
Cooper (1958)	51 fifth-grade children on Guam	California Achievement Test	.80	.54	.77

researchers who compared WISC results with scores earned on various achievement tests. While there is considerable variation in the reported coefficients, it can be seen that most of the correlations between the WISC Full Scale and the measures of achievement are above .60. The same is true for the Verbal Scale. One would expect the Performance Scale scores to correlate less well with measures of academic achievement than the Verbal and Full Scale scores because of the emphasis on verbal skills and ability in school activities.

Construct Validity. The evidence to support a claim of construct validity for the WISC appears to be scant. Gault (1954) conducted a factor analysis of the intercorrelations which appear in the WISC Manual and reported evidence of the existence of four factors. These factors are referred to as a "general eductive factor," a "verbal comprehension factor," a "spatial-perceptual factor," and a "memory factor." The verbal comprehension factor and the spatial-perceptual factor appear to correspond with the Verbal Scale and Performance Scale.

Lotsof et al. (1958, p. 301), however, concluded that "the verbal and performance aspects of the WISC are not independent of each other." In their study they conducted a factor analysis of Rorschach and WISC scores for 72 underachieving children who had reading difficulties. They reported evidence of four factors which they referred to as verbal intelligence, productivity, perceptual movement, and performance speed.

Cohen's (1959) factor analysis of the WISC, discussed in Chapter 4, revealed that the subtests of the WISC showed strong correlations with the factors referred to as verbal comprehension, perceptual organization, freedom from distractibility, and g.

SHORT FORMS OF THE WISC

Carleton and Stacy (1954) devised 21 different short forms of the WISC from the WISC scores of 365 mentally retarded children. After correlating each short form with the Full Scale they found correlation coefficients ranging from .64 for the Comprehension-Vocabulary subtest combination to .88 for the five-subtest combination of Comprehension, Arithmetic, Block Design, Coding, and Picture Completion.

Yalowitz and Armstrong (1955) reported correlation coefficients ranging from .55 to .61 between scores for three short forms and Full Scale intelligence quotients. The 229 subjects in the study were children who had been referred to a child-guidance clinic.

Clements (1963) used test data for 92 children, who were referred to a child-study center, to determine a valid short form of the WISC for a clinical population of reading disability cases. She found that the score for a tetrad consisting of Similarities, Arithmetic, Object Assembly, and Picture Arrangement correlated .947 with the Full Scale score. The addition of either Vocabulary or Picture Arrangement yielded a coefficient of .959. When the data were analyzed for sex differences, Clements found that for the boys in the study the five-test correlation coefficient was .966 and for the girls it was .957.

Yudin (1966) explored the possibility of developing an abbreviated WISC for use with emotionally disturbed children. He rescored the WISC tests of 147 unstable children after selecting certain items from each subtest except Digit Span and Coding, which were left unchanged. The resulting short form of the WISC contained only 56 percent of the items of the regular long form. Yudin reported the following correlation coefficients between IQ scores for the complete WISC scale and scores for the short form: Verbal, .96; Performance, .93; Full Scale, .97. He concluded that the WISC can be shortened without destroying its validity.

The abbreviated form of the WISC which Yudin used was also utilized in a study by Reid, Moore, and Alexander (1968). These researchers investigated the possibility of using the Yudin short form with brain damaged and mentally retarded children. Using data from the test administrations for 77 brain-damaged subjects, the researchers reported the following correlations between the short form and the standard WISC: Verbal, .92; Performance, .87, and Full Scale, .93. For a group of 220 mentally retarded children, the following correlation coefficients were reported: Verbal, .91; Performance, .85 and Full Scale, .92. The researchers concluded that the results of their study indicate that this short form provides results which are comparable to those for the standard WISC. They were of the opinion that this type of short form is useful, (as compared with the type which includes selected subtests) because it eliminates the possibility of unduly penalizing a child who has marked deficits in abilities that are tapped by certain WISC subtests.

Using Wechsler's standardization data for ages 7½, 10½, and 13½, Silverstein (1967) correlated the results of combinations of subtests of the WISC with the standard WISC. He found that the best dyads were I, PA; I,BD; and V, BD. The best triad was I, V, OA, and the best pentad was I, C, A, PA, OA. No tetrad appeared in the data for *all three* age groups. The correlation coefficients which Silverstein reported ranged from .807 for the poorest dyad to .966 for the best pentad.

McKerracher and Watson (1968) reported a correlation coefficient of .96 between the prorated score of the Doppelt short form $[(A + V + PA + BD) \times 10/4]$ and the standard WISC score. The study was based upon data for 127 children at a guidance clinic who were tested with the English version of the WISC. The researchers concluded that the prorated IQ should provide an acceptable indication of the functional intelligence of a subject.

WECHSLER PRESCHOOL AND PRIMARY SCALE OF INTELLIGENCE (WPPSI)

The WPPSI, which is similar to the WISC in organization and content, was developed to meet the need for a scale that could be used to measure the intelligence of children of preschool age. This scale, published in 1967, can be used to test children whose ages range from 4 through 6½ years.

ORGANIZATION OF THE WPPSI

This scale is composed of six verbal and five performance subtests:

Verbal Tests	Performance Tests
Information	Animal House
Vocabulary	Picture Completion
Arithmetic	Mazes
Similarities	Geometric Design
Comprehension	Block Design
Sentences (Supplementary)	

The sentences test is a supplementary test which is not used in computing the verbal-scale score. The Full-Scale score, then, is based on ten tests, five verbal and five performance.

The three tests not found in the WISC are *Animal House, Geometric Design* and *Sentences.* Animal House is a test in which the subject being tested is required to associate signs with symbols (Fig. 6-4). The test may be considered to be a measure of learning ability, with memory, attention span, goal awareness, and ability to concentrate as factors that may be involved (Wechsler, 1967, p. 11). Geometric Design requires the subject to reproduce geometric figures with a sufficient degree of accuracy. It measures abilities which depend primarily on perceptual and visual-motor organization (Wechsler, 1967, p. 11). Sentences is a test which requires that the child be able to repeat verbatim the sentences that are read to him. It is, therefore, a test of immediate recall.

In the usual administration of the *WAIS* and *WISC* all of the verbal tests are administered before the performance tests are administered. In the standard

Fig. 6-4. The Animal House Test of the Wechsler Preschool and Primary Scale of Intelligence. (Courtesy The Psychological Corporation.)

administration of the WPPSI, however, the verbal and performance tests are given in a mixed order: Information, Animal House, Vocabulary, Picture Completion, Arithmetic, Mazes, Geometric Design, Similarities, Block Design, Comprehension and Sentences. Wechsler (1967, p. 7) explains that varying the tests in this way will improve the chances of maintaining a child's interest and cooperation.

STANDARDIZATION OF THE WPPSI

The scale was standarized on a sample consisting of 100 boys and girls in each of six age groups which range from 4 years through 6½ years (Wechsler, 1967, p. 13). The 1,200 cases comprised a sample which was stratified according to age, geographic region, urban-rural residence, color (white-nonwhite) and father's occupation.

RELIABILITY OF THE WPPSI

Reliability coefficients and standard errors of measurement of the subtests and the Verbal Scale, Performance Scale and Full Scale of the WPPSI for the standardization sample are shown in Table 6-7. The reliability coefficients reported in the table are odd-even correlations except for Animal House and the three scales: V, P, and FS. Because Animal House is a speeded test, the test-retest method was used to estimate its reliability. The reliability coefficients reported for the scale IQs were computed by means of a formula for the correlation between two sums of equally weighted scores (Wechsler, 1967, p. 21). The standard errors of measurement reported for the individual tests are in scaled-score units, but for the three scales they are in IQ units.

As one can readily see by examining the data in the table, there is considerable variation in the coefficients of reliability for the eleven subtests. The coefficients range from .62 for Animal House at age 4 to .91 for Mazes at age 5½. The average coefficients for the individual tests for all age groups range from .77 (Animal House) to .87 (Mazes). As one would expect, the reliability coefficients tend to be considerably higher for the three scales (V, P, and FS) than for the subtests. The lowest scale coefficient is .91 for Performance at age 4 and the highest is .97 for Full Scale at ages 5½ and 6. The averages for all ages are .94 for Verbal IQ, .93 for Performance IQ and .96 for Full Scale IQ. These three average coefficients seem quite impressive, and the examiner can feel more confident about the three IQs which the WPPSI yields than about the scaled scores for the individual tests. A great deal of caution should be exercised when one makes judgments based on the results of those subtests which have relatively low reliability coefficients.

In the WPPSI manual, Wechsler (1967) reports test-retest reliability data for a study involving 50 children between the ages of 5½ and 5¾ years. After correction for difference in variability between the smaller sample ($N = 50$) and the standardization group, the test-retest coefficients for the subtests were found to

Table 6-7. Reliability Coefficients and Standard Errors of Measurement of the WPPSI Tests and IQs by Age Group (From Wechsler, 1967, p. 22, by permission of The Psychological Corporation).

N = 200 for Each Age Group[a]

	Age Group												Average
	4		4½		5		5½		6		6½		
Test	r_{11}	SE_m	r_{11}	SE_m	r_{11}	SE_m	r_{11}	SE_m	r_{11}	SE_m	r_{11}	SE_m	r_{11}[b]
Information	.84	1.25	.81	1.31	.77	1.42	.81	1.31	.84	1.25	.75	1.50	.81
Vocabulary	.82	1.28	.84	1.22	.78	1.38	.85	1.18	.87	1.06	.86	1.13	.84
Arithmetic	.81	1.35	.78	1.38	.84	1.14	.86	1.06	.82	1.22	.83	1.23	.82
Similarities	.85	1.19	.82	1.30	.83	1.21	.82	1.32	.84	1.21	.84	1.24	.83
Comprehension	.78	1.43	.83	1.23	.78	1.32	.84	1.19	.82	1.30	.78	1.45	.81
Sentences	.88	1.04	.87	1.12	.83	1.29	.87	1.06	.81	1.35	.84	1.23	.85
Animal House	.62	1.87	.71	1.60	.79	1.37	.82	1.28	.84	1.19	.76	1.45	.77
Picture Completion	.85	1.14	.84	1.19	.81	1.23	.86	1.12	.83	1.23	.81	1.28	.83
Mazes	.85	1.17	.82	1.24	.88	1.03	.91	.87	.87	1.10	.88	1.04	.87
Geometric Design	.80	1.39	.82	1.24	.82	1.31	.84	1.25	.87	1.12	.77	1.42	.82
Block Design	.76	1.53	.78	1.35	.83	1.23	.85	1.17	.88	.99	.81	1.31	.82
Verbal IQ[c]	.94	3.68	.94	3.63	.93	3.61	.95	3.40	.95	3.40	.94	3.69	.94
Performance IQ	.91	4.35	.92	4.02	.94	3.79	.95	3.49	.95	3.44	.92	3.99	.93
Full Scale IQ[c]	.96	3.12	.96	2.99	.96	2.88	.97	2.68	.97	2.66	.96	2.98	.96

Note. The reliability coefficients for all tests except Animal House are odd-even correlations corrected by the Spearman-Brown formula. The SE_m's are in scaled-score units for the tests and in IQ units for the Verbal, Performance, and Full Scale IQs.

[a]The N for Animal House varies from 196 to 200.

[b]The average r_{11} was computed by transforming the 6 reliability coefficients for each test to Fisher's z statistic, and reconverting the mean z value to the equivalent r.

[c]Sentences was not included in the computation of Verbal and Full Scale IQs.

range from .60 (Sentences) to .93 (Picture Completion). The reported coefficients for the three scales are .86 (Verbal), .89 (Performance) and .92 (Full Scale). These reliability coefficients are somewhat lower than the split-half coefficients reported for the standardization sample.

Brittain (1969) used a slightly modified version of the WPPSI with a random sample of 60 British children who were 5½ years of age. He reported split-half reliability coefficients ranging from .73 for Similarities to .90 for Information and Geometric Design. The reliability coefficients for the scales were Verbal .93; Performance, .96; and Full Scale, .97. These figures are quite close to those reported by Wechsler. Brittain concluded that the WPPSI is adequately reliable for use in a clinical situation.

VALIDITY

Because the WPPSI has been in use for such a short time, evidence of validity for the scale is rather meager. We can, however, look at the intercorrelations of the subtests and scales that are reported in the WPPSI manual (Wechsler, 1967), and we can examine the findings of a few studies in which the WPPSI has been correlated with other instruments. Table 6-8 shows the average intercorrelations reported for the subtests and scales of the WPPSI, based on the test results for the six age groups of the standardization sample. It can readily be seen that the average coefficients of correlation between the individual tests vary from .28 between Mazes and Similarities to .60 between Vocabulary and Information and between Comprehension and Information. For the three scales, the lowest average correlation is .44 between Verbal and Mazes, and also between Performance and Similarities. The highest average correlation is between Verbal and Information (.73). The average correlation between the Verbal Scale and the Performance Scale is .66, which indicates a substantial (but far from perfect) positive relationship between Verbal and Performance IQs. In general, it appears that all of the subtests and both the Verbal Scale and Performance Scale are contributing to the measurement of general mental ability.

Wechsler (1967) reports data from a study in which 98 children, ages 60 to 73 months, were administered the WPPSI and three other individual tests of mental ability. The reported correlations between WPPSI IQs and the IQs for the other instruments are shown in Table 6-9.

Judging from the coefficients shown in Table 6-8, there is substantial agreement between the WPPSI Verbal and S-B scores and between the Full Scale, and S-B scores, but only moderate positive correlations between WPPSI results and those of the other two instruments. On the basis of the findings in this study it appears that to a great extent the four instruments are measuring the same quality, probably general mental ability, but the correlation coefficients are not high enough to suggest that the scales are interchangeable.

Yule et al. (1969) used a slightly modified WPPSI to test 76 boys and

Table 6-8. Average Intercorrelation of the WPPSI Tests for 6 Age Groups (From Wechsler, 1967, p. 32, by permission of The Psychological Corporation)
600 Boys and 600 Girls

Test	Information	Vocabulary	Arithmetic	Similarities	Comprehension	Sentences	Animal House	Picture Completion	Mazes	Geometric Design	Block Design	Verbal Score
Vocabulary	.60											
Arithmetic	.58	.49										
Similarities	.53	.49	.46									
Comprehension	.60	.57	.51	.55								
Sentences	.52	.46	.51	.51	.53							
Animal House	.41	.36	.42	.31	.34	.36						
Picture Completion	.47	.45	.42	.36	.42	.35	.38					
Mazes	.37	.35	.41	.28	.33	.30	.36	.44				
Geometric Design	.40	.35	.47	.30	.36	.34	.43	.42	.48			
Block Design	.43	.38	.50	.35	.39	.38	.38	.45	.46	.48		
Verbal Score[a]	.73	.66	.62	.62	.69	.64	.46	.54	.44	.48	.52	
Performance Score[a]	.56	.51	.60	.44	.50	.47	.50	.55	.57	.60	.59	.66
Full Scale Score[a]	.70	.64	.68	.58	.65	.61	.53	.60	.54	.58	.61	—

Note.—The coefficients of correlation were computed from scaled scores.
[a]Verbal Score is the sum of scaled scores on 5 tests, Sentences omitted; Performance Score is the sum of scaled scores on 5 tests; Full Scale Score is the sum of scaled scores on 10 tests, Sentences omitted. Coefficients with these variables have been corrected to remove contamination.

Table 6-9. Correlation of WPPSI IQs with IQs From Three Other
Mental Ability Tests.*

Scale	1960 Stanford-Binet	Peabody Picture Verbal Test (Form A)	Pictorial Test of Intelligence (Deviation IQ)
Verbal IQ	.76	.57	.53
Performance IQ	.56	.44	.60
Full Scale IQ	.75	.58	.64

Source: Wechsler, 1967, p. 34.

74 girls, age five years, on the Isle of Wight. The researchers found no significant differences between girls' and boys' performances except on two subtests. The girls were found to score higher on Animal House, and the boys higher on Mazes. A correlation coefficient of .63 was found between the verbal and performance IQs.

In this study scores from WPPSI were correlated with scores from three other instruments which were administered to the 150 children in the sample. The researchers used a shortened form of the Frostig Developmental Test of Visual Perception, the English Picture Vocabulary Test, and the Auditory Decoding Test of the Illinois Test of Psycholinguistic Abilities. The results are shown in Table 6-10.

It is interesting to note that the only *strong* positive correlations between scores from the WPPSI scales and scores from the other tests are those between the Performance scores and the shortened Frostig scores and between the Full-Scale scores and the Frostig scores. It is interesting, too, that the correlation between the WPPSI Full Scale and the EPVT, .58, was also reported between the WPPSI and PPVT by Wechsler.

Yule and his co-workers found the WPPSI to be "a comparatively well standardized test, interesting to the children and it promises to yield diagnostic information." They caution testers to score the performance items strictly, and they state that the expected Full Scale mean IQ is about 105 for British Children. They also urge that great care be taken in interpreting Verbal-Performance discrepancies, which appear to be larger among British children than among the Wechsler norm group.

They stress that, in their sample, there is a large social-class score differential between the children of "manual" and "nonmanual" parents.

Table 6-10. Correlations Between WPPSI and
Other Tests*

WPPSI	Frostig	EPVT	ITPA
Verbal IQ	.48	.56	.48
Performance IQ	.75	.48	.38
Full Scale IQ	.67	.58	.48

*Source: Yule et al., 1969, pp. 2–3.

SHORT FORMS

Silverstein (1968), using data from the standardization sample, correlated the results of all the combinations of WPPSI subtests with the results for the standard WPPSI. He found that when subtest scores were simply added the best dyad was Information with Block Design (I, BD) which correlated .866 with the WPPSI Full Scale. The best triad was I, A, PC (.910); the best tetrad was I, V, GD, BD (.939); and the best pentad was I, A, C, PC, GD (.957). Similar results were obtained by using the Wherry Doolittle method which tends to select the best short form of each length but utilizes differential weighting of the subtests instead of just the summation of subtest scores. The best combinations found by this method were I, GD; I, C, GD; I, C, GD, BD; and I, C, PC, GD, and BD.

In another study based on the standardization data, Silverstein (1968) constructed an abbreviated form of the WPPSI by reducing the number of items rather than the number of individual subtests. He used every third item on Information, Vocabulary, and Picture Completion and the odd items on the rest of the subtests with the exception of Animal House, which was not altered. Silverstein reported correlations between the WPPSI short form and WPPSI standard form as follows: Verbal, .96, Performance, .97 and Full Scale, .98. These are, indeed, very impressive correlation coefficients.

EVALUATION OF THE WECHSLER SCALES

The Wechsler scales apparently measure the same general mental ability as the Stanford-Binet, judging from the relatively strong positive correlations which have been found between the Wechsler full-scale scores and Stanford-Binet scores.

The Wechsler scales provide three scores—Verbal, Performance, and Full-Scale. This is a very important feature of the scales, for the separate scores can have diagnostic value, especially when subjects have verbal, scholastic, or cultural handicaps.

It should not be assumed, however, that the Performance Scale is an adequate substitute for either the Verbal Scale or for the Full-Scale. The intercorrelations for the three scales are simply not high enough to assume that they can be used interchangeably.

The use of several different subtests, each with its set of similar items, is another asset of the Wechsler scales. Many experienced psychologists are able to derive useful diagnostic information from subject performance on the subtests. The reliability coefficients reported for the subtests, however, are much lower than those for the Verbal, Performance, and Full Scales. This means that a great deal of caution must be exercised in interpreting subtest scores.

The availability of adult norms which extend to age 75 and over makes the WAIS especially suitable for adult testing, and for this purpose the scale is generally preferred over the Stanford-Binet.

One of the limitations of the Wechsler scales is that they do not provide sufficient range to assess adequately the abilities of the very bright or very dull subjects.

Another possible shortcoming is that the WISC and WAIS have not been revised since they were first published in 1949 and 1955 respectively.

In general we find that the Wechsler scales are well-designed, highly reliable instruments which accomplish the objective of measuring general mental ability through the use of a wide variety of interesting tasks. They are suitable for testing most individuals of the age groups for which they are designed.

REFERENCES

Altus, Grace T., "Relationship Between Verbal and Non-verbal Parts of the CTMM and WISC," *Journal of Consulting Psychology* 19 (1955), 143-144.

Anderson, Darrell E., and Morton Flax, "A Comparison of the Peabody Picture Vocabulary Test With the Wechsler Intelligence Scale for Children," *Journal of Educational Research* 62 (1968), 114-116.

Barclay, A., and Patricia Carolan, "A Comparative Study of the Wechsler Intelligence Scale for Children and the Stanford-Binet Intelligence Scale, Form L-M," *Journal of Consulting Psychology* 30 (1966), 6, 563.

Barratt, E. S., "The Relationship of the Progressive Matrices (1938) and the Columbia Mental Maturity Scale to the WISC," *Journal of Consulting Psychology* 20 (1956), 294-296.

———, and Doris L. Baumgarten, "The Relationship of the WISC and Stanford-Binet to School Achievement," *Journal of Consulting Psychology* 21 (1957), 144.

Brengelmann, Johannes C., and Joseph T. Kenny, "Comparison of Leiter, WAIS and Stanford-Binet IQ in Retardates," *Journal of Clinical Psychology* 17 (1961), 235-238.

Brittain, Michael, "A Comparative Study of the Use of the Wechsler Intelligence Scale for Children and the Stanford-Binet Intelligence Scale (Form L-M) with Eight-Year-Old Children," *British Journal of Educational Psychology* 38 (1968), 103-104.

———, "The WPPSI: A Midlands Study," *British Journal of Educational Psychology* 39 (1969), 14-17.

Carleton, F. O., and C. L. Stacy, "Evaluation of Selected Short Forms of the Wechsler Intelligence Scale for Children," *Journal of Clinical Psychology* 10 (1954), 258-261.

Clements, Gladys R., "An Abbreviated Form of the WISC for Children," *Journal of Consulting Psychology* 29 (1963), 92.

Cohen, Jacob, "A Factor-Analytically Based Rationale for the Wechsler Adult Scale," *Journal of Consulting Psychology* 21 (1957), 451-457.

———, "The Factorial Structures of the WISC at Ages 7-6, 10-6 and 13-6," *Journal of Consulting Psychology* 23 (1959), 285-299.

Conroy, R., and W. T. Plant, "WAIS and Group Test Prediction of an Academic

Success Criterion: High School and College," *Educational and Psychological Measurement* 25 (1965), 493–500.

Cooper J. G., "Predicting School Achievement for Bilingual Pupils," *Journal Education Psychology* 49 (1958), 31–36.

Davis, Leo. J., "The Internal Consistency of the WISC with the Mentally Retarded," *American Journal of Mental Deficiency* 70 (1966), 714–716.

Doppelt, Jerome E., "Estimating the Full Scale Score on the Wechsler Adult Intelligence Scale from Scores on Four Subtests," *Journal of Consulting Psychology* 20 (1956), 63–66.

Duke, Robert B., "Intellectual Evaluation of Brain-Damaged Patients With a WAIS Short Form," *Psychological Reports* 20 (1967).

Estes, Betty, "Relationship Between the Otis, 1960 Stanford-Binet and WISC," *Journal of Clinical Psychology* 21 (1965), 296–297.

Frandsen, Arden N., and Higginson J. B., "The Standford-Binet and the Wechsler Intelligence Scale for Children," *Journal of Consulting Psychology* 15 (1951), 236–238.

Freeman, Frank S., *Theory and Practice of Psychological Testing*. 3rd ed. New York: Holt, 1962.

Gage, Gerald, and F. F. Naumann, "Correlation of the Peabody Picture Vocabulary Test and the Wechsler Intelligence Scale for Children," *Journal of Educational Research* 58 (1965), 446–468.

Gault, Una, "Factorial Patterns on the Wechsler Intelligence Scales," *Australian Journal of Psychology* 6 (1954), 85–90.

Gehmen, I. H., and R. P. Matyas, "Stability of the WISC and Binet Tests," *Journal of Consulting Psychology* 20 (1956), 150–152.

Giannell, A. S., and C. M. Freeburne, "Comparative Validity of the WAIS and Stanford-Binet with College Freshmen," *Educational and Psychological Measurement* 23 (1963), 557–567.

Glasser, Alan J. and Irla L. Zimmerman, *Clinical Interpretation of the Wechsler Intelligence Scale for Children*, New York: Grune and Stratton, 1967.

Guertin, Wilson H., et al., "Research with the Wechsler Intelligence Scales for Adults: 1960-65, *Psychological Bulletin* 66 (1966), 385–409.

Himmelstein, Philip, and James D. Herdon, "Comparison of the WISC and Peabody Picture Vocabulary Test with Emotionally Disturbed Children," *Journal of Clinical Psychology* 18 (1962), 82.

Kitzinger, Helen, and E. Blumberg, "Supplementary Guide for Administering and Scoring the Wechsler-Bellevue Intelligence Scale (Form I)," *Psychological Monograph* 65, No. 319, (1951), 1-20.

Knox, Alan B., Arden Grotelueschen, and Douglas Sjogren, "Adult Intelligence and Learning Ability," *Adult Education* 18 (1968), 188–196.

Littell, W. M., "The Wechsler Intelligence Scale for Children: Review of a Decade of Research," *Psychological Bulletin* 57 (1960), 132–156.

Lotsof, E. J., et al., "A Factor Analysis of the WISC and Rorschach," *Journal of Projective Techniques* 22 (1958), 297–301.

Martin, A. W., and J. E. Wiechers, "Raven's Colored Progressive Matrices and the Wechsler Intelligence Scale for Children," *Journal of Consulting Psychology* 18 (1954), 143–144.

Maxwell, Eileen, "Validation of Abbreviated WAIS Scales," *Journal of Consulting Psychology* 21 (1957), 126.

McLeod, Hugh N., and Joseph Rubin, "Correlation Between Raven Progressive Matrices and the WAIS," *Journal of Consulting Psychology* 26 (1962), 190–191.

McKerracher, D. W., and R. A. Watson, "Validation of a Short Form WISC with Clinic Children," *British Journal of Educational Psychology* 38 (1968), 205–208.

Mogel, Steve, and Paul Satz, "Abbreviation of the WAIS for Clinical Use: An Attempt at Validation," *Journal of Clinical Psychology* 19 (1963), 298–300.

Monroe, K. L., "Note on the Estimation of the WAIS Full Scale IQ," *Journal of Clinical Psychology* 22 (1966), 79–81.

Mussen, P., S. Dean and Margery Rosenberg, "Some Further Evidence of the Validity of the WISC," *Journal of Consulting Psychology* 16 (1952), 410–411.

Olsen, Inger A., and Gerald D. Jordheim, "Use of WAIS in a Student Counseling Center," *Personnel and Guidance Journal* 42 (1964), 500–507.

Quereshi, M. Y., "The Internal Consistency of the WISC Scores for Ages 5 to 16," *Journal of Clinical Psychology* 24 (1968), 79–85.

Rapaport, D., M. Gill, and R. Schafer, *Diagnostic Psychological Testing.* Vol. 1, Chicago: Year Book Publishers, 1945.

Reid, Walter, Dana Moore, and Dwayne Alexander, "Abbreviated Form of the WISC for Use With Brain-Damaged and Mentally Retarded Children," *Journal of Consulting and Clinical Psychology* 32 (1968), 236.

Richardson, Helen M., and Elise F. Surko, "WISC Scores and Status in Reading and Arithmetic of Delinquent Children," *Journal of Genetic Psychology* 89 (1956), 251–262.

Rohrs, F. W., and M. B. Haworth, "The 1960 Stanford-Binet, WISC, and Goodenough Tests, with Mentally Retarded Children," *American Journal of Mental Deficiency* 66 (1962), 853–859.

Ross, Robert, and June Moreledge, "Comparison of the WISC and WAIS at Chronological Age Sixteen," *Journal of Consulting Psychology* 31 (1967), 331–332.

Satz, Paul, and Steve Mogel, "An Abbreviation of the WAIS for Clinical Use," *Journal of Clinical Psychology* 18 (1962), 77–79.

Shaw, Dale J., "Estimating WAIS From Progressive Matrices Scores," *Journal of Clinical Psychology* 23, (1967), 184–185.

——— , Charles Mathews, and Hallgrim Klove, "The Equivalence of WISC and PPVT IQs," *American Journal of Mental Deficiency* 70 (1966), 601–604.

Silverstein, A. B., "Validity of WISC Short Forms at Three Age Levels," *Journal of Consulting Psychology* 31 (1967), 635–636.

——— , "Validity of a New Approach to the Design of WAIS, WISC and WPPSI Short Forms," *Journal of Consulting and Clinical Psychology* 32 (1968), 478–479.

——— , "Validity of WPPSI Short Forms," *Journal of Consulting and Clinical Psychology* 32 (1968), 229–230.

Smith, L. M., and Arline R. Fillmore, "The Ammons FRPV Test and the WISC for Remedial Reading Cases," *Journal of Consulting Psychology* 18 (1954), 332.

Stacy, C. L., and F. O. Carleton, "The Relationship Between Ravens Colored Progressive Matrices and Two Tests of General Intelligence," *Journal of Clinical Psychology* 11 (1955), 84‒85.

Stroud, J. B., P. Bloomers, and Margaret Lauber, "Correlation of WISC and Achievement Tests," *Journal of Educational Psychology* 48 (1957), 18‒26.

Turner, R. K., A. Mathews, and S. Rachman, "The Stability of the WISC in a Psychiatric Group," *British Journal of Educational Psychology* 37 (1967), 194‒200.

Wechsler, David, *The Measurement of Adult Intelligence*. Baltimore: Williams & Wilkins, 1939.

——, *Manual for the Wechsler Intelligence Scale for Children*. New York: Psychological Corporation, 1949.

——, *Manual for the Wechsler Adult Intelligence Scale*. New York: Psychological Corporation, 1955.

——, *The Measurement and Appraisal of Adult Intelligence*. (4th ed.) Baltimore: Williams & Wilkins, 1958.

——, *Manual for Wechsler Preschool and Primary Scale of Intelligence*, New York: Psychological Corporation, 1967.

Yalowitz, J. M., and Renate G. Armstrong, "Validity of Short Forms of the Wechsler Intelligence Scale for Children (WISC)," *Journal of Clinical Psychology* 11 (1955), 275‒277.

Yudin, Lee, "An Abbreviated Form of the WISC for Use with Emotionally Disturbed Children," *Journal of Consulting Psychology* 30 (1966), 272‒275.

Yule, W., et al., "The WPPSI: An Empirical Evaluation With a British Sample," *British Journal of Educational Psychology* 39 (1969), 1‒13.

Zytowski, D. G., and J. Hudson, "The Validity of Split-Half Abbreviations of the WAIS," *Journal of Clinical Psychology* 21 (1965), 290‒294.

Tests for Special Purposes

There are circumstances under which it would be inappropriate to use scales such as those described in Chapters 5 and 6 as measures of general mental ability. A superficial knowledge of the procedures used in administering those instruments leads one to realize that the validity of the tests depends upon the examinee's being free of severe physical handicaps. Inspection of the content of those scales makes it apparent that in order for the subject to respond successfully to many of the items he must have in his background those experiences that will enable him to answer the questions or solve the problems. Thus for some physically handicapped individuals and for people who have not had the relevant experiences, scales like the Stanford-Binet and Wechsler are of limited value.

The use of the word intelligence to describe what was being measured by the early tests was unfortunate in that some people came to believe that the tests gave a pure measure of an innate capacity. The scores also came to be interpreted as indices of a person's potential, and as such, were used to identify people who were especially "gifted" and should be given special encouragement. Similarly, the "less talented" could be given special training commensurate with their limited potential. It was believed that IQ scores represented a measure of an amount of ability, and on this basis it was said that a person *was* an idiot, or that a person *was* a genius. Consequently, the scores were believed to represent an innate quality within the individual, and this attitude resulted in children and adults being denied opportunities to improve their intellectual and economic status, for it was assumed that they did not have the inborn potential to benefit from training. That this was an unfortunate use of the scores is rather apparent.

The question as to whether tests of general mental ability measure an innate capacity appeared to have been resolved when the heat from the nature versus nurture controversy cooled many years ago. However, the issue reappeared with the publication of Jensen's (1969) controversial paper. During the earlier period, a considerable amount of debate and research was generated by such questions as: "Is intelligence the result of hereditary factors or does it arise as a consequence of experience in the environment?" and "Is the IQ constant, or does it change with age and circumstances?" The latter question obviously refers to a test score; the former (though not so obviously) also does because intelligence is usually measured by tests. The generally accepted answer to these questions is that behavior which we consider to be intelligent is the result of an interaction between heredity and environment; that intelligence test scores are determined to a large extent by the cultural milieu in which a person is reared and lives, and as a consequence the scores are subject to change as circumstances and the functions measured by the test change.

The resolution of this problem did not adequately filter through to all the levels at which psychological tests were being used. Many psychologists, guidance counselors, teachers, and personnel workers continued to use mental ability tests as though they were valid estimates of the level of general intellectual functioning of everyone regardless of the conditions under which the examinee might have been reared. The consistently low scores of Negroes, Mexican-Americans, and children from the lower socioeconomic classes continued to be regarded as signs of inborn defects.

A consequence of the belief that intelligence tests measured innate capacity became apparent as school integration brought large numbers of "culturally disadvantaged" into previously all white and middle-class schools. The majority of these students scored below expected levels on the tests administered by the schools. They also did poorly in their school work. Since it was frequently believed that the tests measured innate capacity, teachers felt that the students were doing as well as they could "considering their ability." Therefore they were expected to do little. In some instances no effort was made to institute remedial procedures for such students, because it was assumed that people who "score like that" could not benefit from such instruction. Thus many children who could most benefit from remedial instruction have been denied it because of their "lack of ability."

Current concern for the rights of minorities has made the inadequacies of psychological tests fairly common knowledge among some individuals working to assure those rights. Educators and employers have become increasingly wary of the practice of using psychological tests for selection and classification decisions. Unfortunately there has been some tendency to eliminate tests rather than to demand more professional use of the tests (Gilbert, 1966; Loreton, 1965). Tests, properly used, could be a great aid in assuring that every child is given equal opportunity regardless of his racial or ethnic heritage, for as Gardner (1961, pp. 48–49) asserted: "The tests couldn't see whether the youngster was in rags or in tweeds, and they couldn't hear the accents of the slum. The tests revealed intellectual gifts at every level of the population."

CULTURE-FAIR TESTS

A variety of attempts to overcome the effect of cultural bias have been made over the years. Some early workers hoped to be able to develop "culture-free" tests (previously discussed on page 93) which would enable them to make cross-cultural comparisons of mental ability; others hoped to develop tests which would enable them to study innate ability. The researchers usually attempted to eliminate items which were culturally specific or those test requirements which would penalize members of one or another culture.

Language, speed, literacy, and verbal test content are among the factors known to be affected by culture. As a consequence, tests have been developed which virtually eliminate the need for language in any form. In many of these instruments, however, the examinee must be able to recognize such things as fountain pens, globes, irons, and chickens, which are obviously not items prevalent in all cultures. The search for tests which are entirely free of cultural influence has been virtually abandoned because we have come to recognize that heredity and environment interact at all stages of development to produce that behavior which a culture calls intelligent. In other words, intelligence is culturally defined. This being the case, it is unlikely that a practical psychological test can be developed which is equally "fair" in all cultures. Of immediate practical concern in the United States is the fact that tests developed as measures of general ability for our culture seem to be "unfair" to subcultures and minority groups within our culture.

Two frequently heard criticisms of many tests are: (1) they place too much stress on language and (2) they show a middle and upper-class bias in their content. As a consequence, individuals attempting to construct culture-fair tests have tried to minimize the need for language and/or have attempted to present item content which emphasizes presumably noncultural type problems such as abstract pictorial analogies, or they have used as content various problems and situations familiar to all groups for whom the tests were intended (Davis and Eels, 1953). The scales reported in this section are examples of scales considered culture-fair by their authors.

THE CULTURE-FAIR INTELLIGENCE TEST

This is a paper-and-pencil test developed by Cattell and Cattell (1959) and published by the Institute for Personality and Ability Testing (IPAT). The test is available for three levels: Scale 1, for children 4 to 8 years of age and mentally retarded adults; Scale 2, for ages 8 to 14; and Scale 3, for high-school age students and adults. Parallel forms are available for each level.

The purpose of the test is to provide a measure of ability which separates the evaluation of natural intelligence from that contaminated and obscured by education. The authors believe the test can be used for all the purposes to which other intelligence tests are being applied (Cattell and Cattell, 1959).

With the exception of Scale 1, which contains some verbal comprehension material, the Scales contain four tests composed of nonverbal, figural, and geometric designs (Fig. 7-1).

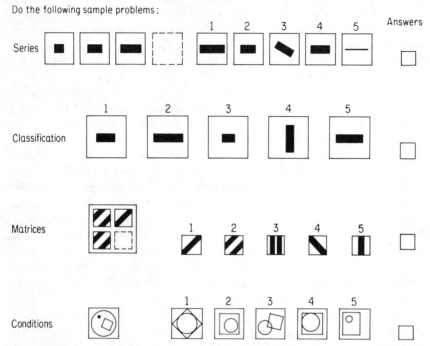

Fig. 7-1. Sample test items for the Culture Fair Intelligence Test. [Reproduced with permission of Institute for Personality and Ability Testing (IPAT). Copyright 1949, 1957. All rights reserved.]

The Series test requires the subject to select from the response alternatives the drawing which will complete the series presented in the stem. On the Classification test, the subject must select the item in each row which does not belong. The Matrices test requires the subject to mark the drawing which completes the pattern. On the Conditions test the subject selects from the response alternatives the drawing into which he could place a dot which would fulfill the conditions given in the sample design.

Reliability coefficients from a number of studies are reported in the handbook (Cattell and Cattell, 1959). Internal consistency estimates for the total test range from .51 (Kuder-Richardson Formula 21, Scale 3, Form A) to .97 (Split-half, Scale 2). Most of the reported coefficients are .70 and below. Reported retest coefficients are in the .80's. Alternate-forms reliability coefficients range from .55 (Scale 3) to .72 (Scale 2).

Cattell prefers to describe the validity of the test in terms of its factorial validity and indicates a high "saturation" on Spearman's g factor. Correlations between the *Culture-Fair Intelligence Tests* and a variety of other tests range between .34 and .85. Unfortunately, evidence for the concurrent and predictive validity of the test for nontest criteria is scant. The few correlations reported in the manual range from .23 to .46 for studies in which school grades were used as criteria.

The handbook reports IQ scores of two types: (1) a "classical" IQ which has a mean of 100 and a standard deviation of 24, and (2) a "standard score" IQ which has a mean of 100 and a standard deviation of 16. In addition, percentile norms are provided. In using these scores it is important that the test interpreter know which IQ has been reported. Since the standard deviation of 16 makes the IQ more comparable to other tests yielding IQ scores, the standard score IQ is the preferred IQ score.

Scale 1 requires individual administration for some of the tests; the others may be administered individually or in groups. The tests are timed, but some norms are available for untimed versions. Verbal instructions are required, but the authors apparently believe that giving the instructions in another language or in pantomime will not change the difficulty of the test.

Most examiners require that a test be demonstrably related to nontest criteria. The lack of evidence of this type of validity for this test seriously limits its usefulness. On the other hand, the test has been administered in several countries other than the United States and the results have been essentially the same in cultures similar to ours. In very dissimilar cultures, however, the results are significantly different from those obtained with the standardization sample. The reported reliability coefficients are lower than those usually demanded for the purpose of making decisions about individuals.

PROGRESSIVE MATRICES TEST

This nonverbal test was developed in Great Britain by Raven and is published by H. K. Lewis and Co., Ltd. It is distributed in the United States by The Psychological Corporation. The test is available for several levels. The 1938 form consisted of sets A, B, C, D, E and was considered suitable for persons ranging in age from 3 to adult. A special colored version of Sets A and B was prepared for children 3 to 8 years of age. The 1947 form provided a set Ab which was intended as a transitional set of problems which were placed between Sets A and B to provide a wider dispersion of scores for children 5 to 11. The Advanced Set II was prepared for adolescents and adults of above-average intelligence (Raven, 1965).

The *Progressive Matrices Test* is composed of 60 matrices or designs from each of which a part has been removed. The 60 designs are arranged into five sets of 12 matrices per set. The items are arranged throughout the sets in order of increasing difficulty. The subject is required to select the design from the response alternatives which will provide the missing part. Sets A, Ab, and B in the

1947 form are in color. Items for the whole series range in difficulty from very simple to extremely complex.

Reliability coefficients from a large number of studies and a variety of populations are reported by Burke (1958). Test-retest coefficients for normal late adolescents and adults range from .79 to .93. Retest coefficients for normal children are somewhat lower, ranging from .71 to .88. Reported split-half and Kuder-Richardson Formula 20 coefficients vary within about the same limits as the retest coefficients. Reliability coefficients for non-English-speaking subjects are of about the same magnitude as those reported for English-speaking examinees.

Evidence for the validity of the Progressive Matrices has been demonstrated in the usual ways. Correlations between the Progressive Matrices and the Stanford-Binet vary from .41 to .86. Similar results are found when the test is correlated with the Wechsler scales. Most of the correlations are in the .60's and .70's. Correlations with verbal group tests range from .27 to .67, most correlations being in the .40's. Correlations with performance or nonverbal tests vary from .22 to .80, with most correlations between .30 and .58. A limited amount of nontest evidence (primarily academic criteria) for the validity of the test is available. The correlations are primarily in the .20's and .30's (Burke, 1958).

No adequate American norms are available for the Progressive Matrices. Raven provides percentile norms based on samples of British children, adult civilians, and adults in military service during World War II.

The test may be administered individually or in groups. It is available in booklet form, or as a form board in which the subject actually fits the proper piece into place. The directions are simple with a limited need for verbal understanding. It is possible to eliminate the verbal element by using pantomime. The Progressive Matrices may also be administered either as a timed or untimed test.

The manual for this test is quite inadequate. It gives very little information on reliability and validity. The flexibility which the examiner has with regard to the administration of the test and the absence of sufficient evidence indicating that the results of the various procedures are comparable make it difficult to evaluate the effectiveness of the test. The *Progressive Matrices Test* is less dependent on education than most tests, and therefore it is useful for identifying examinees who have good ability but who have not developed verbal skills.

GOODENOUGH-HARRIS DRAWING TEST

This test is an extension and revision of the *Goodenough Drawing Test* (1926) prepared by Harris (1963) and published by Harcourt Brace Jovanovich. The test may be used with children 5–15 years of age.

The test is designed to evaluate a child's intelligence by means of his drawings of a man and a woman. It may be used for such purposes as a screening test, a rapid, usually nonthreatening means of gaining an impression of a child's general ability level, and as a means of estimating the mental ability of children for whom the usual verbal tests of ability are inappropriate.

The test booklets provide three spaces for the child to produce his drawings —one for the drawing of a man, one for the drawing of a woman, and one for a "self" drawing. Beside each space 73 blanks are provided for scoring purposes. In administering the test the child is asked to draw the very best picture he can of a man, a woman, and himself. He is cautioned to make a whole person, not simply a head-and-shoulders view. There is no time limit for the test, but according to Harris (1963), young children rarely take more than ten to fifteen minutes. The test may be administered either as a group test or as an individual test. Harris recommends a short rest period between the second and third drawing for children under age 8 or 9. He also most emphatically states that the examiner is to avoid making any suggestions except to remind the child to draw a whole person.

Over the years the Draw-A-Man has been subjected to a considerable amount of research. Most of the data collected are applicable to the Harris revision (at least on the man scale). Interscorer reliability coefficients around the .90's have been reported by Dunn (1967), Harris (1963), and McCarthy (1944). Intrascorer reliability estimates are of the same magnitude (Dunn, 1967; McCarthy, 1944). A number of studies have reported retest reliability coefficients ranging from .94 for a one-day interval between testings (Goodenough, 1926), to .65 for a three-year interval between testings (Vane and Kessler, 1964). Most of the retest coefficients are in the .60's and .70's (Brill, 1935; McCarthy, 1944; McCurdy, 1947). Split-half coefficients of .77 and .89 were reported by Goodenough (1926) and McCarthy (1944).

The validity of the Draw-A-Man has been demonstrated primarily by correlating the Draw-A-Man scores with scores on other tests. Correlations with the Stanford-Binet range from .43 (Estes et al., 1961) to .74 (Goodenough, 1926). Correlations with other tests are of about the same range and magnitude; Estes et al. (1961) found a correlation of .43 with the WISC; Coleman, Iscoe, and Brodsky (1959) reported correlations ranging from .51 to .72 between the Draw-A-Man and the Total Score on the *California Test of Mental Maturity*.

The scoring of this test is not based on the subject's artistic skill but upon the presence of essential details and their relationship to each other. Credit is given for the inclusion of such things as individual body parts, clothing details, proportion and perspective. Scorable items were selected on the basis of age differentiation, relation to the total score on the test, and the relation to scores on group intelligence tests. There are 73 scorable items on the Man Scale and 71 scorable items on the Woman Scale.

Norms for the Man-and-Woman Scales were established on samples of 300 children at each age level from 5 to 15 years. They were selected to be representative of the population of the United States with regard to father's occupation and geographic region. The manual provides standard-score norms which have a mean of 100 and a standard deviation of 15. There are also percentile equivalents for the standard scores (Harris, 1963).

PERFORMANCE TESTS

A performance test is one in which the use of language is restricted to instructions or is not required. When the instructions are given in pantomime, the subject does not have to respond verbally at all; he is just required to make an overt motor response.

Performance tests represented one of the early attempts to overcome the difficulties associated with testing people who, for a multitude of reasons, could not be expected to perform adequately on traditional psychological tests. Early tests (or forms of them) which have been incorporated into scales that are currently in use include the Seguin Form Board (included in Fig. 7-4), developed by Seguin (1866) for use with mentally retarded children; the Healy-Fernald test series (included in Fig. 7-4), developed primarily for use with juvenile delinquents (Healy and Fernald, 1911); and tests developed by Knox (1914) for testing immigrants. Originally, performance scales were considered substitutes for the Stanford-Binet, but it is currently believed that they can best be used as supplements to scales such as the Binet and other highly verbal scales. Correlations between these performance tests and verbal tests generally are in the .50's.

THE LEITER INTERNATIONAL PERFORMANCE SCALE

The *Leiter International Performance Scale*, 1948 revision, and the *Arthur Adaptation, Leiter International Performance Scale* (1959) are published by C. H. Stoelting Company. The tests are graded in difficulty beginning at age 2 and continuing through age 18. The Arthur Adaptation is suitable for ages 2 through 12.

The scale is designed to be a culture-free, nonverbal scale for measuring general mental ability. The Leiter has been used with different ethnic groups in Hawaii, with African groups, and with other nationalities.

The test materials consist of a response frame (Fig. 7-2) to which the examiner attaches a card which contains pictures. The subject is presented with a set of blocks, which also have pictures on them and which the subject must place in the correct stalls to get credit for the tests. The item shown in Fig. 7-2 is an Analogous Designs Test from the 9-year level. The test is divided into three trays: Tray 1 for years 2 to 7, Tray 2 for years 8 to 12, and Tray 3 for years 14 to 18. The items call for the subject to match forms, to match figures or colors, to complete block designs, to classify objects, to complete number series and to solve similarities. The test yields an MA and a ratio IQ.

Reliability studies of the Leiter (for various populations) have yielded relia-

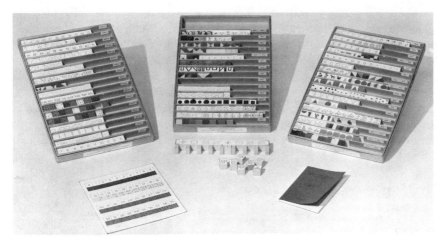

Fig. 7-2. Analogous Designs Test of The Leiter Scale. (Courtesy of C. H. Stoelting Company.)

bility coefficients that are generally in the .90's (Arnold, 1951; Leiter, 1959; Sharp, 1958). The coefficients are predominantly internal consistency estimates. Sharp's study, however, yielded a retest coefficient of .91.

Evidence for the validity of the scale is primarily in the form of correlations with other measures of mental ability, usually the Stanford-Binet. These correlation coefficients, derived from a variety of populations, range from .56 ("slow learners," Sharp, 1957) to .94 ("feeble-minded," Arnold, 1951). Most of the coefficients are in the .60's and .70's (Arnold, 1951; Bessent, 1950; Beverly and Bensberg, 1952; Bensberg and Sloan, 1957; Gallagher, Benoit and Boyd, 1956). Sharp (1957), from a sample of "slow learners," reports the following correlations with the WISC: Verbal IQ, .78; Performance IQ, .80 and Total IQ, .83. Alper (1958) found somewhat lower correlations derived from a group of "mental defectives": Verbal IQ, .40; Performance IQ, .79; and Total IQ, .77.

Descriptions of the groups which comprised the standardization samples for the various revisions of the Leiter Performance Scale are very inadequate. Neither the *Examiners Manual* (Leiter, 1969a) nor the *General Instructions* (Leiter, 1969b), nor the basic literature on the test (Leiter, 1950, Leiter, 1959) provide sufficient information. Leiter (1949) has reported data from several studies (theses and dissertations primarily) which show average IQs and MAs for age levels 5–18.

Administration of the scale proceeds, much as the Stanford-Binet does, by finding a basal year at which all tests are passed and continuing until all tests at two consecutive year levels are failed. The scale is administered individually, with no time limit, and may be administered almost completely without instructions, verbal or pantomimed. The examiner may take the subject's hand and lead him through the response to show him what to do. The score is expressed as months of Mental Age, but because [according to Leiter, (1969b)] the test is scaled about six months too difficult, the ratio IQs that are derived using the obtained MAs must be corrected by adding five IQ points. This necessitates an adjustment in MA which is accomplished through the use of tables provided in the manual.

The fact that the Leiter can be administered without the use of language may make it quite useful in some settings, provided the user is very cautious in the interpretation of the scores. The lack of adequate norms and the apparent misplacement of some tests are factors that limit the general usefulness of the scale.

THE POINT SCALE OF PERFORMANCE TESTS

The *Point Scale of Performance Tests*, devised by Arthur (1930, 1947), is available in two forms. Form I from C. H. Stoelting Company, and Form II from The Psychological Corporation. The tests are intended to be used with persons from five years of age to adulthood.

The purpose of the scale is to provide a means of measuring the ability of deaf children, children suffering from reading handicaps, and non-English-speaking children. The Revised Form II was specifically designed to serve as an alternate for Form I.

The Arthur Point Scale, Form I is a restandardization of eight tests from the Pintner-Paterson scale (described in Chapter 1) plus the Kohs Block Design (Kohs, 1923) and Porteus Maze Tests (Porteus, 1950, 1959). The tests from the Pintner-Paterson are as follows:

1. Knox Cube
2. Seguin Form Board
3. Two-Figure Form Board
4. Casuist Form Board
5. Manikin
6. Feature Profile Test
7. Mare and Foal
8. Healy Picture Completion I

The *Kohs Block Design Test* was developed as a supplement to, or substitute for, the Stanford-Binet. This test and revisions of it have been used by psychologists for diagnostic purposes in a variety of settings. The test utilizes a set of multicolored cubes, each identically colored. A set of cards, each of which bears a colored design, is presented to the subject one at a time. The subject must reproduce the design by assembling the blocks appropriately. The number of blocks required varies with the complexity of the design. It is a timed test and the score depends on both time and correctness of performance. The test requires little or no language.

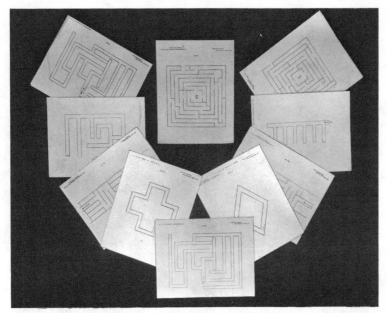

Fig. 7-3. Porteus Maze Test. (Courtesy of C. H. Stoelting Company.)

The *Porteus Maze Test* (Fig. 7-3) is composed of a series of line mazes which increase in difficulty. Each maze is printed on a separate sheet of paper. The subject is required to trace with a pencil the shortest path from the entrance to the exit of the maze without lifting the pencil from the paper. When the subject makes an error he is stopped and the copy of the test is immediately removed. The subject is then given another chance on the same maze. The number of trials given depends upon the level of difficulty of the maze. Scoring is based on the level of difficulty successfully reached and the number of errors made.

The Revised Form II (Arthur, 1947), shown in Fig. 7-4, consists of only five tests, Knox Cube Test, Seguin Form Board Test, Porteus Maze Test, Healy Picture Completion II, and a new test, the Stencil Design Test I. This new test (Fig. 7-5) requires the subject to reproduce a series of designs by superimposing cut-out stencils on a solid card. The designs may have from two to six colors and they increase in complexity. This test replaced the Kohs Block Design Test which, according to Arthur, was too subject to practice effect.

The reliability and validity data reported in the manuals for both forms are very meager. In the Revised Form II manual, for example, the only reliability data presented are the median score differences between Form I and Form II. Evidence for the validity of the Revised Form II is reported in terms of differences between Stanford-Binet IQ scores and Arthur IQ scores. Other investigators have reported correlations in the .70's between the Point Scale and the Stanford-Binet (Cohen and Collier, 1952; Tate, 1952; Hamilton, 1949; Wallin,

Fig. 7-4. Arthur Point Scale of Performance Tests. (Courtesy of The Psychological Corporation.)

1946). Cohen and Collier (1952) reported coefficients of .77, .81, and .80 between the Verbal, Performance, and Total IQs on the WISC and scores on the Arthur. A correlation of .80 was found between the Arthur and the *Leiter International Performance Scale* (Tate, 1952).

The standardization sample for Form I is described as " ... about 1,100 public school children of a good middle-class 'American' district" (Arthur, 1943, pp. 2-3). The norms for Form II are based on the scores of " ... 968 pupils from the same middle-class 'American' district used in standardizing Form I ... " (Arthur, 1947, p. 21). Mental age norms are provided for the Total Point Score. Scores are generally reported in terms of mental age or ratio IQ.

Instructions for administering the scale are reasonably clear. Some of the tests are timed. Raw scores for each test are converted into a point value, and these point values are added to obtain a Total Point Score, which is then converted to a mental age and ratio IQ.

The manuals for both forms of the test are less than adequate by today's standards. The standardization is less than satisfactory, and evidence of the validity of the tests for the purposes and populations described above is meager.

Fig. 7-5. Stencil Design Test. (Courtesy of The Psychological Corporation.)

THE GESELL DEVELOPMENTAL SCHEDULES

The *Gesell Developmental Schedules* are a product of the work of Arnold Gesell and his associates at the Yale Clinic of Child Development and are available through The Psychological Corporation. The Gesell provides tests at two levels: the Infant Schedule which is intended for use with children between the ages of four weeks and fifty-six weeks; and the Preschool Schedule, which is used with children from fifteen months to six years.

The Schedules were developed to provide the clinician with a systematic method of observation for the purpose of the developmental diagnosis of infant behavior. According to Gesell and Amatruda (1947), the Schedules may be useful in determining patterns of development in normal, subnormal and superior children. They also may be useful in the diagnosis of developmental deviations and neurological impairment. In addition, they provide information concerning emotional traits and the organization of personality.

At each age level the Schedules are intended to assess the level of the child's development in four areas:

    1. *Motor behavior.* How well the child controls gross body movements and finer motor coordination. This is measured by analysis of such

behavior as reaching and grasping, manipulation of objects, posture, head balance, standing, creeping, skipping, and throwing.

2. *Adaptive behavior.* How well the child solves problems, has gained eye-hand coordination in obtaining objects, removing obstacles. This area is really a kind of analysis of the child's ability to deal with his environment. Examples include observation of the child's reaction to such things as cubes, a dangling ring, ringing bell, simple form boards, counting, addition and subtraction.

3. *Language behavior.* How well the child is able to communicate. The observations include all forms of communication including gestures, postures, vocalizations, speech, obeying directions and color naming.

4. *Personal-social behavior.* How well the child has learned to react to social training. It involves studying feeding, toilet training, knowledge of numbers, the child's ability to dress himself, cooperative play, ability to differentiate A.M. from P.M.

Reliability and validity data of the usual sort were not developed for the Schedules. For the most part, the items on the schedules are observations and cannot be considered tests in the usual sense. It has been shown, however, that examiner reliability of .95 can be obtained when the examiners have had adequate training and experience with the scales. The population sample from which the behavioral norms were derived was small and restricted to middle-class children (Freeman, 1962).

The procedures used for examining a child are described in the manuals for each level (Gesell and Amatruda, 1947; Gesell et al., 1940). The techniques described for the Infant Schedule are primarily suggestions on how to elicit the desired response. In scoring the developmental schedules the child is given a+ for emitting age-typical response, a++ for exhibiting more mature responses, and a - for not making responses typical for his age. The child's maturity level is "at that point where the aggregate of + signs changes to an aggregate of - signs" (Gesell and Amatruda, 1947). The procedures for administering, scoring, and interpreting the scales are not so well standardized as those used for most psychological tests. Despite the limitations described above, in the hands of an experienced examiner the scales are valuable for appraising an infant's developmental level at the time of the examination.

THE CATTELL INFANT INTELLIGENCE SCALE.

The *Cattell Infant Intelligence Scale* was constructed by Cattell (1940) and is available through the Psychological Corporation. The scale extends from two months to thirty months.

Cattell's purpose in developing the scale was to provide a well-standardized, objective procedure for measuring the intelligence of infants. The scale was constructed to be a downward extension of the Stanford-Binet.

The scale is arranged so that there are five test items at each month through twelve months, then at two-month intervals to thirty months. The items are of the type frequently found in infant tests, but Cattell tried to reduce the subjectivity of procedures found in other scales and to reduce the influence of items highly influenced by home training. She also tried to minimize the number of items that measure primarily motor control. At the lower age levels the items are composed of such tasks as attending to a voice, following a dangling ring or person with the eyes, and head lifting. At older age levels the scale requires more complex behavior, such as manipulating blocks, spoons and cups, pegboards, and form boards. There is also an increasing use of verbal functions and oral instructions. At the upper age levels Binet items are mingled with other items in the scale. If a child passes an item at the thirty-month level, the examiner proceeds to the Stanford-Binet, beginning at Year-Level III. Scores are expressed in terms of MAs and IQs.

Reliability was determined by use of the split-halves technique. The reported reliability coefficients vary from .56 at the three-month level to .90 at the 18-month level. Most of the coefficients are in the .80's (Cattell, 1940). Cattell attributes the relatively low reliability coefficients to the heterogeneity of the item content.

Validity of the scale is expressed in terms of the increase in percent passing each item at successive age levels and in terms of correlations with scores on the Stanford-Binet administered at 36 months of age. The validity coefficients range from .10 (3-month level of Cattell Scale) to .83 (30-month level of the Cattell Scale). Tests administered below nine months of age are of little value in predicting later measured status. "The standardization is based on 1346 examinations made on 274 children at the ages of three, six, nine, twelve, eighteen, twenty-four, thirty and thirty-six months" (Cattell, 1940, p. 25). The children represented a rather restricted sample from the "lower middle classes" (Cattell, 1940, p. 13).

In administering infant tests, examiner characteristics are extremely important, so Cattell, in her general instructions, emphasizes the personal and training prerequisites for an adequate examiner. The instructions for administering the scale are quite clear, but much depends upon the examiner's being an alert observer. The tests are untimed, but Cattell recommends that the examiner work as rapidly as is compatible with the maintenence of an unhurried atmosphere. For the small baby the examination takes from 20 to 30 minutes, and for the older child about 30 minutes. In scoring, each item passed at the 2- to 12-month age level is given a credit of .2 months; from 14 to 24 months each item passed is worth .4 months credit, and from 27 to 30 months each passed item is given a credit of .6 months of Mental Age.

The scale is considered by some psychologists to be one of the most satisfactory scales for testing infants. Several factors should be noted for the user, however: the very restricted normative sample, the relatively low reliabilities, and the fact that all the children in the standardization sample were not tested with the same items. The scale that finally emerged from the project was different from the scale which was used at the beginning.

THE BAYLEY SCALES OF INFANT DEVELOPMENT

These scales are the culmination of forty years of work by Bayley (1969). They are intended to be used with children from 2 through 30 months of age and are available through The Psychological Corporation.

The scales are designed to yield a three-part evaluation of a child's developmental status during the first 2 $\frac{1}{2}$ years of life. It is believed that the parts complement each other, yet each makes a unique contribution to the clinical evaluation of the child.

According to Bayley, "The *primary* value of the development indexes is that they provide the basis for establishing a child's current status, and thus the extent of any deviation from normal expectancy." (Bayley, 1969, p. 4)

Functions of the Bayley Scale

1. The Mental Scale is designed to assess sensory-perceptual acuities, discriminations, and the ability to respond to these; the early acquisition of "object constancy" and memory, learning and problem-solving ability; vocalizations and early evidence of the ability to form generalizations and classifications, which is the basis of abstract thinking. Results of the administrations of the Mental Scale are expressed as a standard score, the MDI, or Mental Development Index.
2. The Motor Scale is designed to provide a measure of the degree of control of the body, coordination of the large muscles and finer manipulatory skills of the hands and fingers. As the Motor Scale is specifically directed toward behavior reflecting motor coordination and skills, it is not concerned with functions that are commonly thought of as "mental" or "intelligent" in nature. Results of the administration of the Motor Scale are expressed as a standard score, the PDI, or Psychomotor Development Index.
3. The Infant Behavior Record is completed after the Mental and Motor Scales have been administered. The IBR helps the clinician assess the nature of the child's social and objective orientations toward his environment as expressed in attitudes, interests, emotions, energy, activity, and tendencies to approach or withdraw from stimulation. (Bayley, 1969, pp. 3–4)

The items on the Mental Scale are the familiar type—responding to a bell, following a ring with the eyes, vocalizations, picking up cubes, discriminating strangers, following oral instructions, picture vocabulary, and paper folding.

The Motor Scale items involve such actions as lifting the head, efforts to sit, rolling over, standing, throwing a ball, jumping, hopping, and walking down steps. The Infant Behavior Record is composed of rating scales descriptive of behaviors of children up to 30 months of age. Tables are provided for each age level which show the percent of the standardization group assigned a given rating on a nine-point scale. Descriptions of behavior characteristic of each age group are also provided.

Bayley recognizes that later "mental" functions are dependent in part upon the development of motor skills, since they influence the quality of the child's interaction with his environment. She considers the .50 to .60 correlations between the Motor and Mental Scales, as well as the clinical observation that poor motor coordination may be an early indicator of neural damage, as evidence of the relationship between early motor skills and later mental development.

Split-half reliability coefficients for the Mental Scale range from .81 to .93, with a median value of .88. Split-half coefficients for the Motor Scale range from .68 to .92, with a median of .84. Bayley attributes the lower coefficients for the Motor Scale to the fact that it has about half as many items as the Mental Scale (Bayley, 1969).

Evidence for the validity of the tests is limited, the primary evidence being an increase in performance with an increase in age. Bayley also reports correlations between the MDI's of the BSID and Stanford-Binet IQs for groups of children 24, 27, or 30 months of age. The correlations range between .47 for the thirty-month group to .57 for the total group.

The scales were standardized on a sample of 1,262 children selected to reflect the proportion of children from 2 through 30 months of age in various subgroups (sex, race, socioeconomic status, rural-urban residence, geographic region) as described in the 1960 United States Census (Bayley, 1969). This painstaking effort to select a representative sample of this population makes the Bayley standardization population superior to that of any other infant scale. The standardization sample for the Infant Behavior Record is only a part of the sample used to standardize the Mental and Motor Scales. About half the sample of infants 15 months and below did not get IBR's. Bayley urges caution in interpreting ratings at these younger levels.

Raw scores are converted to normalized standard scores having a mean of 100 and a standard deviation of 16. The score derived from the administration of the Mental Scale is called the *Mental Development Index* (MDI). The score derived from the administration of the Motor Scale is called the *Psychomotor Development Index* (PDI). It is also possible to find age equivalents for each scale. Ratings on the IBR for a subject are compared to the frequency with which such ratings were assigned to the children in the standardization group who are the same age as the subject.

The scale manual contains many helpful suggestions for the examiner which will aid his efforts to get a reliable estimate of the developmental status of the child. This is especially true with regard to the need for the examiner to establish rapport with the child and the need to continuously evaluate the relationship with the child.

TESTS AND SCALES FOR THE HANDICAPPED

Psychologists, teachers, and counselors who work with the blind, the deaf, and the physically handicapped have long been aware of the limitations of the

Binet and Wechsler scales for measuring the intellectual functioning of such subjects. These limitations become acute when the handicap limits the development of language, since both instruments require that the examinee be able to understand language and respond verbally. The concern of individuals who work with the handicapped has led to continuing efforts to develop tests that will provide more adequate estimates of the general mental ability of these individuals.

The usual problems that confront the test constructor are aggravated when he attempts to develop a test for the handicapped. How does one get a representative sample of the blind, deaf, or orthopedically handicapped? What is the effect of age at the onset of the handicap on the scores? How can it be shown that his test of mental ability for the handicapped measures constructs similar to those measured by tests for normal subjects? Such problems may partially be responsible for the limited development of tests for the handicapped.

Some of the tests presented in this section were selected because they fulfill an urgent need, and because they have been fairly well constructed; others must be considered experimental. The "experimental" tests are presented here in an attempt to bring them to the attention of individuals who have need for such tests.

THE PICTORIAL TEST OF INTELLIGENCE

The *Pictorial Test of Intelligence* was developed by French (1964) and is available through Houghton Mifflin Company. The test is intended for use with children from three to eight years of age.

In testing the orthopedically handicapped it is quite frequently found that it is possible for the subjects to receive auditory and visual test stimuli, but because of severe motor disturbances these subjects are not able to respond orally, or in writing, or perhaps not even by pointing. The *Pictorial Test of Intelligence* makes it possible to test some of these youngsters. The scale was designed to be used in assessing the general intellectual ability of children, *normal* and *handicapped*, between the ages of 3 and 8. The author's purpose in developing the test was to provide an objective, reliable estimate of the young child's ability through a testing procedure that would not require manipulative or speaking responses, and which would be standardized on a representative sample of the three- to eight-year-old population of the United States.

The scale consists of 137 large Response cards and 54 Stimulus cards (Fig. 7-6). Each Response card contains four line drawings from which the subject must choose the correct response. Three of the six subtests require the use of a series of Stimulus cards. These cards are three inches square with a line-drawing centered on each card. On two of the subtests that require the card the child matches the drawing on the Stimulus card with the correct drawing on the Response card. The Response cards are eleven inches square with the line drawings centered along each of the outer edges of the card. The subject can indicate

Fig. 7-6. Materials for the Pictorial Test of Intelligence.

his response choice *by pointing or simply by looking* at the chosen answer. The arrangement of the drawings on the Response cards makes it possible for the examiner to observe the subject's eye movements.

The scale is composed of six subtests described below.

1. *Picture Vocabulary.* This test measures verbal comprehension. It requires the child to recall previously acquired verbal meanings. The subject must respond to a word spoken by the examiner by selecting the drawing on the Response card which best represents a meaning of the stimulus word. Twenty-nine Response cards and 32 words are used in the Picture Vocabulary subtest.
2. *Form Discrimination.* This subtest measures the child's ability to match forms and to differentiate between shapes. The subject must match a drawing on the Stimulus card with one of four on the Response card. Twenty-four Response cards and 27 Stimulus cards are used in the subtest.
3. *Information and Comprehension.* This is a test of knowledge and general understanding which also reflects the subject's verbal comprehension. The responses reflect the subject's alertness to his environment and to available educational cultural opportunities. Twenty-four Response cards are used to obtain 29 answers.
4. *Similarities.* The subject is shown a card on which three of the drawings have common elements; the fourth is different. The subject must indicate which drawing does not belong. The responses to these items reveal the subject's ability to generalize. There are 22 items in the subtest.
5. *Size and Number.* This subtest attempts to measure the ability to retain perceptions of size, space and form relationships. The subject is permitted to view a design on a Stimulus card for five seconds.

> The card is then removed. The subject must then select the same design from a Response card.

Reliability estimates using Kuder-Richardson Formula No. 20 range from .87 for three-year-olds to .93 for six-year-olds. Most of the correlations are in the .90's. A special Short-Form for three and four-year-olds has reported K-R estimates of .86 and .88 respectively. Retest reliabilities range from .69 for a time lapse of 54–56 months to .96 for a time lapse of three to six weeks (French, 1964).

Data on a preliminary form of the PTI are presented in the scale manual as evidence for the predictive validity of the test. The groups from which the rank-order correlations were derived were extremely small. The time lapses were from three to five years for the various groups, and the criteria were achievement and ability-test scores. The reported correlations range between .68 and .82, with most being in the .70's. The manual also reports concurrent validity for first graders based on a comparison of scores on the PTI with the Stanford-Binet, the WISC, and the *Columbia Maturity Scale*. The correlations were found to be .72 with the Stanford-Binet, .65 with the WISC and .53 with the Columbia. Similarly, the correlations between the *subtests* of the PTI and the above-mentioned scales show a greater relationship between the PTI and the S-B than between the PTI and the other two scales.

The PTI was standardized on a sample of 1,830 children between the ages three through eight, with 260 to 341 subjects tested at each age level. The sample was selected to be representative of the U.S. population with regard to geographic region, community size, and occupational level. The final sample included about 16 percent nonwhite children as compared to approximately 11.4 percent in the estimates of the 1960 United States Census. The author does not consider this difference to be important because he considers the major control to be socioeconomic. The standardization sample contained 906 males and 924 females. The manual provides Deviation-IQ Norms, Mental-Age Norms, and Percentile Norms.

In administering the test the box which contains the test material is placed between the subject and the examiner. The Response cards are placed before the subject who may respond verbally, by pointing, or by a "looking response." The examiner records the subject's response by marking whether the child selects the Top, Left, Right, or Bottom figure on the Response card. The instructions are clear and easily understood. Testing time will usually run from 35 to 45 minutes.

The scale is a valuable addition to the instruments available to the clinician. It is especially valuable because of its potential usefulness in measuring the ability of the handicapped.

Other tests which have been used with the orthopedically handicapped include the previously described *Progressive Matrices Test*, the *Peabody Picture Vocabulary Test* and the *Columbia Mental Maturity Scale*.

TESTS FOR THE DEAF OR HARD OF HEARING

Since most of our general mental ability tests are highly verbal in nature, the deaf are usually handicapped with respect to these tests because of retarded language development. Some of the previously cited tests (The Pintner-Paterson Performance Scale and the Arthur Point Scale) were developed in part for the purpose of providing tests of general mental ability for the deaf. The norms for these tests were developed on normal children but, as Anastasi (1968) points out, in situations pertaining to the education of deaf children norms based on deaf children would be useful. Such norms are provided by the *Nebraska Test of Learning Aptitude* (Hiskey, 1966). Separate norms are provided for hearing children who are given scale. The subtests of the Hiskey scale are of the familiar types, such as paper folding, spatial reasoning, memory tests, and picture analogies. Reported reliability and validity coefficients indicate that the test has promise for use with the deaf.

TESTS FOR THE BLIND

In testing the blind it has been possible to administer orally special adaptations of verbal tests. The instruments most frequently adapted for the blind are the Stanford-Binet and Wechsler scales. The *Interim Hayes-Binet Scale* is composed of those items from Forms L and M of the Stanford-Binet which do not require vision. In addition, some subtests devised for an earlier Hayes-Binet are included in the scale. The scale is predominantly oral, but a few items require braille material. The reported reliability and validity coefficients are comparable to those found with tests for sighted persons.

Currently, considerable use is being made of the Wechsler scales for testing the blind. The major adaptation of the Wechslers consists of omitting the performance tests. On the average, blind subjects do as well as or better than sighted subjects when the Wechsler is used (Shurrager and Shurrager, 1964). The use of a strictly verbal test does not, however, tap all the ability of the blind subject. Furthermore, scores on the verbal measures are highly influenced by formal education. As a consequence, there have been efforts to develop mental ability tests of the performance type.

HAPTIC INTELLIGENCE SCALE FOR ADULT BLIND

This scale was developed by Shurrager and Shurrager (1964) and is available in limited numbers through Psychology Research. The test was designed to be used with blind adults, age 16 and older.

The instrument was developed for the purpose of providing a performance scale which would "measure abilities not adequately assessed either by verbal tests of intelligence or existing performance tests designed or adapted for the blind" and which would, when combined with a verbal test of intelligence, provide a comprehensive evaluation of the intelligence of blind persons (Shurrager and Shurrager, 1964, p. iii). A complete assessment would consist of the Verbal Scale of the Wechsler Adult Intelligence Scale and the Haptic Performance Scale. At this time the test must be considered an experimental instrument. It is reported at length here to show how it attempts to directly translate parts of the Wechsler Performance Scale to a performance scale for the blind and also to bring the test to the attention of a broader range of potential users.

The *Haptic Intelligence Scale for Adult Blind* is composed of six subtests, some of which are virtually direct translations of Wechsler items from a visual to a tactile mode. The subtests which comprise the Haptic are as follows:

1. *Digit Symbol.* The subject is required to match numbers (raised dots) with a series of geometric forms which have been embossed on plastic. Key columns, in which the forms with the numbers to be associated with each form are superimposed on the plate, are arranged so that the subject may explore the key with his nonpreferred hand and the test forms with his preferred hand. The subject's responses are given orally.
2. *Object Assembly.* This test requires the subject to assemble common objects which have been dissected into several pieces. The objects are three-dimensional. They are a block, a doll, a ball, and a hand.
3. *Block Design.* This test is composed of four 1½-inch blocks, the sides of which have varied texture (two smooth sides, two rough sides and two diagonally bisected into half rough and half smooth). The subject is required to arrange the blocks into a pattern identical to one which has been presented to him on a plate. The subject feels the design on the plate and then attempts to arrange the blocks to conform to the pattern.
4. *Object Completion.* Sixteen familiar objects, each of which has one important part missing, are presented to the subject. He must identify the missing part in each object.
5. *Pattern Board.* This test consists of a square board with twenty-five round holes arranged in rows of five. Pegs can be inserted into the holes to form patterns. A fixed peg in the center hole serves as a reference point. The subject is asked to examine a pattern with his fingers and then reproduce it after the pegs are withdrawn.
6. *Bead Arithmetic.* The test's apparatus consists of an abacus which contains five spokes, each with five large beads below a broad horizontal divider and two above it. The level of difficulty of the items varies from reading one-digit numbers entered by the tester to solving addition problems entered by the subject.

Reliability coefficients for the subtests range from .70 for Object Assembly to .81 for the Pattern Board subtest. Retest coefficients for the full scale are not reported in the manual because not all of the subjects in the total sample had taken the final form of the Bead Arithmetic Test on the first testing. However, the test-retest coefficient for the sum of the scale scores for five subtests (excluding Bead Arithmetic) was .91 for a sample of 124 subjects (Shurrager and Shurrager, 1964).

The only evidence presented in the manual for the validity of the Haptic is a table showing correlations between the Haptic and the WAIS Verbal. Most of them are in the .30's and .40's, the range being from .17 to .65, with the latter coefficient being found between the Verbal score for the WAIS and the total Haptic score.

The standardization sample, as the scale's authors point out, cannot be considered a representative sample of the blind population of the United States. The difficulties involved in attempting to obtain such a sample are described in the manual. The normative sample was composed of 700 subjects between the ages of 16 and 64 who had " . . . vision not exceeding 5/200 central visual acuity in the better eye with proper correction . . . " and no other sensory handicaps (Shurrager and Shurrager, 1964, p. 9). The subjects were divided into seven age groups: 16-17, 18-19, 20-24, 25-34, 35-44, 45-54, and 55-64, with 50 males and 50 females in each group. A proportional representation of whites and non-whites was maintained and regional representation closely matched that of the 1950 United States Census. Most of the subjects tested were selected from the files of agencies and industries which employ or aid the blind.

All the tests are administered with time limits. Raw scores are converted to scale scores which have a mean set at 10 and a standard deviation set at 3. The total score is a deviation IQ which has a mean of 100 and a standard deviation of 15. The instructions which accompany the manual are clearly written, but anyone using the scale must have considerable practice in the administration of the subtests.

From the discussion regarding the reliability and validity of the scale it is readily apparent that more research is needed to determine whether the scale should be used routinely to measure the intelligence of the adult blind. The scale's authors hope to be able to make the scale more generally available for such research in the near future.

REFERENCES

Alper, A. E., "A Comparison of the WISC and the Arthur Adaptation of the Leiter International Performance Scale with Mental Defectives," *American Journal of Mental Deficiency* 63 (1958), 312-316.

Anastasi, Anne, *Psychological Testing.* 3rd ed. New York. Macmillan, 1968.

Arnold, G. F., "A Technique for Measuring the Mental Ability of the Cerebral Palsied," *Psychological Service Center Journal* 3 (1951), 171-178.

Arthur, Grace, A. *A Point Scale of Performance Tests* (Form I). New York. Commonwealth Fund, 1930.

———, *A Point Scale of Performance Tests* (Rev. Form II). New York. Psychological Corporation, 1947.

Bayley, Nancy, *Manual: Bayley Scales of Infant Development,* New York. Psychological Corporation, 1969.

Bensberg, G. J., and W. Sloan, "Performance of Brain-Injured Defectives on the Arthur Adaptation of the Leiter," *Psychological Service Center Journal* 3 (1957) 181-184.

Bessent, T. E., "A Note on the Validity of the Leiter International Performance Scale," *Journal of Consulting Psychology*, 14 (1950), 234.

Beverly, L., and G. J. Bensberg, "A Comparison of the Leiter, the Cornell-Coxe and Stanford-Binet with Mental Defectives," *American Journal of Mental Deficiency* 57 (1952) 89-91.

Brill, M., "The Reliability of the Goodenough Draw-a-Man Test and the Validity and Reliability of an Abbreviated Scoring Method," *Journal of Educational Psychology* 26 (1935), 701-708.

Burke, H. R., "Raven's Progressive Matrices: A Review and Critical Evaluation," *Journal of Genetic Psychology* 193, (1958), 199-228.

Cattell, Psyche, *The Measurement of Intelligence of Infants and Young Children.* New York. Psychological Corporation, 1940.

Cattell, R. B., and A. K. S. Cattell, *Handbook for the Culture Fair Intelligence Test.* Champaign, Ill.: Institute for Personality and Ability Testing, 1959.

Cohen, B. D., and M. J. Collier, "A Note on the WISC and Other Tests of Children Six to Eight Years Old," *Journal of Consulting Psychology* 16 (1952), 226-227.

Coleman, J. M., Ira Iscoe, and M. Brodsky, "The "Draw-A-Man" Test as a Predictor of School Readiness and as an Index of Emotional and Physical Maturity," *Pediatrics* 24 (1959), 275-281.

Cronbach, L. J., *Essentials of Psychological Testing.* 3rd ed. New York. Harper, 1970.

Davis, A., and K. Eells, *Davis-Eells Test of General Intelligence.* New York. Harcourt, 1953.

Deutsch, M., et al., "Guidelines for Testing Minority Group Children," *Journal of Social Issues* (supplement) 22 (1964) 24-35.

Doppelt, J. E., and G. K. Bennett, "Testing Job Applicants From Disadvantaged Groups," *Test Service Bulletin* 57 (1967).

Dunn, J. A., "Inter-and Intra-Rater Reliability of the New *Harris-Goodenough Draw-a-Man Test,*" *Perceptual and Motor Skills* 24 (1967), 269-270.

Estes, Betty, M. E. Curtin, R. A. DeBurger, and C. Denny, "Relationships Between 1960 Stanford-Binet, 1937 Stanford-Binet, WISC, Raven, and Draw-a-Man," *Journal of Consulting Psychology* 25 (1961), 388-391.

Eells, K., et al., *Intelligence and Cultural Differences.* Chicago: U. of Chicago Press, 1951.

Freeman, Frank S., *Theory and Practice of Psychological Testing.* 3rd ed. New York. Holt, 1962.

French, J. L., *Manual: Pictorial Test of Intelligence.* Boston. Houghton Mifflin, 1964.

Gallagher, J. J., E. P. Benoit, and H. F. Boyd, Intelligence in Brain Damaged Children," *Journal of Clinical Psychology* 12 (1956), 65-72.

Gardner, J. W., *Excellence.* New York. Harper 1961, pp. 48-49.

Gesell, A., et al., *The First Five Years of Life.* New York. Harper, 1940.

_____ and C. S. Amatruda, *Developmental Diagnosis*. 2nd ed. New York. Hoeber, 1947.

Gilbert, H. B., "On the IQ Bab," *Teachers College Record* 67 (1966) 282-285.

Goodenough, F. L., *Measurement of Intelligence by Drawings*. New York. Harcourt, 1926.

Hamilton, M. E., "A Comparison of the Revised Arthur Performance Test (Form II) and the 1937 Binet," *Journal of Consulting Psychology* 13 (1949), 44-49.

Harris, D. B., "A Note on Some Ability Correlates of the Raven Progressive Matrices (1947) in the Kindergarten," *Journal of Educational Psychology* 50 (1959), 228-229.

_____, *Children's Drawings as Measures of Intellectual Maturity: A Revision and Extension of the Goodenough Draw-a-Man Test*. New York. Harcourt, 1963.

Hiskey, M. S., *Hiskey-Nebraska Test of Learning: Manual*. Lincoln, Neb. Union College Press, 1966.

Healy, W., and G. M. Fernald, "Tests for Practical Mental Classification," *Psychological Monographs* 13 No. 2 (1911).

Jenson, A. R., "How Much Can We Boost IQ and Scholastic Achievement?," *Harvard Education Review* 39 (1969), 1-123.

Knox, H. A., "A Scale Based on the Work at Ellis Island, for Estimating Mental Defects," *Journal of the American Medical Association* 62 (1914), 741-747.

Kohs, S. C., *Intelligence Measurements: A Psychological and Statistical Study Based Upon the Block-Design Tests*. New York. Macmillan, 1923.

Leiter, R. G., "Caucasian Norms for the Leiter International Performance Scale 1949," *Psychological Service Center Journal* 1 (1949), 136-138.

_____, "Part II of the Manual for the 1948 Revision of the Leiter International Performance Scale," *Psychological Service Center Journal* 2 (1950), 259-343.

_____, "Part I of the Manual for the 1948 Revision of the Leiter International Performance Scale," *Psychological Service Center Journal* (1959), Vol. 2, 1-72.

_____, *Examiner Manual for the Leiter International Performance Scale*. Chicago. Stoelting, 1969a.

_____, *General Instructions for the Leiter International Performance Scale*. Chicago. Stoelting, 1969b.

Loreton, J. O., "The Decline and Fall of Group Intelligence Testing," *Teachers College Record* 67 (1965), 10-17.

McCarthy, D., "A Study of the Reliability of the Goodenough Test of Intelligence," *Journal of Psychology* 18 (1944), 201-216.

McCurdy, H. G., "Group and Individual Variability in the Goodenough Draw-a-Man Test," *Journal of Educational Psychology* 38 (1947), 428-436.

Pintner, R., and D. G. Paterson, *A Scale of Performance Tests*. New York. Appleton Century, 1917.

Porteus, S. D., *The Porteus Maze Test and Intelligence*. Palo Alto, Calif.: Pacific Books, 1950.

_____, *The Maze Test and Clinical Psychology*. Palo Alto, Calif. Pacific Books, 1959.

Raven, J. C., *Guide to the Standard Progressive Matrices*. London. H. K. Lewis, 1960. (Distributed in the U. S. by The Psychological Corporation.)

_____, *Advanced Progressive Matrices*. London. H. K. Lewis, 1965.

Sharp, H. C., "A Comparison of Slow Learner's Scores on Three Individual Intelligence Scales," *Journal of Clinical Psychology* 13 (1957), 372-374.

_____, "A Note on the Reliability of the Leiter International Performance Scale 1948 Revision," *Journal of Consulting Psychology* 22 (1958), 320.

Shurrager, H. C., and P. S. Shurrager, *Haptic Intelligence Scale for the Adult Blind*. Chicago. Psychology Research, 1964.

Tate, M. E., "The Influence of Cultural Factors on the Leiter International Performance Scale," *Journal of Abnormal and Social Psychology* 47 (1952), 497-501.

Thompson, J. M., and C. J. Finley, "The Relationship Between the Goodenough Draw-a-Man Test and the Stanford-Binet Form L-M in Children Referred for School Guidance Service," *California Journal of Educational Research* 14 (1963), 19-22.

Vane, J. R., and R. T. Kessler, "The Goodenough Draw-a-Man Test: Long Term Reliability and Validity," *Journal of Clinical Psychology* 20 (1964), 487-488.

Wallin, J. E. W., "A Comparison of the Stanford 1916 and 1937 (Form L) Test Results with Those From the Arthur Performance Scale (Form 1) Based on the Same Subjects," *Journal of Genetic Psychology* 69 (1946), 44-55.

Test Administration
and Scoring

Each test manual has specific directions for administering and scoring the various items of the instrument. Because each examiner is expected to follow the manual closely, we shall discuss only those aspects of test administration and scoring which apply in general to mental ability tests, dealing first with *individual* scales and then with *group* tests.

INDIVIDUAL MENTAL ABILITY SCALES

TESTING ENVIRONMENT

It is highly desirable that individual mental testing take place in a suitable setting. Ideally, a relatively small room with perhaps 80 to 100 square feet of floor space should be used. The room should have adequate lighting, heating, and ventilation. It should be free from distracting influences whether they originate within the room or from outside. Attractive toys, unusual artifacts, paintings, or Playboy calendars might be distracting within the testing room; the slamming of doors, loud conversations, or the ringing of bells outside the room also could divert a subject's attention or make concentration difficult.

In order to keep people from coming into the testing room inadvertently and disrupting the testing, the examiner should hang a "Testing in Progress" sign outside the door. The matter of avoiding disruptions is stressed because it is known that the test performance of some individuals is adversely affected by visual or auditory stimuli which are noticeable but not part of the testing procedure. In testing we should endeavor to provide optimum conditions, for we wish to assess, if possible, the subject's *best* performance.

Within the testing room very little is needed in the way of furniture, but that which is present should be suitable for use with the particular individual being tested. A table or desk, a chair for the subject, and a chair for the examiner generally will suffice for individual testing, although some examiners like to use a small table or another chair for the purpose of holding the test kit or test materials. The use of an additional table or chair for the materials allows the examiner to keep the top of the desk free of test materials that could be in the way or could be distracting. The table or desk used for testing should be of suitable height for testing (or adjustable), and the subject's chair should be both comfortable and of appropriate size. If there is a window in the room, it is best to have the subject facing away from it to avoid having him distracted by the scenery, objects, people, or events which may be seen through the window. Or, of course, the drapes could be drawn.

The testing materials should be arranged in such a way that they are easily reached when needed. If the tester has to search for the materials he needs, time will be wasted and the examinee may become bored or annoyed.

It is generally not advisable to allow a third person (such as a parent) to be in the room during the testing session. The presence of a third person would be a departure from standardized procedure, and the effect of having the other person there would be very difficult or impossible to assess.

While the room, furniture, materials, and various equipment which are part of the physical environment of testing, are important, attention must also be paid to the psychological environment. In other words, the examiner should strive to create a situation in which the subject will be willing to be tested and will be likely to attempt to do his best. The most important factor in the creation of a good psychological environment for testing is *rapport*, which we shall define as a harmonious relationship between the subject and his examiner. Rapport does not insure optimal performance on the part of the examinee, but without rapport one can assume that the examinee will perform less well than he should.

ESTABLISHING AND MAINTAINING RAPPORT

The establishment of rapport generally begins when the person who is to be tested first meets the examiner. A smile and a friendly greeting by the examiner often are effective in putting the subject at ease, but in some cases a short, friendly conversation may be necessary.

When a child is tested, it may be advisable to ask him whether he knows why he is being tested, and then explain the reason for the examination if he doesn't know or seems uncertain about it. A phrase like "This test will help us to find out how we can help you" may be helpful in providing understanding and in alleviating apprehension.

It is generally more difficult to establish rapport with *young* children than with older children or adults, because the young are less likely to have the understanding of the test situation which older subjects have. Certainly the examiner who works with young children should be patient and understanding, and perhaps should have a high level of frustration tolerance. It is not uncommon for very young children to be extremely shy, active, curious, or uncooperative.

Many examiners like to begin testing young children by saying something like "Johnny, I'd like to play some games with you," and this usually is an effective way to provide a little explanation of what is about to take place. Older children probably wouldn't care for the "game" bit.

Some examiners use the Draw-a-Man Test to reduce anxiety and at the same time obtain some additional evaluative data.

It is not advisable to offer the child a "bribe" or incentive of some sort to effect cooperation. One of the present authors recalls a case in which the examiner gave a youngster a lollipop at the beginning of a testing session. As it turned out, the child was more interested in the candy than the tests, and the result was a "sticky" situation.

There are times when a child simply is too frightened, upset, or uncooperative to be tested. In these instances the examiner should try to establish rapport, but if reasonable efforts fail, the testing should be postponed until another attempt can be made.

With young children as well as with older subjects there are ways to foster rapport *during* a testing session. For example, the examiner can use the subject's name occasionally, thereby diminishing somewhat the impersonal or formal aspect of testing. The tester also can use a friendly smile and pleasing tone of voice to promote rapport. It helps, too, if the examiner gives some verbal support and encouragement from time to time. When the subject has experienced noticeable difficulty with an item, and seems to be anxious or discouraged, the examiner might say something like, "That seemed a little hard, didn't it? Let's try another one." Occasionally a comment such as, "Fine!," or "You're doing well, Mary," will provide the useful positive reinforcement which some individuals need in a testing situation. It must be emphasized, however, that the tester should not indicate to the subject that the responses are either correct or incorrect. If the examiner were to make some positive comment following each correct answer or performance, after a while the examinee probably would realize that no comment indicated a poor response and perhaps disapproval. We are saying, then, that positive reinforcement is valuable, provided it is used skillfully and appropriately.

ADMINISTERING THE SCALE

Adhering to the Manual

Whenever tests or scales are administered it is essential that the examiner follow the directions and procedures which appear in the manual. This applies to both group and individual instruments, but especially to the latter. There are two reasons for this concern. First, the author of the test or scale has chosen directions which are superior to other directions that might be used, in terms of clarity and ease of administration. Second, the instrument has been standardized on the basis of the procedures which are specified in the manual. If the designated directions and procedures are not followed, it is highly unlikely that the standardization data, such as the scale norms, are applicable.

To what extent should the examiner adhere to the *exact* wording of the directions in the manual? This question arises when college students are learning to administer individual scales, such as the WISC or Stanford-Binet. If the examiner reads word for word from the manual, his attention will be focused on the manual rather than on the examinee. Furthermore, the subject may wonder whether the examiner is sufficiently familiar with the test to give it. Ideally, the examiner should be so familiar with the directions and procedures that he need only glance at the manual occasionally. For the beginner, though, we recommend reading from the manual rather than adding, deleting, or altering words in the directions. We also strongly urge the tester to become thoroughly familiar with the directions and procedures as quickly as possible, so that an occasional glance at the manual will be all that is necessary when tests are being given.

Repeating Questions

In giving a subject the directions for a subtest the examiner should speak distinctly and with sufficient voice volume to enable the subject to hear and understand the question or problem without undue difficulty. Occasionally an examinee may ask that a question be repeated. Generally speaking, questions or directions may be repeated verbatim or in part. In fact, if it is known that the examinee was distracted for some reason, the question should be repeated. The repeating of questions is also recommended to encourage an examinee to respond if he has remained silent after a question is given. Certain items, however, should *never* be repeated. In this category are the memory questions, such as those requiring that the examinee repeat digits or sentences. Again, it is imperative that the examiner be familiar with the special rules that govern the administration of the subtests of the specific scale that is to be used.

Recording Responses

All verbal responses should be recorded in the scoring booklet exactly as they are given by the individual being tested. This practice is important because the final scoring of the subtests must be done after the testing is terminated, and at that time completely recorded responses permit more accurate scoring than partial answers. Complete recording of the responses also is important because it improves the examiner's chances of collecting information concerning unique or repetitive answers which can be useful in the evaluation of a subject's overall performance. There may be times when an examinee's responses are too lengthy to fit in the space provided in the booklet. In this case the examiner must either use a supplementary sheet to record portions of answers or select the most essential parts of the responses and record these in the booklet.

When the examinee doesn't respond to a question, the tester should write in NR (no response). If the response is "I don't know," the recorded response should be DK (don't know). The practice of writing in either DK or NR is useful because it lets the examiner know later why no response was recorded for the particular item.

Sometimes the examinee's verbal responses are ambiguous or unclear, and in this case it is necessary for the examiner to attempt to get the subject to clarify his answer. If this were not done it would be difficult or impossible to score an item as passed or failed or to know how much credit to give for the response. In order to help a subject clarify his answer, the examiner might say: "Tell me more about it," or "Explain what you mean." These kinds of queries are neutral, and they neither help nor hinder the subject. They are used to facilitate scoring, but not to help the examinee get the correct answer.

Whenever a response has been questioned the examiner should write Q (for questioned) after the first recorded answer, and then record any additional responses which the examinee makes.

At times the individual being tested will give more than one response to a question. In this instance the accepted practice is to give the subject credit for the best response as long as one of his responses or part of a response does not indicate that he really does not know the answer. Perhaps an actual incident will illustrate this point. When one little boy was asked the meaning of the word *brave*, which was part of a vocabulary test, he responded by saying: "Well, if a great, big monster came to a town and a man went out to fight it, he would be brave . . . or stupid." Most of us would be inclined to give the full credit for this response.

Some of the items of the individual scales are timed, and it is essential that the exact time required by the subject to answer such questions be recorded. A stopwatch is necessary in individual testing, and the beginning tester should become familiar with it before using it in a testing situation. We should like to suggest also that in using the stopwatch during testing the examiner try to make it as inconspicuous as possible, for some subjects become anxious when they know they are being timed. For some of the easier items of the Wechsler scales (for which responses can come rapidly) it may be better not to start and stop the watch for each item, but to note carefully the starting and finishing time for the items. This practice will eliminate much of the clicking noise which may bother some examinees.

Note Taking

In addition to recording the responses to items the examiner should take notes during the testing sessions. The notes, which can be written on the record form or on another form or sheet, may provide information concerning the subject's appearance, attitude during testing, significant remarks, mannerisms, unusual behavior, apparent or suspected handicaps, and the like. The information can be very useful in the evaluation of an examinee's test performance. Some psychologists have their receptionists or secretaries take notes on the initial appearance and behavior of the subjects when they arrive at the office for testing.

Fatigue in Testing

Because an individual testing period can require a considerable amount of time, sometimes more than an hour, the performance of a young child can be adversely affected by fatigue or boredom. The examiner should be aware of this and should be prepared to take a short break in the session if necessary. This matter of temporarily calling a halt to testing should not be overdone, however, as it was in the following instance.

One of the authors, teaching a class in individual mental testing, stressed the importance of noting the presence of fatigue or boredom in young children. He suggested that a break could be taken if this occurred during the testing session. It was apparent that this suggestion had been taken seriously by one very conscientious student who, during a testing session in a large observation room, stopped testing, went over to a piano in the room, and then proceeded to play a lively tune for his examinee. This was going beyond the call of duty, perhaps. Ordinarily a large room would not be used for testing, but in this case that was the only room available. Also, one ordinarily would not have a piano in the room, but there is an advantage to this: one can easily reach "a chord" with the student. Incidentally, this testing session was observed through a one-way screen.

ORDER OF SUBTEST ADMINISTRATION

Ordinarily the items on subtests of an individual ability scale are administered in the sequence in which they appear in the manual, and this is the *standard* method of administration. However, if in the judgment of the examiner it would be advantageous, the order of presentation of the items for a particular examinee may be altered. The reasons for using some method other than the standard method generally will be based on the physical or emotional status of the person being tested.

When the *serial* method is used, for instance with the *Stanford-Binet Intelligence Scale*, the examiner starts with a relatively easy item of a specific type and continues to give this type of item until it is failed by the subject. This could be done for such items as Memory Span for Digits, Comprehension, and Abstract Words.

The *adaptive* method involves the alternation of easy and difficult items, starting with an easy item of a particular type. If used with the Stanford-Binet, the examiner will start below the subject's expected mental age so that there is likely to be success on the first item. Then the examiner proceeds to test upward and downward to determine the basal and terminal ages as quickly as he can. If used with the Wechsler scale, the examiner will start with an item of some type which is believed to be easy for the subject—for example, one that does not involve lengthy verbal directions or much concentration. Then easy and difficult items will be more or less alternated.

The adaptive method is used in order to prevent discouragement on the part of subjects who are afraid of failing or doing badly on tests. If there is much emotional involvement, the subject may experience a few successive failures on items and may give up too soon. The adaptive method, by giving the anxious or insecure examinee continued opportunity for success, is likely to enhance test motivation and performance.

SCORING

It goes without saying that the most perfectly administered test or scale would yield invalid results if serious mistakes were made in the scoring that follows the administration of the instrument. The scoring of individual scales is much more complex than it is for group tests because each scale consists of a number of subtests (each of which must be scored), and because the responses to many of the items of the individual scale must be evaluated subjectively.

The scoring process for individual scales typically involves three basic operations: scoring the responses, totaling and recording the correct responses or points of credit, and using the appropriate tables to obtain scaled scores and/ or IQs. In order to carry out these operations properly, the examiner must be thoroughly familiar with the items in the scale, the principles and techniques of scoring, and the use of the appropriate tables. In short, the examiner must be familiar with the entire scale and the scoring directions in the manual. He should also be conscientious about evaluating responses and checking all computations and clerical work.

A relatively simple but nevertheless important task related to scoring is the calculation of the chronological age of the examinee. The problem, of course, is to subtract the birthdate from the testing date without making an error in the process. In using the method illustrated below, 30 days may be borrowed from the month or 12 months from the year to simplify subtraction. Three different examples follow.

	Year	Month	Day
Date tested	1957	11	20
Date of birth	1940	10	8
Age	17	1	12
Date tested	1945	7 6	15 45
Date of birth	1905	3	20
Age	40	3	25
Date tested	1970 69	9 14	18 48
Date of birth	1960	8	27
Age	9	6	21

In these examples the first CA is written 17-1, to show an age of seventeen years and one month. The second CA is recorded as 40-3 when the WAIS is used or 40-4 when the Stanford-Binet is used. The third CA is 9-6 for the WISC and 9-7 for the S-B. Whether the additional days beyond the year and months are dropped or not depends upon which scale has been used. With the Wechsler scales the extra days always are disregarded, but with the Stanford-Binet an additional month of CA is recorded when the additional days exceed half a month.

GROUP MENTAL ABILITY TESTS

Up to this point we have been discussing the administration and scoring of individual mental ability scales. Now we shall consider group instruments which are often used in schools and colleges to assess mental ability. Various group instruments are described in Chapter 12.

In many respects the principles and procedures which are essential in individual testing also apply to group testing. Certainly rapport is important in both kinds of testing situations. For both situations it is recommended that the person who administers the test be one who can gain the cooperation of the examinees. He should also be a person who has a positive attitude toward testing.

Both kinds of testing situations require that the examinees be comfortable and at ease during the testing period, so this requires that attention be given to seating, lighting, heating, ventilation, and freedom from distraction in the larger group testing room as well as the smaller room used for individual testing.

Group tests, like the individual scales, should be administered and scored according to the directions in the manual, and the administrator should be an alert, thorough, and conscientious worker.

Although there is much in common between group and individual testing procedures, there are a few aspects of group testing which deserve special attention. A brief discussion of the somewhat unique elements of group testing follows.

ADMINISTRATION OF GROUP TESTS

A distinct advantage of group testing over individual testing is that in the group situation many persons can be tested in a relatively short period of time. It is possible to test hundreds of subjects with a group test in the same amount of time required to administer an individual scale to a single person. Obviously, a relatively large room is required for group testing, and with the large room there must be some special considerations. One of these considerations has to do with the seating of the examinees.

The group-testing room should be large enough to permit the seating of examinees in alternate seats. The use of every other seat is important for at least three reasons: it permits better observation of the subjects who are being tested, it reduces the possibility of cheating, and it gives the subjects a lot more "elbow room" which enhances comfort a bit.

Of course, the desks at which the examinees sit should be comfortable and the writing surfaces should be smooth and sufficiently large. Each seat or desk used should be in good condition, so that no difficulty occurs because of a faulty seat or poor writing surface. Also, left-handed persons should have "left-handed" desks or seats.

The use of a large testing room for a large number of subjects necessitates paying special attention to the acoustics of the room. It goes without saying that each subject in the room should be able to hear the directions distinctly. Whether or not a sound-amplifying system is used, the person who gives the test should speak with a clear, well-modulated voice.

The administrator of a group test should be familiar with two sets of directions—the set which guides the administrator himself and the set which explains what the examinees are to do in taking the test. Familiarity with the directions facilitates rapport and reduces the chances of confusion or misunderstanding. It is often advisable for the test administrator to take the test himself prior to administering it in order to become more familiar with it.

Most group tests of mental ability have strict time limits to which the test administrator is expected to adhere. A mechanical timer or watch with a sweep-second hand usually will suffice for accurate timing. As previously noted, if a timer is used, it is advisable for the tester to learn how to operate it before using it in a testing situation.

Systematic procedures for handing out test copies, answer sheets, pencils, and scratch paper are essential in group testing. A well-planned operation will save time, avoid confusion, and reduce the possibility of losing tests or answer sheets. With large groups, proctors should be used to assist with the handling of materials. Proctors also may be needed to prevent cheating and to help students who need assistance (other than the answering of test questions).

SCORING

Although the scoring process for group tests tends to be much more routine and less complicated than for individual scales, group-test scoring still requires careful attention. Faulty scoring can render group-test results invalid as readily as it can the results of individual scales.

These days much of the scoring of the answer sheets for group tests is done electronically by machine, but enough hand scoring is still being done to warrant a brief discussion of this important phase of testing.

Obviously, the person who has the responsibility for the scoring of answer sheets should be familiar with the scoring procedures for the test in question. Directions for scoring generally are discussed in the test manual.

Before a set of answer sheets is scored, each answer sheet should be scanned to determine whether the marking is satisfactory. Answer sheets which have been mismarked in some way (such as having more than one response marked for an item) require special consideration, and in some cases should be discarded.

It is advisable to use a red pencil in marking the incorrect responses on the answer sheet. This makes the marks stand out for easier tallying. It is generally recommended that each answer sheet be rescored to catch any errors that may have been made during the initial scoring. If time does not permit a total rescoring, a partial check of some of the answer sheets is advisable.

Frequently the person who does the scoring also has the responsibility for recording scores on record forms, and this often requires the use of tables for converting raw scores to percentile ranks or standard scores. It is absolutely essential that the individual who has this responsibility be alert and careful. Careless performance or the use of the wrong tables would be extremely unfortunate, to say the least.

CHARACTERISTICS OF COMPETENT EXAMINERS

Not all individuals who have an interest in testing, or are required to use tests, possess the attributes of a competent examiner. Indeed, there may be many testers at work today who are unsuited for the administration of tests. Ideally, we should be able to select people for this very important task on the basis of whether they possess those qualities which are essential to good test administration. Among the characteristics that we would especially want to consider (though not necessarily in this order) are the following.

1. *Conscientiousness*. The person who administers tests must be willing to become familiar with the instruments he uses, must be willing to follow the principles and procedures of good testing, and must strive for self-improvement. The indifferent or careless worker cannot be expected to provide valid test data and useful psychological reports.

2. *Friendliness*. An important asset for the examiner is the ability to relate well to the subjects that he tests. The friendly person finds it easy to put the examinee at ease and then to maintain a good working relationship during the testing session. Examinees (especially children) tend to respond better to the warm, friendly person than to the emotionally cool individual.

3. *Thoroughness*. It is important for the examiner to take the time and expend the effort required to go through all of the necessary steps that will minimize errors and insure valid results. A considerable amount of work of the tester is clerical in nature, and it is not likely to be exciting to the person who dislikes routine activities. Yet unless attention is paid to details, the time spent in testing may be time wasted. An error made in figuring a score or in using a table may result in a very inaccurate test result.

4. *Ability to Observe*. The person who administers tests should always be alert for information about the examinee which may be significant in some way. The subject's appearance, attitudes, mannerisms, remarks, facial expressions, and personality traits may have an important bearing on test performance, and therefore they should be noted prior to, during, and following the testing session.

5. *Adequate Verbal Ability*. It is not possible to say just how high a level of verbal ability a tester should have; perhaps the higher the level the better. In individual testing he must be able to understand the numerous verbal concepts that appear in the test items, and he must be able to make fine verbal discriminations in evaluating a subject's responses. A verbally deficient person generally would not be competent in testing.

6. *Knowledge of Tests and Measurements*. This important attribute was alluded to in connection with conscientiousness, but it needs to be emphasized. To be considered competent the examiner must possess sufficient knowledge to be able to use various instruments effectively. Experience can be a valuable asset, of course, but reading and research also lead to knowledge in this area.

7. *Objectivity*. The competent tester is able to maintain an objective attitude toward testing and his subjects. He neither helps his examinees with answers to questions nor hinders them as they strive to arrive at answers. This does not mean that he is indifferent during a testing session; rather, he has a neutral attitude. Some excellent teachers are poor testers because their strong desire to help children transfers to the testing situation, where they may tend to help the subjects with the answers to questions.

ETHICAL STANDARDS

The individual who administers, scores, interprets or uses test results in a professional position has a responsibility to himself, his profession, his subjects, and the public to carry out his duties in an ethical manner. On page 208 of the publication *Ethical Standards*, prepared by the American Personnel and Guidance Association, are found nine statements pertaining to ethical standards for testing. We feel that these statements clearly spell out the ethical responsibilities of those who are engaged in testing.

1. The primary purpose of psychological testing is to provide objective and comparative measures for use in self-evaluation or evaluation by others of general or specific attributes.
2. Generally, test results constitute only one of a variety of pertinent data for personnel and guidance decisions. It is the member's responsibility to provide adequate orientation or information to the examinee(s) so that the results of testing may be placed in proper perspective with other relevant factors.

3. When making any statements to the public about tests and testing care must be taken to give accurate information and to avoid any false claims or misconceptions.
4. Different tests demand different levels of competence for administration, scoring, and interpretation. It is therefore the responsibility of the member to recognize the limits of his competence and to perform only those functions which fall within his preparation and competence.
5. In selecting tests for use in a given situation or with a particular client the member must consider not only general but also specific validity, reliability, and appropriateness of the test(s).
6. Tests should be administered under the same conditions which were established in their standardization. Except for research purposes explicitly stated, any departures from these conditions, as well as unusual behavior or irregularities during the testing session which may affect the interpretation of the test results, must be fully noted and reported. In this connection, unsupervised test-taking or the use of tests through the mails are of questionable value.
7. The value of psychological tests depends in part on the novelty to persons taking them. Any prior information, coaching, or reproduction of test materials tends to invalidate test results. Therefore, test security is one of the professional obligations of the member.
8. The member has the responsibility to inform the examinee(s) as to the purpose of testing. The criteria of examinee's welfare and/or explicit prior understanding with him should determine who the recipients of the test results may be.
9. The member should guard against the appropriation, reproduction, or modification of published tests or parts thereof without express permission and adequate recognition of the original author or publisher.

REFERENCES

American Personnel and Guidance Association, "Ethical Standards," *Personnel and Guidance Journal* 40 (1961), 206–209.

Anastasi, Anne, *Psychological Testing.* New York: Macmillan, 1968.

Cronbach, Lee J., *Essentials of Psychological Testing.* 3rd ed. New York: Harper, 1970.

Freeman, Frank, *Theory and Practice of Psychological Testing.* New York: Holt, 1962.

Goodenough, Florence, *Mental Testing: Its History, Principles and Applications.* New York: Holt, 1949.

Glasser, Alan J., and Ira Zimmerman, *Clinical Interpretation of the Wechsler Intelligence Scale for Children.* New York: Grune and Stratton, 1967.

Greene, Edward, *Measurement of Human Behavior.* rev. ed. New York: Odyssey Press, 1952.

Terman, L. M., and Maude Merrill, *Measuring Intelligence.* Boston: Houghton Mifflin, 1937.

_____, *Stanford-Binet Intelligence Scale: Manual for the Third Revision, Form L-M.* Boston: Houghton Mifflin, 1960.

Wechsler, David, *Manual for the Wechsler Intelligence Scale for Children.* New York: Psychological Corporation, 1949.

_____, *Manual for the Wechsler Adult Intelligence Scale.* New York: Psychological Corporation, 1955.

_____, *Manual for the Wechsler Preschool and Primary Scale of Intelligence.* New York: Psychological Corporation, 1967.

Test Interpretation: Normative Data

Test interpretation is the process of extracting meaning from the numerical data acquired in a testing session. Test interpretation always occurs within the framework of some larger objective, usually the purpose of answering rather specific questions. Can I be admitted to University X? Should we hire this person? What kind of person is he? Why is Mary doing so poorly in school? What caused her problem? Should we put her in a special school? These are the kinds of questions that the psychologist frequently is asked to answer, or assist with. It is apparent that they are not all of equal complexity nor are they equally weighted with regard to the consequences of their resolution.

In addition to illustrating the types of problems with which the examiner might be confronted, the above-mentioned questions also indicate the various levels at which interpretations may be made. Further, they point to the several procedures that may be used in drawing inferences on the basis of test results. In essence, the questions require predictive, descriptive, and diagnostic approaches to test interpretation, and each of these may be approached at different levels and by different means.

The data collected in a psychological evaluation can be viewed in three ways. First, when the examiner attempts to answer the question, "What kind of person is he?" the data from the evaluation are treated as a *sample* of the person's behavior and current status. Second, when the questions, "Can I be admitted to College X?" and "Should we hire this person?" require answers, the data are viewed as *correlates* of something else. The correlated behavior may be outside the testing situation (relationship between test results and academic success or success on the job) or it may be intrapersonal (people who exhibit behavior X may also be expected to exhibit behavior Y). Third, when answering the question, "Why is Mary doing so poorly in school?" the data are viewed as *signs* or *cues* pointing to the possible underlying causes of the behavior. In practice, the data from any given case may be viewed in all three ways.

The different ways of viewing the data make different demands upon the validity of the test. By now it should be apparent that content validity requires that the test constitute a *sample* of behavior drawn from a defined "universe" of situations; that concurrent validity is required to estimate a person's *present status* with regard to an attribute *external* to the test; that test predictive validity is needed to predict *future* performance on some external variable; and that construct validity, while required for all of the above, is essential when drawing inferences with regard to the psychological meaning of a "sign."

Test interpretation involves a process of reasoning in which the psychologist observes a bit of data and then draws inferences about the person or formulates hypotheses about the person. The inferences and hypotheses may be at different levels of abstraction, ranging from simple empirical statements to complex explanatory generalizations rather far removed from the data.

Certain uses of tests actually involve very little inference. The first question at the beginning of this chapter, "Can I be admitted to College X?", can be answered simply by knowing the student's test score and the cut-off score used by the university. The test data are directly related to the answer. At the next level of abstraction the examiner might observe Mary during the examination and note that she looks up from the test whenever someone passes in the hall, when any noise from outside the testing room is heard, when the examiner moves, or when the thermostat clicks, and he might infer that she is easily distracted. He might note that she moves around a lot in her chair, stands up, walks away, has her hands in motion most of the time, kicks her feet when she's seated, and then infer that she is hyperactive for a girl of her age. He may note that her drawings on a test are asymmetrical and characteristic of children younger than Mary and then infer immature perceptual-motor skills. On the basis of these inferences drawn from observations of behavior and his knowledge of the behaviors associated with the disorder, he may hypothesize minimal brain dysfunction and conclude that this is the cause of her poor performance in school. This is an abstraction in which the relationship between inferences has led to an empirical conclusion that was generalized to the school setting.

Such is the process of test interpretation. The further one departs from the concrete test performance and the objective data associated with it, the more speculative and less dependable the inferences, hypotheses, and conclusions become. As a consequence, it is essential that the examiner use the best objective data available. This means that he may frequently find it necessary to collect data himself.

The immediate product of administering and scoring a test is a number. In the case of general mental ability tests the number usually represents the number of correct responses made by the examinee. This number, of course, is the raw score. Except for tests in which each item has been assigned some kind of age-related value, raw scores are virtually meaningless. For example, if Harry had correctly spelled 60 of 100 spelling words, this is all that we would know about his performance. We would be hard pressed to know whether to congratulate him or be disappointed. In order to make a raw score meaningful, it is necessary to change it into some derived score and to obtain information about the typical performance of some comparison group on the test. Then the derived score can be compared with the scores that the members of the group made.

DERIVED SCORES

PERCENTILE RANKS

The most commonly used derived score is the percentile rank. The percentile rank of a score designates the percentage of cases or scores below it. For example, if a person has a percentile rank of 30, then 30 percent of the group with which he is being compared made scores lower than he did. Through the use of percentile ranks it is possible to determine a person's relative position in a group on the characteristic being measured. Procedures for calculating percentile ranks were presented in Chapter 2.

The great advantage in the use of percentile ranks is that they are easily understood and explained. A serious disadvantage to the test user is that, while test scores are usually distributed normally, percentile ranks have a rectangular distribution. The result is that rather small raw-score differences near the middle of the distribution produce relatively large differences in percentile ranks, whereas relatively large raw-score differences at the extremes of the distribution result in small percentile differences. The interpreter must bear this in mind or face the danger of misinterpreting large differences in percentile rank near the middle of the distribution which represent insignificant differences in actual performance. A further disadvantage is that percentile ranks cannot be legitimately added, subtracted, multiplied, or divided, so they are of limited value in research.

Z-SCORES

Previous discussion in Chapter 2 gave the rationale and computation for Z-scores. It will be recalled that these scores are derived from the z-score distribution by setting the mean at 50 and the standard deviation at 10. In effect, the score describes the examinee's performance in terms of the departure of his score from the mean of the distribution. The transformation serves to eliminate the decimals and negative numbers associated with the z-score without changing the shape of the raw-score distribution. A person with a Z-score of 50 would be at the mean of the distribution. A Z-score of 70 would indicate that the person's score was two standard deviations above the mean. In highly skewed distributions, interpretation of these scores is severely limited. In distributions which approximate normality, however, they may be interpreted in the same manner as the *T*-scores described below.

T-SCORES

The *T*-score is a normalized standard score (Chapter 2) with a mean of 50 and standard deviation of 10. The score is derived by converting the raw scores to percentile ranks and then, by referring to a table of areas of the normal curve (Table B, Appendix), converting the percentile ranks to z-scores. The effect is to transform the raw scores from a nonnormal or skewed distribution to a distribution which is normal. The *T*-scores are then found by using the same procedure that was used in calculating the Z,

$$T = 50 + 10z$$

the z in this case being from the normalized distribution.

A very great advantage of *T*-scores (and other scores derived in this way) is that they can be referred directly to the normal curve and be interpreted not only as deviations from the mean but as percentile ranks. Thus a person with a *T*-score of 60 $(+1\sigma)$ would have a percentile rank of 84.

STANINES

The stanine scale is a nine-point standard score scale with score values that range from 1 to 9. When distributed normally, stanines have a mean of 5 and a standard deviation of about 2. With the exception of stanines 1 and 9 each stanine will be one-half standard deviation in width. Table 9-1 shows the way in

Table 9-1. Stanine Values for a Normal Distribution of Scores

	Stanine								
	1	2	3	4	5	6	7	8	9
Percent of Cases Assigned	Lowest 4	Next 7	Next 12	Next 17	Middle 20	Next 17	Next 12	Next 7	Highest 4
Interpretive Description	Low	Below Average			Average			Above Average	High

which stanine scores are distributed and provides interpretive descriptions. In nonnormal distributions the percents will only be approximated.

An advantage in the use of stanines is the fact that each stanine represents a band of scores, which effectively prevents the interpretation of an individual score as a precise point on a scale.

NORMS AND NORM GROUPS

Let us return to Harry's spelling-test score to pose further questions. Was the spelling list prepared for people of Harry's age and education? Did Harry spell more or fewer words than other children tested? A person's raw score takes on meaning only when it is compared to the performance of a relevant group of individuals. If Harry took the test with his class in school we could compare his score to the scores of other members of the class and determine where he ranked in his class. If the same test had been given to all children in a school who were in the same grade as Harry, we could compare his performance to the performance of all of those children. Similar comparisons might be made on a citywide or nationwide basis. Harry's score would then permit a number of interpretations.

The groups with which an individual's score might be compared are called *norm groups*, a norm simply being a statistic which describes the performance of a specified group on a test. Such statistics are usually presented in the form of tables, called norms tables, such as the example in Table 9-2. The statistic used to describe the performance of the groups in Table 9-2 is the percentile, so it is a table of percentile norms. Other tables may present *T*-score norms, IQ norms, stanine norms, and so on. In some instances the norm will simply be the mean representing the average performance of some group.

Table 9-2 is a rather special norm table in that it shows the performance of several groups on the test. As was pointed out above, an individual's performance takes on meaning only when it is compared to the performance of a specified group and its meaning changes when the comparison group changes. From Table 9-2 it may be seen that a person with a raw score of 63 on the test of scholastic aptitude would have a percentile score of 12 in College A, 21 at College B, 42 at College C, and 54 at College D. Assuming that the test is a valid predictor of academic performance at each of these schools, this individual would certainly have a different experience in each.

The manual for the test which was used in deriving the norms for the four colleges in Table 9-2 also provides "national" freshman college norms for the test. Using those norms, the raw score of 63 would have been at the 48th percentile. Assuming that the "national" norms are truly representative of entering college freshmen, the 63 would have indicated that the scorer was a fairly typical entering freshman with regard to scholastic aptitude as measured by this test. However, had the person gone to College A or B on the basis of such advice as "Your score is like that of the average college freshman," he would have been badly misled because at College A only about 3 percent of the *graduates* have scores this low or lower, and at College B only about 16 percent of the *graduates* score this low or lower.

The above discussion illustrates several points with regard to the use of tests and norms. In the first place, the test used must be appropriate for the purpose of the testing. No amount of score juggling, or "clinical" maneuvering will help if the wrong test is administered to a subject, or if a test is used for purposes other than those intended. Second, there must be *evidence* presented that the test is valid for the specific purpose for which it is being used. Test validity is

Table 9-2. Norm Table Showing the Performance of Entering Freshmen at Four Colleges on a Test of Scholastic Aptitude

Percentile	Raw Scores			
	College A	College B	College C	College D
99	106 +	104 +	99 +	98 +
98		103	97–98	96–97
97	104–105	101–102	95–96	93–95
96	103	100	93–94	91–92
95	102	99	92	89–90
94		98	91	88
93	101	97	90	87
92	100	96	88–89	85–86
91	99			
90	98	95	87	83–84
89	97	94		
88		93		
87	96	92	85–86	82
86	95		84	81
85		91	83	
84	94			79–80
83			81–82	
82		90		77–78
81				
80	93		79–80	
79	92	88–89		76
78			78	
77				
76	91			74–75
75		87		
74			76–77	
73	90	86		72–73
72				
71				
70			75	
69	89	84–85		70–71
68				

Percentile	Raw Scores			
	College A	College B	College C	College D
67	88			
66	87	83	73–74	68–69
65				
64	86	81–82	71–72	66–67
63				
62				
61	85			
60		79–80	69–70	64–65
59				
58	84			
57				
56	83	78	67–68	63
55				
54				
53	82	76–77	66	61–62
52				
51	81			
50	80	75	64–65	59–60
49				
48				
47				
46				
45				
44	79	73–74	62–63	58
43				
42	78			
41				
40				
39				
38	77	72	60–61	56–57
37				
36				
35				55

Percentile	Raw Scores			
	College A	College B	College C	College D
34	76	70–71	59	54
33	75			
32	74	68–69	57–58	52–53
31				
30				
29	73	67	56	51
28	72			
27				
26				
25	71	65–66	54–55	49–50
24				
23				
22	70	63–64	52–53	48
21	69			
20	68			
19				
18	67	62	51	47
17	66			
16	65	60–61	49–50	45–46
15				
14	64	59	48	44
13	63			
12	62	56–58	46–47	43
11				
10	61	55	44–45	41–42
9				
8	60	53–54	43	40
7	59	52	42	39
6	57–58	49–51	40–41	38
5	55–56	47–48	39	36–37
4	54	45–46	37–38	34–35
3	51–53	43–44	35–36	32–33
2		41–42	34	30–31
1	50	40	33	29

specific, and if no validity data are available there is no way of knowing what the test measures—that is, the norms cannot be meaningfully interpreted. Third, the norms must be relevant. They must be based on a group of people who are similar to the individual tested, or a group similar to the people with whom he will be associated should he choose a given course of action.

Test manuals usually provide what are purported to be "national" norms. When using such norms the examiner should avoid simply accepting the statement that the norms are based on a national population. Most of the norm groups will not be composed of an entire population; they are samples drawn from the relevant population. It is important that the sample be as representative as possible of the population with which the test will be used. A sample purported to be a national sample, but which was drawn primarily from the Midwest, would be biased.

Representativeness of the sample could be assured if the individuals were selected at random from the target population. For large samples like those used in test development, however, such a procedure would be too time-consuming and expensive. The most frequently used procedure in testing is the stratified random sample in which the target population is divided into relevant subgroups so that the subgroups will appear in the sample in proportion to their numbers in the population. Ideally, the individuals who comprise the sample from each subgroup (or stratum) are selected randomly. Populations are frequently subdivided proportionally (on the basis of United States Census data) according to such characteristics as rural-urban residence, age, sex, race, socioeconomic status, geographic region, and so forth. Failure to use a sample representative of the population will bias the normative data and make interpretation of the test results difficult.

The sample from which the norms are derived must be clearly described. The relevant characteristics of the norm group will be determined by the purposes for which the test will be used, and a concise description of those characteristics should be presented in the test manual. Furthermore, when it is known that subgroup differences are related to test performance, it is desirable and sometimes necessary that separate norms be reported for the subgroups. Upon occasion the test manuals report population samples that are extremely large. The absolute size of the norm group is not so important as the extent to which the group is representative of the population to which the test will be applied. It is true that the larger the sample the more stable the statistics based on the sample will be, but a representative sample of moderate size is more desirable than a large, poorly defined group.

One other caution concerning the use of national norms seems appropriate. Norms are not standards of performance. If the norm group is representative of the target population, then the norms represent the performance of a typical group, not the level of performance that should be attained by all groups or individuals.

LOCAL NORMS

Very frequently the test user will find that norms presented in the test manuals are inadequate for his purposes. When his use of tests requires that he try to predict success in a variety of situations, he needs information about his examinee's rank when compared to individuals in those situations. Without such data his predictions are little better than reading tea leaves. The gross statement regarding the "about average college freshman" score (p. 200) is a useful example. At College A the person would almost surely fail. The use of general norms in this manner has resulted in a lot of skepticism regarding the usefulness of psychological tests in making such decisions. Some school counselors have been known to overgeneralize from published test norms. To avoid this problem, knowledgeable test users develop norms for the populations they serve. Such norms are called *local norms*. Table 9-2 is a table of such norms derived for the purpose of aiding school counselors in their attempts to assist students in the selection of a college. With this information students at least know where they stand at each college. Similarly, employment counselors need norms for local industries and jobs, and personnel workers need local norms for placement decisions. Examinees about whom decisions are made on the basis of test scores deserve to be compared to the group with which they will be competing. The use of both national and local norms will enable the test user to extract the maximum amount of information from the test scores.

One of the reasons why local norms are so difficult to obtain is that test users sometimes leap to unwarranted conclusions regarding the institutions that might supply the norms. For example, the students in the colleges in Table 9-2 differ considerably in terms of student ability, but this difference does not necessarily indicate that a superior or inferior education will be obtained at one or the other. The fact is that two of the colleges are large, state-supported institutions at which more than half the undergraduate classes are taught by teaching assistants, whereas School D is a church related undergraduate school where all teaching is done by full-time faculty with a great deal of emphasis placed upon individual attention. Tutoring is available when required and requested. While it is true that a person with a lower score is likely to do better at school D, it does not necessarily follow that high-scoring individuals would not be challenged.

A variety of tables have been prepared for test users to aid them in their interpretive efforts. Table 9-3 was prepared to make it easy to transform the IQ scores derived from most tests into percentile ranks. The column headed *Binet IQ* may be used for tests which yield IQs having a standard deviation of 16.

One danger in using tables such as these lies in assuming that because two IQ scores show the same percentile rank they share the same meaning. Such an assumption is unwarranted because the tests have different content and probably measure somewhat different psychological functions, and because the tests do

Table 9-3. Percentile Ranks for IQs in the American Population

Binet IQ (SD = 16)	Wechsler IQ (SD = 15)	Percentile Rank	Binet IQ (SD = 16)	Wechsler IQ (SD = 15)	Percentile Rank
135+	133+	99	99	99	47
134	132	98	98	98	45
133	131	98	97	97	42
132	130	98	95-96	96	39
131	129	97	94	95	37
130	128	97	93	94	34
129	127	96	92	93	32
128	126	96	91	92	30
127	125	95	90	91	27
126	124	95	89	90	25
124-125	123	94	88	89	23
123	122	93	87	88	21
122	121	92	86	87	19
121	120	91	85	86	18
120	119	90	84	85	16
119	118	88	83	84	14
118	117	87	82	83	13
117	116	86	81	82	12
116	115	84	80	81	10
115	114	82	79	80	9
114	113	81	78	79	8
113	112	79	77	78	7
112	111	77	75-76	77	6
111	110	75	74	76	5
110	109	73	73	75	5
109	108	70	72	74	4
108	107	68	71	73	4
107	106	66	70	72	3
106	105	63	69	71	3
104-105	104	61	68	70	2
103	103	58	67	69	2
102	102	55	66	68	2
101	101	53	65	67	1
100	100	50			

not share a common normative group. The table simply provides a quick reference for changing IQ scores to percentile ranks.

Table 9-4 provides a convenient means of approximating stanines for intelligence tests which have means of 100 and standard deviations of 16 or 15. In addition, the table permits the examiner to approximate the percentage of cases which fall within each score range and to locate percentiles that define the limits of the score range.

Other interpretive aids provide evaluative descriptions of the examinee's performance. Those shown in Tables 9-5 and 9-6 seem to characterize the examinee and not the test score.

There are some very obvious dangers to using these classifications. It becomes very easy to forget that the descriptions must *in fact* refer to scores on the test, *not* to the examinee. In addition, if such descriptions are placed on records, persons who use the records might not be so cautious as the examiner in

Table 9-4. Stanine Approximations for IQ Tests Having a Mean of 100 and a Standard Deviation of 15 or 16

Stanines	Range in z units	IQ Range (SD = 16)	IQ Range (SD = 15)	Percentile Range
9	+ 1.75 and above	129+	127+	97+
8	+ 1.25 to + 1.75	121–128	120–126	90–96
7	+ .75 to + 1.25	113–120	112–119	78–89
6	+ .25 to + .75	105–112	104–111	61–77
5	– .25 to + .25	96–104	97–103	41–60
4	– .75 to – .25	88–95	89–96	24–40
3	– 1.25 to – .75	80–87	81–88	12–23
2	– 1.75 to – 1.25	73–79	75–80	5–11
1	below – 1.75	72 and below	74 and below	4 and below

Table 9-5. Intelligence Classifications for the Stanford-Binet Intelligence Scales

IQ Range	Classification	Percent of Cases Included
148 and above	Near-genius	.1
124–147	Very superior intelligence	6.5
112–123	Superior intelligence	16.0
88–112	Normal or average intelligence	54.7
76–87	Dull	16.0
64–75	Borderline deficiency	5.5
below 64	Feeble-mindedness	1.2

Adapted from S. R. Pinneau, *Changes in Intelligence Quotient from Infancy to Maturity* (Boston: Houghton Mifflin, 1961).

Table 9-6. Intelligence Classifications for the Wechsler Intelligence Scales

IQ Range	Classification	Percent of Cases Included
130 and above	Very superior	2.2
120–129	Superior	6.7
110–119	Bright normal	16.1
90–109	Average	50.0
80–89	Dull normal	16.1
70–79	Borderline	6.7
69 and below	Mental defective	2.2

Source: D. Wechsler, *Manual for the Wechsler Adult Intelligence Scale* (New York: The Psychological Corporation, 1955), p. 20.

the use of the description. As a consequence, it seems much more reasonable to use a classification which describes the score as "high" or "average" or "very low." There is little chance of this type description being mistaken for a qualitative evaluation of the person.

STANDARD ERROR OF MEASUREMENT

As Goldman (1961) points out, the use of norms to locate an examinee in a group is the simplest of the statistical procedures used as aids to test interpretation. This involves comparing a person's score with others' scores in a table of norms. There are complications in the use of norm tables, however. Usually the test user finds the subject's raw score and then looks in the table to find its equivalent in terms of some converted score (norm) which describes the performance of the group. Thus it might be found that a raw score of 130 is equal to an IQ score of 110. The problem arises when this converted score is interpreted as though it represented an absolute measure of a person's ability. It is in fact an *estimate* of his ability based on a test score that is subject to measurement error. Because of this measurement error an estimate of the person's "true" score is all we get from his performance on the test. His obtained score is only one of a large number of possible scores that he might achieve if a different sample of questions were used or if the test were administered at another time. Therefore to say that the examinee mentioned above "has an IQ of 110" is not correct.

Knowing that the subject has a potential range of IQ scores, the first step in interpreting the score is to set up a *confidence interval* about the score. The confidence interval is a range of scores that will include the individual's "true" score a designated percent of the times that it is used. A 95 percent confidence interval or band would, if the person were tested repeatedly, include his "true" score 95 times out of every 100 times it was applied. In other words, if a 95 percent confidence interval is set up around the person's score there would be 1 chance in 20 that the "true" score would lie outside the limits of the interval. A 68 percent confidence interval would include the "true" score about 68 times out of every 100 times it was applied. The confidence interval chosen will depend upon the degree of assurance the examiner requires that the interval will include the "true" score. Usually an 85 percent confidence interval is adequate and many examiners are satisfied with a 68 percent confidence interval.

If we assume that the test which yielded the IQ score of 110 has a standard error of measurement of 6, the 85 percent confidence interval (rounded) would be:

$$\text{Confidence interval} = 110 \pm 6(1.44) = 110 \pm 8.64 = 101\text{--}119$$

There is an 85 percent probability that the "true" score lies within the score limits 101–119. A confidence interval for any score can be established as follows:

1. Multiply the standard error of measurement by the z-value (Table 9-7) associated with the desired confidence interval.

2. Add the product to and subtract it from the subject's score.

3. Round the results to the nearest whole number.

According to Nunnally (1959), the above statements hold true only when the confidence interval is set up around the estimated "true" score, but the amount of error introduced by estimating from the obtained score is negligible.

TABLE 9-7 Values of z Used to Establish Confidence Intervals at Selected Levels

Confidence Interval	z-Value
99 percent	2.58
95 percent	1.96
85 percent	1.44
68 percent	1.00

More importantly, the consistent use of this band of scores in interpreting test scores will eliminate the false impression of a precise measurement of ability. It will also reduce the tendency to overvalue a particular point on the scale. The *School and College Ability Tests* use a 68 percent confidence interval expressed in terms of percentile ranks. The scores are reported as *percentile bands*, which consist of a *range* of percentile scores.

INTERPRETING DIFFERENCES BETWEEN SCORES

Many mental ability tests now yield multiple scores. The Wechsler Scales yield Verbal, Performance, and Total IQs. The California Test of Mental Maturity and the Lorge-Thorndike Intelligence Tests both yield Language and Non-language IQ scores. Scholastic-aptitude tests, such as the School and College Ability Tests, and multiple-aptitude tests, such as the Differential Aptitude Tests, yield multiple scores. A question which very frequently arises when interpreting such scores concerns the person's relative strengths in the different areas. Does he perform better on the Language Section than on the Nonlanguage Section? Is his Quantitative Score really lower than his Verbal Score?

Some test publishers have devised report forms which enable the tester to determine whether the various scores within the test differ significantly from each other. The SCAT, for example, is reported in percentile bands which are based on the obtained score and its standard error (Fig. 9-1).

Each percentile band covers a distance of approximately one standard error of measurement on either side of the obtained score. In interpreting the profile no importance is attached to differences between scores whose percentile bands overlap. This type of procedure can be used by the test interpreter even when the publishers do not provide such bands, by marking off one standard error of measurement on either side of the obtained score.

The bands may also be used with standard scores. When using this procedure the examiner must be sure that the standard error of measurement is expressed in the same units as the obtained score. Some manuals report the standard error in raw-score units only. When this occurs, the interpreter must add the standard error to the obtained raw score and then change the sum into the converted score. Next he must subtract the standard error from the obtained raw score and convert the remainder into the converted score. The range of scores between upper and lower limits of the interval constitutes the band.

Another approach to this problem is through the use of the *standard error*

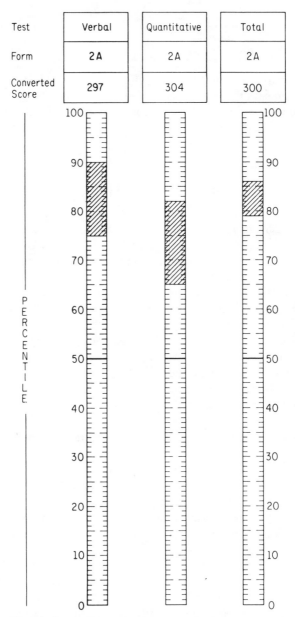

Fig. 9-1. Percentile bands. (Reproduced by permission of the copyright owner, Educational Testing Service, Princeton, N.J.)

of the difference between two test scores. This procedure involves setting up a level of significance at which one is willing to say that a difference is "really a difference." The 5 percent level of significance is a sufficiently stringent requirement for most practical work. In using this procedure one must first calculate the standard error of the difference, which may be found from the standard errors of measurement of the two scores by the formula

$$SE_{diff} = \sqrt{\sigma^2_{meas_1} + \sigma^2_{meas_2}}$$

where σ_{meas_1} = standard error of measurement for Test 1
σ_{meas_2} = standard error of measurement for Test 2

Since the two scores have to be expressed in terms of the same scale—for example, *T*-scores or deviation IQs, the standard deviations will be the same and the statistic may be calculated directly from the reliability coefficients by the formula

$$SE_{diff} = \sigma\sqrt{2 - r_1 - r_2}$$

where σ = standard deviation of the tests
r_1 = reliability coefficient for Test 1
r_2 = reliability coefficient for Test 2

The Technical Report for the California Test of Mental Maturity Series, 1963 Revision (California Test Bureau, 1965), reports the standard error of measurement for the Language Section of Level 5 of the Long Form to be 4.9 IQ points. The standard error of measurement of the Non-Language Section is reported to be 6 IQ points. The standard deviation of both sections is 16 IQ points. Using the first formula presented above, the standard error of the difference between two test scores would be

$$SE_{diff} = \sqrt{(4.9)^2 + (6)^2} = 7.82$$

To determine how large a score difference could be obtained by chance at the .05 level, we multiply the standard error of the difference between the two scores by 1.96 (a normal-curve value). The result is about 16. This means that a difference of 16 or more IQ points between the Language and Non-Language Sections would occur as a result of measurement error only 5 percent of the time. Thus one could say at the 5 percent level of significance that a difference of about 16 IQ points or greater is a "real difference."

EXPECTANCY TABLES

The meaningful use of norm tables in test interpretation requires that the test have some degree of validity, so that one can say that high scores on the test indicate a greater probability of obtaining high scores on the criterion than low scores. The relationship is not explicit, however, and therefore much of the potential usefulness of the relationship is lost. A type of comparison technique which combines the normative data and the validity data is the *expectancy table*. In the expectancy table the relationships between the test scores and criterion scores are shown directly. Usually the expectancy table shows how a group of people with a given test score performed on the criterion. An example of an expectancy table was used in Chapter 3 to illustrate how such a table can be used to assess a test's validity. The one that follows (Table 9-8) is presented to illustrate its use in test interpretation.

Table 9-8 was devised as an illustration of how expectancy tables could be used to determine the probability that a student with a given test score would be

Table 9-8. Expectancy Table Showing DAT Sentences Test Scores and Grades Earned in Rhetoric*

Total No.	Number receiving each grade					Test Scores	Percent receiving each grade					Total Percent
	F	D	C	B	A		F	D	C	B	A	
1					1	80-89					100	100
5				1	4	70-79				20	80	100
22			3	14	5	60-69			14	63	23	100
23			9	8	6	50-59			39	35	26	100
22		3	13	6		40-49		14	59	27		100
16	1	3	9	3		30-39	6	19	56	19		100
8	1	4	3			20-29	13	50	37			100
2		2				10-19		100				100
1	1					0-9		100				100
100	2	13	37	32	16							

*From *Expectancy Tables—A Way of Interpreting Test Validity, Test Service Bulletin* No. 38. By permission of The Psychological Corporation, 1949.

successful in a specified course. In interpreting a score falling in the interval 60–69, the test interpreter could say "Of the people who scored like this, 23 percent earned A's, 63 percent earned B's, and 14 percent earned C's." He could also say, "86 percent of the people who scored like this earned B or better grades." Adaptations of this type of table can be made for a multitude of purposes.

It is also possible to construct more complex tables which have two predictors (Wesman, 1966). Table 9-9 is an example of such a table.

The great advantage of double-entry expectancy tables is that they permit simultaneous presentation of relationships among two predictors and a criterion. For example, it can be seen in the table that of the people who scored 40 and above on both the numerical language usage tests, 5 earned A's, 2 earned B's and 1 earned a C. Being able to combine the information from two predictors may held considerably in predicting the criterion performance, since low scores on one predictor may be compensated by higher ability on the other. Expectancy tables are an extremely useful means of presenting and interpreting test data. Considering how easy it is to construct such tables, it is surprising that they are not more generally used. Table 9-9 was empirically derived—that is, it is composed of results actually reported by the school. It is possible to derive tables on

Table 9-9. Relationship Between APT-N and APT-LU Scores, and Grades in Science Seventh Grade Students (N = 294)*

Numerical Score	Language Usage Score									Raw Total	
	19 and below		20-29 N		30-39 N		40 and above				
40 and above	A B C D E		A B C D E	2	A B C D E	6 6 1	A B C D E	5 2 1	A B C D E	11 8 4	
30-39	A B C D E	1 2 1	A B C D E	1 7 8	A B C D E	4 12 12	A B C D E	5 10 3	A B C D E	11 29 25 1	
20-29	A B C D E	2 3 9 8 3	A B C D E	3 7 25 6 7	A B C D E	 6 17 1	A B C D E	1 8 2	A B C D E	6 24 53 15 10	
19 and below	A B C D E	1 2 22 19 19	A B C D E	1 2 18 6 4	A B C D E	1 1 1	A B C D E		A B C D E	3 4 41 25 24	
									Grand Total		
Column Total (by grade)	A B C D E	4 5 33 27 23	A B C D E	5 16 53 12 11	A B C D E	11 24 31 1 1	A B C D E	11 20 6	A B C D E	31 65 123 40 35	

*From *Double-Entry Expectancy Tables, Test Service Bulletin* No. 56. By permission of The Psychological Corporation, 1966.

a theoretical basis using correlation and regression theory, but this of course involves appropriate knowledge of statistics.

USING THE RESULTS OF RESEARCH

Some of the most valuable normative data are the means and standard deviations reported in professional journals. The journals frequently report such information on groups with whom one might wish to compare an examinee's score. Table 9-10, for example, presents means, standard deviations, and sample sizes for the occupational levels of the fathers of children used in standardizing the WISC. The WISC manual presents the standard error of measurement for the scale. Suppose that Mary's father is employed in an occupation which fits into the bottom category and Mary obtains an IQ score on the WISC of 100. Does her score differ significantly from the average score of children whose fathers are so employed? This can be determined by using a formula presented by Davis

Table 9-10. Means, Standard Deviations, and Sample Sizes for the Occupational Groups Represented by Fathers of Children Who Participated in the WISC Standardization*

Occupational Group	Mean	SD	N
Profession and semiprofessional	110.3	13.3	176
Proprietors, managers, and officials	106.2	12.4	256
Clerical, sales, and kindred	105.2	11.1	280
Craftsmen, foremen, and kindred	101.3	12.4	393
Operatives and kindred	99.1	12.2	363
Farmers and farm managers	97.4	14.0	222
Domestic, protective, and other service.	97.0	12.5	122
Farm laborers, foremen, and laborers	94.2	12.8	303

*Adapted from H. Seashore, A. Wesman, and J. Doppelt, "The standardization of the Wechsler Intelligence Scale for Children," *Journal of Consulting Psychology* 14 pp. 99–110 (1950).

(1964) for comparing an individual's score (X) with the average score $(\overline{X})$ for a group of which he is not a member:

$$SE_m (X - \overline{X}) = SE_{m_x} \sqrt{\frac{N + 1}{N}}$$

where $SE_m (X - \overline{X})$ = standard error of measurement of the difference between X and $\overline{X}$.

SE_{m_x} = standard error of measurement of test
N = number of people in group

Substituting the data for the WISC,

$$SE_m (X - \overline{X}) = 3.36 \sqrt{\frac{304}{303}} = 3.36$$

By multiplying the value 3.36 by 1.64 the magnitude of the difference needed to be significant at the 10 percent level of significance can be established. That value, 5.5, indicates that a difference of 5.5 is the smallest difference that we can consider significant at the 10 percent level of significance. In Mary's case, we can say that her score is significantly different from the average score for the group.

The importance of this statistic becomes apparent when it is interpreted in light of other data known about Mary's socioeconomic level. The absolute value of Mary's score (100) is the mean for the national norm group of the WISC, and ordinarily no special significance would be attached to such a score. However, since Mary comes from a group known to obtain lower-than-average scores, and since her score is significantly higher than the average score for her group, Mary may be an exceptional person and interpretations usually accorded a score of 100 may be inappropriate. At a time when the value of psychological tests for use with a number of minority groups is being challenged, the simple statistics presented above can be used as a safeguard against underestimating the value of scores which depart significantly from the mean scores for such groups. In the example given the SE_m $(X-\overline{X})$ had the same value as the SE_m. This will not be the case if the comparison group is very small.

It is frequently desirable to compare an individual's score with the average score for a group of which he is a member. Because of the wide departures of many groups from the national norms these statistics have their usefulness when one wishes to make intragroup comparisons. For example, suppose Sam's school uses the California Test of Mental Maturity to measure general mental ability. The school is in a low socioeconomic, predominantly Negro, neighborhood. Sam is a black fifth-grader. The mean IQ score for 60 fifth-graders in Sam's school is 88, and Sam's score is 96. The school counselor wants to know whether Sam's score departs significantly from the class average to determine whether he should be given special work. The manual for the CTMM reports the standard error of measurement for children in Sam's grade to be 5. Assuming that the test is as reliable for this group as for the group that the standard error was calculated on (a risky assumption to say the least), Sam's score could be compared to the class average by using the following formula (Davis, 1964):

$$SE_m \ (X - \overline{X}) = SE_{m_x} \ \sqrt{\frac{N-1}{N}}$$

Substituting the data for Sam's class,

$$SE_m \ (X - \overline{X}) = 5 \ \sqrt{\frac{59}{60}} = 4.9$$

Again setting the level of significance at 10 percent, we multiply the SE_m $(X-\overline{X})$, 4.9, by 1.64 and find that a difference between the mean and a score must be about 8 points to be considered significant. Sam's score is therefore significantly higher than that of his class and the special work seems appropriate.

REFERENCES

Anastasi, A., *Psychological Testing*, 3rd ed., New York: Macmillan, 1968.

Davis, F. B., *Educational Measurements and Their Interpretation*, Belmont, Calif.: Wadsworth, 1964.

Goldman, L., *Using Tests in Counseling*, New York: Appleton-Century, 1962.

Nunnally, J. C., *Tests and Measurements: Assessment and Prediction*, New York: McGraw-Hill, 1959.

Pinneau, S. R., *Changes In Intelligence Quotient From Infancy To Maturity*, Boston: Houghton-Mifflin, 1961.

Seashore, H., A. Wesman, and J. Doppelt, "The Standardization of the Wechsler Intelligence Scale for Children," *Journal of Consulting Psychology* 14 (1950), 99-110.

Wechsler, D., *Manual for the Wechsler Adult Intelligence Scale*, New York: Psychological Corporation, 1955.

Wesman, A. G., "Expectancy tables - a Way of Interpreting Test Validity," *Test Service Bulletin No. 38*. New York: Psychological Corporation, 1949.

——, "Double-Entry Expectancy Tables," *Test Service Bulletin No. 56*. New York: Psychological Corporation, 1966.

Test Interpretation:
Clinical Uses of the
Wechsler Scales
and the
Stanford-Binet / CHAPTER 10

The use of intelligence tests for diagnostic purposes has received considerable criticism in recent years. Probably the most important reason for the criticism has been the accumulation of research that reveals the shortcomings involved in diagnostic procedures. For example, many of the "signs" used with the Wechsler-Bellevue scale have not held up in validation studies.

Meehl (1954) and Cronbach (1956) have presented extensive reviews of research relating to the controversy over the merits of clinical versus statistical prediction. The conclusions reported in these reviews tend to indicate that in the process of working with a large amount of complex, meaningful data, the diagnostician generally does a rather poor job when compared with the statistician. That is, when it comes to predicting human behavior, the psychologist who relies on statistical procedures will have better results than the one who relies on clinical judgment. It would be unwise, however, to throw out all clinical data obtained in the administration of a mental ability test. Rather than feed the results into a computer and get answers in this fashion, it appears that the most effective route in diagnostic testing at the current time is to make use of validation studies and statistical procedures so that the test administrator may rely heavily on actuarial data as well as clinical hunches. In other words, test administrators should be familiar with actuarial procedures yet be able to make good use of clinical cues.

This chapter deals with clinical applications of test data obtained from the Wechsler scales and the Stanford-Binet.

THE WISC AND THE WAIS

Since scores are obtained for each subtest of the Wechsler scales, it is a natural inclination to attempt to use subtest scores in a diagnostic manner. Unfortunately, research studies have not completely justified this procedure. The major reason why diagnosis on the basis of subtest data is extremely difficult is that the scores can vary for many reasons. Variation in subtest scores may be attributed to a wide variety of determiners, including the following.

1. *The general factor, g.* Each subtest on the Wechsler, to a degree, is measuring general intelligence *g*. While the amount of *g* measured by each subtest varies among the tests and at different age levels, the measurement of *g* may account for as much as half of the variance in any one subtest.
2. *Nonintellectual determiners.* Anxiety, testing conditions, environmental and cultural influences, bodily concerns, examiner's influence, need for achievement, age, sex, educational level, etc., may influence the scores of any subtest.
3. *Primary factors.* Factor-analysis studies have indicated that frequently a subtest may contribute to a factor that is present in a variety of other subtests and these factors, called primary factors, account for varying degrees of subtest variability.
4. *Measurement error.* Variance accounted for by the lack of test reliability, and reported in the manual as a standard error of the measurement, accounts for an additional portion of score variation.
5. *Subtest specifics.* Unique factors that may be attributed to a particular subtest account for a very small amount of the variance exhibited by the subtest.

These comments should not be construed to mean that subtest scores are worthless. The performance of the subject during a particular subtest may indeed be rich with cues concerning the individual's approach to a problem situation. The qualitative aspects of a subject's performance may be as important as the quantitative results. Each of the Wechsler subtests is discussed below and examples of the type of qualitative responses that should be observed are indicated. Frequently these observations should be considered as *tentative hypotheses* to be verified by other means.

CLINICAL ANALYSIS OF THE SUBTESTS

Information

Since information is usually the first test given, the behavior of young children during the subtest should be noted carefully and a verbatim account of their responses recorded. Evidence of immature speech, evidence of dependent behavior, attempts to impress the examiner, and similar initial behaviors should be noted and contrasted with later tests to see whether these behaviors persist or are just an initial reaction to an adult. While the Information items generally can be answered by very specific responses, attempts to elaborate, to impress the examiner, or to show knowledge should be noted. When asked, "From what animal do we get milk?" children who wish to impress the examiner may bring up the concept of mammals rather than respond simply with "cow." After a subject is asked "What must you do to make water boil?" the explicitness involved in his answer should be noted. Frequently a meticulous youngster will give a very long and explicit response to this question. When asked who discovered America, the more knowledgeable youngsters often will bring up the Erickson-Columbus controversy. If asked where the sun sets, precocious youngsters may contest the question and indicate that, in reality, rotation of the planets is involved. Following the question about what the stomach does, the examiner should note whether a simple or complicated answer involving digestion is given. It should be noted, too, that an answer stating that the stomach holds food is qualitatively different from an answer explaining the digestive process.

The inclination of the subject to guess during this subtest should be noted. This sometimes becomes evident on questions concerning the height of the average American man and the distance from New York to Chicago.

The perseveration of responses should be carefully noted. Perseveration refers to the repeating of an answer that was previously given to a question but which is not appropriate for the present question. For example, a subject is asked how many pennies make a nickel and he responds "five"; but then he responds "five" to a subsequent question about the number of days in a week. With young children this may indicate desire for examiner approval or the inability to shift from one item to the next.

Some responses, such as an inappropriate numerical answer to an item following an item where a numerical response is appropriate, may indicate that the subject is a slow learner. With other children it may be simply a matter of being ill at ease.

The items that are missed should be examined to determine both the level of difficulty and the degree of cultural bias. Frequently children from impoverished homes miss what should be fairly easy items and then are able to answer more difficult items that appear later in the test. The question "Who wrote *Romeo and Juliet*?" is a culturally biased item that frequently is missed by children from impoverished homes. These children also frequently miss the item concerning the location of Chile because of their greater concern about food than about geography.

With adults, the initial reaction to the information test may be one of feeling threatened or defensive. Comments concerning reasons for not knowing an item, or the evidence of hostile behavior when an item is missed, should be noted. Whether the subject tends to give explicit, general, brief, or verbose answers also should be noted. (Items such as "How does yeast cause dough to rise?" may elicit a very brief or very involved explanation.)

The nature of the items missed by adults may be important. Items such as, "Who wrote Hamlet?" tend to show more cultural bias than other items. Rapaport et al. (1968) report that on the Wechsler-Bellevue failures in the middle ranges of the test frequently are indications of an impoverished educational or cultural environment. This hypothesis would tend to be verified if the individual missed many of the middle items but knew many of the later items in the test. Rapaport et al. contend that failures on the initial items plus success on the later items, when coupled with inappropriate ideation, frequently indicate either a reflection of temporary inefficiency or psychotic disorganization.

Information generally is described as being a test of verbal ability that reflects cultural background and memory. Factor-analysis studies by Cohen (1957, 1959) indicate that this test is a good measure of g and that it contributes to a factor labeled Verbal Comprehension I. Its subject specificity (measurement of unique functions) is low at most ages, and this emphasizes the danger of attempting to interpret an Information score in isolation.

Comprehension

Because Comprehension tends to elicit complex explanations, it can be rich in clinical cues. For young children, questions concerning what to do when you cut your finger, or lose one of your friend's toys, can elicit responses that are either dependent and immature, or independent. A child may consistently indicate the tendency to seek help from his mother or others when confronted with these kinds of situations, or he may indicate that he would cope with the situation in an independent and effective manner. Questions concerning what to do when a fellow much smaller than yourself starts a fight with you, or why criminals are locked up, allow the subject to verbalize situations containing aggression or hostility. A child can respond to these questions in ways that indicate independence, desire to manipulate others, naive perceptions of problems, cooperative solutions, verbalized hostility, or aggression. This subtest also gives the subject an opportunity to give either fairly short or quite elaborate responses. Unfortunately, many of the items in the test provide higher scores when more than one reason is given, instead of awarding equal scores for single acceptable reasons. This tends to penalize the individual who gives rather brief, concise answers. An important aspect of the clinical assessment of comprehension involves the determination of whether the subject is parroting socially learned responses or is able to produce abstract concepts based on an understanding of a complex situation.

Rapaport et al. (1968) characterize this test as one measuring judgment in reality situations that require the delay of impulses. The researchers differentiate between those who have an abstract comprehension of the function of judgment, those who have a steroryped comprehension of the function of judgment, those who have a steroryped answer, and those whose judgment may have deteriorated but who are still able to give superficial responses that may be scorable.

Qualitative differences may be found between those who come up with succinct answers, those who see too many possibilities to make up their minds, and those whose judgment seems to be in constant struggle with their impulses. There is a qualitative difference implied between people who keep away from bad company because of the possibility of a bad influence and those who consider bad company uninteresting. Then there are subjects who may not want to keep away from bad company because they wish to be like them, and there are others who are so strong that they will not be influenced by bad company but will learn from them. Rapaport et al. (1968) consider failure of very easy items by adults to be characteristic of certain psychotic categories when more difficult items are passed. Undoubtedly, the ideation expressed by psychotics in answer to specific questions is of more diagnostic significance than the score on the test.

Cohen's (1957) factor analysis studies indicate that Comprehension is a moderately good measure of *g*. The test, however, shows an unusual relationship to the factors Verbal Comprehension I and Verbal Comprehension II that changes with age. For younger children, the test contributes to Verbal Comprehension II which involves the ability to express verbally some form of social or practical judgment. At the adult level the test tends to contribute to Verbal Comprehension I which reflects knowledge of formally learned, socially correct responses. At the 13½-year level it contributes to both of these factors. Cohen thus concludes that the test measures verbal judgment at younger ages and formally learned responses at older ages while, at the 13½-year level it tends to measure both and functions as a pivotal point. Cohen (1957) also maintains that the WISC has low specificity, especially for essentially normal individuals, and that singling out the score of this test for unique interpretation is unjustified.

Arithmetic

Wechsler indicates that Arithmetic essentially measures concentration and arithmetic reasoning, with concentration being affected by fluctuations of tension or a transient emotional reaction, and arithmetic reasoning being affected by education and occupation. Rapaport et al. (1968) classify Arithmetic as mainly a test of concentration and feel that the scores could be affected by anxiety. Cohen (1957, 1959), on the basis of factor analysis, finds that Arithmetic is a moderately good measure of *g* in the WISC but only a mediocre measure in the WAIS. At the 7½- and 10½-year levels, he finds that the test enters into the Verbal Comprehension I Factor, which is knowledge impressed by formal education. At the 13½-year level, this test shifts to measuring Freedom from Distractability, and it has a large loading on this factor at adult age levels. In addition, Cohen finds a great deal of subtest specificity and concludes that Arithmetic could be used as a measure of arithmetic ability at all ages except the age 7½ level. Cohen's studies thus seem to indicate that Wechsler's assessment is essentially accurate, and that Arithmetic appears to be measuring both concentration and arithmetic reasoning, being a better measure of concentration at the older levels than at the younger levels.

Arithmetic, Digit Span, and Coding (or Digit Symbol) have long been looked upon as measures of anxiety. Cohen's findings would raise the possibility that anxiety is not reflected in arithmetic performance as one grows older. In testing age 13½ and above, test administrators are faced with the problem of attempting to determine the amount of influence that both concentration and arithmetic ability have on the test scores obtained. Frequently clinical cues may be used to help make this distinction. Since the subject may verbalize minimally on this test, the examiner is frequently left with only a few physical or verbal expressions of a spontaneous nature unless he investigates performance. Many examiners, when evaluating the qualitative aspects of this test, point out wrong responses to the subject to see whether he can correct them. This is done in the attempt to differentiate between temporary inefficiencies and the inability to understand the concepts involved. Temporary inefficiencies are likely to show up on easier items due to the pressure of speed. Some examiners encourage the subjects to think out loud when they are working with problems in an attempt to differentiate between temporary inefficiencies and the lack of arithmetic ability. These procedures are recommended only for experienced examiners.

In summation, clinical cues may be obtained from the examinee either from verbal or physical expressions, to help determine whether anxiety or lack of arithmetic ability is influencing the score earned on this particular subtest. Hopefully, the clinical cues may be combined with the scores and with other data, such as educational-occupational status, to attempt to determine the exact function of this test for an individual subject.

Similarities

One of the important observations that can be made during the Similarities Test is whether the subject tends to function on a concrete, functional, or abstract level in his attempt to answer the questions. Subjects who are unable to abstract well are frequently concerned with the concrete detail of the two terms presented in an item. For example, when asked in what way an axe and a saw are alike, such a subject may visualize the teeth of the saw in contrast to the smooth blade of an axe and indicate that they are not alike. Another individual who operates in a concrete fashion at a slightly higher level may indicate that they are alike because they are made of metal—an answer which does not merit any credit. A person who tends to stress the functional aspects of objects may say that the axe and saw are used to cut wood. The subject who is able to abstract well may come up with the answer that they are both tools. When observing these three levels of conceptualization, the tester should keep in mind that for certain items of this subtest, concrete or functional answers may or may not be awarded points because the scoring is based on statistical procedures. Hence, if the subject were to say that an axe and a saw are alike because they are made of metal, he would receive no credit; if he said a coat and dress are alike because they are made of cloth, he would receive one point.

The typical level of conceptualization should be observed throughout this test. When doing this, the examiner must bear in mind that toward the end of the test when the items become more difficult there is generally a tendency for the subject to return to a more concrete or functional response because he cannot successfully produce an abstract response.

This test may be quite frustrating for individuals who tend to be concrete or functional in their conceptualizations, so another important observation that can be made is the subject's response to this frustration. Sometimes it is difficult to distinguish between a negativistic person who is resisting the test and someone who is operating near the concrete level and genuinely does not perceive the similarity involved. Occasionally, too, when a child indicates that two items are not alike, his response results from confidence and independence rather than a negative attitude. This type of child tends to look upon the items as "trick" questions and may not be negativistic at all.

Another type of clinical observation that may be made involves responses that relate to *one* of the stimulus words rather than *both*. When given the item "A knife and a piece of glass both _____," a subject may respond with "break." In this case he probably is reacting to glass but not to knife. In a similar fashion, when asked how scissors and a copper pan are alike, a child's response may indicate that scissors are perceived as weapons. A response indicating unusual stimulus value for one of the words to the exclusion of the other frequently portrays a preoccupation that the child has.

When analyzing this subtest the examiner should remember that many of the abstract responses are quite conventional and may be available to well-informed subjects even though they lack the ability to perform abstract thinking. As an example, it is quite easy to think of dogs and lions as animals because of their typical classification. The perception of similarity in *fly* and *tree* because of their having life does not generally stem from conventional information. An abstract response, then, may be a simple parroting of available information rather than the result of abstract conceptualization.

Wechsler indicates that Similarities is a test that measures the individual's ability to perceive common elements in the terms he is asked to compare. The test requires verbal comprehension for success, and at higher levels it assesses the ability to bring terms together under a single concept. The WISC is thought to assess logical and abstract thinking ability. Rapaport et al. (1968), categorize Similarities as a test of verbal concept formation, but they point out that conventional verbal responses may be operative. Cohen's studies (1957, 1959) indicate that the test is a good measure of g and enters into the Verbal Comprehension I Factor at all age levels. At the ages of 13½ and 18–19, it also contributes to the Verbal Comprehension II Factor. A tentative interpretation would be that the test measures verbally retained knowledge at all levels, but at the 13½ and 18–19 level it may measure the ability to form concepts and use logic and judgment.

Vocabulary

Vocabulary has long been recognized as one of the best tests for providing clinical insight into the intellectual functioning of subjects. Vocabulary scores tend to be quite resistant to impairment by either temporary or long-standing inefficiencies and deterioration. However, when intellectual deterioration does take place, the level of functioning on Vocabulary tends to change. Frequently, severely impaired individuals (such as those who are schizophrenic) will retain much of their functioning on Vocabulary but will be identifiable by an analysis of their responses. Peculiar verbalizations (such as associations rather than definitions, sound alliteration, or extreme intellectualization) are cues to severe impairment. Grossly impaired individuals also are likely to fail on easier items because of their ideation.

The examiner must be careful in generalizing about a subject's failing easy items, however, since frequently this is also an indication of cultural impoverishment. The qualitative analysis of the response frequently indicates which of the possible conditions may be operative. As Vocabulary is one of the most stable subtests, the vocabulary performance is frequently compared to the total scores on the verbal and performance tests to see whether there appears to be deterioration on the other tests. This process should be done very carefully, however, and should be coupled with an assessment of the intellectual level and cultural background of the individual.

Vocabulary responses tend to give cues concerning the amount of verbal information and the range of ideas available to the subject, and the test is believed to be highly dependent on early experience and education. The responses often give definite cues concerning the cultural background of the subject, especially his experiences during his younger years.

An analysis of the responses also tends to provide insight into the level of verbal expression typical of the subject. Appropriate synonyms are usually considered one of the highest levels of verbal functioning. Critical uses or qualities constitute a less desirable level, noncritical uses or qualities constitute an even lower level, and the use of the word in a sentence is the lowest level of functioning.

Many cues concerning the handling of aggression, social development, and life experiences are reflected in the responses of children. The examiner, however, should be very careful not to overreact to these clues. Frequently, responses to the word "sword" are quite aggressive among younger boys and do not necessarily reflect anything but an appropriate response to the stimulus word. If aggressive replies are used in response to more "innocuous" types of words, then aggressive tendencies may be suggested.

Wechsler indicates that Vocabulary is a good measure of general intelligence that reflects schooling and learning. The test also indicates the amount of verbal information that the subject possesses and the range of his ideas based upon experience and education. Rapaport et al. (1968) feel that the test is quite dependent upon the cultural wealth of early education and environmental experiences and is quite resistant to improvement by later schooling or experience. Cohen (1957, 1959) concludes that Vocabulary is a good measure of *g* either when used by itself or in combination with other subtests. At the age-10½ level it contributes to the Verbal Comprehension II Factor. It is generally acknowledged that Vocabulary is one of the best measures of intellectual functioning.

Digit Span

Since the subject is required only to repeat digits either forward or backward on this test, a minimum amount of observation is possible. This subtest is believed to measure attention, concentration, memory, or freedom from distractability, and is believed to be subject to interference by anxiety or temporary inefficiencies. It is very important to observe the performance of the subject on this test in order to attempt to determine which of the above-mentioned factors are operative in the performance. One of the crucial observations is whether the subject repeats the digits as a series or attempts to group them. Rapaport et al. (1968) indicate that simply repeating the digits may test attention, but if the subject groups the digits he is altering the function of the test and the test then may actually measure concentration.

Another observation is concerned with whether the subject attempts to visualize the digits or whether he attempts to reproduce them auditorily. Frequently, experienced examiners will inquire about the method used by the examinee. When the subject fails a particular series, the examiner should note whether this is done by transposing digits, interjecting incorrect digits, or producing more or less than the number of digits originally given. Rapaport et al. (1968) suggest that reversing two digits may indicate temporary inefficiency or negativism, and that negativistic subjects are more likely to do better on digits backward than digits forward.

The examiner also should observe whether the subject can adapt to the rhythm of the examiner in repeating the digits. Occasionally, neurotic or highly anxious subjects are unable to achieve on this series because of the speed with which the digits are presented and they may comment on this. If, after testing, the examiner alters the speed and the subject is then able to perform this task, it may be assumed that the person is lacking in the flexibility that is needed for him to adapt to the rhythm of the examiner.

During this test the examiner should observe whether the subject seems to perform in an effortless manner or with a great deal of concentration. If the subject gives an effortless performance the test is likely to be measuring attention, but if the individual is anxious he frequently finds it necessary to exert a great deal of concentration on his performance—and this is what is measured. Other types of observation involve noting whether easier series are failed while the more difficult series are completed, and noting the amount of discrepancy between digits forward and digits backward. Kitzinger and Blumberg (1951) feel that distractability is generally indicated by intratest variability. A wide discrepancy between digits forward and digits reversed, with the digits-forward score being much greater, is generally indicative of mental disturbance, while a larger score on digits reversed may indicate compulsive or negativistic trends.

Wechsler describes Digit Span as mainly a measure of attention and rote memory, and he suggests that extreme difficulty with this test often has diagnostic significance for predicting mental deficiency or organic impairment. When organic impairment is not indicated, poor performance on this test may be due to anxiety or inattention. Rapaport et al. (1968) classify Digit Span mainly as a test of attention unless grouping occurs, in which case it may also measure concentration. Cohen (1959) indicates that when combined with Arithmetic, Digit Span is a good measure of Factor C (Freedom from Distractability) in the WAIS and upper WISC levels. He also indicates that at adult levels it appears to have a minor unique function. Lutey (1966, p. 71) concludes that

> Although Digit Span may function most consistently and effectively as an assessment of Freedom from Distractability in all age groups *for most subjects*, beyond this, it has a differential meaning for special groups and its interpretation, singly or as a part of a cluster of subtests, can be appropriately made *only* by reference to other characteristics of the given subject; e.g., in older individuals the memory aspect may be prominent; in neurotics, the anxiety effects are pronounced, in brain-damaged, the significance of performance on digits backward appears highly diagnostic; in pre-school children it seems to have a strong affinity to the Verbal Comprehension I Factor and enters into an undefined factor called "Picture Arrangement"; in adolescents and adults it appears to be involved in a factor labeled "General Technical Sophistication," the prominence of which increases with age; in mental retardates it has special diagnostic value as a measure of "Trace" or short-term memory, etc.

In addition, Lutey hypothesizes that the anxiety measured by Digit Span may be test anxiety in subjects who recognize that they are test-anxious. She further hypothesizes that the specific factor measured by Digit Span is the ability to inhibit, control, delay, or confine responses.

Digit Span has long been associated with what is termed the "anxiety triad." In the event that Digit Span, Arithmetic, and Digit Symbols (or Coding) all are low, anxiety is frequently postulated. Digit Span also has been associated with what is called the Trace measure. The Trace measure is composed of Arithmetic, Digit Span, and Coding, and when all three of these subtests tend to be low when compared with the individual's own mean, it is generally an indication of mental retardation. From the above descriptions, it is apparent that the score on Digit Span may be affected by a wide variety of variables, and that the interpretation of scores achieved on this subtest must be made with extreme caution.

Picture Completion

Picture Completion is another subtest that does not elicit much observable behavior. One of the crucial behaviors that may be observed, however, is whether the subject points to the missing item or is able to verbalize concerning the missing portion. If he verbalizes concerning the missing portion, it is important to note the *level* of his response. On the *fly item* there is a difference between indicating that a whisker or "that little thing sticking out" is missing, versus "an antenna is missing." It is generally assumed that a higher level of abstraction is reached by the child who can respond to each missing part with a correct verbal symbol.

A very typical response on the part of children and some adults is the comment that there is "nothing missing." This may be interpreted in several ways. The first interpretation may simply indicate a lack of attention to the instructions with the result that the subject is structuring the task to be one of indicating whether or not there is something missing. Other subjects may say there is nothing missing in a defensive manner, indicating that they are not able to see anything and believe that they are being tricked.

The perseveration of responses should be carefully noted. Frequently, a child who is retarded or disturbed will perseverate. Occasionally perseveration may be noted in the very young child who has assumed approval was given for a previous answer and is dependent enough to want to elicit this same type of approval.

Rapaport et al. (1968) indicate that a high score on this subtest is characteristic of a paranoid-ego structure due to a perceptual overalertness. Research has failed to bear out this hypothesis. Some children may do well on this test because of previous training to attend to detail, whereas others may do poorly simply because of impulsiveness. Observation of the subject may shed some light on whether the score was influenced by impulsiveness or critical observation.

Wechsler describes Picture Completion as a measure of the subject's ability to differentiate between essential and nonessential detail. The test involves the use of basic perceptual and conceptual abilities, visual recognition, and the identification of familiar objects and forms. Wechsler refers to this test (in the WISC) as a test of visual alertness and visual memory. Rapaport et al. (1968) indicate that Picture Completion measures the ability to concentrate on visually perceived material. The tasks in the test involve the ability to discover an inconsistency or deficiency, to appraise relationships in a limited time, and to concentrate. The items are based on common information from everyday life and do not require any special background. Cohen (1957, 1959) states that Picture Completion is an excellent measure of *g* in the WAIS, but is a poor measure of *g* in the WISC. In both the WISC and the WAIS the test loads on Cohen's Factor D (application of judgment to situations following some implicit verbal manipulation).

In the WISC the test also contains loadings on Perceptual Organization at the ages of 10½ and 13½. A factor analytic study by Saunders (1960) indicates that Picture Completion produces three factors which he labels Maintenance of Contact, Maintenance of Perspective, and Effect of Uncertainty. He suggests that Maintenance of Contact is a unique contribution of Picture Completion and refers to contact with reality. His Maintenance of Perspective Factor is somewhat similar to Cohen's Verbal Comprehension Factor II.

In summary, it appears that Picture Completion tends to contribute to the Relevancy Factor (Cohen's D Factor) at all ages. At the adult level it appears to measure what Saunders calls Maintenance of Contact and Effect of Uncertainty. The Effect of Uncertainty should not be interpreted unless it is combined with Object Assembly as suggested by Saunders.

Picture Arrangement

One of the crucial observations to be made when one is administering this subtest to children is whether the subject progresses from right to left, or left to right. Experienced examiners occasionally ask the child to tell a story describing his arrangement of the pictures. This allows the examiner to determine the sequencing direction and whether an incorrect placement of pictures may be due to a creative interpretation of the situation or to simple randomness. With adults who appear to be highly disturbed it frequently is helpful for the examiner to have them tell a story so that he may gain insight into the reason for an unusual sequence of pictures. Eliciting stories from the subject is not recommended for all of the items on this test because it will have a tendency to result in a spuriously high score.

Another observation that should be made is whether the subject realizes that he is being timed on the test. A child who does not recognize the time element involved, or a subject who is rather deliberate and does not hurry on this task, is likely to be penalized. When a subject receives a rather high number of points but few (if any) time bonuses, his score may be the result of particular personality traits, and this should be noted. Wechsler describes Picture Arrangement as a test which assesses the subject's ability to comprehend or size up a total situation, and performance on it depends upon the subject's ability to get the idea of the story. In the WISC it also is considered to be a test requiring interpretation of social situations. Rapaport et al. (1968) describe Picture Arrangement as essentially a test of planning and anticipation. The planning element or "anticipating the future" implies both attention and judgment. Concentration enters into this task only when the subject is able to distinguish essential from nonessential elements in the pictures. Cohen concludes that Picture Arrangement in the WAIS is a mediocre measure of g and is a very weak and ambiguous measure of four of the five factors. In the WISC, Picture Arrangement is the best measure of g among the performance subtests—particularly at the ages of $7\frac{1}{2}$ and $10\frac{1}{2}$. Picture Arrangement thus appears to be an excellent measure of g in the WISC, but its function beyond this is not clear.

Block Design

The subject's approach to this test should be observed very carefully. Some subjects utilize a trial-and-error approach and rapidly manipulate the blocks in an attempt to reproduce the design. Other subjects approach the task in a very systematic way, analyze the design, and then place each block very deliberately. Neither of these approaches is as efficient as a combination of the two techniques. Some subjects approach the task by using a whole-design approach, while others break the design into segments. Since the designs become progressively difficult, the whole-design approach becomes less and less effective and, if the subject is not able to switch to another approach, his score on the test may be depressed.

Some children rotate their bodies or heads to get a better perspective of the design, and some find it necessary to leave space between the blocks in the assembled design. If either of these behaviors is pronounced, a visual-perception problem may be present and the visual-perception abilities of the child should be checked. Occasionally a child will assemble the pattern using the wrong colored blocks. This is not usually due to a color-vision defect, but rather an inability on the part of the child to pay attention to more than one modality at a time (form).

Adult performance should be observed carefully, particularly on the first items. Psychotics and severely depressed subjects frequently are unable to perform on even the simple items. Some severely disturbed subjects are able to perform the task, but their performance is based on a random shifting of the blocks in a rather aimless manner.

Block Design has long been regarded as a test which measures, indirectly, neurological functioning. One of the problems associated with the use of this test in determining neurological dysfunction is that the dysfunction may be visual, perceptual, or motor in nature, and hence difficult to analyze. Correlations with the EEG are not very high because the EEG is fairly inadequate in picking up mild neurological dysfunctions. When a child achieves a severely depressed Block Design score which is not due to his approach to the task, it is generally desirable to perform a neurological examination.

Wechsler regards Block Design as an excellent measure of *g* and nonverbal intelligence in general. The test involves the ability to perceive and analyze forms—to analyze the whole into its component parts. Block Design in the WISC is believed to measure the ability to analyze and form abstract designs. Wechsler tends to stress its qualitative values in indicating how subjects approach the task, and in revealing differences in attitudes and temperament. He feels that it has diagnostic value in assessing mental deterioration, brain disease, or visual-motor impairment. Rapaport et al. (1968) regard Block Design as a test which measures visual-motor coordination that is reproductive rather than imitative or productive. They describe the test as one that combines visual organization with visual-motor coordination, and involves differentiating a design into parts and then reproducing it based upon concept formation. Cohen (1959) indicates that among the performance tests, Block Design is a fair measure of *g* in the WAIS and one of the best measures of *g* in the WISC. Block Design, like Object Assembly is a good contributor to the Perceptual Organization Factor. In the

WISC it provides a substantial measure of a specific factor which Cohen labels "spatial visualization ability." It measures this same factor, to a degree, in the WAIS.

Object Assembly

Object Assembly is another subtest which has excellent qualitative features. One of the significant observations that should be made is the subject's approach to the task—that is, his working habits and his persistence. Wechsler characterizes approaches to the task as follows: (1) an immediate perception of the whole, along with an understanding of the parts; (2) rapid recognition of the whole, but difficulty in relating the parts to the whole; (3) complete failure to take in the whole, with insight following periods of trial-and-error.

Observations can indicate the manner in which the subject perceives the task and the degree to which he uses trial-and-error procedures. This test also affords the examiner an opportunity to observe how subjects react to their mistakes and attempt to rectify them, and the manner in which they handle the frustration that results from abortive attempts.

Retarded children often pile up the pieces rather than fit them together and frequently end up with extra pieces when they feel they have accomplished the task. Highly disturbed adults frequently are unable to perceive the whole, yet may obtain fairly adequate scores on a planless, trial-and-error performance.

Wechsler describes Object Assembly as a task which requires the subject to put things together into a familiar configuration. For the WISC he regards the test as one which measures the ability to put together concrete forms. Rapaport et al. (1968) describe Object Assembly as a test measuring visual-motor coordination that is not influenced greatly by motor speed. They stress the need for an actively structured visual-organizing process that is anticipatory in nature. Cohen (1959) states that for both the WISC and the WAIS, Object Assembly is a poor measure of g. When combined with Block Design, it contributes to the Perceptual Organization Factor and loads on no other factor except Freedom from Distractability at the $10\frac{1}{2}$-year age level. Lutey (1966) concludes that Object Assembly tends to relate to the Effects of Uncertainty described by Saunders (1960). She also concludes that perceptual sets influence the performances of many subjects. Object Assembly appears to be a test that provides qualitative information, but there are some differences of opinion concerning the factors to which it contributes.

Digit Symbol (WAIS) and Coding (WISC)

Digit Symbol involves the performance of a somewhat novel task and is sensitive to a variety of impairments. Observation should be very precise to attempt to obtain cues concerning the type of performance which affects the obtained score. Wechsler indicates that older subjects are slower on Digit Symbol because they are mentally "slowed up." He also indicates that neurotics and unstable subjects tend to do poorly on this test. He believes that the test measures mental deficiency rather than impairment, and that emotional reactions may cause the neurotic to have difficulty concentrating or applying himself. Performance on this test also relates to the level of energy of the subject. Anxious hesitancy, obsessive doubt, or a very meticulous approach which involves an attempt to reproduce the symbols exactly, are important characteristics. For all subjects, the inability to concentrate on the task for any length of time should be noted, as well as fluctuations in speed and attention. The necessity to refer constantly back to the key, or to erase, or the inability to perceive the symbols are important aspects to be observed.

Hewitt and Massey (1969) list the following variables that the examiner should be sensitive toward in his observations of children:

(a) Which hand does the child use? (laterality)

(b) How does he slant his paper? (visual-perceptual development)

(c) Does he use his non-active hand to hold the paper still? (well-developed laterality and separation of sides)

(d) Does he see the time urgency? (intelligence)

(e) Is his attention span adequate to complete the two-minute assignment without pauses? (concentration)

(f) Does he look back to the sample at the top or at previously completed designs? (organizational ability, memory)

(g) Does he skip spaces? (visual tracking problems)

(h) Does he erase and lose time? (compulsive or dull)

(i) Does he use two hands to turn the pencil over to erase, or does he lay the pencil down and pick it up by the other end rather than manipulating it with one hand to reverse ends? (brain damage, poor muscle control)

(j) Is neatness more important than speed? (compulsive)

(k) Does speed seem to be the most important factor? (bright)

(l) Does he ask numerous obvious questions? (dependent, uncertain)

The variables listed above should be used to develop hypotheses and the examiner should not assume that each of these necessarily indicates the characteristic in parenthesis.

Wechsler considers Coding in the WISC to be measuring speed of learning and writing symbols, with the subject's score being dependent upon speed and accuracy. Visual acuity and motor coordination are not especially important, but motor speed is. Rapaport et al. (1968) describe Digit Symbol as a measure of visual-motor coordination measuring psychomotor speed and initiative activity. The emphasis is upon visual activity, motor activity, and a learning process. The learning process is one of a momentary noting rather than one of an integration into the subject's general frame of reference, and is described as a visual-organizing motor task. Cohen (1959) indicates that neither Coding nor Digit Symbol is a very good measure of *g*. Both have a high loading on factor E which Cohen has not described, but has left as a specific factor.

In an excellent review of the research, Lutey (1966) indicates that Digit Symbol is sex-linked, with females scoring significantly higher than males, which tends to obscure an interpretation of the subtest unless sex is considered. Digit Symbol and Coding also appear to be related to age and associated with memory for older age groups. For normal subjects, the test appears to function more as an assessment of perceptual and psychomotor speed than learning. Digit Symbol tends to cluster with Arithmetic and Digit Span at certain ages to reveal what Davis (1956) calls Numerical Facility. Digit Span, Arithmetic, and Coding (or Digit Symbol) form the "anxiety triad." Neurotic subjects with anxiety states as well as disturbed children tend to score low on these three tests. Digit Symbol and Coding contribute to the Trace or short-term memory factor which tends to differentiate between mental retardates and normals. Digit Symbol also appears to contribute to a factor which Davis (1956) has labeled Fluency (tendency to be responsible and uninhibited with a free flow of responses to stimulation).

Mazes

The three major variables to be observed in the Maze test are planning ability, impulsiveness, and visual-motor coordination. Impulsiveness and planning ability tend to interact on this test: an individual who is very impulsive and yet has good planning ability is likely to achieve a lower score than an individual with less planning ability but who is not impulsive. The subject should be observed carefully to see which of these two factors seems to be governing his performance. Visual-motor coordination generally is observed by noting the subject's ability to stay within the lines. This should also be related to impulsivity, since impulsivity may be the factor that accounts for the subject's crossing of lines, rather than the lack of good visual-motor coordination.

Wechsler considers the test to be one that requires planning and following a visual pattern, with performance generally being affected by the subject's approach to the task. Cohen (1959) indicates that the Maze Test makes a relatively weak contribution to *g*. At the 7½ and 10½ age levels it contributes to the Perceptual Organization Factor, and at the 10½ to 13½ age levels it contributes to the Freedom from Distractability Factor. It also tends to have a high loading on a specific factor which Cohen refers to as Planning Ability. Lutey (1966) hypothesizes that Mazes could logically be expected to affiliate with Object Assembly and Picture Completion in the Effects of Uncertainty Factor.

Scatter Analysis

One measure of score *scatter* that has received a great deal of attention over the years has been the difference between the Performance IQ and Verbal IQ on the Wechsler tests. Wechsler (1958) indicates that for most mental disorders subjects perform better on the verbal than on the performance tests, and that a difference of 15 IQ points between the verbal and performance scores can be interpreted as "diagnostically significant" in most instances. He is careful to point out that the significance of the difference between the Verbal and Performance scales must depend upon such characteristics as level of intelligence, education, occupation, cultural and possibly racial differences. There have been a great many studies published concerning the Verbal-Performance difference on the Wechsler tests, and it is quite safe to say at this point that many factors may produce such a discrepancy. Since this difference may be pushed in opposite directions by different factors, frequently they tend to cancel out, which results in the conclusion on the part of many investigators that the Verbal-Performance discrepancy concept should be abandoned. The failure of many researchers to find a valid method for diagnostic prediction relates to the lack of control of many of the variables involved.

Two major problems that must be faced in utilizing the Verbal-Performance difference involve (1) establishing levels of significance, and (2) determining the diagnostic significance of these differences. Field (1960) points out that there is a difference between significance in the "abnormal" as compared with the *statistical* sense. He states that a discrepancy in the WAIS of 13 points would occur only once in 100 times by chance, and hence any discrepancy over 13 points could be considered statistically significant. In the standardization population, however, discrepancies of 25 points occur once in every 100 subjects in the population. Thus one could say that a discrepancy is not significant until it reaches approximately 25 IQ points or more.

Another way of determining statistical significance would be to add the standard error of measurement to and subtract it from the Verbal and Performance scores, to get bands or ranges for these scores. If the resultant bands do not overlap, one can say that it is quite probable that there is a statistically significant difference between the Verbal and Performance scores. Whether one should use the standard error of measurement, or a difference of 15 points, or a difference of 25 points in attempting to establish the significance of a difference, depends upon the use that he plans to make of this difference, and whether this difference is for groups or for individuals. When using individual test results, the examiner usually will want a higher level of significance than when comparing group scores.

While the results of the reported research are not conclusive, it appears that certain groups tend to have either higher Performance or higher Verbal IQs. Groups for whom the *Performance* score is generally higher than the *Verbal* score are

1. Mentally retarded subjects (with the possible exception of Negroes).
2. Bilingual subjects (excepting Jewish subjects).
3. Subjects from lower socioeconomic or lower occupational levels.
4. Delinquent sociopathic or psychopathic subjects in general.
5. Retarded or problem readers.

6. Children labeled as "underachievers."
7. Subjects with brain damage in the left hemisphere.

Groups likely to exhibit a significantly higher Verbal than Performance score are

1. Intellectually gifted subjects.
2. Subjects with higher levels of education.
3. Unilingual Jewish subjects.
4. Urban subjects.
5. Schizophrenics.
6. Children with learning problems based on perceptual difficulties.
7. Persons having brain damage in the right hemisphere.
8. Depressed, hysterical, or neurotic subjects (research results are inconclusive).

While differences between the Verbal and Performance IQs listed above have been found for these *groups*, it is a questionable practice to conclude that one may observe a Verbal-Performance discrepancy and, from this, indicate that an individual belongs to one of the particular groups listed. For example, when the Verbal IQ is significantly greater than the Performance IQ, it may simply be a result of higher intelligence, higher level of education, urban living, perceptual problems, neurosis, or brain damage in the right hemisphere. On the other hand, it may merely be due to an error of measurement.

Hence, all the generalities listed above, while they may be used as diagnostic cues, should be corroborated by a great deal of additional evidence before a diagnosis is made. An individual may have a significantly higher Verbal or Performance IQ and not necessarily belong to one of the diagnostic categories listed above. Hence, at the present time, Verbal-Performance differences may provide cues and may be significant for groups, but they should only be used to generate *hypotheses* when one is working with an individual.

Another method of scatter analysis is intertest scatter. Wechsler (1958) states that intertest variability is expected to be very high in the verbal subtests for schizophrenics. Many methods of subtest scatter have been advocated, but none has proven to be especially useful. However, subtest scatter may provide useful information when combined with other data. A subtest which deviates significantly may be considered in relation to clinical cues obtained during the test administration, to the functions of the subtest, to the results of factor analyses, and to the subtest's relationship to other subtests.

In determining scatter, Lutey (1966) recommends that subtest scatter be calculated by adding the standard error of the measurement to each subtest score and substracting it from the subtest score to achieve a range. The standard error of the measurement for the total test is also added to and subtracted from the total test score to obtain a band for the total test. Any subtest whose score range falls outside of the range for the complete test is designated as one that deviates significantly. Lutey (1966, p. 87) suggests that some scatter is indicated if one or two subtest scores fall outside the full-scale range, and extreme and significant scatter is indicated if as many as half of the scores fall outside the full-scale range. This same procedure may be repeated for the Verbal and Performance tests separately, in which case one subtest score outside the average range indicates some scatter, two scores considerable scatter, and half of the scores extreme and significant scatter. The use of scatter analysis will be discussed in more detail after a consideration of the results of factor analysis.

THE LUTEY APPROACH

Students learning to interpret the Wechsler tests are usually awed at the vast amount of material available concerning these tests, and find it almost impossible to assimilate all the information in a meaningful way. They soon learn that the interpretation of subtests on the Wechsler is exceedingly difficult since, after the *g* factor is eliminated and measurement error is considered, there is frequently little specific measurement left for them to use. Experienced clinicians may be aware of many of the studies involving Wechsler tests but find it difficult to remember and adequately utilize the results of these studies. Many of the factor analytic studies are so complex and involve such variability in the loadings at different age levels that it is difficult for examiners to use these studies objectively.

Lutey (1966) has produced a highly structured approach based upon a critical survey of the literature. Her system allows the test interpreter to consider a wide variety of factors and evaluate their significance without having to refer to a large number of outside sources. Lutey divides the factors to be used into two groups—the primary factors which are largely based on Cohen's factor-analysis studies, and the tentative factors which are not entirely supported by research but which have some evidence to indicate their existence. The tentative factors should be used with a great deal of caution at the present time. The following section describes the primary and tentative factors.

Major-Factor Scores

The Major-Factor Scores are based upon factors discovered in Cohen's studies, but they are adapted in the following ways:

1. Instead of using the Full Scale or Verbal IQ as recommended by Cohen for a measure of *g*, the four subtests loading highest in the *g* factor are used for this calculation.
2. All of the subtests loaded to a significant degree (the .20 criterion) on a given factor for the subject's age level are used rather than the same tests for all age levels.
3. Factor E, which is a specific factor found in coding, has been switched to the tentative factors.

Listed below are the major factors and a brief description of what each appears to be measuring.

1. G (general)—present general intellectual ability or function.
2. VC (verbal comprehension)—verbally retained knowledge impressed by formal education.
3. PO (perceptual organization)—the ability to interpret and/or organize visually perceived materials.
4. FD (freedom from distractability)—the ability to remain undistracted, to attend and/or concentrate.
5. R (relevance)—the ability to apply judgment to situations—using verbal skills in new situations.

The subtests which contribute to each of the factors described above are shown in Table 10-1 for the WAIS and Table 10-2 for the WISC. The subtests which contribute most highly to each factor are indicated by an X. For example, when referring to Table 10-1, the G factor for the 16-23 age group is composed of the subtests Information, Similarities, Vocabulary, and Picture Completion. An *asterisk* indicates those performance tests which contribute highly to G. The standard errors of measurement indicated have been rounded except for those followed by +, the symbol indicating that the standard error has been estimated.

Tentative Factors

The tentative factors have been derived from the interpretation of a wide variety of research studies which have not been verified directly. Their use, then, should be restricted to hypotheses concerning the performance of subjects and should be verified by other sources. The tentative factors are

1. A:N (anxiety or numerical facility). The subtests contributing to this factor are Digit Span, Arithmetic, and Digit Symbol (or Coding). As the term implies, this factor may be indicative of either anxiety or numerical facility. If the factor is reflecting anxiety, the anxiety is a disturbed or uneasy state and not the chronic anxiety found in psychiatric groups. The anxiety measured may be specifically related to test-anxiety and may not be an habitual characteristic of the subject. On the other hand, this factor may be indicative of numerical facility as defined by Davis (1956). He describes this as the ability to manipulate simple spatial symbols as contrasted to verbal symbols. If all three subtests are high, and if this factor score differs significantly from the subject's other scores, the test results would generally be a reflection of good numerical facility. If the three scores are significantly low for the subject, the factor measured may be anxiety, lack of numerical facility, or both. Anxiety may be suspected when the factor score is significantly low and the following conditions exist:
(a) Arithmetic and Digit Symbol are higher than Digit Span.

Table 10.1. Rounded Standard Errors of Measurement and Factor Composition of the Subtests of the WAIS†

Subtests	(16–23)							(23–40)							(40 and Over)						
	SE$_m$	G	VC	PO	FD	R	S	SE$_m$	G	VC	PO	FD	R	S	SE$_m$	G	VC	PO	FD	R	S
Information	.9	X	X					.9	X	X					.9	X	X				
Comprehension	1.4		X					1.5		X					1.5	X	X				
Arithmetic	1.4	X	X		X			1.4	X			X			1.2+		X		X		X
Similarities	1.1+		X			X	X	1.2		X					1.3+		X		X		
Digit Span	1.6				X			1.8	X			X			1.7+				X		
Vocabulary	.7	X	X					.7	X	X					.7	X	X				X
Digit Symbol	.9	X						1.0#	X				X	X	1.0#	X				X	X
Picture Completion	1.2	*		X		X	X	1.1+	*		X				1.2	*		X		X	X
Block Design	1.2			X		X	X	1.3			X		X	X	1.2	*		X		X	X
Picture Arrangement	1.7			X				1.7+			X				1.4					X	
Object Assembly	1.7			X				1.7			X				1.6			X			

	IQ Pts.	IQ Pts.	IQ Pts.
V IQ	3.0 (2.5 age SS pts.)	3.0 (2.5 age SS pts.)	3.0 (2.5 age SS pts.)
P IQ	4.0 (2.4 age SS pts.)	4.0 (2.4 age SS pts.)	3.7 (2.4 age SS pts.)
FS IQ	2.6 (2.3 age SS pts.)	2.6 (2.0 age SS pts.)	2.6 (2.4 age SS pts.)

Age Groups

†After Lutey, 1966, p. 85.

Table 10.2. Rounded Standard Errors of Measurement and Factor Composition of the Subtests of the WISC†

Subtests	Age Groups																				
	(5-0 to 8-11)							(9-0 to 11-11)							(12-0 to 16-0)						
	SE$_m$	G	VC	PO	FD	R	S	SE$_m$	G	VC	PO	FD	R	S	SE$_m$	G	VC	PO	FD	R	S
Information	1.8	X	X				X	1.3+	X	X					1.3	X	X				
Comprehension	1.9+					X		1.6					X		1.6		X			X	
Arithmetic	1.8+	X	X					1.2	X	X					1.4+	X			X		
Similarities	1.8		X			X		1.3		X			X		1.4	X	X			X	
Vocabulary	1.4+	X	X					.9	X						1.0	X	X				
Digit Span	1.9				X			1.9				X			2.1				X		
Picture Completion	1.9+						X	1.8			X		X		1.7			X		X	
Picture Arrangement	1.6	X			X			1.6	*		X				1.6	*		X			
Block Design	1.2	*		X			X	1.1			X			X	1.0	*		X			X
Object Assembly	1.8+			X				1.8			X	X			1.6			X			
Coding	1.9				X			1.9#				X			1.9#	*			X		
Mazes	1.4			X			X	1.3			X			X	1.5				X		X

IQ Pts.			IQ Pts.			IQ Pts.		
V IQ	5.2 (2.1 SS pts.)		3.0 (2.4 SS pts.)			3.0 (2.3 SS pts.)		
P IQ	5.6+ (2.0 SS pts.)		5.0 (2.1 SS pts.)			4.7+ (2.1 SS pts.)		
FS IQ	4.3 (1.9 SS pts.)		3.4 (2.0 SS pts.)			3.7 (2.0 SS pts.)		

†After Lutey, 1966, p. 86.

(b) Scores on the timed tests are lower than those on the untimed tests.

(c) Picture Arrangement is higher than Digit Span.

(d) The subject exhibits overt signs of anxiety.

(e) It is known from other sources that the subject does achieve well in tasks requiring numerical facility.

2. M (Memory). The subtests contributing to this factor are Information and Arithmetic for long-range memory retention and Digit Span and Coding (or Digit Symbol) for immediate recall. The factor is described as the subject's ability to reproduce or recall any of the written or verbal-form knowledge or symbols to which he has been exposed. This factor is usually related to the FD (Freedom from Distractability) factor. It may be hypothesized that if FD and M both are high or low, the major measurement involved in both is likely to reflect Memory. If these two factors vary away from each other, it may be hypothesized that the Freedom from Distractability factor is emphasizing the degree of vulnerability to distraction.

3. F (Fluency). The subtests contributing to this factor are Comprehension, Digit Span, and Digit Symbol (or Coding). Davis (1956) describes this factor as "a tendency to be responsive and uninhibited, with consequent free flow of responses to stimulation." This factor appears to be essentially a nonintellective factor and is usually corroborated by reference to observed behavior during the test.

4. U (Effects of Uncertainty). The subtests involved in this factor are Picture Completion, Object Assembly, and Mazes (in the WISC). This factor is defined as the degree to which a subject's performance is affected by his willingness to respond when he is uncertain of the accuracy of his answer. The subtests related to this factor present stimuli which are incomplete or involve an unknown element. Saunders (1960) indicates that Picture Completion is the crucial subtest involved in this factor. Evidence of the factor is usually corroborated by observations of the subject during the test. If the subject is seeking support while performing these subtests, his performance may well be handicapped.

Subtest Specifics

The subtests listed in this category are those that have been found by factor-analysis studies to measure a unique function. The specifics are indicated by an X under S in Tables 10-1 and 10-2. Since the measurement error for each of these subtests is fairly large, they are placed in the tentative category. These subtests may be interpreted as measuring a specific function only when they deviate significantly from scores on other subtests.

1. Information. This subtest measures a unique function only at the 5-0 to 8-11 age levels. Osborne (1963) labels this factor as Expressive Psycho-

linguistics. The abilities measured appear to involve either object-naming or indicating the use of an object. This function may be partially verified by examining the subject's responses to the vocabulary subtest to determine whether *use* is significant in his definitions of words. The Information score should not be considered significant unless it deviates at least three points from the total-test average.

2. Arithmetic. This subtest has a specific function at all levels in the WAIS and above the nine-year level in the WISC. At these age levels, this test appears to measure ability to solve arithmetic problems. To be significant, the scores should depart two or three points from the Verbal average.

3. Digit Span. This is a specific of the WAIS. It is defined as the ability to inhibit, control, delay, and/or confine responses. This definition has the connotation of the ability to exercise mental control where it is required. The score on this test should deviate from the total-test average by at least three points to be considered significant.

4. Picture Completion. This is a specific of the WAIS. Saunders (1960) labels this factor Maintenance of Contact, referring to contact with reality. Rapaport et al. (1968) hypothesize that a poor performance on this test may be indicative of inability to concentrate and impairment of contact with reality. The Picture Completion score must depart by at least two or three points to be considered significant.

5. Block Design. A specific at all levels in the WAIS and WISC. Cohen (1959) describes the unique function of Block Design as measuring spatial-visualization ability. To be significant, Block Design must vary from the Performance average by at least two or three points.

6. Mazes. A specific at all levels in the WISC. Cohen (1959) refers to the unique measure of Mazes as Planning Ability. To be significant, Mazes should depart from other subtests, especially Block Design and Object Assembly, by two or three points.

The Trace Factor

This factor is not calculated unless the IQs obtained by the subject are very low. The subtests generally used in calculating the Trace Factor are Arithmetic, Digit Span, and Coding (or Digit Symbol), with Picture Arrangement and Block Design used as supporting subtests. The Trace Factor is defined as a short-term memory factor by Baumeister et al. (1962a,b, 1963). The definition is based on the stimulus-trace concept of Ellis (1963) which describes the Trace Factor as being physiologically based and dependent upon the ability to attend during both the reception and the reproduction phases of the memory process. If the Trace Factor is significantly low, a diagnosis of mental retardation may be indicated for those subjects obtaining very low Full Scale IQs.

Plotting Profiles

To facilitate the use of factor scores, scatter, and Verbal versus Performance differences on the WISC and WAIS, Lutey (1966) has devised profile sheets which present all of this information in one compact form (see Tables 10-4 and 10-5). In preparing these profile sheets, the scaled scores from the WISC and the age-scale scores from the WAIS (see pages 101–110 of the WAIS Manual) are used. The age-scale scores are used for the WAIS because this allows one to compare the subject's performance to others of his same age. The scaled scores (WISC) or age-scale scores (WAIS) are plotted on the profile sheet by marking with an X. The standard error of measurement for each score is then added to and subtracted from the score to obtain a band within which the subject's true score is expected to fall. The averages for the Verbal, Performance, and Full Scale scores are computed and, again, the estimated standard errors of measurement for the scale scores are added to and subtracted from these averages to produce bands within which the true scores are likely to fall.

To calculate the factor scores, Tables 10-1 and 10-2 are used and the scaled scores, or age-scales scores, are recorded on the profile sheet to show where they contribute to a factor. Those subtests which contribute to a factor are indicated by an X in Tables 10-1 and 10-2. Since the tentative factors are the same for all age groups on both the WAIS and the WISC, these are automatically entered with the exception that specifics are indicated by an x when these are appropriate for a particular age level. The average of the factor scores is computed and then compared to the Full Scale average. The factor-score average is then labeled as being high, low, or average. Using a method suggested by Cohen, standard deviations of the factor scores are then added to and subtracted from the average of the factor scores to form a band similar to that obtained by using the standard error of the measurement (in previous calculations). Rounded standard deviations are used rather than the standard error of the measurement to discount the influence of *G* or *g*. (See Table 10-3.) Those factor scores which are significantly high or low when compared to the full-scale average are then designated with an asterisk as being significant. By now it should be apparent that a great deal of information is available on the profile sheet.

Referring to Table 10-4, initially one would hypothesize a moderate amount of scatter by visual inspection. When the standard error of measurement is added to and subtracted from the Full-Scale average, the resulting band ranges from the 9.3 to the 13.3 level. Three test bands (Comprehension, Vocabulary, and Block Design) fall beyond this range, verifying the moderate amount of scatter based on statistical analysis. The performance average appears to be higher than the verbal

Table 10-3. Rounded Standard Deviations of Factor Scores

Factor	G	VC	PO	FD	R	A:N	M	F	U
WISC	2.2	2.5	2.4	2.2	2.4	2.3	2.2	2.2	2.3
WAIS	2.7	2.7	2.5	2.2	2.3	2.5	2.5	2.4	2.2

TABLE 10-4. WISC Profile

NAME __LOPEZ, JUVENTINO__ AGE __15–10__ SCHOOL __Kennedy High__

TEST DATE __7/11/70__ EXAMINER __Ray Rivas__

Scaled Scores

00 01 02 03 04 05 06 07 08 09 10 11 12 13 14 15 16 17 18 19 20

(Red)

(Blue)

(Green)

(Black)

Verbal Average	Performance Average	Full Scale Average
10 ± 2.3	12.5 ± 2.1	11.3 ± 2.0
(Blue Line) 7.7 – 12.3	(Green Line) 10.4 – 14.6	(Red Line) 9.3 – 13.3

After Lutey, 1966, p. 108.

	General	Verbal Comp.	Perceptual Org.	Distractability	Relevance	Anx: #Facility	Memory	Fluency	Uncertainty	Specific	Total	Ave.	Factor SD	Eval
Info	10	10					10			—	39	9.8	2.2	L
Comp	—	6		8	6	8	8	6		x	37	9.2	2.5	L
Arith	8	—	11		13	8				x	41	13.7	2.4	H*
Sim	13	13	16								33	11	2.2	A
Voc	8	8	14	15	—	15	15	15			30	10	2.4	L
D S	—				11	15	15	15			38	12.7	2.3	H
P C	x		11	—	11				11	x	48	12	2.2	A
P A	x			—							36	12	2.2	A
B D									14		35	11.7	2.3	A
O A						15				x				
Cod	x			10		15	15	15	10	x				
Mazes														

*Significant

TABLE 10-5. WAIS Profile

Name __HILL, CAROL__   Age __20__   Non-Stud.____   Student __x__
School __Voc. – Tech.__   Grade ____   Major __Clerical__
Test Date __7/19/70__   Examiner __Dave Jones__

Age-Scale Scores

Score columns: 00 01 02 03 04 05 06 07 08 09 10 11 12 13 14 15 16 17 18 19

(Blue)   (Red)   (Black)   (Green)

	Verbal Average	Performance Average	Full Scale Average
	6.7 ± 2.5	5.2 ± 2.4	6.0 ± 2.3
	(Blue line) 4.2 – 9.2	(Green line) 2.8 – 7.6	(Red line) 3.7 – 8.3

After Lutey, 1966, p. 108.

Factor grid:

	General	Verbal Comp.	Perceptual Org.	Distractability	Relevance	Anx: #Facility	Memory	Fluency	Uncertainty	Specific
Info	5	5					5			
Comp	—	7		7		7	7	7		x
Arith	5	5								
Sim	7	7		9		9	9	9		x
D S							7			
Voc	7	7				9	9	9		x
D Sym	4			4	4	8	8	8	4	x
P C			6							
B D			5		5					x
P A			3						3	
O A										
Total	21	24	14	16	9	24	29	24	7	
Ave.	5.3	6	4.7	8	4.5	8	7.3	8	3.5	
Factor SD	2.7	2.7	2.5	2.2	2.3	2.5	2.5	2.4	2.2	
Eval.	A	A	L	H	L	H	H	H	L*	

*Significant

average. The verbal-average band (10 plus and minus 2.3) shows a range from 7.7 to 12.3 and this range does not overlap with the performance average of 12.5. This indicates that there is a significant statistical difference between the verbal and performance IQs. Since this type of analysis generally has the effect of discounting the effects of general intellectual functioning, it seems safe to say that the performance average is statistically greater than the verbal average.

A review of the factor scores indicates that three of the factor scores—General, Verbal Comprehension, and Relevance—are more than 1 point lower than the Full-Scale average and hence are labeled low. Perceptual Organization and Anxiety:Facility are over one point above the average and are labeled high. Distractability, Memory, Fluency, and Uncertainty are all within one point of the Full-Scale average and are labeled average. When the rounded standard deviations are added to and subtracted from the factor averages, only one factor stands out as being significant in relation to the subject's own Full Scale average. This factor is Perceptual Organization. The subject appears to have a significantly high ability to interpret and/or organize visually perceived materials. When the factor scores are compared with the general population, we find that Perceptual Organization is still above the band for the general population (8 to 12), as is the Anxiety:Facility factor. Since the Anxiety:Facility Factor is high while the subject's Arithmetic score is fairly low, we would tend to hypothesize that this factor is measuring numerical facility rather than anxiety.

Arithmetic is one of the specifics indicated in this profile. Since it is two points below the verbal average, it is approaching significance. When one compares the Arithmetic score with the score for Coding, it appears that the subject's Numerical Facility score is reflecting his ability to manipulate simple spatial symbols other than mathematical symbols. The other specific that is significantly high is Block Design, since this falls out of the band calculated for the Full Scale average. Again this can be interpreted to mean that the subject has the ability to perform well in tasks measuring spatial visualization.

Because the subject comes from a home where both Spanish and English are spoken, the three performance tests contributing the most to $G(g)$ at this age level were used to calculate a performance G. These three factors are Picture Arrangement (Scaled Score = 9), Block Design (SS = 16), and Coding (SS = 15). The average of these three performance tests is 13.3, which is significantly higher than both his General Factor score and his Full Scale average. One would tend to hypothesize that either a linguistic or an educational handicap is operative with respect to his General Factor and that the subject exhibits a high intellectual functioning on tasks that are not verbal.

The profile in Table 10-5 does not appear to show a significant amount of scatter. This is verified in that no test falls out of the Full Scale band of 3.7 to 8.3. While the Verbal average is higher than the Performance average, the Verbal range overlaps the Performance range, so this difference is not considered to be significant. A review of the factor scores reveals that only one tentative factor

(Effects of Uncertainty) is significant, and this is significantly low. This would suggest the hypothesis that perhaps the subject's test performance is adversely affected by her unwillingness to respond when she is uncertain about the accuracy of her answer. This hypothesis should be verified by observation made during the test performance or by other sources.

Of the four subtests designated as specifics, only two—Digit Span and Picture Completion—approach significance, with DS being high, and PC being low. A high Digit Span score raises the hypothesis that the subject is able to exercise sufficient mental control to inhibit control, delay and/or confine her responses. The low Picture Completion score suggests the hypothesis that the individual, when dealing with an object, may have trouble assuming that it is a familiar object which she can cope with, and therefore may have difficulty concentrating upon it. Whether there is any serious inability to maintain contact with reality should be investigated with other sources of information. The subject's Full Scale IQ is 74, so the Trace Factor has been calculated. This was calculated on the basis of scores on Arithmetic (SS = 7), Digit Span (SS = 9), and D Sym (SS = 8). Since the average of these subtests is a scaled-score average of 8 and is higher than the Full Scale average rather than lower, a physiological basis for retardation is contraindicated. The possibility of functional retardation should be investigated through the use of other sources of information.

The brief descriptions given above, based on the profile sheets, are very incomplete since no other data are included. Many of the hypotheses suggested by the profile sheets would have been verified during the test administration or tested through the use of other sources of information to corroborate them. It is strongly advised that anyone who wishes to use the Lutey method should obtain and utilize the Lutey manual, *Individual Intelligence Testing* (Dr. Carol L. Lutey, 4709 Kiowa Drive, Greeley, Colorado 80631).

THE WPPSI

Since the WPPSI is relatively new and little research has been done with it, the clinical uses of the results tend to be limited at the present time. The correlations between the subtests and the Full Scale IQ are higher on the WPPSI than on the 7½-year age group of the WISC for both the Verbal and Performance sections of the test. This would seem to suggest that the WPPSI is a better indicator of *g* than the WISC, and that the use of a Performance *g* factor as an estimate of general ability is justifiable.

Except for the Block Design, the reliabilities of the WPPSI appear to be better than those of the WISC at all age levels, resulting in smaller standard errors of measurement. The WPPSI thus appears to be a little more reliable than the WISC.

Since the factor scores previously discussed have not been validated for the WPPSI, it would appear that these should be used only on an experimental basis at this time. Some of the subtests of the WPPSI are sufficiently different from those of the WISC to suggest that the loadings for factors may be quite different for the two instruments. Wechsler (1967) suggests that on initial and retest administration a new score be calculated for the WPPSI that involves the scores obtained on ANIMAL HOUSE. It is hypothesized that this may be an estimate of a child's ability to learn a simple task. This score, called a Speed of Learning Score (SL), will require additional research before its function is known.

The test performances of young children are quite variable, which means that the testing of these children with the WPPSI should incorporate a great deal of astute observation so that the validity of the test may be assessed. Lutey (1967) has suggested that an involvement rating be made for every WPPSI and that the validity of the WPPSI be assessed on the basis of this rating. In a study involving 40 subjects, Lutey found that there tended to be a higher obtained IQ with higher ratings of involvement, that the involvement rating was generally higher for older subjects, and that ratings on the first two and last two subtests of the WPPSI appeared to be consistent. Lutey has identified a number of factors that seem to be important in assessing involvement:

1. The amount of time that eye contact was maintained during the testing session.
2. Whether the examiner enjoyed being with the child and felt comfortable versus finding it difficult to relate to the child and feeling uncomfortable.
3. Whether the child appeared to be attentive to the examiner and test situation rather than objects in the room and past experiences.
4. Whether the child appeared relaxed or tense, fearful, nervous, or tired and disinterested.
5. Whether the child's conversation was directed toward aspects of the test or other experiences.
6. Whether the test was completed or whether it had to be discontinued.

Lutey's study would seem to indicate that keen observation is extremely essential when testing young children, not only for acquiring information but for estimating the validity of the test results. Since the WPPSI's construction closely parallels that of the WISC and the WAIS, hopefully in the near future research will verify that many of the factors previously found may be applicable to the WPPSI. Until research has verified these, however, it would seem that the WPPSI should serve mainly as a test of general ability. Observations of the examiner should be used to suggest hypotheses concerning the performance of the child and to assess the validity of the test.

STANFORD-BINET INTELLIGENCE SCALE

Because the Stanford-Binet was constructed to measure global or general intelligence, it does not measure differential intellective abilities as well as the

Wechsler scales. The S-B is, however, highly regarded as a test of general mental ability, especially for use with children. The single score, which may be either the MA or the IQ, should be regarded as the major score when the Stanford-Binet is used.

A content analysis of the test reveals that it is strongly weighted toward measuring verbal abilities, and that it is based upon experiences common to the urban culture of the United States. Hence, it would seem to be of dubious value for bicultural or bilingual groups. Even for the middle-class subject who is not bilingual or bicultural, several conditions related to validity are important and these will be discussed.

VALIDITY AND RELIABILITY

Since the Stanford-Binet is designed to obtain a measure of general mental ability, one method of evaluating the validity of the test *for an individual* is an analysis of the items (subtests) to determine whether those that correlate highly with total-test score are included in the tests passed, or whether the items contributing greatly to the total score are items generally showing a *low* correlation with the total-test score. If the items passed by the subject are mainly those that correlate best with the total score on the Stanford-Binet, one may assume that the score obtained probably is a valid measure of general ability. If the tests passed tend to be items that are low in correlation with the total-test score, one may assume that the scale in general is not adequately measuring the g factor.

Another method of assessing the validity of the Stanford-Binet is to observe the subject carefully during his performance on the scale to determine whether nonintellective factors are contributing significantly to the test results. This is especially crucial with young children. Subjects should be carefully observed to see whether they are involved and interested in the tasks; whether they are operating at an effective level of activity or tend to be overactive or lethargic; whether they are independent and initiate activity or need to be urged; whether they are at ease with the examiner or tend to be shy, reserved, or ill at ease; whether they appear to trust their own abilities; whether they are anxious or self-assured; whether they tend to persist or give up easily on tests; whether they react unfavorably to failure or difficult tasks; and, in general, whether the relationship between the examiner and the subject is positive or negative.

With adults, responses should be carefully recorded so that any unusual verbalizations may be examined. The Stanford-Binet offers an excellent standardized clinical situation that allows the examiner to observe behavior and assess various aspects of performance besides the MA or IQ that is eventually obtained.

The reliability of the test data should also be assessed to determine the amount of stability that can be assumed. One available index of reliability for the Stanford-Binet is that of internal consistency, or the extent to which a subtest correlates with the total scale score. These data are available in Appendix B of the S-B manual. The subtests passed by a subject may be compared to the average correlations to determine whether the tests passed tend to correlate higher or lower than the average of the subtests, thus giving an indication of internal consistency for the subject.

In general, the S-B has greater reliability at the lower IQ levels than at the high IQ levels and is more reliable at the older ages than at the younger ages. For example, the reliability coefficients listed in the Manual (page 10) range from .83 (for IQs 140-149) to .91 (for IQs 60-69) for the 2½-to-5½ age groups. The range for the 14-to-18 age group is from .95 (for IQs 140-149) to .98 (for IQs 60-69).

Another method of evaluating the reliability is to add and subtract the standard error of measurement from the obtained score to obtain a band within which the subject's true score is likely to fall. While adequate data concerning the standard errors of measurement for the 1960 revision of the Stanford-Binet are not available, SE_m's can be calculated for the various age groups (See Chapter 2).

SCATTER AND DIFFICULTY LEVEL

It has been apparent for a long time that there is a wide variation among individuals with respect to the distance between basal and ceiling age. Some individuals have scores that seem to cluster around the MA score while others are scattered over a very broad range of age levels. There has been much research aimed at attempting to quantify the scatter and to establish the meaning of this variation, but results in this area have proved to be quite disappointing, and exactly what scatter indicates has not been established to date.

The lack of definitive research concerning scatter should not prevent the tester from analyzing the degree of scatter and the items contributing to the scatter. The items missed at the lower age level should be compared with the items passed at the higher age level to determine whether a particular type of test was passed or failed at each level. The cues obtained from this analysis frequently can be related to the behavior of the subject during testing to see whether personality characteristics seem to be entering into this pattern. The scatter also can be related to the other information available about the subject to determine whether tenable hypotheses can be evolved.

Closely related to the analysis of scatter is an analysis of the difficulty level of items passed or failed. An exact interpretation of the performance of a subject who seems to fail some items that are generally regarded as easy at a particular age level and passes other items that are difficult at that age level is difficult to make. However, when the level of difficulty is related to the scatter, the examiner may obtain cues that may lead him to conclude that particular educational or environment factors may be affecting the scores on the scale. These hypotheses, of course, should be verified by other observations or data.

SUBTEST GROUPING

McNemar (1942) factor-analyzed the 1937 edition of the Stanford-Binet. He concluded that a single common factor would explain most of the performance on the Stanford-Binet. Jones (1949) factor-analyzed four separate age levels of the Stanford-Binet and discovered the presence of group factors. In the 1960 revision of the Stanford-Binet the scale's authors retained all of the tests high in the *g* factor, and excluded many of the tests which were low. This has improved the Stanford-Binet as a measure of the *g* factor. Despite this evidence, clinicians continue to group the subtests according to function in an effort to obtain greater clinical insight into the performance of subjects. Lutey (1966), Sattler (1965), and Valett (1965) have evolved methods of grouping the items according to the different abilities involved. These groupings are based upon the factor-analytic studies of McNemar and Jones as well as an analysis of the content of the subtests and their descriptions. There is general agreement among these three systems. Lutey's classification is presented in the following pages.

MANIPULATION TESTS

These tests measure the ability to utilize objects and materials in performing tasks that depend largely on visual-motor skills. This category appears at the earlier age levels.

Age Level	Test	Age Level	Test
2	1. Three-Hole Form Board	5	2. Paper Folding: Triangle
2	4. Block-Building: Tower	5	4. Copying a Square
2–6	A. Three-Hole Form Board: Rotated	5	A. Knot
3	1. Stringing Beads	7	3. Copying a Diamond
3	3. Block-Building: Bridge	9	1. Paper Cutting
3	5. Copying a Circle	13	A. Paper Cutting
3	6. Drawing a Vertical Line	AA	A. Binet Paper Cutting

VOCABULARY AND LANGUAGE TESTS

Vocabulary. Tests which measure the ability to use words to indicate meanings and/or definitions in response to actual objects or pictures for younger subjects, and words for older subjects.

Age Level	Test	Age Level	Test
2	5. Picture Vocabulary	11	3. Abstract Words 2
2–6	3. Naming Objects	12	1. Vocabulary
2–6	4. Picture Vocabulary	12	5. Abstract Words 1
3	2. Picture Vocabulary	13	2. Abstract Words 2
4	1. Picture Vocabulary	14	1. Vocabulary
6	1. Vocabulary	AA	1. Vocabulary
8	1. Vocabulary	AA	8. Abstract Words 3
10	1. Vocabulary	SA 1	1. Vocabulary
10	3. Abstract Words 1	SA 2	1. Vocabulary
10	5. Word Naming	SA 3	1. Vocabulary

Language Comprehension. Tests which measure the ability to demonstrate an understanding of verbal stimuli that psycholinguistically may be termed "decoding" ability.

Age Level	Test	Age Level	Test
2	3. Identifying Parts of Body	3–6	1. Comparison of Balls
2	A. Identifying Objects by Name	3–6	A. Comparison of Sticks
2–6	1. Identifying Objects by Use	4	4. Pictorial Identification
2–6	2. Identifying Parts of Body	4–6	4. Materials
2–6	6. Obeying Simple Commands	A	Pictorial Identification

Language Usage. Tests which measure the ability to use or place words in context to convey meanings; corresponds to psycholinguistic process of "encoding" ability.

Age Level	Test	Age Level	Test
2	6. Word Combinations	12	6. Minkus Completion 1
5	3. Definitions	13	5. Dissected Sentences
9	4. Rhymes: New Form	SA 1	3. Minkus Completion 2
9	A. Rhymes: Old Form	SA 1	5. Sentence Building

MEMORY TESTS

Tests which measure the ability to recall verbal or visual stimuli, usually dependent upon immediate recall or rote learning. This ability may include attending and concentrating.

Age Level	Test	Age Level	Test
2	2. Delayed Response	9	6. Repeating 4 Digits Reversed
2–6	5. Repeating 2 Digits	10	6. Repeating 6 Digits
3	4. Picture Memories	11	1. Memory for Designs 1
3	A. Repeating 3 Digits	11	4. Memory for Sentences 2
4	2. Naming Objects from Memory	12	4. Repeating 5 Digits Reversed
4	A. Memory for Sentences 1	12	A. Memory for Designs 2
4–6	5. Three Commissions	13	3. Memory for Sentences 3
7	6. Repeating 5 Digits	16	6. Copying a Bead Chain from Memory
7	A. Repeating 3 Digits Reversed		
8	2. Memories for Stories: The Wet Fall		
9	3. Memory for Designs 1	SA 1	4. Repeating 6 Digits Reversed
		SA 2	6. Repeating Thought of Passage 1. Value of Life
		SA 3	6. Repeating Thought of Passage 2. Tests

DISCRIMINATION TESTS

Perceptual Discrimination. Tests that measure the ability to visually perceive differences and similarities in stimulus objects or identify missing parts of incomplete figures. This group of tests appears at younger ages and tends to measure level of maturity of perceptual ability.

Age Level	Test	Age Level	Test
3–6	3. Discrimination of Animal Pictures	4–6	3. Pictorial Similarities and Differences 1
3–6	5. Sorting Buttons	5	1. Picture Completion: Man
4	5. Discrimination of Forms	5	5. Pictorial Similarities and Differences 2
		6	3. Mutilated Pictures

Verbal Comparisons. Tests which measure the ability to perceive similarities and/or differences in sets of verbal stimuli (similar to Sattler's "conceptual thinking").

Age Level	Test	Age Level	Test
4	3. Opposite Analogies 1	14	6. Reconciliation of Opposites
4–6	2. Opposite Analogies 2	AA	3. Differences Between Abstract Words
6	2. Differences		
6	5. Opposite Analogies 1	AA	7. Essential Differences
7	2. Similarity: Two Things	SA 1	6. Essential Similarities
7	5. Opposite Analogies 3	SA 2	5. Essential Differences
8	4. Similarities and Differences	SA 3	3. Opposite Analogies 4
		SA 3	A. Opposite Analogies 5

REASONING AND PROBLEM-SOLVING TESTS

Verbal Reasoning. Tests which measure the ability to give verbal responses to problem situations generally requiring application of knowledge and/or judgment.

Age Level	Test	Age Level	Test
3–6	4. Response To Pictures: Level 1	10	A. Verbal Absurdities 3
3–6	6. Comprehension 1	11	2. Abstract Word 2
4	6. Comprehension 2	11	A. Finding Reasons 2
4–6	1. Aesthetic Comparison	12	2. Verbal Absurdities 2
6	A. Comprehension 3	12	3. Picture Absurdities 2
7	1. Response to Pictures: Level 3	13	4. Problems of Fact
7	4. Comprehension 4	14	3. Reasoning 1
8	3. Verbal Absurdities 1	AA	5. Ingenuity 1
8	5. Comprehension 4	SA 2	2. Finding Reasons 2
8	6. Naming the Days of the Week	SA 3	3. Proverbs 2
8	A. Problem Situations 1	SA 3	A. Codes
9	2. Verbal Absurdities 2	SA 3	2. Proverbs 3
10	4. Finding Reasons 1	SA 3	5. Reasoning 2

Nonverbal Reasoning. Tests which measure the ability to demonstrate by behavior the application of judgment and/or knowledge to problem situations. Also assessed is the ability to visualize and plan ahead.

Age Level	Test	Age Level	Test
3–6	2. Patience: Pictures	14	5. Orientation: Direction 1
5	6. Patience: Rectangles	AA	6. Orientation: Direction 2
6	6. Maze Tracing	SA 3	4. Orientation: Direction 3
13	1. Plan of Search		

Numerical Reasoning. Tests which measure the ability to solve problems of various degrees of complexity involving numbers, either as the response or the stimulus.

Age Level	Test	Age Level	Test
6	4. Number Concepts	14	A. Ingenuity 2
9	5. Making Change	AA	2. Ingenuity 1
10	2. Block Counting	AA	4. Arithmetical Reasoning
14	2. Induction	SA 1	2. Enclosed Box Problem
14	4. Ingenuity 1	SA 2	4. Ingenuity 1

The grouping of subtests discussed in the preceding pages should be used with a great deal of caution. An analysis of this grouping will reveal that at certain age levels some of the categories are not tested at all, while at other age levels they may be tested three or four times. This should not prevent the examiner from analyzing the pattern of successes, however. If he were to discover that all of the items involving memory had been failed, this would be too obvious a clinical cue to disregard. An analysis of the subtests frequently can be combined with other data to uncover variations in intellective functioning.

TESTING ETHNIC GROUPS

When testing members of various ethnic groups, it is not enough to be unprejudiced, empathic, and objective. While these characteristics are necessary to obtain maximum results in the testing of subjects in general, the examiner also should be well acquainted with the culture and verbal patterns of the group being tested. If he is not, it is questionable whether he can establish an adequate relationship, communicate adequately, or be sufficiently sensitive to the non-intellective behavior of the subject. The type of sensitivity needed cannot be obtained by reading the literature; it almost necessitates a fairly prolonged contact with the group in question.

Most of the tests used for individual mental testing do not adequately represent some of the ethnic groups that an examiner may encounter. The Stanford-Binet, as previously indicated, is highly verbal and generally reflects the culture of the white, middle-class subject. Subjects from the other ethnic groups often do poorly on this scale. While the WAIS and WPPSI include black subjects in the norming group, other ethnic groups were not systematically considered. The WISC includes only white students in the standardization sample. Since certain ethnic groups were not systematically included, the scoring criteria frequently discriminate against responses made by the members of those groups. This leaves the examiner with the problem of attempting to score these responses according to his understanding of the ethnic group in question.

While there have been a few isolated studies investigating the effect that race or sex might have upon the performance of a subject in a testing session, there does not appear to be any comprehensive research in these areas. Rosen (1964), in reviewing the literature, indicates that attributes of religion, sex, and race have been avoided as topics of study. Carkhuff and Pierce (1967) have reported that the race of both the client and counselor appear to have a significant effect upon the depth of self-exploration in initial clinical interviews.

The militant stance taken by many leaders of ethnic groups in recent years has resulted in an increase in research on ethnic groups. The effect that the current demands for recognition and consideration might have upon the test behavior of discrete ethnic groups has not been systematically studied because of the recency of the movement for status.

Two important factors that enter into the problem of testing members of ethnic groups are the acculturation level and the socioeconomic level of the subject. Many individuals from ethnic groups possess the middle-class value structure to the extent that testing poses no great problem for them, but others possess cultural values that hinder both the relationship needed for adequate testing and the test performance itself. The socioeconomic level of the subject is important in testing because the members of a low socioeconomic group, in effect, have a cultural system which frequently inhibits their performance on tests. A typical subject from a distinct minority group is likely to have both cultural and socioeconomic characteristics that operate against successful test performance. When evaluating test-taking behavior and test scores, the acculturation level and socioeconomic level both should be considered by the examiner.

The purpose for which the test results will be used also should constantly be kept in mind when one tests members of minority groups. Although the test may discriminate against members of a certain group, if the test is to be used for predicting academic success this discrimination will not necessarily diminish the predictive validity of the test. If the examiner wishes to obtain an estimate of a minority individual's level of intellectual functioning, he can use a nonverbal or noncultural scale.

Unfortunately, there are no clear-cut answers to the problems related to the testing of members of divergent ethnic groups. Some of the difficulties encountered in the testing of two such groups, black subjects and Spanish-speaking subjects, will be discussed briefly.

THE BLACK SUBJECT

Currently, American black people have become active in their search for recognition as a unique ethnic group. It has long been recognized that many Negroes have harbored hostile feelings toward white people as a result of prejudicial treatment. Generally this hostility has been more overt and noticeable in the northern Negro than in the southern Negro. In their search for identification, the blacks frequently perceive whites as their foes or antagonists. How a reflection of these feelings may distort scores on an intelligence test has not been systematically investigated, but it can be assumed that distortion exists in varying degrees. This problem cannot be overcome simply by having black test administrators, because many blacks may see other blacks in this position as persons who have "gone over to the establishment." Vontress (1968) indicates that the black client sometimes sees the white counselor as an enemy and the black counselor as a collaborator.

While it may be assumed that each individual examinee will react to a test situation somewhat differently, the test administrator must consider the current social picture when attempting to interpret the scores that black people achieve on intelligence tests. The militant stance taken by some black groups undoubtedly has an effect on younger children as they become exposed to the struggles of the adults. It is very difficult for a test administrator to separate lack of knowledge from a lack of desire to cooperate; and since the social climate is changing so rapidly, the problem is difficult to evaluate by means of research. Research that may be applicable at one particular time could be out of date by the next year. This means that the test administrator **probably** is saddled with the difficult job of attempting to consider the personal reaction of the subject when attempting to interpret the results of tests. Since this procedure involves a high degree of subjectivity, a great deal of caution should be used in the interpretation of test results for black subjects.

The black person who is caught up in the current social struggle is likely to have feelings of anger, anxiety, or self-hatred, and these feelings may result in a reluctance to reveal himself to others. English (1957) indicates that many black people feel their minority status so deeply that they are reluctant to bare their feelings to anyone, even people close to them. Vontress (1970) indicates that the hesitancy to be self-disclosing is particularly apparent in the black male. Vontress also indicates that frequently by middle age the original resentment has burned out and the older black is likely to respond in a stereotyped ritualistic manner.

Another problem encountered in the testing of many black subjects concerns the accent and colloquialisms that hinder communication. Hewitt and Massey (1969) indicate that many ghetto children misinterpret many of the words appearing in the WISC. *Join* may be interpreted as enjoying, *fur* as four, *coal* as cold, etc. While a black subject may misinterpret the words of the test administrator, the reverse situation is also true. Frequently attempts on the part of the subject to respond are in communications typical of the black ghetto and this places the responsibility of interpretation upon the examiner. If he is not knowledgeable in ghetto types of communication he is not likely to be able to understand the subject. This may result in a kind of penalty as far as test scores are concerned.

The *culture* of the black ghetto is also apparent in the responses of many black children. The ghetto child is likely to be given independence at an earlier age than most middle-class white children, and is also likely to verbalize aggressive behaviors because these are frequently necessary for survival in the ghetto. Items such as knives, scissors, or broken glass are more apt to be considered for their potential as a weapon than for other purposes.

The ghetto child is also likely to have a different perception of crime and law than the typical white child. Adults who may view the law as punitive and prejudicial frequently inculcate these attitudes in the child. The black child's responses to questions such as, "Why are criminals locked up?" are not likely to be based on a knowledge of the function of law. The burglar sequence in Picture Arrangement is also likely to be interpreted so that the thief escapes the policeman (Hewitt and Massey, 1969). Other cultural differences stressed by Hewitt and Massey involve time orientation. The black ghetto resident is not likely to be very conscious of time, and many of the test concepts based upon time or future orientation are militated against by the ghetto culture. A lack of concern for time may also be reflected in test tasks that are timed.

The poverty of the ghetto is likely to be reflected in how children respond to questions such as, "Why is it better to pay bills by check than by cash?" This question and others (such as the meaning of "C.O.D.") are not within the realm of experience of the poverty-stricken child. The effects of poverty also are likely to be revealed in concern for some of the basic necessities of life, such as food and clothing.

THE SPANISH-SPEAKING SUBJECT

The various populations that are grouped under the label "Spanish-speaking" actually are a rather diverse group. It would be a mistake to assume that all of these people are identical. On the other hand, there are several common elements that create problems in individual mental testing. The two major areas of concern are linguistic ability and degree of enculturation. To place the results of the intelligence tests in proper perspective, it would undoubtedly be desirable to have indices of both linguistic ability and enculturation before interpreting the test for a Spanish-speaking subject. Even with these indices, it would be difficult to place tests in proper perspective because most standardized intelligence tests were not constructed using discreet Spanish-speaking groups. Thus the scoring frequently does not reflect their linguistic abilities or cultural values.

It would be incorrect to assume that many of the Spanish-speaking subjects are proficient in Spanish and simply have not developed fluent English. Many of the Spanish-speaking groups actually are deficient in both Spanish and English and speak in a combination of the two languages without a depth of knowledge in either. These subjects frequently are at a greater disadvantage than the subject who comes from a foreign country with a well-developed grasp of Spanish. Spanish-speaking subjects with just a rudimentary grasp of Spanish have not learned the concepts that frequently are tested in intelligence tests. These subjects exhibit a deficiency in linguistic ability and are not able to transfer knowledge from the Spanish language to the English language very readily. Therefore, attempts to translate intelligence tests into Spanish often are doomed to failure as far as these people are concerned.

Earlier the technique of comparing verbal and nonverbal tasks was discussed. While this process may allow the tester to gain some information concerning linguistic difficulties, it has to remain as a highly questionable procedure with all Spanish-speaking subjects. There is little evidence to indicate that these people are not as handicapped on performance items (due to linguistic or cultural background) as they are on verbal items. Certainly one would expect that the Spanish-speaking subject is likely to perform better on performance items than verbal items, but to interpret his performance IQ as an index of general intelligence could be quite misleading. Performance items may still require verbal comprehension in terms of instruction and they demand a certain amount of experiential background for success.

The Spanish-speaking subject frequently confuses "how" with "what" and "why." Because of the contamination of the Spanish background, many English words, such as *chair* and *share* are misinterpreted. A much more subtle aspect of the linguistic problem is the reluctance of many Spanish-speaking children to display their knowledge to adults. In many of the groups the child is not encouraged to express his knowledge or ability, and frequently he feels reluctant to do so with adults.

Many Spanish-speaking subjects come from low socioeconomic backgrounds and exhibit many of the same characteristics that the black ghetto subjects have. For example, the Spanish-speaking subject is likely to show little concern for time, and is frequently handicapped in those tasks that require rapid performance. He is also likely to operate at a rather concrete functional level in many of his verbalizations. If he lives in poverty, there will be the emphasis on the basic necessities of life, and this sometimes results in a rather apathetic approach to all tasks that do not provide visible reward.

Many of the characteristics described above are also accentuated by the cultures of the Latin American countries. In most of these cultures a child is not encouraged to be competitive and aggressive; rather, he is expected to be cooperative in the family and to remain somewhat dependent upon the family. Since most of our intelligence tests presume a middle-class orientation of competitiveness, the Spanish-speaking child is frequently handicapped. He may have to learn during the test that he expected to perform rapidly. The degree to which the subject will react to the speed factor involved in testing varies tremendously, and his reaction may have a great impact upon the score achieved. Frequently the culture from which he comes stresses traditional ways of doing things and traditional answers to problems; it does not reward innovative problem-solving techniques. The Spanish-speaking subject therefore frequently assumes that there is one method of doing a particular task, and he rather rigidly sticks to this method instead of seeking a flexible approach.

Other cultural values also may seriously hinder this subject's performance on the test. Many of the groups have not stressed the value of education in the past, and it is questionable whether their members will be well motivated to perform if they view the test as an educational enterprise. Their previous failures in tasks that are typically "educational" may cause them to give up on a task like an intelligence test. For many of the males, values such as the "machismo concept" may interfere with performance. Many Spanish-speaking males still hold quite highly to the ideal of being "macho," or "masculine." If the task is viewed as one that is not particularly masculine in nature, many of the Spanish-speaking males will not be motivated to do well.

Like the Negroes, many of the groups in the United States that speak Spanish are involved in militant activities in an attempt to achieve recognition. Some of the subjects tested will show the element of distrust that one finds in the Negro population. This distrust frequently is aggravated by their individual exposure to the process of enculturation. During enculturation, many people go through cycles in which they will either reject their own culture or reject the dominant culture as well as people identified with each of these cultures. Thus, the same problems that exist for the black subject are likely to exist for the Spanish-speaking subject. The Spanish-speaking subject may be actively antagonistic towards the "Anglo" or he may be attempting to emulate him. How this attitudinal set influences his performance generally is difficult to ascertain, especially when this attitude may be masked by overt cooperative behavior.

REFERENCES

Alimena, B., "A Note on Norms for Scatter Analysis on the Wechsler Intelligence Scales," *Journal of Clinical Psychology* 17 (1961), 61.

Balthazar, E. E., and D. H. Morrison, "The Use of the Wechsler Intelligence Scales as Diagnostic Indicators of Predominant Left-Right and Indeterminate Unilateral Brain Damage," *Journal of Clinical Psychology* 17 (1961), 161–165.

Baumeister, A. A., "Use of the WISC with Mental Retardates: A Review," *American Journal of Mental Deficiency* 69 (1964), 183–194.

———, and C. J. Bartlett, "A Comparison of the Factor of Normals and Retardates on the WISC," *American Journal of Mental Deficiency* 66 (1962a), 641–646.

———, "Further Factorial Investigations of WISC Performance of Mental Defectives," *American Journal of Mental Deficiency* 67 (1962b), 257–261.

———, and W. F. Hawkins, "Stimulus Trace as a Predictor of Performance," *American Journal of Mental Deficiency* 67 (1963), 726–729.

Bernstein, A. S., E. B. Klein, L. Berger, and J. Cohen, "Relationship Between Institutionalization, Other Demographic Variables and the Structure of Intelligence in Chronic Schizophrenics," *Journal of Consulting Psychology* 29 (1965), 320–324.

Carkhuff, R. R., and R. Pierce, "Differential Effects of Therapist Race and Social Class Upon Patient Depth of Self-Exploration in the Initial Clinical Interview," *Journal of Consulting Psychology* 31 (1967), 632–635.

Cohen, J., "A Factor-Analytically Based Rationale for the Wechsler-Bellevue," *Journal of Consulting Psychology* 16 (1952a), 272–277.

———, "Factors Underlying Wechsler-Bellevue Performance on Three Neuropsychiatric Groups," *Journal of Abnormal Social Psychology* 47 (1952b), 359–365.

————, "The Factorial Structure of the WAIS Between Early Adulthood and Old Age," *Journal of Consulting Psychology* 21 (1957a), 283–290.

————, "A Factor-Analytically Based Rationale For the Wechsler Adult Intelligence Scale," *Journal of Consulting Psychology* 21 (1957b), 451–457.

————, "The Factorial Structure of the WISC at Ages 7-6, 10-6, and 13-6," *Journal of Psychology* 23 (1959), 285–299.

Conry, R., and W. T. Plant, "WAIS and Group Test Predictions of an Academic Success Criterion: High School and College," *Educational and Psychological Measurement* 25 (1965), 493–500.

Cropley, A. J., "Differentiation of Abilities, Socio-Economic Status and the WISC," *Journal of Consulting Psychology* 28 (1964), 512–517.

Cronbach, L. J., "Assessment of Individual Differences," in P. Farnsworth and A. McNemar (eds.), *Annual Review of Psychology*, Vol. VII. Stanford, Calif.: *Annual Reviews*, (1956), pp. 173–196.

Davis, J. C., "The Scatter Pattern of a Southern Negro Group on the Wechsler-Bellevue Intelligence Scale," *Journal of Clinical Psychology* 13 (1957), 298–300.

Davis, P. C., "A Factor Analysis of the Wechsler-Bellevue Scale," *Educational Psychological Measurement* 16 (1956), 127–146.

Ellis, N. R., "Stimulus Trace and Behavioral Inadequacy," in N. R. Ellis (ed.), *Handbook of Mental Deficiency*, New York: McGraw-Hill, (1963), pp. 134–158.

English, W. H., "Minority Group Attitudes of Negroes and Implications for Guidance," *Journal of Negro Education* 26 (1957), 99–107.

Field, J. G., "Two Types of Tables for Use With Wechsler's Intelligence Scales," *Journal of Clinical Psychology* 16 (1960), 3–7.

————, "The Performance-Verbal IQ Discrepancy in a Group of Socio-paths," *Journal of Clinical Psychology* 16 (1960), 321–322.

Furth, H. G., and N. A. Milgam, "Verbal Factors in Performance on WISC Similarities," *Journal of Clinical Psychology* 21 (1965), 424–427.

Gainer, W. L., "The Ability of the WISC Subtests to Discriminate Between Boys and Girls Classified as Educable Mentally Retarded," *California Journal of Educational Research* 16 (1965), 85–92.

Guilford, J. P., *Fundamental Statistics in Psychology and Education*. New York: McGraw-Hill, 1950.

Hewitt, P., and J. O. Massey, *Clinical Clues From the WISC: Wechsler Intelligence Scale for Children With Special Sections on Testing Black and Spanish-Speaking Children*, Palo Alto, Calif.: Consulting Psychologists Press, 1969.

Hirst, Lynne S., "The Usefulness of a Two-way Analysis of WISC Sub-Tests in the Diagnosis of Remedial Reading Problems," *Journal of Experimental Education* 29 (1960), 153–160.

Jones, H. Gwynne, "The Evaluation of the Significance of Differences Between Scaled Scores of the WAIS: The Perpetuation of a Fallacy," *Journal of Consulting Psychology* 20 (1956), 319–320.

Jones, L. V., "A Factor Analysis of the Stanford-Binet at Four Age Levels," *Psychometrika* 14 (1949), 299–331.

Kallos, G. L., J. M. Grabow, and E. A. Guarino, "The WISC Profile of Disabled Readers," *Personnel and Guidance Journal* 39 (1961), 476–478.

Kitzenger, Helen, and E. Blumberg, "Supplementary Guide for Administering and Scoring the Wechsler-Bellevue Intelligence Scale (Form 1)," *Psychological Monographs* 65, No. 319 (1951), 1–20.

Levinson, B. M., "Traditional Jewish Culture Values and Performance on the Wechsler Tests," *Journal of Educational Psychology* 50 (1959), 177–181.

Littell, W. M., "The Wechsler Intelligence Scale for Children: Review of a Decade of Research," *Psychological Bulletin* 57 (1960), 132–156.

Lutey, C., *Individual Intelligence Testing: A Manual.* Greeley, Colo.: Executary, Inc., 1966.

———, *Individual Intelligence Testing: A Manual Supplement: Wechsler Preschool and Primary Scale of Intelligence (WPPSI).* Greeley, Colo.: Colorado State College Bookstore, 1967.

McDonald, A. S., "Intellectual Characteristics of Disabled Readers at the High School and College Levels," *Journal of Developmental Reading* 7 (1964), 97–101.

McNemar, Q., *The Revision of the Stanford-Binet Scale: An Analysis of the Standardization Data.* Boston: Houghton-Mifflin, 1942.

———, "On WAIS Difference Scores," *Journal of Consulting Psychology* 21 (1957), 239–240.

Meehl, P. E., *Clinical vs. Statistical Prediction.* Minneapolis: U. of Minnesota Press, 1954.

Ogdon, D. P., "WISC IQs for the Mentally Retarded," *Journal of Consulting Psychology* 24 (1960), 187–188.

Osborne, R. T., "Factorial Composition of the Wechsler Intelligence Scale for Children at the Pre-school Level," *Psychological Reports* 13 (1963), 443–448.

Prado, W. M., and Schnadt, F., "Differences in WAIS-WB Functioning of Three Psychiatric Groups," *Journal of Clinical Psychology* 21 (1965), 184–186.

Rapaport, D., with the collaboration of M. Gill and R. Schafer, *Diagnostic Psychological Testing.* Vol. I. Chicago: Year Book Publishers, 1945.

———, M. Gill, and R. Schafer, *Diagnostic Psychological Testing.* Ed. by Robert E. Holt. rev. ed., New York: International U. Press, 1968.

Rashkis, H. A., and G. S. Welsh, "Detection of Anxiety by the Use of the Wechsler Scale," *Journal of Clinical Psychology* 20 (1964), 354–357.

Reed, H. B. C., Jr., and R. M. Reitan, "Intelligence Test Performance of Brain Damaged Subjects With Lateralized Motor Deficits," *Journal of Consulting Psychology* 27 (1963), 102–106.

Rosen, A., "Client Preferences: An Overview of the Literature," *Personnel and Guidance Journal* 52 (1964), 459–462.

Sattler, J. M., "Analysis of Functions of the 1960 Stanford-Binet Intelligence Scale, Form L-M," *Journal of Clinical Psychology* 21 (1965), 173–179.

Saunders, D. R., "A Factor Analysis of the Picture Completion Items of the WAIS," *Journal of Clinical Psychology* 16 (1960), 146–149.

Silverstein, A. B., P. J. Mohan, R. E. Franken, and Doris E. Rhone, "Test Anxiety and Intellectual Performance in Mentally Retarded School Children," *Child Development* 35 (1964), 1137–1146.

Stone, F. Beth, and V. N. Rowley, "Educational Disability in Emotionally Disturbed Children," *Exceptional Children* 30 (1964), 423–426.

Valett, R. E., *Description of a Clinical Profile for the Stanford-Binet Intelligence Scale (L-M)*. Palo Alto, Calif.: Consulting Psychologist Press, 1965.

Vontress, C. E., "Counseling the Culturally Different in Our Society," paper presented at the National Conference of State Employment Service Counseling Supervisors, Detroit, 1968.

———, "Cultural Barriers in the Counseling Relationship," *Personnel and Guidance Journal* 48 (1969), 11–17.

———, "Counseling Blacks," *Personnel and Guidance Journal* 48 (1970), 713–719.

Wechsler, David, *The Measurement of Adult Intelligence*. 3rd ed. Baltimore: Williams & Wilkins, 1944.

———, *Manual: Wechsler Intelligence Scale for Children*. New York: Psychological Corporation, 1949.

———, *Manual for the Wechsler Adult Intelligence Scale*. New York: Psychological Corporation, 1955.

———, *The Measurement and Appraisal of Adult Intelligence*. Baltimore: Williams & Wilkins, 1958.

———, *Manual for the Wechsler Preschool and Primary Scale of Intelligence*. New York: Psychological Corporation, 1967.

The Psychological Report

GENERAL CONSIDERATIONS

The primary function of the psychological test is to provide data which will enable a psychologist or some other specialist to make a decision about another person or group of people or, in guidance, to help a person to make a decision about himself. Test data alone, however, are rarely sufficient for this function. The test results must be interpreted and integrated with information from the testing session and the subject's background. With the exception of some counseling functions, such interpretation and integration requires a written report.

Since the 1940's increasingly large numbers of persons with diverse educational backgrounds and professional affiliations have included the use of psychological tests among their professed competencies. Such persons include psychologists, vocational guidance workers, educational consultants, and personnel managers. All of them may expect at some time to be required to write a report of a psychological examination. Although some of these specialists will serve multiple or overlapping functions, each specialist presumably will have to satisfy the demands of his special clientele.

These demands determine not only the nature of the material that will be emphasized in the report but also the complexity or level of sophistication with which the report will be written. Requests for psychological reports come from such diverse sources as psychologists, psychiatrists, other physicians, counselors, guidance workers, school teachers, school administrators, employers, social workers, parents, and the examinees themselves. Not all of these people are interested in gaining the same information from a report; they have their own specific needs, and their ability to deal with psychological jargon and measurement terms is as diverse as the needs themselves.

259

The requirements of the client, therefore, will determine to a great extent the content of the report. Unfortunately, report writers have not "tailored" their work to meet these requirements in a way which their clientele find satisfactory. Tallent (1963) and Reiss (1959) have presented a large number of complaints regarding the way in which psychological reports are written. Among the most frequently registered are the following.

1. Too much or too little raw data included in the report.
2. Omission of essential information.
3. Irresponsible interpretation.
4. Unlabeled speculation.
5. Not practical or useful; misplaced emphasis.
6. Too much jargon.
7. Too vague and ambiguous.
8. Generalized (cookbook) interpretations.

Such complaints grow out of the psychologist's failure to consider the needs and competencies of his individual client. If a report does not contain the information required by the reader it is worthless. In order to write a truly useful report the psychologist must have a thorough understanding of the reader's needs.

SPECIFIC CONSIDERATIONS

THE EXAMINER'S RESPONSIBILITIES

A primary consideration for the examiner in determining what the reader expects in a report is the purpose for which the evaluation is being requested. Before accepting the responsibility for doing an evaluation the examiner should attempt to determine what specific decisions will be made on the basis of his evaluation. If he has this information he can also determine whether he has the competencies required to meet the needs of his client. *The Ethical Standards of Psychologists* contains two statements which bear directly on the psychologist's qualifications in this regard: "[A] psychologist does not claim either directly or by implication professional qualifications that differ from his actual qualifications . . ." (APA, 1967, p. 65) and "Test results or other assessment data used for evaluation or classification are communicated to employers, relatives or other appropriate persons in such a way as to guard against misinterpretation or misuse." (APA, 1967, p. 70) Similar statements appear in the *Ethical Standards of the American Personnel and Guidance Association.* The only way a psychologist can avoid violating these ethical standards is by requiring his clientele to specify how the test information is to be used.

The professional literature contains a number of examples of the types of reports that can be written with little or no reference to data gathered during an evaluation. Two of the most famous of these are the *Aunt Fanny Description* (Tallent, 1958) and the *Barnum-type* character reading. The Aunt Fanny type report consists of a collection of general statements which might apply to any one in a given population. The report writer simply needs to keep in mind the conflicts, mechanisms, and peculiarities of that population and then write statements which would, in part, apply to nearly everyone in the population. As an example of this type, Tallent (1963) presented a "psychological report" prepared by Dr. Norman Sundberg (Sundberg and Tyler, 1962, pp. 236–237). The "report" follows.

Completely Blind Analysis of the Case
of a Schizophrenic Veteran

—Norman D. Sundberg

Written before the writer knew *anything* about the patient except that he was a new admission to a Veterans Administration hospital and his case was to be worked up for a state psychological association meeting, January, 1956, Salem, Oregon.

This veteran approached the testing situation with some reluctance. He was cooperative with the clinician, but was mildly evasive on some of the material. Both the tests and the past history suggest considerable inadequacy in interpersonal relations, particularly with members of his family. Although it is doubtful whether he has ever had very close relationships with anyone, the few apparently close relationships which he has had were tinged with a great deal of ambivalence. He has never been able to sink his roots very deeply. He is immature, egocentric and irritable, and often he misperceives the good intentions of the people around him. Projection is one of his prominent defense mechanisms. He tends to be basically passive and dependent, though there are occasional periods of resistance and rebellion against others. Although he shows some seclusiveness and autistic trends, he is in fair to good contact with reality. Vocationally, his adjustment has been very poor. Mostly he has drifted from one job to another. His interests are shallow and he tends to have poor motivation for his work. Also he has had a hard time keeping his jobs because of difficulty in getting along with fellow employees. Though he has had some affairs, his sex life has been unsatisfactory to him. At present he is mildly depressed, although a great deal of affect is not shown. What physical complaints he has appear mainly to have a functional origin. His intelligence is close to average, but he is functioning below his full capacity. In summary, this is a long-term inadequate or borderline adjustment pattern. Test results and case history, though they do not give a strong clear-cut diagnostic picture, suggest the diagnosis of schizophrenic reaction, chronic undifferentiated type. Prognosis for response to treatment appears to be poor.

This completely blind analysis is based on the following assumptions:

1. The usual veteran referred for psychological testing is not likely to be an obvious or clear-cut diagnostic case. There is no need for testing unless there is indecision about what steps

might be taken in his behalf. Consequently, hedging is to be expected in a report anyway.

2. There are some modal characteristics of patients coming to VA hospitals. In placing bets on what the patient is likely to be like, the best guess would be a description of the modal personality. For instance, most of the veterans coming to this hospital are chronic cases who have not succeeded in jobs or in family life. Also, the best guess on intelligence would obviously be average intelligence, but since the person is a psychiatric patient it is likely that he is not functioning at his best.

3. This is a schizophrenic case (according to the plan for the program). Given the general classification schizophrenia, one can work back to some of the characteristics which belong to such persons and have a fair chance of being right.

4. Certain modal behaviors of the clinical staff provide clues. They use certain words, resort to jargon. They have a preference for certain diagnoses. A large percentage of the cases wind up with the diagnosis of schizophrenic reaction, chronic undifferentiated type.

5. There are some "universally valid" adjectives which are appropriate for almost any psychiatric patient, such as *dependent*, *immature*, *irritable*, and *egocentric*.

6. In the less clear areas where modal characteristics do not stand out, it is safe to write a vague statement or one which can be interpreted in various ways. Readers can be counted on to overlook a few vague misses and to select the descriptions which jibe with their own preconceptions.

7. All of this is intended to say that we have much in common with the old fortune teller, and that what we need are better ways of dealing with individuality. Knowing modal personalities is very useful; it certainly adds to ease of social communication; however, we are sometimes fooled into thinking that we know persons when actually all we know are our own stereotypes.

The second kind of generalized description also is based on generalities which have the "feel" of being valid because they are based on high population base rates. Furthermore, the descriptions are generally flattering, and the mild negative statements can be overlooked or made acceptable by the general tone of the description. The reader of the description can read into it what he pleases. This method has been labeled the *Barnum* effect after a fake report prepared by D. G. Paterson entitled *Character Reading at Sight of Mr. S. According to the System of Mr. P. T. Barnum* (Thorne, 1961, p. 31).

> Abilities: Above average in intelligence or mental alertness. Also above average in accuracy—rather painstaking at times. Deserves a reputation for neatness—dislikes turning out sloppy work. Has initiative; that is, ability to make suggestions and to get new ideas, open-mindedness.

Emotions: You have a tendency to worry at times but not to excess. You do get depressed at times but you couldn't be called moody because you are generally cheerful and rather optimistic. You have a good disposition although earlier in life you have had a struggle with yourself to control your impulses and temper.

Interests: You are strongly socially inclined, you like to meet people, especially to mix with those you know well. You appreciate art, painting and music but you will never be a success as an artist or as a creator or composer of music. You like sports and athletic events but devote more of your attention to reading about them in the sporting page than in actual participation.

Ambitions: You are ambitious and deserve credit for wanting to be well thought of by your family, business associates and friends. These ambitions come out most strongly in your tendency to indulge in daydreams, in building air-castles, but this does not mean that you fail to get into the game of life actively.

Vocational: You ought to continue to be successful so long as you stay in a social vocation. I mean if you keep at work bringing you in contact with people. Just what work you pick out isn't as important as the fact that it must be work bringing you in touch with people. On the negative side you would never have made a success at strictly theoretical work or in pure research work such as in physics or neurology.

It is apparent that such reports would be of no value as an aid in the decision-making process. They provide no specific information about the *individual* and are not directed toward some purpose. It is only when the report is individualized and purposeful that such quackery is avoided. Aside from those psychologists who are knowingly unethical in their practice, there are test users who produce "canned" reports because they do not have some of the competencies which would enable them to practice effectively. A person professing to use tests as a part of his practice must first of all know his tests. While such a statement might appear trite, there are unfortunately some persons who use tests with no more knowledge of them than the information presented in the manual. It is essential that individuals who employ tests in their practice know the research on the tests they use. Test users also should stay abreast of new developments in testing. Furthermore, they need to keep records on their own successes and failures, thereby creating a means of determining the validity of their predictions.

A second requirement for the test user is that he must have great depth and breadth in his understanding of people. There are several ways that the human being can be conceptualized; for example, sociologically, anthropologically, and psychologically. While it is true that the psychological consultant is primarily interested in the psychological aspects of man, it is equally true that the consultant is called upon to help make decisions about individuals in situations in which extensive knowledge about these other areas is essential. This means that his preparation should include the study of personality, individual differences, developmental psychology, sociology, and anthropology—to mention only a few relevant areas. Such depth is necessary if the examiner is to explain adequately the subject's performance on a test, and is to be able to make accurate predictions from test scores about the subject's behavior outside the consulting room, especially his behavior in the specific situation which led to the referral.

A third requirement is that the test user must be able to take an objective view of his work. He must maintain an empirical approach to testing which will enable him to evaluate critically any new data that might lead him to modify or reject previous hypotheses regarding tests and examinees. In effect, what we are saying is that the psychological examiner must be a practitioner-scientist, which to Pepinsky and Pepinsky (1954), means that his procedures must follow a special set of rules:

1. He must specify the observations upon which his inference is based.
2. He must rephrase his inferential statement in the form of an answerable question.
3. He must confront his hypotheses with observations independent of those upon which the inference was founded.

Obviously all of this cannot be done in a report, but the process is necessary if the examiner is to write up his evaluations objectively. The examiner must clearly distinguish between observation and inference in his report. This might be done by reporting representative examples of the behavior from which the inference was drawn. The process of test interpretation involves a number of observations from which the examiner draws inferences which lead to hypotheses about the examinee and result in a model of the examinee as he is likely to function in the situation which led to the referral. Figure 11-1 is a schematic representation of the process (Goldman, 1961, p. 189).

Since the examiner must report on the "model in a situation," the fourth requirement is that the examiner must have intimate knowledge of the environments in which his test subjects will function. If he is a psychologist working as a vocational counselor he must know jobs, job requirements, and the vocational implications of test scores. If he is to help determine the proper therapy or therapist for a client he must know about the responses of individuals with certain characteristics to specific therapy and/or particular therapists. The school psychologist must know the school, teachers, counselors, administrators, and remedial teaching procedures for particular disabilities. Such information is acquired through direct experience and observation, through classes, and through reading the professional literature. Only when the above requirements are met should the examiner feel qualified to write individualized psychological reports instead of generalized or "canned" reports.

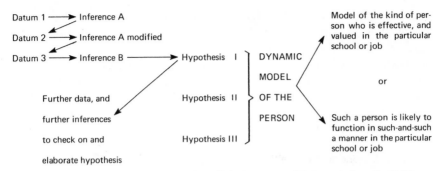

Fig. 11-1. Schematic representation of a clinical process of interpretation. L. Goldman, *Using Tests in Counseling.* New York: Appleton-Century-Crofts, Educational Division, Meredith Corporation, 1961, p. 189.

THE STYLE AND CONTENT OF THE REPORT

The style and content of a psychological report are determined by the purpose for which the report is being written, the needs and sophistication of the reader, the preferences of the writer, and in some instances institutional requirements. A variety of outlines have been developed as aids to the preparation of psychological reports. Some examples of outlines are presented later in this chapter. A rigid adherence to these forms tends to result in a segmented presentation of test results with a concomitant segmentation of the personality of the subject of the report. Because of this tendency some psychologists would abandon all such forms and use a flexible, idiosyncratic approach to report writing. When this approach is used, the organization of the report is determined by the purpose of the report, the results are presented in a narrative style, and the content is limited to the psychologist's interpretation of the data. Other psychologists prefer a more technical, detailed report in which a test-by-test interpretation is made and test scores are included in the report. Such reports usually contain an integrated summary which may include the important characteristics of the narrative report. Very few psychologists would advocate the inclusion of raw responses to individual items except in unusual circumstances.

Regardless of the form used, psychological reports usually cover such things as (1) basic identifying information, such as the subject's name, age, sex, marital status, occupation, education; (2) the reason for the assessment, which serves as an orientation for the reader to the rest of the report; (3) behavioral observations of the examinee during testing, the purpose of which is to describe the tone of the testing situation and provide any information (attitudinal, physical, or environmental) which might influence the results and interpretation of the test scores; (4) assessment procedures used (tests, observations); (5) a report of the subject's intellectual functioning; (6) a description of the subject's personality and personality dynamics (attitudes, adjustment mechanisms, conflicts, etc.) and the source of such information; (7) when appropriate, diagnostic impressions and prognosis; (8) when appropriate, recommendations for disposition of the case.

L'Abate (1964, p. 132) proposes a variant (Chart A) on this scheme which separates the *descriptive* content from the *explanatory* content in report writing. In the descriptive division, personality functioning is differentiated into self-presentational and phenotypical levels. In the explanatory division, personality is differentiated into the genotypical and historical levels.

Chart A A Working Proposal for Personality Functioning*

A. Description
  1. Self-presentational level—*How* does the patient present himself?
     (a) attire
     (b) test-taking attitudes
     (c) interaction with examiner
     (d) other characteristics pertinent to this level
  2. Phenotypical level—*What* is the patient like?
     (a) congruency or incongruency of this level with level 1
     (b) functioning proper—major conflict area or thesis
         (1) emotional and psychosexual organization
         (2) intellectual and cognitive organization
     (c) defensive structure and organization
     (d) other characteristics pertinent to this level

B. Explanation
  1. Genotypical level—*Why* does the individual behave the way he does?
     (a) congruency or incongruency of this level with above levels
     (b) *Where?* possible intrapsychic determinants
         (1) intellectual retardation
         (2) psychosexual identification
         (3) cerebral dysfunction
         (4) dependency or hostility or other impulses
     (c) other intrapsychic determinants
  2. Historical level—*When* did the individual acquire such genotype?
     (a) possible or speculative antecedents or determinants
         (1) parental deprivation
         (2) early sources of identification
         (3) chronicity or abruptness of cerebral trauma
     (b) congruency or incongruency of this level with above levels

*Source: L. L'Abate, *Principles of Clinical Psychology* (New York: Grune and Stratton, 1964), p. 32.

Discussions of levels in report writing quite frequently lead the reader into a maze of ambiguity because, as L'Abate (1964) points out, quite frequently the various types of levels are not defined. He differentiates between levels of organization, levels of integration, levels of functioning, and levels of interpretation. In writing about personality or intelligence it is possible to describe each of the component parts of the personality or intelligence in terms of its level of complexity—that is, in terms of the number of variables involved, degree of fragmentation, variability, and controllability. In doing so the writer is discussing the organization of personality or intelligence.

When he discusses the component parts in terms of their relationship with each other, the writer is describing the integration of personality. It is apparent that personality is always organized but may not be integrated. That is, there may be serious conflicts and discrepancies between components; for example, between aspirations and ability, between one's real self and ideal self, or among values. Or there may be an overdevelopment of one component of personality or ability at the expense of other components.

In describing the behavior associated with the subject's level of integration the writer may choose to discuss it at various levels of functioning, including descriptions of or hypotheses about the causes of the lack of integration. In L'Abate's scheme these levels may be Self-Presentational, Phenotypical, Genotypical and Historical, or Situational.

Finally, the levels of interpretation may range from an empirical description (which may simply be a statistical interpretation of the data) through a logical development of the data to generalizations, conclusions, and predictions about the global personality. Chart B (L'Abate, 1964, p. 39) summarizes L'Abate's scheme for the use of levels in clinical work.

Super and Crites (1962) have presented a list of principles of test interpretation which complements L'Abate's scheme and provides a guide for the conceptualization of reports more limited in scope. The substance of their statements follows.

1. Scores should be interpreted statistically in light of the appropriate norm groups.
2. Any behavior which occurred during the testing session and which might have affected the subject's performance on the test should be described and its relationship explained.
3. In the event that other scores in the battery have a bearing on a given score the report should include the implications. This is crucial in the case of discrepancies, as, for example, between level of interests and ability.
4. Interpretations must be modified in the light of any personal characteristics or case-history data which would indicate that the subject was grossly different from the norm group.
5. The test results should be expressed first in psychological terms and then in terms of the behavior relevant to the purpose for which the evaluation was done.
6. The result should be summarized in such a way as to point up the subject's potentialities and liabilities and to provide a dynamic, integrated picture of the individual as he is functioning and can be expected to function in the future.

The following outline is presented by Freeman (1962 pp. 338–340) as an example of the type of form used in teaching students to write reports of intelligence tests. This particular form is of value because of its wealth of suggestions for observation as well as the fact that its function is restricted to intelligence tests.

Chart B   Types of Levels in Clinical Psychology*

(a) Levels of Organization

(c) Levels of Interpretation

Empirical Description   Logical Explanation

Levels of Abstraction

	I	II	III	IV
Ranging from most simple, biochemical to most complex, social level. Increase in organization according to: Number of Variables Variability Modificability Controllability	Test responses and results; raw data resulting from physical and psychological organization	Clusters of responses; patterns of whole scores, ratings, etc., summary of observations	Inferences drawn from results of observations	Relationships between inferences leading to empirical conclusions and generalizations	Relationships of conclusions and generalizations to general principles and laws

(b) Levels of Psychological Functioning

Self-Presentational   Phenotypical   Genotypical   Historical or Situational

*Source: L. L'Abate, *Principles of Clinical Psychology* (New York: Grune and Stratton, 1964), p. 39.

Psychological Examination

Name: (last, first, middle)   Date:
Age: (in years and months)   Date of Birth:
Referred by:

I. Introductory Statement
   a. by whom tested
   b. reason for testing
II. Name (in full) of the test used
III. State the individual's general attitude and response to the test situation and to the examiner.
IV. Test findings:

Stanford-Binet   WAIS or WISC

   a. Mental Age   a. Verbal IQ
   b. Intelligence Quotient   b. Performance IQ
   c. Basal   c. Full-Scale IQ
   d. Terminal Year   d. Classification
   e. Classification (average
      superior, etc.)
V. Test Evaluation
   a. Analyze the performance on:
      1. verbal materials
      2. nonverbal materials
   b. Compare the MA and IQ with the Vocabulary test score
   c. Point out the quantitative and qualitative aspects of the results:
      1. strengths
      2. weaknesses
      3. scatter analysis
      4. quality of language (word definitions, use of language, grammar, richness of vocabulary, nuances, etc.
VI. A summary statement of test performance
VII. Subject's behavior while being tested
   a. Reaction time:
      1. Were responses delayed, blocked, irregular?
      2. Was there any indication of negativism?
      3. Were responses given quickly or impulsively?
   b. Nature of responses:
      1. Are some nonsensical, immature, childlike?
      2. Are they, on the whole, of good quality; or are they inconsistent?
      3. Is there confabulation?
      4. Does the subject ask for help?
      5. Is the subject critical of his responses?
   c. Depth of responses:
      1. Are they "surface" responses?
      2. Do they show depth of understanding?
      3. Does the subject try to appear penetrating?
      4. Does the subject adopt a "playful" (defensive) attitude?
   d. Self-references:
      1. Is the question or answer referred to the self? (Describe and analyze the references.)

    2. Are the responses in terms of the subject's own or immediate experiences, or in terms of someone else's?

    3. Does the individual give expression to his feelings during the testing (orally or by body movements)?

  e. Evidence of confusion or doubt:

    1. Do test questions have to be repeated?

    2. Does the subject change his answers? (Under what conditions?)

    3. Are questions misunderstood or misinterpreted? If so, explain in what way.

  f. Verbalization:

    1. Is the subject verbose?

    2. Is he spontaneous in responding?

    3. Does he have peculiarities of speech?

  g. Organizational methods:

    1. Is the individual careful or overmeticulous?

    2. Does he plan and work systematically? Or is his a random approach?

    3. Does he make many false starts?

    4. Does he generalize readily?

    5. Is there evidence of perseveration?

  h. Adaptability:

    1. Does the subject shift readily from one test to the next?

    2. Is his interest sustained in all types of test items?

  i. Motor coordination:

    1. Are the gross and finer movements skillful or awkward?

    2. Can he smoothly execute bilateral movements?

  j. Effort:

    1. Is the subject cooperative?

    2. Does he give evidence of trying hard?

    3. Does he attend with ease or difficulty?

  k. Mood:

    1. Was the individual readily upset, irritable, argumentative, stuporous, happy, sad, depressed?

    2. Were there any emotional outbursts?

    3. Did his mood undergo change during the testing?

    4. Was he, on the whole, cheerful?

    5. In what mood was the individual when he left the testing room?*

More comprehensive outlines have been constructed for use when a complete assessment is to be done. The following form is a composite of several such outlines.

  I. General Observations

    A. Appearance

      1. Dress, outstanding features

      2. Mannerisms, posture, gestures

      3. Coordination

      4. Physique

    B. Adjustment to the Testing Situation

      1. Initial reaction

      2. Signs of tension

      3. Attitudes toward tests and examiner

*Source: F. Freeman, *Theory and Practice of Psychological Testing* (New York: Holt Rinehart and Winston, Inc., 1962), pp. 338–340.

      4. Cooperation and effort during evaluation
      5. Reaction to praise and encouragement
   C. Spontaneous Responses
      1. Clarity of speech
      2. Quality of verbal production
      3. Vocabulary
   D. Rapport
  II. Mental Functioning
   A. Results of Intelligence Tests
      1. Interpretation of results
      2. Relationship between potential and performance
      3. Evidence of organic involvement, if appropriate
      4. Educational implications
      5. Vocational implications
   B. Results of other tests of intellectual functioning
      1. Visual-motor test
      2. Memory
      3. Concept Formation
      4. Achievement
      5. Vocational Aptitude
 III. Personality Functioning
   A. Results of Personality Tests
      1. Interpretation of tests in relation to behavior
      2. Signs of psychopathology
      3. Drives and needs
      4. Perception of self
      5. Conflicts
      6. Defense mechanisms
      7. Emotional control
   B. Data from other sources
      1. Sources of social-emotional disturbance
      2. Frustrations
      3. Interpersonal relations
      4. Goals
      5. Value system
 IV. Summary and Recommendations

As previously stated, some psychologists object to detailed outlines such as these because such formats appear to segment the personality of the subject rather than present a picture of an integrated functioning individual. Furthermore, there is a tendency for reports that follow detailed outlines to be test-oriented rather than person- and purpose-oriented. Such outlines can be useful, however, when they are used as guides to help the writer organize his results.

PREPARATION OF THE REPORT

The preparation of the report actually starts with the selection of the tests to be used in the evaluation, because the tests selected will be determined by the purpose for which the evaluation is being done. At the end of a testing session the psychologist is confronted with a mass of raw test data, a large number of specific observations of the subject, occasionally some case-history data, and some subjective feelings about the examinee. If the examiner wishes to do a thorough job, he will solicit data from every available source.

DATA REDUCTION

A major task in the preparation of the report is the reduction in the amount of data with which the examiner must deal. There are, in fact, several steps to this aspect of report writing. The first step is to review the primary purpose of the evaluation. It should be written out together with secondary uses which might influence the nature of the material included in the report.

The second step is to prepare a list of factors known to be of importance in predicting criterion performance or known to be relevant with respect to the purpose of the evaluation. In preparing a report for vocational guidance, for example, one must consider aptitudes, interests, other personality characteristics, finances, training and job opportunities, and the relationship between these variables and job success and satisfaction. Other topics might be attitudes, emotional controls, goals, interpersonal relations, needs, perception of self and environment, and values.

The third step is to review the case-history data and write up the observations made during the testing session. At this point the writer should not attempt to edit the observations to any great extent —it is best to err on the side of overinclusion. These data provide a valuable source of interpretive hypotheses.

The fourth step is to prepare an interpretation for each test. This interpretation should be preceded by a statement of the purpose that the test was to serve in the evaluation. At this point it is important that the specific source of the interpretation be included, e.g., "The gross difference between the Verbal and Performance scores on the WAIS," or "The elevations on scales 2 and 7 of the MMPI." The behavior of the examinee in response to the various aspects of the test is also a rich source of interpretive hypotheses. At this stage it is best to resist the temptation to make high-level inferences from these bits of data (See Fig. 11-1 and Chart B).

The fifth step is to review all of the data and eliminate the obviously irrelevant and trival. In part this may be done simply by referring to the purpose, but several criteria may need to be applied. Tallent (1958), in discussing the importance of individualizing clinical evaluations, offers suggestions which might serve as guides for evaluating the statements to be used in reports. The substance of these suggestions follows.

1. Consider whether it is important to mention a finding which is true of many persons.
2. Show the unique aspects of a trait by indicating how it is manifested.
3. Indicate trait strength because trait significance is partially dependent on the strength of the trait.

4. State the level at which a trait occurs.
5. Describe the circumstances in which behavior becomes overt or important.
6. Specify the manner in which traits interrelate, rather than simply mention them separately.
7. Avoid "shot-gun" reporting of all possible findings. Always ask, "Will this statement help my reader understand the client as an individual?"

The use of a list such as this encourages the beginning writer to report results thoroughly and also to recognize that when thoroughness is not possible some types of information should be left out or labeled as speculation. It also makes it possible to determine the confidence with which the psychologist's conclusions can be stated. The more certain he is of the cues that led to his conclusions, the more selective he can be about the material to be included in the report. A problem which sometimes arises at this point is the occasional appearance of a characteristic which so dominates the personality of the subject that the examiner feels it should be placed in the report even though it may not be relevant to immediate decision. In such instances the information should probably be included because the report will probably also function as a record.

The sixth step is to arrange the interpretive statements into a hierarchy of significance for the report. Again it is necessary to consult the stated purpose of the report because different purposes may result in different hierarchies. If the purpose is simply to describe the present functioning of the individual, the data should be presented in a manner that will most effectively represent the subject's performance at the time of testing. If it is a diagnostic report, on the other hand, the data might be presented in a stepwise fashion as evidence building to a diagnostic conclusion. If recommendations for treatment are to be made it might be essential that information regarding the origin of a symptomatic bit of behavior be included in the report.

ORGANIZATION OF THE REPORT

Although psychological evaluations are usually requested for rather specific purposes, the reports may be read and used by individuals other than the referring agent. This will almost certainly be true when a team approach to decision making is used and when the report is to become a part of a record. It is also quite likely that in such situations the readers will vary in their knowledge of psychology and psychological terms. The psychologist should take this into account in his report. Lay readers are not likely to be willing to struggle through endless technical terminology, while professionals may want such material included in the report. For this reason we are of the opinion that the dual report (Hammond and Allen, 1953, p. 53) will generally be the most suitable plan for the report.

The dual report is described as one consisting of "(1) a brief nontechnical resumé of the psychologist's findings, directed at the untrained reader, stressing conclusions and recommendations, and making no attempt to represent the full complexity of the case, followed by (2) the full, detailed technical report which sets forth the complete picture of the psychologist's findings for the reader trained in psychology and which may also be useful for further research." As Hammond and Allen point out, this plan is extremely flexible. The first part could be very short and nontechnical or it can be detailed and appropriate only for a trained psychologist. The nature of the second part of the report would be determined by the completeness and technical level of the first. When the introductory summary is written in nontechnical, everyday language relevant to the purpose of the evaluation, the lay reader is spared the problem of wading through technical data, and the professional will not find it necessary to turn back from an end summary to check details. In addition, it is possible to present the subject as a whole unified personality.

The material from step five (p. 272) can form the basis for the detailed section of the report. This section will include the detailed analysis of the test results, and perhaps illustrative quotations from interviews and the test protocols.

At this point the writer should prepare an outline of his report. He should begin by reviewing the material from step six (p. 273) and selecting from this the most salient aspects of the subject's personality and performance. It is not possible to make general statements about what a psychologist should emphasize in a report; this is a matter which will vary from psychologist to psychologist and and from report to report. Some things that should be considered in the review are (1) the frequency with which a theme occurs, (2) the intensity of subject involvement with a theme, recurrent or not, and (3) the consequences of a characteristic with regard to the purpose of the evaluation. These selected features should be the ones most characteristic of the subject so that they can provide the major topic headings of the outline. The subheadings will be short statements and examples of the major characteristics as they relate to the purpose of the evaluation. In this form the outline may be used as a framework for writing an opening summary for the report, which in turn may provide an outline for the rest of the first section of the report.

As implied above, the opening summary must be written after the detailed part of the report is finished. When compiling the report the psychologist begins by writing a sentence or so to orient the reader to the purpose of the report and to the procedures used in the evaluation. The sentence of the opening summary may state some central theme which might run through the report, or the writer might briefly state his conclusions and recommendations. The writer then may consult his outline, which is composed of the major results of the evaluation, and write a sentence or two about each of the findings that he has selected as being most characteristic of the subject. It is important that the psychologist show the relationships between the points he makes and how these points are related to his conclusions. When the writer has presented the main points in the order in which they appear in the report, the opening summary is complete. Obviously many details are omitted from such a summary, but its purpose is simply to present the central ideas of the complete report in the order in which they appear in the report.

The writer is now ready to complete the first part of the dual report. A frequent criticism of the reports of beginning writers and of some experienced report writers is that their reports are segmented—that is, the various sections are not integrated. There are several techniques for achieving integration in a report, but one of the most important is parallel construction. The reader will note that the opening summary is composed of general statements that are derived from the outline and are presented in the order in which they appear in the complete report. In the writing of the remainder of the first part of the dual report these sentences or paraphrases of them become the topic sentences of each major section of the report. The extent to which the writer elaborates upon these sentences depends upon how detailed this part of the report is to be (see p. 265). The major sections may be paragraphs or larger units, but in any case the use of such parallel construction will do much toward integrating the report.

By following a few suggestions with regard to paragraph organization the writer may also improve the organization and effectiveness of the report. The suggestions are as follows.

1. Each paragraph should encompass one main idea.
2. The paragraph should be organized so that the most general, important aspects appear at the beginning of the paragraph followed by the more specific statements concerning the general topic.
3. Related points should be kept together and arranged in a logical sequence, so that the point that is essential for understanding another will be presented first.
4. Points the writer wishes to emphasize should be placed at the beginning or the end of the paragraph. Emphasis is greatest at the beginning of the paragraph.

A well-organized, integrated first part of the dual report will adequately satisfy most of the requirements of the referring agent. Nonetheless, the second detailed section of the report must be carefully organized so that the reader may find the data from which the interpretations in the first section were drawn. Outlines such as those presented on pp. 269-271 may help in the organization of the second part of the report. An example of the first part of a dual report follows.

Date: 6-9-72
To: Mrs. Ima Helper
Pleasant Town Public Schools
Re: Emma Blank

Purpose   Miss Emma Blank was referred to the Psychological Service Center by Mrs. Ima Helper, guidance counselor, at the request of Mrs. Blank, Emma's mother. The purpose for the referral was to determine the reasons for Emma's poor progress in school and to aid in planning an appropriate educational program for her.

During the examination, the Wechsler Intelligence Scale for Children, the Wide-Range Achievement Test, the Bender Visual-Motor Gestalt Test and the House-Tree-Person Technique were administered. Additional information from the school and interviews with Mrs. Blank and Emma were used in determining Emma's current intellectual and emotional status.

Data from the above sources suggest that Emma is a child of low average intelligence who, while not seriously disturbed emotionally, is functioning poorly in the classroom due to her immaturity and a generalized fearfulness. These characteristics may be the result of the interaction of two factors: (1) the unfortunate circumstances surrounding her premature birth, and (2) a reaction to an unwholesome family background.

She needs definitely structured tasks and support in her educational efforts as well as consistency and support in her home to reduce her apprehensiveness. Teaching methods should be of the multi-modal type, involving simultaneous presentation to all avenues of perception. Professional family counseling would undoubtedly help to foster more constructive patterns of interpersonal relationships in the home.

Intellectually, Emma is functioning at a low-average level. The WISC yielded a verbal score of 87, a performance score of 94, and a total IQ of 90. Although her performance in the classroom is definitely inferior, her performance on the achievement test indicated a deficit of only a few months. The grossly inferior performance in the classroom is probably the result of her inability to focus on a problem for even moderate lengths of time. Unless she is supervised and supported she becomes fidgety and inattentive. In addition, she seems unable to deal with abstract or generalized ideas; that is, her thinking is very concrete. When, for example, she was asked to work arithmetic problems she was successful but it was necessary for her to count on her fingers.

The need to reduce things to a concrete operation may be a function of her general immaturity and a desire for the security of certainty. Although she is physically average for her age, she is poorly coordinated in both gross and fine muscle control. There is about a year's lag in her visual-motor perception. In addition, her speech and conversation are immature. She seemed generally unsure of herself and apprehensive with regard to her status during the examination. She was quite dependent upon my support and needed continual reassurance that she was performing adequately. This strong need for structure, reassurance, and support undoubtedly interferes with her performance in the classroom.

Expansion
on second
sentence
in opening
summary

These aspects of Emma's personality probably reflect her background and home environment. Her mother's health was "poor" during pregnancy and labor had to be induced because of "difficulties." Emma was born a jaundiced, two-month premature baby into a family in which the father was a diabetic alcoholic and the mother a "high strung," impatient, inconsistent woman. The father alternated between abusing the child when drunk and attempts to "make up" for it when sober. This highly unstable environment lasted through the first three years of Emma's life; then it was made even more complicated by the birth of a brother, and shortly thereafter, the divorce of her parents. These events probably increased her feelings of insecurity, since she is reported to be jealous of her brother and to "aggravate" both the mother and the brother to get attention. For a child such as this, structure, reassurance, and "concreteness" are essential elements of safety and security. The mother's recent marriage to a man who is "steady" and "calm" may provide some stability in the home.

Elaboration
of third
sentence of
opening
summary

The use of teaching methods which utilize simultaneous presentation of visual, auditory, and kinesthetic stimulation seems most appropriate in light of her test performance and past history. She exhibits many of the characteristics associated with children manifesting *minimal neurological dysfunction*; i. e., visual-motor deficit, heightened motor activity, concrete orientation, complications at birth, a developmental history of clumsiness, and generalized immaturity. However, because of her premature birth and the added complication of the disturbed family relationship, such a diagnosis is unwarranted. The teaching methods recommended above provide factors needed by Emma. The tasks are structured, usually require the active participation of the pupil, and provide many opportunities for the teacher to support the pupil. Competition should be minimized.

Mrs. Blank needs help in learning to cope with Emma and with herself. It is quite likely that if professional counseling is not sought the present family situation will deteriorate due to Emma's continuous demands for attention and reassurance and Mrs. Blank's immature response to the demands. The parents need to learn to establish a stable, supportive, secure home situation in which discipline is consistent and predictable.

S. R. Bond, Ph. D.

Recognizing the fact that psychological reports will vary considerably in format and content, the following section in this chapter presents a few examples of reports written by different psychologists. These reports are not meant to serve as models. They are presented to show how psychologists integrate various kinds of information in a psychological evaluation. The first example concerns the subject whose test profile is shown in Table 10-4, page 240.

PSYCHOLOGICAL TEST REPORT

Name: Juventino Lopez   Test: WISC
Birth date: 9-9-54   Grade: 10
Test date: 7-11-70   School: Kennedy H. S.
Age: 15-10   Examiner: Ray Rivas

Summary

The subject's Full Scale IQ (109) places him near the top of the average range of mental ability as compared to others his age in the general population. His Verbal IQ of 100 is significantly lower than his Performance IQ of 118.

The subject comes from a home where both English and Spanish are spoken. The pattern of scores achieved on the subtests support the hypothesis that the significantly lower Verbal score may partially stem from a language handicap. The pattern of subtest scores, coupled with an apparent lack of motivation for testing, indicates that the Full Scale score underestimates his intelligence. Regardless of the cause of his performance, the results indicate that the subject should be able to achieve adequately at his grade level. Conferences with the subject and his parents are recommended to clarify the subject's plans and attitudes toward school. If the subject returns to school, the results of testing and conferences should be referred to the school to help provide better placement and assistance.

The Testing Situation

The subject was referred to a special summer project by his English teacher who indicated that although he was doing minimal work in her class, she felt that he was an extremely bright person. His school records revealed about an equal number of C's and D's in his subjects, with D's predominating in any subject having to do with mathematics. His mathematics teachers indicated that although he was able to do the work, he could not be encouraged to exert more than very minimal amounts of effort in this area. The only previous testing was performed in the seventh grade where he obtained a Full Scale IQ of 106, a Performance IQ of 116, and a Verbal IQ of 97 on the Lorge-Thorndike Intelligence Test.

The subject was accompanied to the testing situation by his mother who indicated that her son did not wish to return to school next fall. She indicated that he felt that he did not like school, especially mathematics classes, and that school was too hard for him. The mother indicated that both she and her husband wanted very much for their son to reenter school in the fall.

The test was administered in the counselor's office. Ventilation and lighting were adequate, and there were no distracting influences during the testing session.

The subject is of approximately average height and weight for his age. He was neatly dressed in casual clothes and seemed comfortable, although he did not volunteer much information. An adequate level of rapport was rather quickly established, but the subject at no time seemed very enthusiastic about the testing situation and at no time volunteered information. Before testing he simply stated that he did not like school and was thinking about quitting. When questioned further he simply said that he did not like the teachers and felt that he could earn money by obtaining a job and helping with the family's financial situation.

The subject comes from a low-income family of Spanish descent. While the father is employed regularly, the subject has five younger brothers and sisters, so there is a financial problem. Both the subject and his mother speak with a decided accent but appear to have adequate comprehension of English.

During the test the subject appeared to prefer the performance subtests to the verbal subtests. He did not seem to mind the Block Design Test and worked methodically on this and the Object Assembly Test. On most of the verbal tests he would respond to questions fairly readily, but seemed to give up if there was any question in his mind that he knew the correct answer. At this point he would simply shake his head and would not offer more information when questioned.

Discussion of Results

One of the important features of the subject's test results is the 18-point difference between his Verbal and Performance IQ's. This difference can be expected to occur in only 20 percent of the subjects taking this test. When the effects of general intellectual functioning are removed, his performance ability is still significantly superior to his verbal ability. When the three Performance tests contributing most highly to the general intelligence level at this age are calculated (Picture Arrangement, Block Design, and Coding), the average of these Performance tests is a score of 13.3, which is significantly higher than both his General Factor score and his Full Scale average. It is hypothesized that a linguistic handicap depressed his obtained score. When the pattern of scores is related to his rather apathetic performance throughout the test administration, it is concluded that his obtained IQ definitely underestimates his intellectual functioning.

The amount of scatter shown by the subject's scores is moderate in that three subtests deviate significantly from total performance, with scaled scores ranging from the 6 to the 16 level. The scores for Comprehension and Vocabulary are significantly low, while the Block Design score is significantly high. When compared to the general population, his Verbal and Full Scale IQ fall within the average range and his Performance IQ falls in the bright-normal range. These scores indicate that the subject has the ability to complete school.

When the subject's major and tentative factor scores are considered (compared to his own performance on the test), perceptual organization is significantly high. This tends to indicate a high ability to interpret and/or organize visually perceived materials. When compared to the general population, Perceptual Organization and the Anxiety: Facility Factor are high. Since the subject's Arithmetic score is fairly low, one can hypothesize that the Anxiety: Facility Factor is measuring the ability to manipulate spatial symbols other than mathematics symbols. When compared to the general population, none of the subject's factor scores is significantly low. At this age range, the Arithmetic Test measures, to a degree, specific ability in performing mathematical tasks. Thus it can be assumed that, to a degree, the subject lacks some ability in this area.

In conclusion, the subject's test results show a great deal of strength in performance and perceptual abilities. His major weakness appears to be in Arithmetic. His high scores on Performance items provide evidence that he has the capacity to improve his skills in academic areas if he is given assistance and is motivated to improve. If the school can provide a situation that will result in the subject's being more interested in achieving, he probably can succeed reasonably well.

PSYCHOLOGICAL EVALUATION

Cindy G.
Birth date: April 4, 1964
Date of evaluation: June 22, 1972

Purpose of Referral: Evaluation of a learning problem.

History: Cindy was born at term after six hours of labor weighing six pounds, ten ounces. The pregnancy was uneventful. The child's health has been normally good. She is the youngest of five children. The mother has been married three times, as a result of which Cindy has three older siblings from the union between her mother and her first husband, deceased, and one sibling from a marriage which ended in divorce. All of the children use the surname of Cindy's father, although they have not been legally adopted.

Cindy has a devoted mother whose emotional instability interferes with her capacity for using good judgment at times in the rearing of the children. During periods of instability, dissension in the home produces anxiety in the children. Cindy's father is an insecure individual who is nine years older than his wife. He has no history of prior marriages. His relationship to all of the children is that of a parent, and he apparently considers them his children. Both of the parents are highly intelligent. The father's earning capacity is limited due to the lack of formal education, and the family is frequently harrassed by money problems. Cindy was brought to the examiner because of a learning problem.

Techniques Employed: The Wechsler Intelligence Scale for Children, the Bender-Gestalt Test, and the House-Tree-Person Test.

Specific Findings: On the WISC, Cindy had a Verbal Scale IQ range of 96 through 99, a Performance Scale IQ of 97, and a Full Scale IQ range of 96 through 98. She was eight years, two months of age at the time of the testing.

AREAS OF STRENGTH:

The ability to abstract common qualities or similarities ranged from the ten year, two month level to the ten year, ten month level, at least two years above age level.

The ability to learn symbolic material and commit it to writing ranged from the eight-year, ten-month level to the nine-year, two-month level, at least one-half year above age level.

Visual awareness, as evidenced by the ability to be aware of missing elements in pictures ranged from the eight year, six month level to the eight year, ten month level, at least one-half year above age level.

Form and size perception, figure-ground discrimination, and the ability to analyze and synthesize block designs where depth is a factor ranged from the eight year, six month level to the eight year, ten month level, at least one-half year above age level, as compared to form and size perception in a neutrally colored object assembly which ranged from the six year, six month level to the six year, ten month level, at least two and one-half years below age level.

Immediate auditory recall ranged from the seven year, six month level to the eight year, ten month level, from over one-half year below age level to over one-half year above age level.

Vocabulary ranged from the seven year, ten month level to the eight year, two month level, at least at age level.

AREAS OF INADEQUACY were:

Comprehension and judgment of the adequate manner of handling situations ranged from the seven-year, six-month level to the seven-year, ten-month level, at least one-half year below age level.

Acquired information ranged from the seven-year, two-month level to the seven-year, six-month level, at least one-half year below age level.

Arithmetical reasoning ranged from the six-year, ten-month level to the seven-year, six-month level, at least one year below age level.

Social judgment as demonstrated by the ability to grasp a pictured situation and predict the sequence of events was performed at the six-year, six-month level, over one and one-half years below age level.

On the House-Tree-Person Test, the drawings revealed a higher level of intelligence and creativity than was manifested on the intelligence scale. Some difficulty in reality orientation was also manifested.

On the Bender-Gestalt Test, Cindy displayed fair form and size perception. She had some difficulty with the oblique plane. A reversal tendency was also noted.

Conclusions and Recommendations: This is a child of at least average normal intelligence, the scatter of whose scores on the intelligence scale and on other tests suggests a higher potential level of intelligence than is presently manifested. The directionality problem noted in the responses to the Bender-Gestalt is usually found in the records of children who develop reading problems. There is a possibility that the anxiety, fostered by the emotional climate, affected this youngster's ability to function in the area of arithmetical reasoning, the subtest on the intelligence scale which is most easily affected by anxiety or lack of reality orientation. Cindy would benefit from a small class in which individualized instruction and supervision is possible, in which the pace is slow, and perceptual training is available as a basis for the acquisition of reading skills. The parents have been referred by the examiner to a family service agency for supportive therapy.

Examiner: L. Solomon, Ph. D.

WISC RESULTS

Name: Cindy G.   Age: 8-2   Sex: F

	Year	Mo.	Day		Scaled Score	IQ
Date tested	1969	6	22	Verbal Scale	47–49	96–99
Date of birth	1961	4	4	Performance Scale	48	97
Age	8	2	18	Full Scale	95–97	96–98

Verbal Tests	Raw Score	Scaled Score	Performance Tests	Raw Score	Scaled Score
Information	8	8	Picture Completion	9	11
Comprehension	8	9	Picture Arrangement	8	7
Arithmetic	5	7–8	Block Design	10	11
Similarities	9	13	Object Assembly	12	8
Vocabulary	23	10	Coding	29	11
(Digit Span)	8	9–10	(Mazes)		
Sum of Verbal Tests		56–58	Sum of Performance Tests		48

PSYCHOLOGICAL EVALUATION
July 22, 1969

Subject: Shirley Sweet
Date of birth: 3-19-62
Chronological age: 7-4

REASON FOR REFERRAL:

The subject entered Sunshine Elementary School in September, 1968. She failed the first grade. The subject's parents are seeking diagnostic evaluation in an attempt to determine the most appropriate academic setting for this child.

PREVIOUS PSYCHOLOGICAL CONTACTS:

This subject previously was seen for intellectual evaluation by psychologist U. R. Wright at the Children's Clinic. At CA 7-0 administration of the Wechsler Intelligence Scale for Children yielded a VSIQ of 74, a PSIQ of 92, and a FSIQ of 80. In summary, it is reported that this is "A child with possible cerebral dysfunctioning and a definite verbal language disability. She is learning in the verbal area at a preschool level."

TECHNIQUES USED:

Stanford-Binet Intellegence Scale, Form L-M: CA = 7-4 MA = 5-6 DIQ = 73
Wechsler Intelligence Scale for Children: VSIQ = 84 PSIQ = 86 FSIQ = 83
Bender-Visual-Motor Gestalt Test: developmental age 6-6 to 6-11 Wide-Range Achievement Test: rd. gr. = 1.1 sp.gr. = prekindergarten 1 arith. gr. = kindergarten 2
House, Tree and Person Technique (chromatic)
Interview

BEHAVIORAL OBSERVATIONS:

This slightly small, fully ambulatory, appropriately groomed, seven-year-old Caucasian female was brought by her mother. The subject was somewhat reticent and reserved on contact, but she readily accepted the examiner's invitation to accompany him to the evaluation area. Although she was initially diffident and somewhat ill at ease, a positive relationship was relatively easy to establish after a period of conversation and reassurance. As the session progressed, she became very responsive and spontaneous; she readily accepted all tasks presented, attended to instructions, invested adequately, and appeared to enjoy the individual attention.

Auditory and visual acuity are considered adequate for testing purposes. Sentences are complete and fairly easy to understand, but speech is immature for her age. Gross color discrimination is adequately developed. Gross muscle movements are within average limits; coordination for refined motor tasks is below expectations. Orientation with respect to person, time, and place is fairly poor but not unrealistic for one of her level of intellectual functioning. Lateral dominance is assessed to be left for eye, right for hand, and incomplete for foot. Mood and affect were appropriate throughout the session. Anxiety level and psychomotor activity were not significantly elevated.

TEST RESULTS:

Current overall intellectual functioning, including verbal and nonverbal functioning is assessed to be in the low Dull Normal to mid Border Line range of intelligence. Present overall functioning correlates fairly well with full-scale results obtained on the previous intellectual evaluation.

Funds of general information are restricted, but she appears well able to utilize that knowledge which she has required in responding appropriately to social and practical situations. Word knowledge and verbal concept development are slightly below expectations for her age group, and her thinking tends to be rather concretistic. She is readily able to perceive the difference in concrete objects but she has marked difficulty in seeing the likenesses or common attributes in objects. Moreover, she has difficulty abstracting and defining words which lack concrete references.

Abilities to attend and concentrate, on both visual and oral stimuli, are very poorly developed, as are memory functions. Her difficulty in perceiving visual stimuli in a situation restricts her ability to do puzzlelike tasks, as does her random, trial-and-error approach to such materials. Graphic reproductions are characterized by distortion and difficulty with angles and curves.

Current level of academic attainment, as assessed on the WRAT, is at grade level 1.1 in reading, prekindergarten 1 in spelling, and kindergarten 2 in arithmetic. This level of academic attainment is below the expectations for a child of her presently assessed level of intellectual functioning. One strongly suspects that factors in the emotional realm are depressing the full expression of the intellectual capabilities she possesses. She does not know her ABC's, she counts on her fingers, and cannot spell or read any words. She will very likely require a special remedial, individualized classroom situation, as well as professional counseling and environmental modification.

Shirley appears to be a very immature, insecure, and anxious individual with rather marked passive-aggressive tendencies. She has a rather concrete orientation to the environment, requiring a great deal of supportive structuring in order to respond and behave appropriately. Moreover, she seems to view the environment (especially the mother) as failing to meet her needs. This perception of the mother, coupled with displacement by a younger brother at age 15 months, has resulted in resentment and hostility expressed in passive resistance and aggressive acting out. Additionally, her inability to compete with, and relate successfully with, peers and siblings has engendered marked feelings of inadequacy, defeat, and rejection. Presently observed self-feelings, perceptions, etc., resulting in behavioral problems characterized by passive resistance, aggression, insecurity, felt inadequacy, and immaturity are related to her lowered intellectual capabilities as well as her early environment. The first year of her life was reportedly very traumatic and deprived, marked by extreme disharmony in the home, three changes of residence, and desertion by the father. Also, mother reports she had very little time for this child during the first year of her life. When the subject was 15 months of age, a brother was born. The mother started to work five days after the birth. Since that time the mother has always worked. Mother reports that the subject frequently wears the younger brother's clothes and always attempts to play the part of "baby." Her desire not to grow up, thus being the "baby," together with her lack of success in competing with sibling and peers, has greatly mitigated her motivation to grow up or mature. In other words, by not maturing she becomes the "baby" and also removes herself from competition. Even though this child lacks the intellectual capabilities to achieve academically like an "average" child, one strongly suspects her current level of academic attainment, to a great extent, reflects passive-aggression and a desire not to mature.

SUMMARY:

The subject currently is functioning intellectually in the lower Dull Normal to mid Border Line range of intelligence. Even though current intellectual functioning is significantly below average, academic progress is depressed in relation to the expectations for one of her intellectual status. It is obvious that she will require a specialized academic program and professional guidance.

RECOMMENDATIONS:

1. A remedial, individualized learning situation.
2. Professional counseling and/or environmental modifications in attempt to foster more constructive patterns of interpersonal relationship in the home.
3. Reevaluation in approximately 1 year.

Gus Schtalt, Ph.D.
Psychologist

PSYCHOLOGICAL EXAMINATION

Name: Mark Lane   Date: December 29, 1972
Age: 5-6   Date of birth: July 6, 1967

I. Introductory Statement:

The subject was tested for two reasons: (1) as a practice administration required for a testing course and (2) as a follow up of an earlier test, the WISC, on which he scored dull normal.

II. Name of Test:

Stanford-Binet, L-M

III. Subject's General Attitude and Response to Test Situation and Examiner

The subject was tested willingly, and he particularly enjoyed the individual attention he received. His attitude was good, and he worked earnestly. Although he seemed comfortable in adult company, he was rather shy and did not volunteer any extra information. Perhaps this was due to his inability to communicate well because of speech and language problems. He showed no signs of restlessness and moved easily from one test level to the other.

IV. Test Findings

Stanford-Binet
a. Mental Age: 5-7
b. Intelligence Quotient: 102
c. Basal Age: 5-0
d. Terminal Year: 8
e. Classification: Average

V. Test Evaluation

The subject performed better on the nonverbal items of the test than on the verbal ones. Out of a total of thirty items, he performed correctly on six out of eighteen verbal items and nine out of twelve nonverbal items; in other words, he got one-third of the verbal items and three-fourths of the nonverbal items correct. It seems likely the subject would perform better on nonverbal items than verbal items because of his language and speech problems, but on the WPPSI he earned a verbal IQ of 94 and a performance IQ of 95. However, one cannot compare directly the results of the two tests because the items of the WPPSI measure different kinds of verbal and nonverbal performances than the Stanford-Binet.

The subject earned an MA of 5-7, an IQ of 102, and a vocabulary score of 4; the subject has a CA of 5-7. Since vocabulary scores below the six-year level are not given, it is difficult to compare the subject's vocabulary score with his MA; therefore, the item responses themselves must be examined. The subject's response to the vocabulary items lacked clarity because his vocabulary was limited; if he did have a sufficient vocabulary, he could not put the words together to make a clear statement. For example, he defined straw as "coke" and when questioned said, "Drink coke." On Differences—year six—he did not know what to do because he did not know what "difference" meant. His vocabulary is weak for a child whose IQ is 102, but it must be remembered that he primarily earned the score by performing correctly on nonverbal items.

Out of a total of eighteen items administered above his CA and MA, the subject passed four; out of a total of six items administered below his CA and MA, he passed six. The more abstract and verbal the items became, the less he succeeded on the items above his CA and MA. He passed through four out of five age levels administered to him. (He passed only one item on the last two age levels.)

The quality of the subject's language was poor; he had a limited vocabulary (see preceding discussion); he had difficulty constructing grammatical sentences (frequently left out verbs and used the present tense for the past); and had a speech problem. He mispronounced words; for example, he particularly had trouble pronouncing the consonants *s*, *l*, *r*, and *n* and used *e* for *i* and *a* for *e*. It was difficult to understand him and at times impossible.

VI. Test Performance Summary

The subject performed better on the nonverbal items of the test than on the verbal ones. The more abstract and verbal the items became, the less he succeeded as he passed through the different age levels. His performance can be attributed to language and speech problems and the number of verbal items in the test.

VII. Subject's Behavior

The subject's reaction time to questions was normal throughout the test. Sometimes his responses were nonsensical or inconsistent; for example, if he did not know an answer, he might say anything that came into his head. He appeared to be uncritical of his responses, which can be attributed to his age and level of maturity, but he never asked for help. His responses tended to be surface; for example, when asked, "In what way are a penny and a quarter alike?" his response was "A dime." He did not appear to be either penetrating or defensive, but he may have indicated negativism when he responded, "It not funny," to the items on Verbal Absurdities I and Picture Absurdities II.

The subject was still throughout the testing session and gave no expression of his feelings other than an occasional smile. The subject's responses were in terms of his own experiences and self; for example, his responses to "What's the thing for you to do when you are on your way to school...?" and "What's the thing for you to do if another boy hits...?" were, "I'd run to the school," and "Hit him back." The responses either include a direct self-reference, "I," or an assumed one.

No test questions were repeated and the subject changed none of his answers. He did misunderstand some directions and misinterpret a few questions. For example, he missed all of the items of Differences at year 6. When asked, "What is the difference between a bird and a dog, a slipper and a boot, and wood and glass?" his responses were "a bee, a sock, and a house." Obviously, he did not know what "difference" meant. When asked, "What should you do if you found on the streets of a city a three-year-old baby...?" his answer was, "He'd get run over." He misinterpreted the question.

The subject gave very brief answers to questions—usually only one or two words long. He answered spontaneously and never had to be urged. He had several speech peculiarities which were discussed in preceding paragraphs.

He exhibited inconsistent organizational methods. He worked very carefully and diligently on the mazes (to be sure he went the shortest way and stayed on the walk), but he worked rather carelessly on the drawings of the square and diamond and did no planning. The subject had difficulty generalizing on the Similarities—year 7. When asked, "In what way are wood and coal, an apple and a peach, a ship and an automobile, and iron and silver alike?" his answers were "brick, orange, a car, and hot."

The subject adapted well to each level and seemed interested in all of the items except Verbal Absurdities I, where he displayed possible negativism. (See previous discussion.)

The subject was cooperative and tried to do his best on parts of the test (as was noted earlier on the mazes); however, if he did not know an answer, he gave no indication of trying to think it through. His cheerful mood did not flucuate throughout the test or when he left. He seemed to be rather easygoing and carefree and seemed to be in complete control of his feelings and himself—almost too much so for a five-year old.

Patricia Protocol
Examiner

REFERENCES

American Personnel and Guidance Association, "Ethical Standards," *Personnel and Guidance Journal* 40 (1961), 206-209.

American Psychological Association, *Casebook on Ethical Standards of Psychologists*, Washington, D.C.: The Association, 1967.

Freeman, Frank S., *Theory and Practice of Psychological Testing*. 3rd ed. New York: Holt, 1962

Goldman, L., *Using Tests in Counseling*. New York: Appleton-Century, 1961.

Hammond, K. R., and J. M. Allen, *Writing Clinical Reports*. Englewood Cliffs, N. J.: Prentice-Hall, 1953.

L'Abate, L., *Principles of Clinical Psychology*. New York: Grune and Stratton, 1964.

Pepinsky, H. B., and P. N. Pepinsky, *Counseling Theory and Practice*. New York. Ronald, 1954.

Sundberg, N. D., and L. E. Tyler, *Clinical Psychology*. New York: Appleton-Century, 1962.

Super, D. E., and J. O. Crites, *Appraising Vocational Fitness*. New York: Harper, 1962.

Tallent, N., "On Individualizing the Psychologist's Clinical Evaluation," *Journal of Clinical Psychology* 14 (1958), 243-244.

——, Clinical Psychological Consultation, New Jersey, Prentice-Hall, Inc., 1963.

——, and W. J. Reiss, "Multidisciplinary Views on the Preparation of Written Clinical Reports: III. The Trouble with Psychological Reports," *Journal of Clinical Psychology* 15 (1959), 444-446.

Thorne, F. C., *Clinical Judgment: A Study of Clinical Errors*. Brandan, Vt.: Journal of Clinical Psychology Publishers, 1961.

Group Tests of Mental Ability

Psychologists and guidance workers who do a large part of their practice with children may frequently find it necessary to refer to school reports when collecting case history data on their subjects. Such records rarely include scores on individual intelligence tests, but the majority of the records will have test reports on at least one of the many group tests of mental ability currently in use.

The tests will be variously labeled, as "intelligence tests," "mental ability tests," "mental maturity tests," "academic ability tests," and so on. Whatever they are called, the tests tend to be highly verbal and quantitative in nature and require that the examinee be able to read. Some of the tests employ items which measure nonverbal abilities, such as spatial relations, nonverbal abstract reasoning, and reasoning through the use of pictures. Tests which tap such abilities provide valuable information, especially when the examinee is a bright person who has not developed a facility with the English language. Nevertheless, white persons with upper or middle socioeconomic status and urban residence have a definite advantage when taking these tests because the content reflects, primarily, the experiences that such groups have in their schools.

After the early grades, these tests are as valid and reliable as the individual tests for some purposes. Their reliability coefficients are usually in the .80's and .90's and their predictive validity coefficients (for academic criteria) are frequently in the .60's and .70's.

Except for the multiple-aptitude tests, which are placed last, the tests reviewed in this chapter are arranged according to the extent to which their content reflects formal educational achievement, the first tests being those that have sections not wholly dependent on school-related experiences. The technical information contained in these reviews may be found in the technical manuals and examiners' manuals of the tests. Individuals considering the use of these tests should consult these sources.

CALIFORNIA TEST OF MENTAL MATURITY

Authors
    E. T. Sullivan, W. W. Clark, and E. W. Tiegs
Publisher
    California Test Bureau
    Del Monte Research Park
    Monterey, California 93940
Edition
    1963
Forms
    Short Form
    Long Form

LEVELS FOR WHICH TEST IS AVAILABLE

	Short Form		Long Form
Levels	Grade Range	Levels	Grade Range
0	K–L1	0	K–1
1	H1–3	1	1–3
1H	3–4		
2	4–6	2	4–6
2H	6–7		
3	7–8	3	7–8
4	9–12	4	9–12
5	12–Adult	5	12–Adult

PURPOSE

This test was designed to provide information about the functional capacities that are basic to learning, problem solving, and responding to new situations. It is intended to parallel the *Stanford-Binet Intelligence Scale* as closely as possible (Sullivan, Clark, and Tiegs, 1963).

DESCRIPTION OF TEST

The CTMM Short Form, 1963 Revision consists of seven test units, each of which presumably measures ability in a manner different from the others. The seven test units are grouped according to four factors, and the items are all of the multiple-choice type. The four factors and the test units associated with them are as follows: Factor I–*Logical Reasoning* (Test 1: Opposites, Test 2: Similarities, Test 3: Analogies); Factor II–*Numerical Reasoning* (Test 4: Numerical Values, Test 5: Numerical Problems); Factor III–*Verbal Concepts* (Test 6: Verbal Comprehension); Factor IV–*Memory* (Test 7: Delayed Recall).

The CTMM Long Form, 1963 Revision, contains twelve tests rather than seven and it measures an additional factor, Spatial Relations. The additional tests are Rights and Lefts, Manipulation of Areas (these two comprise the Spatial Factor), Number Series (added to the Numerical Reasoning Factor) and Immediate Recall (added to the Memory Factor). Both forms of the CTMM have their subtests grouped into a Language Section and a Non-Language Section.

RELIABILITY

The *Technical Report* for the CTMM 1963 Revision (California Test Bureau, 1965) reports reliability data for all levels of both forms of the test. With the exception of Level 1 of the Short Form, Kuder-Richardson Formula No. 21 estimates of internal consistency were calculated on the raw-score data. Reliability coefficients are reported for factor, sections, and the total scores for each level of both the Short Form and Long Form. The reliability coefficients for the Language Section of the Short Form range from .70 at Level 0 to .94 at Level 2. With the exception of the Level 0 correlation, the reliabilities are .90 or above. The coefficients for the Non-Language Section of the Short Form range from .59 at Level 0 to .89 at Levels 1 and 2. With the exception of the correlation at Level 0, all of the correlations are .81 or above. The coefficients for the *Total Score* vary from .78 at Level 1 to .95 at Level 2, and all are above .90 except for the correlation at Level 1. Retest correlations (one-year interval) for the Language Section vary from .60 for Level 1 to .93 for Level 3. For the Non-Language Section the retest correlations range from .48 for Level 1 to .78 for Level 2. The retest correlations for the Total Score vary from .62 at Level 1 to .93 at Level 3. Most of the correlations are in the .80's.

Reliability coefficients for the Language Section of the Long-Form range from .71 at Level 0 to .95 at Level 2. Level 1 has a reliability coefficient in the .70's, but the rest are above .90. The reported coefficients for the Non-Language Section of the Long Form vary from .79 at Level 0 to .93 at Level 2, with most of the correlations in the .80's. The standard error of measurement is reported in raw-score units and standard-score units for the factors and sections and in deviation IQ units for the sections and total test.

VALIDITY

All the validity data presented in the *Technical Report* are derived from scores on the Short Form. Evidence for the content validity of the test is presented as an analysis of the CTMM content using the Mental Age of the Stanford-Binet Intelligence Scale, Form L-M, 1960 revision, as the criterion. Correlation coefficients between the S-B and the CTMM IQ scores for each section (L, NL) and the Total IQ score are presented in the *Technical Report*. Test data from approximately 200 persons at each test level were used to obtain the correlations. The correlations between the Binet and the CTMM Language IQs and S-B IQs range from .60 for Level 1 to .77 for Level 3. The Non-Language IQ correlations vary from .56 at Levels 0 and 1 to .65 at Level 3. The correlations between Total CTMM IQs and S-B IQs range from .66 at Level 1 to .78 at Level 3. Other validity data include correlations between CTMM Mental Age scores and S-B Mental Age scores. For the CTMM Total the correlations range from .60 at Level 1 to .80 for Levels 0 and 2. Data concerning the relationship between the CTMM Short Form and several group tests are also presented in the *Technical Report*. Most of the correlations are in the .70's and .80's.

NORMS

Norms for the CTMM were derived from 38,793 cases obtained by testing class samples from 253 schools selected from seven geographic regions representing 49 states. The publisher provides deviation IQ, mental age, standard score, and percentile norms for the section and total scores. Standard score and percentile norms are provided for the factor scores.

ADMINISTRATION AND SCORING

The directions for the administration of the test are easily understood by both the examiner and the examinee. Time requirements for the Short Form vary from 39 to 43 minutes actual testing time, depending on the level being used. Similar variation in time requirements exists for the Long Form, Level 5. The CTMM may be hand-scored or machine-scored. The manual provides clear instructions for scoring the test.

COMMENTS

As with all such tests, the interpretation of individual test scores requires more than a superficial understanding of basic psychometry. Caution must be used in attempting to interpret factor scores, or differences between factor scores, since the *Technical Report* does not report concurrent or predictive validity data for the factor scores. The art work used in the test needs to be improved, and this has been a criticism of the CTMM series for some time. In addition, the paper used for the test is of poor quality. Some sections of the Technical Report are not well written and should be improved. For example, the section which describes the scaling procedures leaves one wondering what the norms represent.

Despite the above criticism, the test has value because the division of the IQ score into Language and Non-Language components provides reasonably reliable information concerning examinees that is not tapped by strictly verbal-type tests.

LORGE-THORNDIKE INTELLIGENCE TEST

Authors
> I. Lorge, R. L. Thorndike, and E. Hagen

Publisher
> Houghton Mifflin Company
> 110 Tremont Street
> Boston, Massachusetts 02107

Edition
> 1964

Forms
A and B for Primary Batteries
1 and 2 for Multilevel Edition

LEVELS FOR WHICH TEST IS AVAILABLE

Multilevel Edition		Primary Battery	
Level	Grade	Level	Grade
A	3–4	1	K–1
B	4–5	2	2–3
C	5–6		
D	6–7		
E	7–8		
F	9–10		
G	11–12		
H	12–13		

PURPOSE

These tests are designed to measure abstract intelligence, which is defined as "the ability to work with ideas and the relationships among ideas" (Lorge, Thorndike, and Hagen, 1966, p. 1).

DESCRIPTION OF TEST

The 1964 Multilevel Edition of the *Lorge-Thorndike Intelligence Test* provides both a Verbal and Nonverbal Battery, for grades 3–13, in a single booklet. There is a graded series of items divided into eight separate scales for use within this grade range. The Verbal Battery consists of five subtests which contain only verbal items. The subtests are: Vocabulary, Verbal Classification, Sentence Completion, Arithmetic Reasoning, and Verbal Analogy. The Nonverbal Battery is composed of items which are either pictorial or numerical. The items are arranged to form three subtests: Pictorial Classification, Pictorial Analogy, and Numerical Relationships. According to the test authors, the Nonverbal Battery yields an estimate of scholastic aptitude relatively independent of reading ability.

RELIABILITY

Most of the reliability data reported in the *Technical Manual* are based on studies involving subjects from two counties in Maryland. Alternate-form reliability estimates for the Verbal Battery vary from .83 to .93, depending on the level and the group. About half of the reported coefficients are in the .90's. The reported reliability coefficients for the Nonverbal Battery are in the .80's. Split-half reliabilities, reported for a sample of the standardization group, range from .92 to .95 for the Verbal Battery and from .90 to .94 for the Nonverbal Battery. Standard errors of measurement are reported for selected score levels.

VALIDITY

Most of the validity information presented in the *Technical Manual* is based on the old Separate-Level Edition of this test. Data reported for the Multilevel Edition show the relationship between two achievement tests (*The Iowa Tests of Basic Skills* and *The Tests of Academic Progress*) and the Multilevel Edition. Correlations between the Verbal Battery and the various subtests of ITBS are mostly in the .60's and .70's. The coefficients reported for the Nonverbal Battery are generally lower but tend to cluster in the .60's. Higher correlations were found between the TAP and the Multilevel Edition. Most of these correlations were in the .70's and .80's for the Verbal Battery and in the .60's and .70's for the Nonverbal Battery. Correlations are also reported between the Multilevel Edition and the CEEB and ACT tests. The correlations for the Verbal Battery cluster in the .60's and .70's as compared with the .30's and .40's for the Nonverbal Battery. The *Technical Manual* also reports correlations between scores from this edition and *Differential Aptitude Test* scores for two groups of eighth-graders. No evidence is presented for the predictive or concurrent validity of this edition of the test with nontest criteria.

NORMS

Norms for the Multilevel Edition of the Lorge-Thorndike were derived from a sample of the population stratified by community size and socioeconomic status. The final norms were based on 72 sampling units that yielded approximately 19,000 students per grade for grades 3 through 12. Four types of norms are presented in the Manual: Deviation IQs (mean = 100; standard deviation = 16), grade equivalents, age equivalents, and grade percentiles. No norms based on combined Verbal and Nonverbal scores are given.

ADMINISTRATION AND SCORING

The directions for the administration of the test are quite precise, but the administrator must carefully study the procedure prior to giving the test. There is no time limit set for the Primary Batteries. The Verbal Battery of the Multilevel Edition requires a total of 35 minutes of actual testing time; the Nonverbal

Battery requires 25 minutes. The authors point out that speed is not a factor in the tests because very few examinees would improve their score with more time. The tests are, therefore, *power* tests. Several types of answer sheets may be used with the tests, and the Manual provides specific directions for each answer sheet. The test may be hand scored or machine scored.

COMMENTS

The multilevel feature of this test provides a great deal of potential flexibility for the examiner to apply sound testing principles in the use of tests. The Manual makes recommendations with regard to the differential use of the various levels of the test according to the socioeconomic status of the group being tested. The multilevel feature also provides for economy of time and material. It is quite likely that initially the format will be confusing to the examinees, so close proctoring is necessary. The lack of validity data for this edition is unfortunate, but people who have used the Separate-Level Edition will probably find this new edition satisfactory. People with solid training in basic psychometry can interpret the results of this test.

PRIMARY MENTAL ABILITIES TESTS

Authors
    L. L. Thurstone and T. G. Thurstone
Publisher
    Science Research Associates
    250 East Erie Street
    Chicago, Illinois 60611
Edition
    1962
Forms
    One form at each level.

LEVELS FOR WHICH TEST IS AVAILABLE

    K-Grade 1
    Grades 2-4
    Grades 4-6
    Grades 6-9
    Grades 9-12

PURPOSE

The SRA *Primary Mental Abilities Tests* "are designed to provide multifactored as well as general intelligence indices for all grade levels from kindergarten through the twelfth grade." (Thurstone, 1965, p. 1)

DESCRIPTION OF TEST

The test is composed of subtests labeled according to the "primary mental abilities" that they are presumed to measure. The tests included at all levels are Verbal Meaning, Number Facility, Perceptual Speed, and Spatial Relations. Reasoning subtest is included at the 4–6 level.

RELIABILITY

The *PMA Technical Report* presents reliability data derived from an unidentified public school system in North Carolina. Retest coefficients are reported for the subtests and for the total score for two time intervals, one week and four weeks. Sample sizes ranged from 14 to 34, with most of them falling below 30. Retesting after a one-week interval yielded retest coefficients for the subtests ranging from .59 (Grade 1, Perceptual Speed, Level K-1) to .95 (Grade 5, Verbal Meaning, Level 4–6; Grade 8, Level 6–9; Grade 11, Level 9–12). Most of the correlations for the Total IQ are above .90, and with the exception of the subtest Perceptual Speed, the subtest correlations are generally in the .70's and .80's.

Retesting after a four-week interval yielded retest coefficients for the subtests ranging from .45 (Grade 4, Perceptual Speed, Level 2–4) to .96 (Grade 4, Verbal Meaning, Level 4–6). Most of the reported subtest correlations are in the .70's and .80's. The four-week retest coefficients for the Total score vary from .83 (Grade 1, Level K-1) to .95 (Grade 5, Level 4–6), and most of them are .85 or above, the exceptions being Grade 1, Level K-1. Standard errors of measurement are also reported.

VALIDITY

Predictive validity coefficients are reported for three elementary schools and four grades of a high school. Concurrent validity is reported for the twelfth grade of the high school, the criteria being year-end grade-point average, and grades in specific subject-matter areas. Fourteen months elapsed between testing and the collection of the criterion data. The data are presented school by school and there is no summary table. This procedure would be useful if there were more data presented, but as it is, the information is slightly more useful than no information. However, correlations between end-of-year average grades and the PMA Total IQ score range from .32 (School D, Grade 10) to .91 (School B, Grade 3). In general, the coefficients are higher for the elementary grades than for high school. Correlations between PMA subtests and end-of-year average grades range from .03 (School D, Grades 10 and 12) for the Spatial Relations subtest to .74 (School A, Grade 8) for the Reasoning subtest. Correlations between PMA Total IQ and grades in specific subjects range from .21 (School D, Science, Drafting) to .67 (School B, Social Studies).

Data are also presented on the relationships between PMA scores and scores from the *Kuhlman-Anderson Test* and the *Iowa Tests of Basic Skills* (Composite Score). The data were derived from School A (not otherwise described).

NORMS

According to the *Technical Report* the norms were developed on a sample of 32,383 pupils from 73 schools representing 39 school systems stratified on the basis of regional location and school size. The Report, however, does not describe the sample other than to show the extent to which the regional sampling was successful. Both the secondary and elementary samples were represented in the proportions by region representative of the secondary school population. The PMA norms are presented as mental-age equivalents for Levels K-1 and 2-4 and deviation IQs (mean 100, standard deviation 16) are provided for the other levels. In addition, percentile and stanine norms are given.

ADMINISTRATION AND SCORING

The Manual provides well-written, clear directions for the administration of the test. Time requirements vary with the level of the test. The Primary Mental Abilities Test may be scored by machine or by hand, and the Manual gives directions for both methods of scoring. In addition, a scoring device is available from the publisher.

COMMENTS

Because of the limited amount of validity data presented in the *Technical Report* this test must be interpreted with a great deal of caution. Training in basic psychometry and experience in testing should be prerequisites to the use of this test.

ACADEMIC PROMISE TEST

Authors
G. K. Bennett, M. G. Bennett, D. M. Clendennon, J. E. Doppelt, J. H. Ricks, Jr., H. G. Seashore, and A. G. Wesman.
Publisher
The Psychological Corporation
304 East 45th Street
New York, New York 10017
Edition
1965 Revision
Forms
A and B

LEVELS FOR WHICH TEST IS AVAILABLE

Grades 6-9

PURPOSE

The APT is designed to provide a broad, differential description of the academic abilities of students in grades 6–9.

DESCRIPTION OF TEST

The APT battery consists of four tests: Verbal (V), Numerical (N), Abstract Reasoning (AR), and Language Usage (LU). The Verbal Test items are of the analogies type. The Numerical Test is composed of a variety of item types, but the emphasis is upon numerical reasoning rather than computation. The Abstract Reasoning Test consists of figure-classification problems. The Language Usage Test contains a combination of grammar, spelling, and punctuation items. Scores are also obtained for combinations of AR+N, V+LU and the APT total-test performance.

RELIABILITY

Delayed alternate-form reliability coefficients are reported for the subtests for each grade level for which the test is applicable and for the combined AR+N, V+LU, and APT total scores. Reliability coefficients for the subtests are reported from .81 (V grade 6, AR grade 9) to .90 (N, grade 9). The AR+N reliability coefficients range from .88 (grade 7) to .92 (grade 8). The V+LU coefficients vary from .90 (grade 6) to .92 (grade 9). The APT total score reliability coefficients range from .93 (grade 7) to .94 (grades 6, 8, 9). Standard errors of measurement are reported for all tests and combinations at each grade level.

VALIDITY

The APT manual reports correlations of APT scores with a variety of mental ability and achievement tests for all of the grade levels at which the test is to be used. The correlations between the APT total-score and the intelligence tests range from .64 (Otis Q–S: Beta, Form EM) to .89 (*Henmon-Nelson Tests of Mental Ability*). The correlations between the APT and various achievement batteries are generally in the .60's and .70's, the exception being for the Abstract Reasoning Test, which generally has correlations in the .40's and .50's.

The Manual also presents detailed validity data which show the relationship between APT scores and grades in a variety of courses from schools in communities of various sizes from four regions of the United States. The correlations are of the magnitude usually found when well-constructed tests are used for this purpose. The median coefficients are in the .40's and .50's.

NORMS

According to the APT manual, more than 34,000 students in grades 6–9 were used in establishing the percentile norms for the APT. The sample was drawn to be representative of the distribution of children enrolled in schools from four regions of the United States and 85 school systems in 37 states. Twenty-three percentile values are designated at each grade level.

ADMINISTRATION AND SCORING

The directions for administering the test are complete and very clear. The test may be hand-scored or machine-scored, and the instructions for scoring are thorough. Scoring services are also available from the publisher.

COMMENTS

The test authors recommend that the scores be interpreted as percentile bands rather than as points on the scale. The profile sheet is so constructed that it is possible to determine whether scores between subtests differ significantly from each other by drawing a vertical line from one-half inch above to one-half inch below the line that shows the percentile rank. If the lines drawn for each score overlap, the scores are not different. This simple procedure also serves to remind the interpreter that the scores should not be interpreted as discrete points on the scale. Interpreters should have training in basic measurement principles.

The test seems useful as a measure of academic aptitude. Statistical data presented in the Manual are clear and detailed. The validity and reliability data point to a promising, fairly short test of scholastic ability.

OTIS-LENNON MENTAL ABILITY TEST

Authors
A. S. Otis, and R. T. Lennon
Publisher
Harcourt Brace Jovanovich, Inc.
757 Third Avenue
New York 10017
Edition
1967
Forms
J and K

LEVELS FOR WHICH TEST IS AVAILABLE

Primary I	Last half of Kindergarten
Primary II	1.0–1.5
Elementary I	1.6–3.9
Elementary II	4.0–6.9
Intermediate	7.0–9.9
Advanced	10.0–12.9

PURPOSE

"The . . . series were constructed to measure verbal, numerical, and abstract reasoning abilities important for success in those facets of American culture where a premium is placed upon the possession of such reasoning abilities." (Otis and Lennon, 1969)

DESCRIPTION OF TEST

The two primary levels contain only pictorial items which measure the mental processes of classification (education of relations), quantitative reasoning, following directions, and comprehension of verbal concepts. The Primary levels contain 55 items. The Elementary I Level contains 80 items and measures, in addition to the functions measured by the primary levels, reasoning by analogy. The tests at the upper three levels contain 80 items each arranged in spiral omnibus form. Various types of items, verbal and nonverbal (synonyms, opposites, verbal analogies, figure analogies, number series) sample a variety of mental processes. The emphasis is placed upon measuring abstract reasoning. The test is a single-score test, and the score is presumed to be a measure of the V:ed part of Vernon's g.

RELIABILITY

The *Technical Handbook* reports estimates of reliability based on alternate forms, split-half, and Kuder-Richardson Formula No. 21 techniques. The reliability coefficients are reported by grades and by typical ages within levels for samples drawn from the national standardization program. Alternate-forms coefficients were derived from data obtained from four school systems in which Form J and Form K were administered in a counterbalanced design to the same pupils within a two-week period. The reported reliability estimates range from .83 (K) to .94 (grades 8, 10, 11) and .81 (age 5) to .94 (age 14). The median alternate-forms reliability coefficient was .92. The split-half reliability estimates, made from the total national standardization sample, varied from .89 (grade 2) to .96 (grade 12), and from .89 (age 7) to .96 (ages 10, 11, 14, 17). The Kuder Richardson Formula No. 21 estimates for the same groups ranged from .88 (grades K, 2) to .95 (grades 5, 6, 8, 9, 11, 12) and from .88 (age 7) to .96 (ages 11, 14). Retest coefficients determined from a one-year follow-up study in one school system ranged from .80 (Primary Level vs. Elementary I) to .94 (Advanced Level vs. Advanced Level). The correlations sometimes were derived from administering different levels of the test on the second testing because the subjects had changed levels in school; in those instances the coefficient cannot be considered a true retest coefficient. Split-half coefficients are also reported for grade according to school-system enrollment and for grade according to socioeconomic level. These correlations are generally in the .90's. Standard errors of measurement are presented in raw-score units by grade for each form, and in Deviation IQ units for the forms combined. In addition, the standard error of measurement data are presented for different points in the DIQ scale.

VALIDITY

The Handbook presents two types of *criterion-related* validity: (1) correlations between the O-L MAT scores and achievement tests (*Iowa Tests of Basic Skills, California Achievement Tests, Ohio Survey Tests: Achievement Section, Metropolitan Achievement Tests, Stanford Achievement Tests* and the *Sequential Tests of Educational Progress*) and (2) correlations between O-L MAT scores and end-of-year course grades. Correlations between the achievement tests and the O-L MAT test scores and grades are generally in the .50's and .60's. The *construct* validity of the test is demonstrated by presenting correlations between the O-L MAT and several tests of mental ability (*Stanford-Binet, Ravens Progressive Matrices, Otis Quick-Scoring Mental Ability Test, California Test of Mental Maturity, Lorge-Thorndike Intelligence Tests* and the *Primary Mental Abilities Tests*). Most of these correlations cluster between .60 and .80. Correlations between the O-L MAT and scholastic-aptitude tests (*School and College Ability Tests, Ohio Survey Test: Aptitude Section, Preliminary Scholastic Aptitude Test, American College Testing Program Examination, National Merit Scholarship Qualifying Test*) range from .52 (SCAT Quantitative, Form 5B) to .93 (SCAT Total, Form 3B), with most correlations ranging between .60 and .80.

NORMS

The *Norms Conversion Booklet* presents normalized Deviation IQs (DIQ) which have a mean of 100 and a standard deviation of 16 for three-month intervals of chronological age. Percentile-rank and stanine norms are provided for the DIQs. Percentile ranks and stanines are also presented by grade for both first and second half-year testings. In addition, mental-age equivalents are reported for the Primary I, Primary II, and Elementary Levels of the test. These mental-age scores represent the median performance of pupils of a given chronological age in the norming sample.

The standardization sample was composed of approximately 200,000 pupils from 117 school systems from all 50 states. The sample was drawn in such a way as to be representative of U.S. school pupils enrolled in grades K-12. A stratified multistage probability sampling technique was used, the basic sampling unit being the school. The variables used in stratifying the school systems were (1) enrollment, (2) type (public, private, church-related), (3) a composite socioeconomic index based upon median family income and adult level of education as reported by the school system, and (4) geographic region. Approximately

12,000 students per grade were tested in grades 1-12 and about 6,000 at the kindergarten level.

ADMINISTRATION AND SCORING

The directions for the administration of the test are clear and concise. Special instructions are provided for the variety of scoring methods and answer sheets which may be used with the test. At the Primary I level each item must be presented orally by the examiner and the test booklet must be scored by hand. Testing time for the primary levels is approximately 30-35 minutes, and for the Elementary I level it is approximately 45-50 minutes. Hand-scoring from the booklet is possible for all levels, but separate answer sheets are available which may be machine scored or hand scored.

COMMENTS

Insofar as it is possible to do so, the *Manual for Administration* which accompanies each level of the test provides guidelines for the interpretation of the test, and it is quite likely that a teacher who understood and followed the guidelines could do an adequate though limited job of interpreting the test. Without specific instruction in basic psychometry, however, teachers will not understand the importance and relevance of the recommendations of the guidelines.

The data in the *Technical Handbook* are presented in a clear, unambiguous manner, which is a relief from the jargon-filled reports that accompany many group tests. The test seems very carefully standardized on a group that is relatively representative of the target populations. For its stated purpose, the test appears to be a relatively valid and reliable instrument.

COOPERATIVE SCHOOL AND COLLEGE ABILITY TESTS

Author-Publisher
Cooperative Test Division
Educational Testing Service
Princeton, New Jersey 08540

Edition
1963

Forms
A, B   Levels 5-1, U
C, D   Level 1 plus sophomores

LEVELS FOR WHICH TEST IS AVAILABLE

Level	Grades
5	4–6
4	6–8
3	8–10
2	10–12
1	College freshmen and sophomores, and superior grade 12
U	Students in the last two years of college

PURPOSE

The SCAT was designed to estimate the "capacity of a student to undertake the next highest level of schooling" by measuring two school-related abilities: Verbal and Quantitative.

DESCRIPTION OF TEST

The tests for each level of the SCAT are composed of four tasks: sentence understanding, numerical computation, word meaning, and numerical problem solving. Verbal, Quantitative, and Total Scores are obtained from these four separately timed sections.

RELIABILITY

Kuder-Richardson Formula No. 20 estimates of reliability are reported for each level of the SCAT. All of the reported coefficients for the Total Score are .95 or above. The reliability coefficients for the Verbal Score are at least .92 and the coefficients for the Quantitative Socres are all above .90, except for Level 5 at which the coefficient is .88. The estimates for the Quantitative Scores may be somewhat high due to the speed factor in the timing for these tests.

VALIDITY

The various *SCAT-STEP Supplements* (1958, 1963) and the *Technical Report* (1957) present detailed evidence of the relationship between the SCAT and test and academic criteria. Since the purpose of the test was to predict academic success, the academic criteria are the most relevant. Average predictive validity coefficients are reported to range from .42 (Total-score with mathematics grades, Grade 11) to .88 (Total-score with grade-point average, Grade 7). The seventh-grade correlations tend to be generally higher than the correlations for other groups. The *Technical Report* also presents data on the relationship between SCAT scores and teacher ratings of their pupils' ability in areas measured by the SCAT. These ratings were taken from fifth-grade teachers who were unaware of the scores of their pupils. Ratings for one school were extremely variable, which resulted in a considerable reduction in the magnitude of the average correlation. Verbal scores correlated .64 (.75 excluding the "variable" school) with teacher ratings, and the Quantitative scores correlated .58 (.69 excluding the "variable" school).

NORMS

Norms for the SCAT were based on scores obtained by testing all of the students in a minimum of 50 schools in each grade from 4 through 12. College norms were based on tests administered to 12 students in each of grades 13 and 14 in 120 colleges. The samples were drawn so that they would be representative of the population in four regions of the United States. The scores are reported in percentile bands rather than percentile ranks in an attempt to insure that interpretations will be more realistic. The percentile bands are approximately two standard errors of measurement in width.

ADMINISTRATION AND SCORING

The directions for administering and scoring the SCAT are clear and easy to follow. The directions suggest that approximately 90 minutes be allowed for a testing session. Actual working time is 70 minutes. The test may be hand-scored or machine-scored. Instructions for both procedures are provided in the examiner's handbook.

COMMENTS

The attempt to build in realistic test interpretation through the use of percentile bands is to be commended. If more publishers were to adopt a similar technique, a substantial amount of the criticism aimed at psychological tests could be avoided. A considerable amount of validity data has been amassed, but the information is published in several different manuals. It should be pulled together and published in one source. The use of percentile bands makes this test one about which it can be said that a teacher can interpret the scores. Nevertheless, persons using this test should have training in basic psychometry.

DIFFERENTIAL APTITUDE TESTS

Authors
G. K. Bennett, H. G. Seashore, and A. G. Wesman
Publisher
The Psychological Corporation
304 East 45th Street
New York, N.Y. 10017
Edition
1963
Forms
Form L
Form M

LEVELS FOR WHICH TESTS ARE AVAILABLE

The tests are designed for use in Grades 8-12

PURPOSE

The primary purpose for the *Differential Aptitude Tests* is to provide an integrated, scientific, well-standardized procedure for measuring the multiple abilities of boys and girls for purposes of educational and vocational guidance.

DESCRIPTION OF TESTS

The DAT yields separate scores from eight tests and also a score resulting from a combination of two of the eight. The eight tests are (1) Verbal Reasoning, a measure of the subject's ability to abstract, or generalize and think constructively with words. This ability is measured by double-ended analogies. (2) Numerical Ability, designed to measure understanding of numerical relationships and facility in handling numerical concepts. The test is composed of computation items. (3) Abstract Reasoning, which measures the subject's ability to reason by requiring him to perceive an operating principle in sets of changing diagrams. (4) Clerical Speed and Accuracy, which measures speed of response in a simple perceptual task. The test involves comparing letter and number combinations from the test booklet with combinations on the answer sheet. The examinee must underline the combination on the answer sheet, which is exactly like the one underlined in the test booklet. (5) Mechanical Reasoning, which measures the ability to reason in the mechanical field as well as the understanding of mechanical and physical principles in familiar situations. Each item consists of a pictorially presented mechanical situation together with a simply worded question. (6) Space Relations, which provides a measure of the ability to deal with concrete materials through visualization. The items involve the mental manipulation of objects in three-dimensional space. (7) Language Usage: Spelling, a test which requires the subject to determine whether a word is correctly spelled or misspelled. (8) Language Usage: Grammar (which measures the examinee's ability to distinguish between good and bad grammar, punctuation, and word usage.

RELIABILITY

Except for the Clerical Speed and Accuracy Test, reliability estimates were calculated using the split-halves procedure corrected by the Spearman-Brown formula. Test-retest and alternate-forms coefficients are reported for the Clerical Speed and Accuracy Test. Reliability coefficients are reported for each grade by sex. For the boys on form L, the coefficients ranged from .85 (Grade 9, Mechanical Reasoning) to .96 (Verbal Reasoning and Numerical Ability), with the average coefficients being in the .90's. Similar but somewhat lower correlations are reported for Form M. Standard errors of measurement are reported for both forms by grade and sex.

VALIDITY

A vast amount of predictive validity data showing the relationship between the test and course grades is presented in the manual. Some of the correlations are in the .70's and .80's, but the median correlations for the three best predictors (VR, NA, VR+NA) are generally in the .50's. Although the relationships between the individual tests and the criteria are what would be expected, the best overall predictor of grades is the VR+NA score. Data regarding the prediction of vocational success are distressingly meager. Data showing the relationship between the DAT tests and several intelligence and achievement tests are also presented in the Manual. As the authors point out, some of the correlations between certain of the DAT tests and the intelligence tests are as high as the correlations between alternate forms of the intelligence tests. Correlations between the achievement tests and the VR, NA, and VR+NA tests are generally in the .60's and .70's. AR correlations with achievement tests are in .50's and 60's.

NORMS

The norms are derived from a sample of more than 50,000 students from 195 schools in 95 communities in 43 states, representing all major geographic areas. The norms for the *Differential Aptitude Tests* are expressed as percentile ranks and stanines. There are separate norms for boys and girls and also for fall semester and spring semester testings. Separate norms are also provided for the Clerical Speed and Accuracy Test for the various answer sheets which may be used with the DAT.

ADMINISTRATION AND SCORING

Detailed directions for administering the test are presented in the Manual. It is important that the administrator be familiar with the procedures required for the answer sheet he wishes to use. Separate instructions are given for each type of answer sheet. Testing time requires about four hours which may be broken into two, four, or six testing sessions. The Manual also provides adequate instructions for hand and machine scoring. Commercial scoring services are available to the user of the test.

COMMENTS

The DAT and its manuals have long been models of test construction, thoroughness of research, and frankness of reporting. The material presented in the Manual is very well written and can generally be understood by a person with a good background in basic psychometry. Instructions for interpreting the test, if followed, will prevent the test user from overemphasizing nonsignificant score differences. The fact that so little information is available on the DAT's ability to discriminate between vocational groups limits its usefulness for vocational guidance.

MULTIPLE APTITUDE TESTS

Authors
  D. Segal and E. Raskin
Publisher
  California Test Bureau
  Del Monte Research Park
  Monterey, California 93940
Edition
  1959

LEVELS FOR WHICH TESTS ARE AVAILABLE

The tests are designed to test Grades 7–13.

PURPOSE

The test battery was designed to provide comprehensive, differential aptitude data to help individuals understand their potentialities, and thus enable them to make wiser academic and vocational decisions.

DESCRIPTION OF TESTS

The *Multiple Aptitude Tests* comprise an integrated battery which yields scores on nine tests and four factors. Factor I, Verbal Comprehension, is composed of two tests: (1) Word Meaning, a vocabulary test, and (2) Paragraph Meaning, a test of reading comprehension. Factor II, Perceptual Speed contains two tests: (3) Language Usage, a measure of the examinee's ability to detect errors in grammar, spelling, punctuation, and capitalization and (4) Routine Clerical Facility, which measures the individual's rate and accuracy in checking likenesses and differences in names and numbers. Factor III, Numerical Reasoning, consists of two tests: (5) Arithmetic Reasoning, which measures the examinee's ability to comprehend a problem, apply the correct principle involved, and determine the correct answer. (6) Arithmetic Computation, a test of the examinee's mastery of arithmetic skills. Factor IV, Spatial Visualization, is composed of three tests: (7) Applied Science and Mechanics, which measures the examinee's understanding and application of principles that explain the actions of fluids, and machines, (8) Spatial Relations—Two Dimensions, and (9) Spatial Relations—Three Dimensions. The last two tests are spatial-visualization tests.

RELIABILITY

Except for Routine Clerical Facility, reliability estimates were calculated using the Kuder-Richardson Formula No. 21. Retest correlations are reported for the Routine Clerical Facility Test. Reliability coefficients are reported by grade and sex for the tests and by grade for the Factors. Reported correlations for the males range from .72 (Grade 8, Applied Science and Mechanics) to .95 (Grade 8, Arithmetic Computation). Reliability Coefficients reported for females vary from .66 (Grade 7, Applied Science and Mechanics) to .95 (Grade 10, Routine Clerical Facility). Average correlations across all grades for both males and females are in the .80's. Reported reliability coefficients for the Factors are in the .90's for all grades. Standard errors of measurement are reported by grades.

VALIDITY

A substantial amount of evidence of predictive validity showing the relationship between the MAT scores and grades in a variety of school subjects is presented in the manual for both Factor scores and individual tests. The intervals between testing and the collection of criterion data vary from one semester to four years. For the most part the correlations are around .40 to .50. Data are also presented in the Manual in the form of graphs of the performance of various occupational groups. In addition, correlations are presented which show the relationship between the MAT and other tests.

NORMS

According to the *Technical Report* (Segal and Raskin, 1959), the norms reflect the performance of 11,004 examinees selected to be a representative sampling of major geographic areas in the United States. The subjects were drawn from 64 schools in eight regions. Percentile and *T*-score norms are reported by grade and sex in the *Technical Report*, but only composite norms are reported in the *Examiner's Manual*. Norms are also reported for a Scholastic Potential score which is a composite of Factor I and Factor III standard scores.

ADMINISTRATION AND SCORING

The examiner is required to read the instructions from a test booklet which does not contain the time limits for each test, so the examiner needs to study the Manual carefully in preparation for the administration of the test. The instructions are clear and easy to follow, but the inclusion of directions for two marking procedures may cause confusion for the examinees. Perhaps such information should be placed in the *Examiner's Manual*. The tests may be hand-scored or machine-scored, and the directions for scoring are adequate.

COMMENTS

Persons using this test should be well trained in psychometry. Caution should be used in interpreting the test scores for educational and vocational purposes unless local validity studies have demonstrated the appropriate relationships between scores on the MAT and the criteria. Although some relationship between the MAT and vocational criteria has been shown, much more needs to be done to establish the test battery's usefulness for vocational guidance.

REFERENCES

Bennett, G. K., et al., *Manual: Academic Promise Tests.* 1965 revision. New York: Psychological Corporation, 1965.

——, H. G. Seashore, and A. G. Wesman, *Manual for the Differential Aptitude Tests.* 4th ed. New York: Psychological Corporation, 1968.

California Test Bureau, *Guide to Interpretation of the California Test of Mental Maturity Series.* 1963 revision. Monterey, Calif.: The Bureau, 1964.

California Test Bureau, *Technical Report on California Test of Mental Maturity Series.* 1963 revision. Monterey, Calif.: The Bureau, 1965.

Cooperative Test Division, *Technical Report: School and College Ability Tests.* Princeton, N. J.: Educational Testing Service, 1963.

Lorge, I., R. L. Thorndike, and E. Hagen, *Technical Manual: The Lorge-Thorndike Intelligence Tests.* Multi-Level ed. Boston: Houghton Mifflin, 1966.

Otis, A. S., and R. T. Lennon, *Technical Handbook: Otis-Lennon Mental Ability Test.* New York: Harcourt, 1969.

Segal, D. and E. Raskin, *Technical Report on the Multiple Aptitude Tests.* Monterey, Calif.: California Test Bureau, 1959.

Sullivan, E. T., W. W. Clark, and E. W. Tiegs, *Examiners Manual: California Test of Mental Maturity.* Monterey, Calif.: California Test Bureau, 1963.

Thurstone, T. G., *Technical Report: Primary Mental Abilities.* 1962 revision. Chicago: Science Research Associates, 1965.

Research and Measurement

Students in classes that cover tests and measurements are likely to be either consumers or producers of research. As *consumers* of research they read research reports or articles and sometimes utilize the information obtained from these sources. As *producers* of research they not only read about the investigations of others, but they also conduct their own research projects.

Whether an individual conducts his own research or uses the research findings of others, he should have some knowledge concerning the purposes and basic procedures of a scientific investigation. When he reads articles or research reports he should be able to do so critically. A great amount of the material that appears in print today and that passes for research is not genuine research because it fails to meet reasonable research criteria. This chapter presents a brief discussion of the fundamental aspects of research in the behavioral sciences and provides criteria that can be used in the evaluation of research.

PURPOSES OF RESEARCH

Generally speaking, the reason for doing research is to "discover answers to questions through the application of scientific procedures." (Sellitz, et al., 1967, p. 2) The assumption is made, of course, that the procedures used in research have been tested and found to be valid and reliable. As Hillway (1956, p. 5) says,

> Research is an instrument which mankind has perfected very slowly over a period of several centuries, and it seems to be at present our most reliable means of advancing our knowledge. Its purpose, like that of other methods, is to discover facts and ideas not previously known to man.

309

There are various types of research, and a great number of different research procedures and techniques are employed in research, but probably all research is designed to serve one or more of the following functions: (1) to determine the status of phenomena (past and present); (2) to ascertain the nature, composition, and processes that characterize selected phenomena; (3) to trace growth, developmental history, change, and status of certain phenomena; and (4) to study cause-and-effect relationships among and between certain phenomena (Turney and Robb, 1971, p. 2).

What motivates individuals to undertake research? This question is indeed extremely difficult to answer. There may be more reasons for different people conducting research than one can imagine. Some researchers seem to have a strong desire to do research because they have a need to find out, to explore or investigate the unknown. Others may just enjoy challenges. Still others have highly creative minds and research is an outlet for the creative urge. Of course, where faculty members are concerned, they may simply prefer to do research instead of teach, counsel, or put down riots. Some faculty members conduct research because there is a certain amount of prestige associated with it. And of course in some institutions of higher learning the "publish or perish" principle operates, and that is enough to stimulate many professors to "produce." Perhaps this "pressure" accounts for some of the psuedo-research that appears in print. Of course, a combination of the reasons just mentioned (or others) may apply to the researcher.

TYPES OF RESEARCH

It is possible to categorize research in a number of ways. For example, it can be referred to as either *pure* or *applied* research, depending on the extent to which the research is directed toward the solution of an existing problem. As Fox (1969, pp. 93-94) explains the comparison:

> At one end of the continuum is pure research which, in its extreme form, is research motivated solely by intellectual interest and directed toward the acquisition of knowledge for knowledge's sake. In this extreme form, there is no known or intended practical application of the findings, even if the research is successfully completed. In contrast, applied research in its extreme form would be directed toward solving a specific practical problem, even though no new knowledge was acquired in the process.

If a researcher merely wished to find out whether the children of today perform better than the children of fifty years ago on mental ability tests, he could design research for this purpose and would then be doing *pure* research. If, however, a researcher wished to complete a study to establish norms for a new test of mental ability, he would be interested in conducting *applied* research. In the second instance the problem is specific and practical, and the research serves a purpose which is of immediate significance to the researcher.

Most research in the behavioral sciences also can be classified as *historical*, *descriptive*, or *experimental.* Each of these types of research will be discussed, but greater emphasis will be placed on descriptive and experimental research because they are more common in the field of mental measurement.

HISTORICAL RESEARCH

Research is classified as historical research if its purpose is to organize and classify data concerning past events, circumstances, or situations. A study of the events that led to the construction of the first Binet scale would be an example of historical research.

If the data collected for historical research can be properly documented, the conclusions that the investigator draws from this research can be just as sound as those based on other types of research. The problems involved in the study of past events can be difficult, however, and at times the desired information cannot be obtained. Furthermore, it may be difficult for the researcher to interpret the historical data after they have been acquired.

Whenever possible, the person who is doing historical research will try to obtain *primary* rather than *secondary* sources of information. A primary source is an original document or the testimony of a person who is or was an eyewitness. A secondary source of data may be a reproduction of an original document or a report of someone who interviewed an actual witness. In measurement, such things as books, manuscripts, tests, test reports, data sheets, and test manuals are examples of sources of historical data.

In the process of conducting historical research the investigator must exercise critical judgment with respect to the sources of information. The researcher must apply two kinds of criticism—*external* and *internal.* External criticism is a term that refers to the authenticity and completeness of a particular document. If a document is found to be counterfeit or incomplete, the researcher cannot use it as a basis for valid conclusions. The investigator himself is responsible for determining the origin and genuineness of his sources of data.

After he has established that a document is authentic and complete, the researcher must apply *internal* criticism—that is, he must analyze the *content* of the document to determine whether the author accurately reported factual information. Clues regarding the authenticity of a document's content can come from the language used, persons or events mentioned, dates reported, and the apparent agreement of the content with other historical documents of the period in question.

DESCRIPTIVE RESEARCH

There are actually several different kinds of *descriptive* research, but in general they deal with the problem of finding out about current situations. In a sense, then, descriptive-research studies are status studies. In this section we shall discuss briefly four types of descriptive research: survey study, case study, correlation study, and developmental study.

Survey Study

Sometimes it is necessary for an institution to conduct a survey to determine its status with respect to some factor or condition before certain changes or improvements can be made. For example, a district's superintendent of schools may wish to determine what kinds of psychological tests are being used in the various schools. Or the guidance director may wish to establish test norms for the school district. In these instances a descriptive survey could be conducted to obtain the necessary data.

Case Study

This kind of research is conducted when the researcher is interested in the characteristics or behavior of a single unit, such as a person, agency or institution. The researcher who carries out a case study may use various procedures, instruments, and techniques to gather biographical, physiological, environmental, or psychological data pertaining to his subject. Of course, a researcher could do several case studies at one time, but each would be limited to one person or unit. Very often the researcher must obtain assistance from other professional people such as physicians, teachers, social workers, and clergymen. A very widely known case study was started by Lewis Terman several years ago and is still being carried on by other researchers. This is the well-known study of gifted children. Since it involves the same subjects over a period of years, it is referred to as a *longitudinal* study. In contrast, a *cross-sectional* study compares (at the same point in time) different people representing different stages of development.

Correlation Study

Much of the research related to psychological measurement is designed to estimate the extent to which different variables are related to each other. Now that computers are within the reach of many researchers we can expect a great deal more of this type of research in the future. Examples of correlation studies are numerous. They include the studies designed to determine test validity and reliability in which tests are correlated with similar tests, or in which test-retest data are correlated, or parts of a test are correlated with the whole test. In other correlation studies a test's results are correlated with measures of specific variables to determine whether a relationship exists. For example, a researcher might determine whether the results of a mental ability test are correlated with a measure of creativity.

Developmental Study

An example of this kind of research is a study in which the researcher examines the growth or development of a group of subjects over a period of time. The researcher may be interested in either qualitative or quantitative changes, and the study can use either the longitudinal or cross-sectional design. As an example, a researcher could conduct a cross-sectional study to determine changes in mental development from birth to old age for the population in general. Of course, this would be a very broad topic and it is likely that only certain aspects of it would be studied in a specific research project.

Lest we give the wrong impression about descriptive research, we must emphasize that it is not simply a matter of collecting and analyzing data. Sound descriptive research requires good planning and careful execution. The researcher must know what data he needs, he must have adequate data-collecting devices, he must know how to analyze and to interpret the data, and he must be able to draw sound conclusions from his findings. These and other aspects of research will be discussed later.

EXPERIMENTAL AND QUASI-EXPERIMENTAL RESEARCH

In experimental research studies the researcher systematically varies a factor (or factors) in order to determine the effect that the varied factor produces during the experiment.

The variable that is changed or manipulated systematically is referred to as the *independent variable* in the experiment. The factor that changes as a consequence of a variation in the independent variable is known as the *dependent variable.* There are other variables in an experiment and these may be referred to as *intervening variables.* The researcher attempts to control or regulate these intervening or confounding variables in his study so that they will not exert an influence on the dependent variable. Ideally, then, whatever change is noted in the dependent variable is the result of change in the independent variable, which the researcher very carefully changes to a known degree.

Many studies that are conducted in schools or other institutions do not have the complete control of the variables that a true experiment has, so these studies should really be referred to as *quasi-experimental studies.* That is, the studies resemble experiments, so we treat them *as though* they were actually experimental studies. For the most part our discussion will pertain to quasi-experimental studies.

For an example of experimental research, assume that a researcher decides to study the effect of anxiety on intelligence-test scores. In this case an experiment can be conducted in which the level of anxiety (independent variable) can be varied to determine the extent to which the variation influences intelligence-test scores (dependent variable).

Experiments may be performed in the laboratory and in this case they are referred to as *laboratory experiments.* If they are carried on outside the laboratory, as they often are, the term *field experiment* is used. Laboratory experiments can be conducted under the most ideal conditions, but they tend to be expensive, exacting, time-consuming, and limited to a very small number of subjects.

PLANNING AND CONDUCTING RESEARCH

The term *research plan* refers to a scheme that an investigator formulates in order to attack some specified problem in a systematic, scientific manner. The steps that a researcher is likely to follow in most research studies are: defining the problem, formulating hypotheses, surveying the literature, designing the study, collecting data, analyzing data, and drawing conclusions from the findings of the study. Each of these steps involves a number of important considerations on the part of the researcher.

SELECTING AND DEFINING A PROBLEM

Before an investigator can begin the study of a problem, he must determine whether the problem is worthy of research and whether it is researchable. There are many problems that are not worth the time and expense required for their investigation, and there are many problems that seem to defy research efforts at this time. In some instances a problem area is an important one, but research tools are not available. The area of human motivation, for example, is one of the most difficult to research, because it is so difficult to measure motivation.

In deciding whether to attack a problem the researcher must consider such important factors as the availability of data-collecting devices (if they are needed), the probable financial requirements of the study, and the probable time required for the study. The research worker also may have to determine whether the necessary facilities, equipment and personnel are available to carry out a particular research project. He must also decide whether he is qualified to carry out the project that he has in mind.

After a researcher has decided that a particular problem is worthy of research and is researchable, he must state the problem in a clear but concise manner so that both he and others have a good grasp of the nature of it.

FORMULATING HYPOTHESES

Many experienced researchers feel that *hypotheses* are useful in research. A hypothesis may be thought of as a stated prediction of an outcome of research. One might say that it is an intelligent guess about what is likely to be found in a research study. A few examples of stated hypotheses follow:

1. There is a positive relationship between mental ability scores and standardized achievement-test scores.

2. First-grade pupils who have had kindergarten experience will have higher intelligence-test scores than pupils who have not had kindergarten experience.
3. There is no difference between the intelligence-test scores of high anxiety and low-anxiety subjects.

The third hypothesis is stated in the "null" form. This means that there is a prediction of no true difference between the two groups. It implies that if a difference in intelligence-test scores is found, it can be attributed to chance. A very important part of research is the testing of hypotheses to determine whether they can be supported by the research findings. This topic will be discussed later.

Researchers use hypotheses in their studies in order to provide a necessary framework for the research. Hypotheses can be useful in the formulation of the statement of the problem, the development of a research design, and the selection of research procedures.

It should be made clear, however, that sound research can be conducted without statements of hypotheses. In fact, some researchers feel that hypotheses bias a researcher toward certain conclusions. Another objection is that by stating one or more hypotheses in a study the investigator may overlook other equally good hypotheses, or he may ignore or overlook conclusions that could be made. Sometimes in place of stated hypotheses the researcher will simply use a direct question or a declarative statement of purpose.

Perhaps the soundest advice that we can give concerning the use of hypotheses is that the researcher should use his best judgment. If hypotheses seem either useful or necessary, they should be employed in a research project.

SURVEYING THE LITERATURE

A systematic review of the literature is a step that every investigator is expected to take when he initiates a research study. The process often takes a considerable amount of time, but it provides important advantages for the researcher. For example, the review of literature helps him identify, define, and limit his problem. It also enables him to acquire new ideas and knowledge that can facilitate the planning and organization of the study.

Although it is generally expected that the researcher will survey all of the writings that relate to his research, it is not expected that he will read in detail every reference that may be available. It is expected, however, that he will attempt to find all of the studies that are closely related to his research topic and then scrutinize them to determine their value. Perhaps only a few of the references that are examined will be useful to the researcher, but these may be especially relevant and useful.

RESEARCH DESIGN

A study cannot be evaluated properly unless its methods and procedures are reported in sufficient detail. In exemplary research the investigator reveals a clear, precise plan of attack directed toward the stated problem.

The specific aspects of research design will, of course, vary with the nature of the study. For example, in a survey study it is generally necessary to describe the locale in which the study was conducted, because without this information a valid interpretation of the findings may not be possible. In an experimental study, it is necessary to explain in detail how the comparision groups were selected if two or more groups were used.

Because research designs must fit the particular problem and research situation, it is not possible to cover all of the important considerations that might confront an investigator. We shall, however, discuss briefly some of the important factors that must be considered in formulating a research design.

Sample Selection

Very frequently when a researcher conducts a study he intends to *generalize* from the findings of his study to a whole population or another situation. For example, if he measures some characteristic (such as mental ability) of a representative group of students in a school system he may want the data that he has collected to apply to all of the students of the school and not just to the study group. Provided that his sampling technique is sound and his data are valid, he can do this.

As explained in Chapter 2, a sample is a selected set of persons, objects, or other things that a researcher has drawn from a larger set, the population. A sample may vary in size from a single case to as large as the population itself. In research, a sample generally is only a small part of a population.

The type of sample that is most basic in research is the *random sample.* It is defined as one that is drawn in such a way that every individual in the population has the same chance of being selected. If the researcher wished to make certain that all of the strata or subpopulations of a population were represented, he could select individuals at random from each of the strata. This sample would be a *stratified random sample.* If this procedure were done properly it could reflect the exact proportion of each stratum to the whole population.

The problem of selecting a truly representative sample is more complicated than it may seem at first glance. A major difficulty that researchers must face lies in defining the characteristics of the population to which an investigator wishes to generalize. It is likely that differences in definitions of populations are responsible for what appear to be discrepancies or contradictory findings in similar research studies. For example, if creativity were defined differently in two different studies the researchers could conceivably draw different conclusions about, say, the relationship between intelligence and creative ability.

Attitudes of Subjects

Some research studies involve the use of human subjects as participants, and this requires that the researcher consider subject attitude as an important factor. Certainly the outcome of an experiment can depend greatly on whether the subjects were cooperative, uncooperative, or indifferent. Volunteers can be used, but then the question arises concerning the possibility of some important difference between volunteers and nonvolunteers. Thus the representativeness of a sample of volunteers must be questioned.

The well known *Hawthorne effect* may operate in some studies if there is no effort made to control it. This term is used to indicate the set or positive attitude that can exist if subjects know that they are taking part in a study. It has been found that some subjects will perform better at a task than they generally do if they realize that they are the participants in research. This condition, if it exists in a study, can exert an unwanted influence on the results of a research project.

In a survey-research project the subjects who are asked to respond to a questionnaire may be extremely conscientious or they may be uncooperative. If the researcher gets a low percentage of returns, or if the forms often are incomplete, he probably will not have a representative sample to use in his study.

Of course, in some research the question of subject attitude is not relevant. This would be the case if the data were collected and correlated without the subjects really being aware of the process.

Measurement of Variables

Most research in the behavioral sciences requires that the investigator measure certain characteristics or variables. In order to accomplish this task, he must select the most appropriate instruments or techniques. The selection process can be difficult, for it involves a careful appraisal of the device or technique in question with special attention given to three elements: objectivity, reliability, and validity. Because these concepts were discussed in Chapter 3, we shall not define them here. Suffice it to say that the instruments or techniques used in research should be highly objective, reliable, and valid; and data should be reported to substantiate any claim that these characteristics are indeed present. If the devices used in a study are seriously deficient in these requirements, the findings and conclusions obviously are subject to question. Unfortunately, there are some human traits, such as motivation, anxiety, self-concept, and attitudes that are at this time extremely difficult to measure. Thus we would urge the reader to be cautious when reading or utilizing research reports that involve such variables.

Comparison of Groups

Many research projects involve the comparison of two or more groups; for example, high achievers and low achievers. Suppose that two *achievement level* groups are compared and their characteristics are analyzed. It may be quite difficult to determine which differences between groups are responsible for high or low achievement. Actually, many variables or combinations of variables could account for the difference in level of performance. Is the difference due to home environment? Is it due to verbal ability or study skills? Is mental ability the important factor? Perhaps all of these factors and others are important. Because so many factors are allowed to vary, or are not *controlled* in this kind of group comparison, the results of such a study are almost impossible to interpret. This problem sometimes can be partially overcome through the use of two matched groups.

Let us suppose that an investigator wished to compare the academic achievement of the seniors of two different high schools to determine whether the students are achieving better in one school than in the other. He could, of course, merely test a sample of students from each school's senior class and then compare their average scores to see whether one class excelled over the other. A better approach, however, would be to form two matched groups of students using sex, age, IQ, and courses taken, as the matching variables. If this were done the two groups would be more comparable, and the researcher could be more certain that the students in the one school really were superior to those in the other school, if a difference were found. Of course the size of the difference would be important, and this matter will be discussed later.

As was mentioned earlier, those variables that may exert an unwanted effect upon the results of a study are referred to as *intervening* or *confounding* variables. While these variables cannot be controlled in all research studies, they can be controlled in some through the use of experimental-research designs which employ *experimental* and *control* groups.

Control and Experimental Groups

A frequently used method of eliminating or limiting the effects of confounding variables in a study is to use a kind of comparison group known as a *control group.* An example will serve to illustrate how a control group might be used in an experiment. Suppose that a researcher decided to study the effect of coaching on intelligence test scores. He could merely choose a group of subjects at random, test them to get their IQs (pretest), coach them for a period of time, and then test them again (posttest) to determine whether their scores had changed. If a statistical test revealed a significant score difference, he might conclude that coaching had produced the difference. But this conclusion would not be completely sound, because confounding variables might have been operating during the experiment and their effect was not controlled. A better design would be one in which two groups were used: experimental and control.

The experimenter could select the two intact groups (already formed, such as two grades in school) and designate one group the control group and the other the experimental group. Then the experimental group would be coached, but the control group would not. Both groups would be administered pretests and post-tests to determine whether IQ changes occurred and the extent of change. Then a statistical test, such as analysis of covariance, would be used to compare the IQ gains or losses of the two groups. Without the use of a special statistical technique (analysis of covariance) to control for differences in the two groups at the *start* of the experiment it would not be sound to conclude that a score difference between the two groups was due solely to coaching.

For this kind of experiment some researchers would prefer to select two groups randomly and designate one as the control group and the other as the experimental group. In this case the assumption is made that any differences between the groups at the start of the experiment are very small and must have occurred by chance. So the assumption is made that if there is an IQ score difference between the groups at the end of the experiment it very likely resulted from the effects of coaching.

Systematic Bias

If the groups are not formed through random selection of the members, the researchers must assume that one group could have an advantage (or more than one) over the other at the start of an experiment. Such an advantage is generally referred to as *systematic bias.* It is even possible for systematic bias to occur when a random-selection procedure is used, and it behooves the researcher to be aware of this possibility. Bias can occur not only through the selection process but also as a result of the use of instruments (an instrument favoring one group over the other), environmental factors, or the nature of the tasks being performed by the groups (if they are easier for one group).

When variables cannot be held constant it is possible to examine their influences through *replication*, or by repeating the experiment. If, in an experiment in which individual intelligence tests were used, either the examiner's personality or testing technique was regarded as a possible intervening variable that was not controlled, the experiment could be repeated with another examiner doing the testing. Then an examination of the results of the two studies might reveal whether the examiner's performance actually was a contaminating variable.

Balancing is a method that can be used to control the effects of variables that cannot be held constant. When balancing is employed in an experimental study, the variables are allowed to vary but they must vary in the same way in the treatment groups. If sex is regarded as an important factor there will be the same proportion of boys and girls in each group. The groups might also be balanced with regard to age, intelligence level, reading ability, attitudes, or other factors, depending upon the nature of the experiment.

This discussion of research designs and their limitations has by no means covered all of the possibilities. There are many ways to design an experimental study, and there are many procedures for trying to cope with contaminating variables. What we have endeavored to do is point out some of the important aspects of research design. The student who wishes to do research can get help from references which discuss research design in detail. Some of these references appear at the end of this chapter.

COLLECTING DATA

After the researcher has determined what data he needs, he must develop appropriate data-collecting procedures. One of the first tasks to be accomplished is the *selection* of data-gathering tools and techniques.

Ordinarily the researcher evaluates the instruments that are available for his study and chooses from among these. If the available devices are not satisfactory, he can modify them or develop original instruments.

In selecting available tools and techniques for the collection of data it is essential that the investigator become familiar with them to the extent that he knows their unique characteristics, strengths, and limitations. This means that an attempt should be made to assess the validity, reliability, objectivity, and usability of each device or technique under consideration.

If a new instrument must be developed, the researcher generally has a lot of work to do. The items must be carefully constructed, which means that a great deal of attention must be given to content as well as to the mechanics of item writing. This applies to questionnaires, interviews, rating scales, and other devices as well as tests. A considerable amount of useful information relative to the construction of data-collecting devices and procedures can be found in advanced psychometrics textbooks.

In some kinds of behavioral research the data-collecting process involves the use of mechanical equipment such as mazes, pursuit rotors, and teaching machines. The researcher may have to become familiar with a mechanical device, or he may have to train someone else to use it. When an appropriate mechanical apparatus is not available, the researcher is faced with the job of constructing one.

Sometimes a research worker will carry out a pilot study in order to try out data-collecting devices or procedures. This step takes additional time, but it may be a timesaver in the long run, for it can reveal defects in the data-collection instruments and techniques that might spoil a research project. Furthermore, a pilot study can provide evidence concerning the feasibility of a study.

Another important aspect of data collecting concerns the use of a sample or population of subjects. If the researcher plans to use an entire population he must be sure that all of the members of it will be available when the data are to be collected. If a random sample is needed, an appropriate procedure must be chosen, perhaps the use of a table of random numbers. When classes of students in schools are to be used, there are various problems involving class schedules, length of class period, availability of rooms for testing, and the like that must be solved. Certainly it behooves the investigator to plan and organize his procedures carefully.

After the data have been collected they must be prepared for the analysis. Quantitative data (such as test scores) in their original form seldom are ready for analysis. If tests have been used, the raw scores and identifying data may have to be transferred from the answer sheets to a data sheet. If the researcher uses a desk calculator for statistical operations he will find it convenient to work from the data sheet. When a computer is used, the data are transferred from the data sheet to punch cards that the computer can read.

If the data are qualitative in nature, as is the case for historical studies and some studies using interviews or questionnaires, analysis often requires the categorizing of data prior to their appraisal and evaluation. Thus qualitative as well as quantitative data require processing after they are acquired.

DATA ANALYSIS

The nature of the study, the stated purposes, and/or the hypotheses determine to a great extent the procedures that will be used in the analysis of the acquired data. Historical data and qualitative data require an appreciable amount of subjective interpretation. Quantitative data, however, can be subjected to *statistical analysis.* Since studies conducted in the field of mental measurement mainly involve the processing of quantitative data, a brief discussion of statistical analysis seems appropriate.

In his statement of purpose or his hypotheses the researcher suggests what he is attempting to do in his research project. When he has acquired the data that he needs he must organize them and then check on the reliability of his findings. In a sense, then, the investigator must determine the likelihood that he could get the same research results again. This knowledge is necessary if the researcher wishes to draw conclusions or generalize from his findings. Statistical techniques are tools that enable the researcher to reach a decision concerning the degree of confidence that he may have in his research results. An example may help explain this point.

Suppose that a researcher decided to conduct an experiment to determine whether the promise of a reward would increase the scores made by subjects on a mental ability test. For this project the investigator draws a random sample of 60 subjects, and then he randomly assigns 30 to an experimental group and 30 to a control group. At the beginning of the study the members of the experimental group are told that a reward will be given at the conclusion of the testing session. The control group subjects, of course, are not offered any type of reward; they simply are informed that they are to take the test. After the testing is completed, the test-score mean (average) is determined for each group and the two group means are compared. The question now arises: Is the difference that is found large enough to be considered a true difference? Or, stated another way, could this difference have occurred just by chance? If the researcher hypothesizes that actually there is no real difference between the groups (null hypothesis) he can apply a statistical test to his research data. In this instance he may decide to apply the *t*-test for a difference between the means.

Without going into detail, we can say that the *t*-test requires that the difference between the two means he compared with a statistic known as the *standard error of the difference between means*. If the difference between the means is sufficiently greater than the standard error of the difference between means, the researcher will reject the null hypothesis and conclude that there is a significant difference between the performances of the two groups. If he draws this conclusion, he is expected to state the level of significance that he has employed. The term *level of significance* is a statistical term which refers to the probability that the null hypothesis can be rejected. Two levels of significance generally are used in behavioral research: the .05 level and the .01 level.

When the .05 level of significance is employed the researcher is saying that the obtained difference between the two groups could have occurred by chance only five times out of 100. That is, the difference is so large that it very likely is not a chance difference. A larger difference between the means would be required to meet a test at the .01 level of significance, for at this level the researcher says that a chance difference of this size will occur only one time in a hundred.

The *t*-test for a difference between means is only one of many statistical tests. Analysis of variance, analysis of covariance, Hotelling's T^2, the sign test, and chi square are just a few of the statistical tests that a researcher may use. Each test is considered appropriate for particular research designs and types of samples. These tests take into consideration the size of the samples used in the study and the amount of variance of the data used.

Not only must *mean* differences be subjected to statistical tests, but other research results as well; for example, *correlation coefficients*. If a correlation is found between two sets of data, the investigator sometimes cannot be sure that a coefficient of that particular size could not have occurred by chance. Thus he must use a formula or a table to determine whether, for his sample, the *r* is large enough to be significant at the stated level of significance (such as the .05 level).

Sometimes, because of faulty design, lack of control of variables, or systematic bias, the researcher makes the mistake of rejecting a true null hypothesis. That is, he concludes that an obtained difference is a true difference when it is not. This kind of error is termed a *Type I error*. A *Type II error* is made when the investigator accepts a false hypothesis, or concludes that two groups are the same when actually they are different.

We have intentionally kept the discussion of statistical analysis brief, but it is in fact a complex topic that is dealt with in detail in textbooks and other references. Certainly, the reader who wishes to do research that requires a statistical analysis is encouraged to consult references that cover this subject in sufficient detail.

CONCLUSIONS

Following his analysis of the research data the researcher is in a position to draw conclusions from the results or findings of the study. In stating his conclusions the researcher should make clear, concise statements based upon his interpretation of the data. The statements should relate to the purpose and/or hypotheses of the study, and they should be formulated with the limitations of the study in mind. The researcher should, of course, avoid the error of overgeneralizing from his findings. The conclusions drawn in some studies can apply only to the sample used in the study because of the small size of the sample, the method of obtaining the sample, the research design, or perhaps other important factors.

EVALUATION OF RESEARCH

The evaluation of research is important for both the producer and consumer of research. The person who *conducts* research should be able to evaluate his own research proposals or completed projects. The individual who *reads about* the research of others should be able to read critically, so that he will be able to determine a study's relevance and worth. Strauss (1969, pp. 165–169) provides a useful set of guidelines for the analysis of the various aspects of a research report:

1. *Problem raised.* A problem is a felt need, a difficulty, an "itch to know." It should be obviously important and worthwhile; also one that has a good chance of being solved with reasonable time and effort. It is, therefore, usually only a small part of a larger problem, a portion small enough to be digestible. It should not be something entirely new but should have arisen as a result of previous work done by the author or by others. A properly posed and stated problem, in declarative or question form, is probably the most important part of the research project. Natural scientists say that a problem well stated is a problem half solved. It must therefore be in terms which are succinct, specific, and precise so that it leads naturally to all the succeeding steps. An unspecified, implied or poorly delineated problem is a serious handicap to the researcher, for "an investigator who begins his study in confusion has nowhere to go but into more of it."

2. *Previous work cited.* There should be evidence of a good literature search and a good grasp of the current "state of the art." Failure to cite previous studies implies discourtesy or ignorance. The most recent papers should be given the most attention, for they (presumably) give the most recent findings and include older sources. While previous papers should be documented and critically appraised by the researcher, too much detail or a long list of references are not necessary. A good project sets out to replicate or extend the previous work with improvements to reduce bias, eliminate flaws, consider pertinent variables, settle unresolved issues, or check contradictory or uncertain findings. An accompanying bibliography should identify other sources for the reader.

3. *Objectives stated.* These are the ultimate goals, the socially useful reasons for solving the problem. They should be limited to a small

number (one is enough), be obviously important, fairly specific in scope, and clearly stated as objectives. They should grow out of the problem naturally as rather broad generalizations which can be broken down into a group of hypotheses.

4. *Hypotheses formulated.* A common trend is to present several objectives and only one or two hypotheses; it should be the reverse. Hypotheses are reasonable and rather narrow generalizations which are to be tested during the study and either accepted or rejected; therefore, the mark of a true hypothesis is that it is testable. Hypotheses may be stated as either positive or negative; if the latter, they are called "null hypotheses." In research it cannot be proved that someting is so; it can only be proved that something is not so. If it is shown to be not "not so" (null hypothesis), then it may be assumed to be so. The whole purpose of a research project is to propose a series of plausible consequences growing out of the objectives based on the problem, and to reach conclusions after testing them as to which of these postulated hypotheses may be accepted and which rejected.

5. *Assumptions made.* It is impossible for an investigator to control all the elements in his project and so he must base his work on many assumptions, somewhat like axioms in geometric proofs. An assumption is a reasonable but presently unprovable factor. The more rigorous the research, the fewer the assumptions, and therefore every one should be justified. If the worker frankly enumerates them in his report, it shows that he is aware of what he is doing and that he is honest. Some assumptions may remain implicit, but others—such as the validity of instruments, adequacy of sampling and control of variables—should be acknowledged.

(Note: In some published papers, the authors fail to present explicitly one or more of the above criteria, and it is up to the reader to formulate them from other portions of the report or by reading between the lines.)

6. *Population studied.* By definition, a population must be clearly described in detail by its characteristics and size. The reasons for selecting the chosen population, such as availability or convenience, should be well explained. It cannot be assumed to be a normal population unless very large and heterogeneous; otherwise the normal distribution must be proved.

7. *Sample drawn.* This is a key factor on which many projects founder. A true sample must be either representative of the population, or drawn by using a table of random numbers so that every member of the population has an equal chance of being selected. In either case the procedure is difficult and complicated, and the size and nature of the sample must be defended as appropriate. With good technique, a small sample correctly drawn is better than a large sample poorly selected. If a control group is used, it must be chosen with equal care. Only with a sample rigorously drawn and free from bias—a rare thing in educational research—can the results be generalized. Most workers describe as a sample what are really the subpopulations with which they are working, even though they call them experimental and control groups, and the findings of their studies can therefore be said to apply only to their particular subpopulations and "all others like them." If the subpopulations are described in detail, the reader can decide whether he can apply the findings to his own situation.

8. *Instruments used.* Poor instrumentation is another common and serious flaw in much educational research. To make certain that the instruments will correctly and consistently measure what is to be measured, they should have at least been pretested in a pilot study or calibrated in some way. A "faint tinge of validity" is not enough. Any original instrument should be described fully and illustrated with examples. It is ridiculous for a worker who has formulated an "armchair" untested measuring device to claim that the results he obtains with its use can be accepted with any degree of assurance. Several poor instruments, when used on the same project, are not necessarily more valid than one. Instruments borrowed or modified from the work of others, with courteous acknowledgments, are good; better yet are well-known, published, standardized instruments with appropriate norms.

9. *Design examined.* In general, the simpler the experimental design, the better. Elaborate designs, which attempt too much, often stumble over themselves and get bogged down. Treatments and data-collection methods should be clearly described. Variables should be recognized, identified as dependent or independent, and controls incorporated whenever possible. The statistical procedures should be a part of the design from the first, not applied after the data have been collected. This highly complex subject is well treated in many books.

10. *Procedure followed.* This is often one of the best parts of most reports. The steps in carrying out the project should be described in sufficient detail so that they may be completely understood; the measure of this is that the entire procedure could be replicated by another worker who would wish to repeat the project. Nothing should be left incomplete or omitted.

11. *Safeguards taken.* Many sources of error and bias creep into research and some of these may be anticipated and guarded against. Plenty of time is one safeguard, to allow for Murphy's law, which says that "If there is anything which can possibly go wrong in research, it usually does." Sampling adequately, pretesting instruments, training assistants, controlling some variables, eliminating the "halo" effect, refining procedures, allowing for errors, and calling on experts for judgments and assistance are some other safeguards commonly employed. The failure to apply adequate safeguards is a serious flaw in much educational research.

12. *Observations recorded.* These are the raw, primary sources of data, which generally consist of test scores and other values measured by the instruments, replies to questionnaires, checklists, rating scales, oral or written reactions, lists of activities, overt behavior, and so on. In a properly reported study, the type of observations are fully and clearly set forth, are discrete and quantitative, and are reproducible by the investigator or by someone else.

13. *Findings assembled.* Observations are usually summarized into tables, graphs, and charts. Tabulations should be as simple as possible and all parts of tables, such as abbreviations, should be explained. Technical jargon should be held to a minimum, for the best tables are those which are self-explanatory to the careful reader. If the reports do not include the tabulated findings, all conclusions and interpretations may be regarded with some suspicion.

14. *Statistics interpreted.* A research report replete with statistical jargon should be regarded with a degree of skepticism. It may represent

an attempt to impress the reader, to substitute technicalities for under-standing, to counterfeit accuracy or to explain away unpalatable facts. In educational research the interest lies in estimating how much the results could have been due to chance and how much could with confidence be ascribed to the treatments used in the procedure. The current practice is to allow no more than 5 percent to chance in order to have the results regarded as statistically significant. This is written as "at the .05 level of confidence" or, if expressed as a probability, as "$P < .05$." The smaller the level of confidence or the P value, the less the probability that chance played a role and the greater the confidence or assurance that the treatments did so. The confidence level or P value is found in the proper tables after (usually) applying the t-test, the chi-square technique or the analysis of variance—depending on the kinds of data and the uses made of them. There is an unfortunate tendency by many to ignore the concept of significant numbers and to show a value, for example, as 56.96 percent, which means to an accuracy of four decimal places; but it is absurd to suppose that the essentially crude data collected in most educational research can be measured to such a high degree of accuracy.

15. *Interpretations discussed.* This refers to what his findings mean to the investigator. The explanations are also useful to people who cannot read tables. Since some readers may look at the same data and derive other meanings, all tabulations must be included in the report. The author may also discuss the implications and usefulness of his findings. A common flaw of researchers is their failure to examine their own findings from many angles and to extract all possible meanings from their data.

16. *Conclusions reached.* Essentially this consists of the acceptance or the rejection of the hypotheses which had been proposed earlier. Some workers find it hard to face the fact that negative conclusions and failures are also thoroughly respectable and worthwhile reporting. Four common and serious flaws may crop up. One is to rationalize away the breakdown of the stated hypotheses and to bring in new elements not previously mentioned. Another is to extrapolate the findings and conclusions to situations and to populations not represented in the sub-populations studied. A third is to lean on the "fudge factor" to reach the expected conclusions. A fourth, and the most serious, is to draw conclusions not warranted by the findings. The AERA Committee on Evaluation of Research (1967) found that the major flaw in research reports (38 percent) was the drawing of unwarranted conclusions.

17. *Limitations recognized.* No matter how carefully planned and executed, every research project has limitations and weaknesses which may or may not be the fault of the investigator. In any case, it is his obligation to be intellectually honest and aware, and to point them out as a caution to the consumers of his research and as a guide for future workers in the area.

18. *Further work projected.* Work on one problem usually raises one or more other problems. It may be the next logical step, or some new related hypotheses, or the application of different techniques, or replication with greater rigor, improved design, better instruments or a more representative sample. In any case, the investigator should be in the best position to suggest related research, and it is his duty to do so.

19. *Improvements suggested.* Valuable ideas may be proposed by the reader as to how the project or the reporting of it could have been improved. A good understanding of the study, plus hindsight and a different point of view, may produce pertinent suggestions as to how the investigation could have been better controlled and the pitfalls that could have been avoided. The comments may be a summary of constructive criticisms made throughout the analysis or some additional and more general statements.

20. *Clarity of report.* The published paper should be written in plain, straightforward language and be easy to follow and understand. Jargon, pompous verbiage, undefined terms, and vague descriptions indicate that the author did not understand what he was doing, cannot express himself meaningfully, or is trying to impress the reader. A poorly organized paper may be the result of haste, carelessness, or lack of insight. If the research report cannot be easily understood by a serious reader—the prospective consumer—the whole project was a waste of time.

Research should be able to withstand a critical analysis. To the extent that a study does not meet reasonable standards of excellence its value is diminished. While the student cannot be sure that a research project was conducted precisely as it was reported, he can at least give the research report a rather critical review. If the research report reveals serious deficiencies in design, procedure, data analysis, or some other important aspect of the research there should be ample reason to disregard the findings and conclusions of the study. With respect to research reports, *caveat emptor* seems to apply.

REFERENCES

Beveridge, William I. B., *The Art of Scientific Inquiry.* New York: Norton, 1950.

Brown, Clarence W., and E. E. Ghiselli, *Scientific Method in Psychology.* New York: McGraw-Hill, 1955.

Davitz, Joel R., and Lois J. Davitz, *A Guide for Evaluating Research Plans in Psychology and Education.* New York: Teachers College Press, 1967.

DuBois, P. H., *Introduction to Psychological Statistics.* New York: Harper, 1965.

Edwards, Allen L., *Experimental Design in Psychological Research.* New York: Holt, 1962.

Fox, David J., *The Research Process in Education.* New York: Holt, 1969.

Freedman, Paul, *The Principles of Scientific Research.* New York: Pergamon, 1960.

Guilford, J. P., *Psychometric Methods.* 2nd ed. New York: McGraw-Hill, 1954.

Hillway, Tyrus, *Introduction to Research.* Boston: Houghton-Mifflin, 1956.

Lathrop, Richard G., *Introduction to Psychological Research.* New York: Harper, 1969.

Lindquist, E. F., *Design and Analysis of Experiments in Psychology and Education.* Boston: Houghton Mifflin, 1956.

McNemar, Quinn, *Psychological Statistics.* 3rd ed. New York: Wiley, 1962.

Roscoe, John T., *Fundamental Research Statistics for the Behavioral Sciences.* New York: Holt, 1969.

Sellitz, Claire, Marie Jahoda, Morton Deutsch, and Stuart Cook, *Research Methods in Social Relations.* New York: Holt, 1967.

Spence, Janet T., Benton Underwood, Carl Duncan, and John Cotton, *Elementary Statistics.* 2nd ed. New York: Appleton-Century, 1968.

Strauss, Samuel, "Guidelines for Analysis of Research Reports," *Journal of Educational Research* 63 (1969), 165–169.

Turney, B. L. and G. P. Robb, *Research in Education.* Hinsdale, Ill.: Dryden, 1971.

Appendix

TABLE A Squares and Square Roots

No.	Square	Square Root	No.	Square	Square Root
1	1	1.000	51	2,601	7.141
2	4	1.414	52	2,704	7.211
3	9	1.732	53	2,809	7.280
4	16	2.000	54	2,916	7.348
5	25	2.236	55	3,025	7.416
6	36	2.449	56	3,136	7.483
7	49	2.646	57	3,249	7.550
8	64	2.828	58	3,364	7.616
9	81	3.000	59	3,481	7.681
10	100	3.162	60	3,600	7.746
11	121	3.317	61	3,721	7.810
12	144	3,464	62	3,844	7.874
13	169	3.606	63	3,969	7.937
14	196	3.742	64	4,096	8.000
15	225	3.873	65	4,225	8.062
16	256	4.000	66	4,356	8.124
17	289	4.123	67	4,489	8.185
18	324	4.243	68	4,624	8.246
19	361	4.359	69	4,761	8.307
20	400	4.472	70	4,900	8.367
21	441	4.583	71	5,041	8.426
22	484	4.690	72	5,184	8.485
23	529	4.796	73	5,329	8.544
24	576	4.899	74	5,476	8.602
25	625	5.000	75	5,625	8.660
26	676	5.099	76	5,776	8.718
27	729	5.196	77	5,929	8.775
28	784	5.292	78	6,084	8.832
29	841	5.385	79	6,241	8.888
30	900	5.477	80	6,400	8.944
31	961	5.568	81	6,561	9.000
32	1,024	5.657	82	6,724	9.055
33	1,089	5.745	83	6,889	9.110
34	1,156	5.831	84	7,056	9.165
35	1,225	5.916	85	7,225	9.220
36	1,296	6.000	86	7,396	9.274
37	1,369	6.083	87	7,569	9.327
38	1,444	6.164	88	7,744	9.381
39	1,521	6.245	89	7,921	9.343
40	1,600	6.325	90	8,100	9.487
41	1,681	6.403	91	8,281	9.539
42	1,764	6.481	92	8,464	9.592
43	1,849	6.557	93	8,649	9.644
44	1,936	6.633	94	8,836	9.695
45	2,025	6.708	95	9,025	9.747
46	2,116	6.782	96	9,216	9.798
47	2,209	6.856	97	9,409	9.849
48	2,304	6.928	98	9,604	9.899
49	2,401	7.000	99	9,801	9.950
50	2,500	7.071	100	10,000	10.000

TABLE B Normal Curve Areas

z	.00	.01	.02	.03	.04	.05	.06	.07	.08	.09
0.0	.0000	.0040	.0080	.0120	.0160	.0199	.0239	.0279	.0319	.0359
0.1	.0398	.0438	.0478	.0517	.0557	.0596	.0636	.0675	.0714	.0753
0.2	.0793	.0832	.0871	.0910	.0948	.0987	.1026	.1064	.1103	.1141
0.3	.1179	.1217	.1255	.1293	.1331	.1368	.1406	.1443	.1480	.1517
0.4	.1554	.1591	.1628	.1664	.1700	.1736	.1772	.1808	.1844	.1879
0.5	.1915	.1950	.1985	.2019	.2054	.2088	.2123	.2157	.2190	.2224
0.6	.2257	.2291	.2324	.2357	.2389	.2422	.2454	.2486	.2517	.2549
0.7	.2580	.2611	.2642	.2673	.2704	.2734	.2764	.2794	.2823	.2852
0.8	.2881	.2910	.2939	.2967	.2995	.3023	.3051	.3078	.3106	.3133
0.9	.3159	.3186	.3212	.3238	.3264	.3289	.3315	.3340	.3365	.3389
1.0	.3413	.3438	.3461	.3485	.3508	.3531	.3554	.3577	.3599	.3621
1.1	.3643	.3665	.3686	.3708	.3729	.3749	.3770	.3790	.3810	.3830
1.2	.3849	.3869	.3888	.3907	.3925	.3944	.3962	.3980	.3997	.4015
1.3	.4032	.4049	.4066	.4082	.4099	.4115	.4131	.4147	.4162	.4177
1.4	.4192	.4207	.4222	.4236	.4251	.4265	.4279	.4292	.4306	.4319
1.5	.4332	.4345	.4357	.4370	.4382	.4394	.4406	.4418	.4429	.4441
1.6	.4452	.4463	.4474	.4484	.4495	.4505	.4515	.4525	.4535	.4545
1.7	.4554	.4564	.4573	.4582	.4591	.4599	.4608	.4616	.4625	.4633
1.8	.4641	.4649	.4656	.4664	.4671	.4678	.4686	.4693	.4699	.4706
1.9	.4713	.4719	.4726	.4732	.4738	.4744	.4750	.4756	.4761	.4767
2.0	.4772	.4778	.4783	.4788	.4793	.4798	.4803	.4808	.4812	.4817
2.1	.4821	.4826	.4830	.4834	.4838	.4842	.4846	.4850	.4854	.4857
2.2	.4861	.4864	.4868	.4871	.4875	.4878	.4881	.4884	.4887	.4890
2.3	.4893	.4896	.4898	.4901	.4904	.4906	.4909	.4911	.4913	.4916
2.4	.4918	.4920	.4922	.4925	.4927	.4929	.4931	.4932	.4934	.4936
2.5	.4938	.4940	.4941	.4943	.4945	.4946	.4948	.4949	.4951	.4952
2.6	.4953	.4955	.4956	.4957	.4959	.4960	.4961	.4962	.4963	.4964
2.7	.4965	.4966	.4967	.4968	.4969	.4970	.4971	.4972	.4973	.4974
2.8	.4974	.4975	.4976	.4977	.4977	.4978	.4979	.4979	.4980	.4981
2.9	.4981	.4982	.4982	.4983	.4984	.4984	.4985	.4985	.4986	.4986
3.0	.4987	.4987	.4987	.4988	.4988	.4989	.4989	.4989	.4990	.4990

TABLE C* Values of *r* at the 5 Percent and 1 Percent Levels of Significance

Degrees of Freedom (d.f.)	5%	1%	Degrees of Freedom (d.f.)	5%	1%
1	.997	1.000	21	.413	.526
2	.950	.990	22	.404	.515
3	.878	.959	23	.396	.505
4	.811	.917	24	.388	.496
5	.754	.874	25	.381	.487
6	.707	.834	26	.374	.478
7	.666	.798	27	.367	.470
8	.632	.765	28	.361	.463
9	.602	.735	29	.355	.456
10	.576	.708	30	.349	.449
11	.553	.684	35	.325	.418
12	.532	.661	40	.304	.393
13	.514	.641	45	.288	.372
14	.497	.623	50	.273	.354
15	.482	.606	60	.250	.325
16	.468	.590	70	.232	.302
17	.456	.575	80	.217	.283
18	.444	.561	90	.205	.267
19	.433	.549	100	.195	.254
20	.423	.537			

Excerpts from R. A. Fisher, *Statistical Methods for Research Workers*, Table V-A, published by Oliver and Boyd, Edinburgh. Printed by permission of the author and publisher.

A Glossary of
Measurement Terms*

Ability The power to perform a designated responsive act. The power may be potential or actual, native or acquired. The term implies that the act can be performed now, without further training, if the necessary circumstances are present.

Aptitude is the capacity to acquire proficiency with training.

Capability, like *capacity*, refers to maximum ability with further training. Capability applies more particularly to potentialities for the near future.

Capacity is potential ability.

Proficiency is the degree of ability already acquired.

Skill is the efficient performance of mental or physical tasks.

Talent is a relatively high order of aptitude. It refers to an individual's susceptibility to an unusually high degree of training.

Genius is superlative ability to invent, originate, or execute. Genius is not a class or type by itself, but is found in the topmost range of the distribution of human abilities.

Achievement age The performance level or achievement test score expressed in terms of the chronological age group for which this performance level or achievement test score is average. If a given score on an achievement test corresponds to an achievement age of 11 years, 2 months, pupils 11 years, 2 months, on the average, will earn this score.

Achievement test A test that measures the amount a pupil has achieved in one or more subject fields or in the general aspects of schooling.

Adjustment inventory Usually a self-report instrument used to uncover personal and social adjustment problems. Synonymous with Personality Test, Mental Health Analysis and Temperament Test.

Age norm Values or scores representing typical or average performance for individuals classified according to chronological age, usually expressed as

*By permission of the publisher, CTB/McGraw-Hill Book Company, Monterey, California.

central tendencies, percentiles, standard scores, or stanines. In achievement tests, which are standardized by grades, it is the "age equivalent" for grades, with interpolation between given reference points. (See *norms*.)

Age-Grade table A table showing the relationship between the chronological ages of pupils and the school grade in which they are classified.

Alternate-Form reliability A measure of the extent to which two equivalent or parallel forms of a test are consistent with each other in measuring whatever they do measure. See *reliability*.

Anticipated achievement* the Anticipated Achievement of a student is the grade placement value obtained from the Anticipated Achievement Grade Placement Norms by using the chronological age, mental age, and school grade classification of the student. This Anticipated Achievement Grade Placement value, when determined for a student, is interpreted as the achievement performance typical of a homogeneous nationwide sample of students who have the same chronological age, mental age, and school grade classification of this particular student. Thus, it is possible, through the use of the Anticipated Achievement Grade Placement Norms to establish a performance standard for an individual student. See *anticipated achievement grade placement norms*.

Anticipated achievement grade placement norms* Anticipated Achievement Grade Placement Norms are systems of norms developed for an achievement test through standardization of the achievement test jointly with a test of mental maturity so that typical achievement test performance may be established for specific groups homogeneous with respect to chronological age, mental age, and school grade classification. See *anticipated achievement*.

Arithmetic mean The sum of a set of scores divided by the number of scores.

Articulated tests A series of tests in which different levels of the test are used for different ages or grades and which have been constructed and standardized so that the same or comparable elements or objectives are measured in the overlapping ranges among the various levels of the test. Well articulated tests have considerable overlapping from level to level in order to test the wide ranges of abilities and achievements in any given grade or class. A well articulated series of test batteries yields the same *derived scores* on a given grade group when either a lower or higher level of the test is used.

Battery A group of several tests of which the results are of value individually, in combination, and/or totally. When the tests have been standardized on the same population, the norms are usually called "integrated."

Ceiling The upper limit of ability that can be measured by a test. Individuals are said to have reached the ceiling of a test when they have abilities that are above the highest performance level at which the test can make reliable discriminations. When the ceiling of a test is reached with an individual or group, the next higher level of the test should be used.

Centile A value on the scoring scale below which are any given percentage of cases. According to some statisticians, the term *centile* is often superfluously called percentile. See *percentile*.

Chronological age equivalent The mean or median test score for a specified chronological age group. See *derived scores*.

*Introduced in 1957 by Dr. William M. Shanner.

Chronological age grade placement A scale indicating the relationship between chronological age and school grade. For any school grade and month in grade, a chronological age equivalent, in years and months or months, may be assigned which represents the average chronological age of pupils classified at this grade placement.

Class interval The divisions of a frequency distribution bounded by upper and lower score values. See *frequency distribution.*

Correction for guessing A technique devised to adjust the number of right answers for a test by using some portion of the wrong answers. The assumption is made that if an examinee guesses on an objective test, the number of right and wrong answers resulting will be proportional to the number of alternate responses in each item. Common correction formulas are

$$R - \frac{W}{3}, \quad R - W, \quad R - \frac{W}{2}.$$

Correlation Coefficient (r) This is the most commonly used measure of relationship between paired facts or of the tendency of two or more variables, or attributes to go hand-in-hand. It ranges in value from -1.00 for perfect negative relationship through 0.00 for none or pure chance to $+1.00$ for perfect positive relationship. Examples are Pearson Product Moment, Bi-Serial, Tetrachoric, Phi.

Criterion A standard, norm, or judgment used as a basis for quantitative and qualitative comparison.

Cross-Validation The process of checking whether a decision derived from one set of data is truly effective when this decision is applied to another independent, but relevant, set of data. Not to be confused with cross-comparison which is the process of comparing the results from two different tests, with neither being considered the criterion instrument.

Decile One of the nine points that divide a ranked distribution into ten parts, each containing one-tenth of all classes. Decile rank is the rank order of the 10 divisions. Thus, the 1st decile rank is the rank of those below the 1st decile point, the 5th decile rank below the 5th decile point, and the 10th decile rank is of those at or above the 9th decile point. See *centile, percentile.*

Decile Point	Percentile	Decile Rank	Percentile Rank
9	90	10	90–99
8	80	9	80–89
7	70	8	70–79
6	60	7	60–69
5	50	6	50–59
4	40	5	40–49
3	30	4	30–39
2	20	3	20–29
1	10	2	10–19
		1	0–9

Derived score A score that has been converted from a qualitative or quantitative mark on one scale into the units of another scale.

1. *Grade Placement Equivalent*
2. *Chronological Age Equivalent*
3. *Chronological Age Grade Placement*
4. *Educational Age*
5. *Intelligence Quotient (IQ)*
6. *Intelligence (MA) Grade Placement*
7. *Mental Age*
8. *Percentile Rank*
9. *Standard Score* (Sigma score, *T*-score, *Z*-score)
10. *Anticipated Achievement Grade Placement*

Deviation I.Q. A measure of intelligence based on the extent to which an individual's score deviates from a score that is normal for the individual's age.

Diagnostic test A test intended for the separate measurement of specific aspects of achievement in a single subject or field. Such tests yield measures of specific skills, knowledges, or abilities underlying achievement within a broad subject. Diagnostic tests are designed to identify particular strengths and weaknesses of an individual. See *prognostic tests, survey tests, ability*.

Difficulty value The percent of a specified group who answer a test item correctly.

Discriminating power The ability of a test item to differentiate between individuals possessing much of some characteristic (skill, knowledge, attitude) from those possessing little of the characteristic.

Duel standardization The procedure of standardizing two tests simultaneously on one sample, thereby integrating the two instruments.

Educational age A pupil's achievement test score expressed in terms of the chronological age group for which his achievement score is average.

Equated scores Derived scores that are comparable from test to test; e.g., Standard Scores, Grade Placements, Mental Ages, etc.

Error of estimate (standard or probable) An expression for the degree to which test scores estimated from a criterion would expect to correspond to scores actually made on the test. See *standard error of measurement*.

Evaluation program The testing, measuring, and appraisal of the growth, adjustment, and achievement of the learner by means of tests and many non-test instruments and techniques. It involves the identification and formulation of a comprehensive set of major objectives of a curriculum, their definition in terms of pupil behavior, and the selection or construction of valid, reliable, and practical instruments for appraising specified phases of pupil behavior. Evaluation includes integrating and interpreting the various evidences of behavior stability and behavior changes into an over-all picture of an individual or of an education situation. An adequate educational evaluation program is one (1) that is comprehensive and well-balanced in terms of both the learner and the curriculum; (2) that is continuous and well-articulated from the first grade through the secondary grades; (3) that is functional and practical for those using it; and (4) that uses integrated and scientific measuring instruments and techniques.

Evaluation and measurement are not synonymous terms. The emphasis in measurement is upon single aspects of subject-matter achievement or specific skills and abilities; emphasis in evaluation is upon broad personality changes and major objectives of the educational program.

Expectancy norms Any of various methods for adjusting achievement test norms with respect to mental ability and chronological age and/or other characteristics of the person or persons to whom the tests are given. See *anticipated achievement grade placement norms.*

Expected grade placement (XGP)* A computed score representing the achievement test performance of an individual based on a regression technique which is a function of both mental age and chronological age and expressed in grade placement units.

Extrapolation A process of estimating values of a function beyond the range of available data.

Face validity Refers to the acceptability of the test and test situation by the examinee or user, in terms of apparent uses to which the test is to be put. A test has face validity when it appears to measure the variable to be tested.

Factor analysis A method (centroid, grouping, principal components) of analyzing the intercorrelations among a set of variables such as test scores. Factor analysis attempts to account for the interrelationships in terms of some underlying "factors," preferably fewer in number than the original variables. It reveals how much of the variation in each of the original measures arises from or is associated with each of the hypothetical factors.

Factored test A test battery for which several scores representing different factors of ability, established by factor analysis, are obtained.

Frequency distribution A tabulation of scores from high to low (or low to high) showing the number of persons who obtain each score or group of scores.

Grade norm The average test score obtained by pupils classified at a given grade placement.

Grade placement equivalent A score or a scale developed to indicate the school grade and month in that school grade which is then assigned to the average chronological age, mental age, test score, or other characteristics of pupils classified at this school grade. A grade placement equivalent of 6.4 is interpreted as the fourth month of the sixth grade.

Intellectual status index A statistically derived index number which indicates the extent to which the chronological age and mental ability of a pupil differ from the chronological age and mental ability characteristics of the basic norming sample for the grade involved. An Intellectual Status Index of 100 indicates that a pupil's chronological age and mental ability characteristics are equivalent to those of the basic norming sample. Values above and below 100 indicate superior and inferior characteristics respectively in an individual pupil as compared with the basic norming sample. See *anticipated achievement.*

Intelligence The ability to perceive and understand relationships, such as logical, spatial, verbal, numerical, and recall of associated meanings. Also called academic aptitude, *scholastic aptitude, mental ability, capacity, and mental maturity.* The types of tests that are used to measure various kinds of intelligence are illustrated below using the *California Short-Form Test of Mental Maturity* as an example:

*Introduced by Dr. Alice M. Horn.

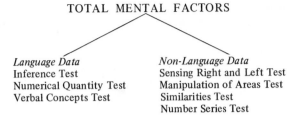

TOTAL MENTAL FACTORS

Language Data
Inference Test
Numerical Quantity Test
Verbal Concepts Test

Non-Language Data
Sensing Right and Left Test
Manipulation of Areas Test
Similarities Test
Number Series Test

Using the same test as an example, the tests that contribute to four mental factors are shown below:

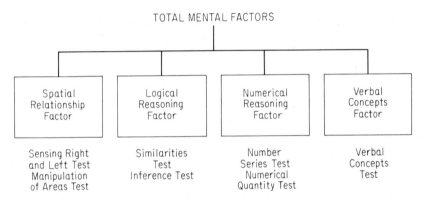

TOTAL MENTAL FACTORS

Spatial Relationship Factor	Logical Reasoning Factor	Numerical Reasoning Factor	Verbal Concepts Factor
Sensing Right and Left Test Manipulation of Areas Test	Similarities Test Inference Test	Number Series Test Numerical Quantity Test	Verbal Concepts Test

Intelligence quotient (IQ) A measure of potential rate of growth up to 16 years of age, expressed as the ratio of mental age to chronological age. The formula is

$$IQ = \frac{MA}{CA} \times 100$$

For ages over 16 years, 192 months is used as the chronological age, the evidence being that, on the average, mental maturity does not increase materially with further increases in chronological age. See mental age.

Intelligence (MA) grade placement (IGP) A mental age scale expressed in terms of the grade placements for which the mental age is average. The IGP for an individual is found by entering a table with the person's mental age and reading the IGP equivalent for the mental age. The mental age grade placement scale, for the California Test of Mental Maturity, corresponds exactly to the chronological age grade placement scale for all values up to and including 9.0 grade placement (MA = CA = 172 months), since at these grades the average IQ is assumed to be 100. Beyond 9.0 the mental age increases more rapidly than the chronological age due to the selection of individuals who remain in school at these higher grade levels. At CA 192 months and higher the mental age and consequent IGP are determined by 192 times the median IQ of the respective grades. At 16.7 grade placement, the grade placement scale is discontinued. Higher mental age grade placement is expressed at this point upward in terms of college graduate percentiles.

Interpolation A process of estimating intermediate values between two known points. In the example, a Mental Age value of 205, by interpolation, would be assigned a MA Grade Placement of 12.9.

EXAMPLE

Mental Age	MA Grade Placement
202	12.5
204	12.8
206	13.0
208	13.2

Item analysis Anyone of several methods used in test construction to determine how well a given test item discriminates among individuals differing in some characteristic. The effectiveness of a test item depends upon three factors: (1) the validity of the item in regards to curriculum content and educational objectives; (2) the discriminating power of the item in regards to validity and internal consistency; (3) the difficulty of the item. See criterion.

Mean The sum of a set of scores divided by the number of scores.

Median The middle score in a set of ranked scores. It is the point above or below which an equal number of ranked scores lie. It corresponds to the 50th percentile.

Mental age The chronological age for which a given score on an intelligence test is average or normal. A raw score of 51 on the Language tests of the CTMM, Junior High Level, corresponds to a mental age of 160 months (13 yrs., 4 mos.). The typical individual in the standardization sample who was 160 months old obtained an average raw score of 51 on the Language part of the test.

Mental age grade placement See *intelligence grade placement, chronological age grade placement, anticipated achievement.*

Mental maturity Intelligence, mental ability. See *intelligence.*

Mode The score or value that occurs most frequently in a distribution.

Normal distribution curve A derived curve based on the assumption that variations from the mean are by chance. It is bell-shaped in form and adopted as true because of its repeated recurrence in the frequency distributions of sets of measurements of human characteristics in psychology and education. It has many useful mathematical properties. In a normal distribution curve, scores are distributed symmetrically about the mean, as many cases at various equal distances above the mean as below the mean, and with cases concentrated near the average and decreasing in frequency the further one departs from it. (See page 339).

Normalized standard score Usually called *T*-scores, made to conform to standard score values of a normal distribution curve by use of percentile equivalents of the normal curved area; and most frequently expressed with a mean equated to 50 and a standard deviation equated to 10. (See p. 339.)

Norms Summarized statistics that describe the test performance of reference groups of pupils of various ages or grades in the standardization group for the test. Grade, age, standard score, and percentile are common types of norms. See *derived scores.*

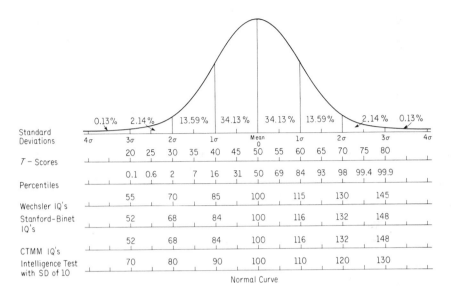

Normal Curve

Omnibus test A test in which items measuring a variety of mental operations are all combined into a single sequence rather than being grouped together by type of operation. The test has one time limit and yields a single score.

Percentile One of the 99 point scores that divide a ranked distribution into groups, each of which contains 1/100 of the scores. A percentile rank is a person's rank in a standard group of 100 persons representative of the full range of the normative population. If a person obtains a percentile rank of 70, his standing is regarded as equaling or surpassing 70 percent of the normative group on which the test was standardized; a percentile rank score of 70 may also be interpreted to mean that 30 percent of the normative group excel this person's test performance. See *centile, decile.*

Performance test Broadly speaking, every test is a performance test whether the performance is oral responses to questions, written responses to an essay test or an objective test, or the application of manual skills in a test situation. However, pencil-and-paper or oral tests are not usually regarded as performance tests. Performance tests generally require the use and manipulation of physical objects and the application of physical and manual skills in situations not restricted to oral and written responses. Shorthand or typing tests in which the response called for is similar to the behavior about which information is desired exemplify work-sample tests which are a type of performance test.

Personality The sum total of everything that constitutes a person's mental, emotional, and temperamental make-up. Personality refers to the manner and effectiveness with which the whole individual meets his personal and social problems, and indirectly the manner in which he impresses his fellows. Personality adjustment status has been evaluated by three levels of projection: Level 1, direct or rationalized questions like the *California Test of Personality* or the *Mental Health Analysis*; Level 2, incomplete sentences or pictures; Level 3, ink blots, clouds, *S-O Rorschach Test.*

Phi coefficient (ϕ) A product-moment correlation coefficient computed from a 4-fold table (double dichotomy). Frequently the dichotomy is between passing or failing a test item and is interpreted as the discrimination effectiveness.

Potentiality Latent power. See *ability, aptitude, capacity.*

Power test A test which is designed to sample the range of an examinee's capacity in particular skills or abilities and which places minimal emphasis on time limits.

Probable error (PE) A value obtained by multiplying the standard error by 0.6745. This provides a value so that a range of one probable error on either side of the mean of a normal distribution includes exactly 50 percent of the cases. Two PE units equal 82 percent of the cases; three PE units equal 95.7 percent of the cases; four PE units equal 99.3 percent of the cases, or "physical certainty."

Prognostic test A test used to predict future success or failure in a specific subject or field. The test usually measures the skills and abilities that are prerequisite for success in the particular subject or task. See *aptitude.*

Projective technique A test situation in which the subject responds to stimuli such as ink-blots, pictures, incomplete sentences, or clouds, in such a manner that he "projects" into his responses manifestations of personality characteristics. See *personality.*

Random sample A sample drawn in such a way that every member of the population has an equal chance of being included, thus eliminating bias of selection. A random sample is "representative" of its total population.

Range The difference reflected by noting the lowest and the highest scores obtained on a test by some group.

Readiness test A test of ability to engage in a new type of specific learning. Level of maturity, previous experience, and mental and emotional set are important factors in readiness.

Reference population The total population from which a sample is selected for measurement. The term is synonymous with Standardization Population. For the *California Test of Mental Maturity* and the *California Achievement Tests*, the standardization or reference population is the total pupil enrollment in public schools (grades one through twelve) in the United States. See *standardization sample.*

Regression effect Tendency for a predicted score to be relatively nearer the mean of its series than the score from which it was predicted is to the mean of its series. For example, if we predict school marks from an intelligence test, we will find that for all pupils who have IQs two standard deviations above the mean, the mean of their predicted school marks will be less than two standard deviations from the mean of the school marks.

Reliability The degree to which a pupil would obtain the same score if the test were readministered to the pupil (assuming no additional learning, practice effects, etc.); trustworthiness of scores. Several types of reliability coefficients should be distinguished:

    (a) *Coefficient of internal consistency* refers to a measure based on internal analysis of data obtained on a single trial of a test. More prominent of these are the analysis of variance method (Kuder-Richardson, Hoyt) and the split-half method.

(b) *Coefficient of equivalence* refers to a correlation between scores from two forms given at essentially the same time.

(c) *Coefficient of stability* refers to a correlation between test and retest with some period of time intervening. The test-retest situation may be with two forms of the same test.

Scaled score A unit in a system of equated scores established for the raw scores of a test so that the scaled score values may themselves be interpreted usually as representative of the mean performance of certain reference groups and so that intervals between any pair of scaled scores may be interpreted as differences in terms of the characteristics of the reference group.

Scaled test (1) A test in which the items are arranged in an order of increasing difficulty. (2) May also refer to a test whose items are assigned weights or values according to the difficulty of the item.

Scholastic aptitude A combination of native and acquired abilities that is needed to do school work. See *intelligence*.

Sigma (σ) Designation for *standard error* and most frequently applied to *standard deviation*.

Skewness The degree to which a unimodal (one-peak) curve departs from symmetry.

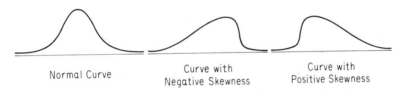

Normal Curve   Curve with   Curve with
                      Negative Skewness   Positive Skewness

Sociometry Measurement of the interpersonal relationships existing among the members of a group. One of the simplest sociometric methods is the "Guess Who" device. This is a test, used first by Hartshorne and May, consisting of descriptions of roles played by children; each child in the group responds to each description by naming any child he thinks the description fits. Another instrument, the *Bonney-Fessenden Sociograph*, is a device for studying the social structure of groups by identifying cliques, hierarchies of leadership, and other social groupings.

Speed test A test in which performance is measured by the number of tasks performed in a given time.

Split-half coefficient A measure of estimating the reliability of a power test by splitting it into comparable halves (usually the odd-numbered items and the even-numbered items, whose respective means and variances are equal), correlating the scores of the two halves, and applying the Spearman-Brown prophecy formula to estimate the correlation. See *reliability*.

Standard A level of performance agreed upon by experts or established by local school personnel as a goal of pupil attainment. Not to be confused with norm. See *norms*.

Standard deviation (S.D.) It is a statistic used to express the extent of the deviations from the mean for the distribution. It is obtained by taking the square root of the mean of the squares of the deviations from the mean of a distribution. If the group tested is a normal one their scores, if plotted graphically, would yield a normal distribution curve. Approximately two-thirds (68.3 percent) of the scores would lie within the limits of one standard deviation above and one standard deviation below the mean. One-third of the scores would be above the mean by one standard deviation, and one-third below the mean by one standard deviation. About 95 percent of the scores lie within the limits of two standard deviations above and below the mean. About 99.7 percent of the cases lie within the limits of three standard deviations above and below the mean.

Standard error of measurement Indicates how closely the individual's score compares with his true score. If the standard error is 3.0, the chances are 2 to 1 that the score lies within 3.0 points either way of his true score, or 19 to 1 that it is not more than 6.0 points (2 times *standard error of measurement*) from his true score.

Standardization of test battery Involves the assignment of a system of derived scores of the tests to facilitate interpretation of the test in terms of reference populations. In the standardization of the California Achievement Tests there were two specific steps: (1) the establishment of a longitudinal scale of grade placement values from grades 1.0 to 16.5, whose function it is to measure the relative status of pupils in relationship to the typical performance of pupils of known school-grade classification, chronological age, and mental ability; and (2) the establishment of a percentile scale at specific school grades, whose function it is to indicate the variation in test scores found for the total population of pupils classified in the same school grade.

Standardization sample Refers to that part of the reference population which is selected for use in norming a test. This sample should be representative of the reference population in essential characteristics, such as geographical representation, age, and grade.

Standardized test A test that is composed of empirically selected materials, has definite directions for administration, scoring, and use, data on reliability and validity, and has adequately determined norms.

Standard score (sigma score, T-score, Z-score) A score expressed as a deviation from the mean in terms of the standard deviation of the distribution (raw score minus the mean, divided by the standard deviation). See *normalized standard score.*

Stanines A unit that divides the norm population into nine groups. Except for Stanines 1 and 9, the groups are spaced in half-sigma units, with the mean at Stanine 5.

Stanine	1	2	3	4	5	6	7	8	9
Percent in stanine	4	7	12	17	20	17	12	7	4

Stratified sample A sample in which cases are selected by the use of certain controls, such as geographical region, community size, grade, age, sex, etc.

Survey test A test that measures general achievement in a given subject area. It is used to test skills and abilities of widely varying types. A survey test may also yield diagnostic information. See *Diagnostic test.*

T-score A derived score based upon the equivalence of percentile values to standard scores, thus avoiding the effects of skewed distributions, and usually having a mean equated to 50 and a standard deviation equated to 10.

Transmutation of scores The changing of scores from various tests to a common or equivalent scale so that the scores may be compared or combined.

Validity A test is valid to the extent that we know what it measures or predicts. The two basic approaches to the determination of validity—logical analysis and empirical analysis—are diagrammed below:

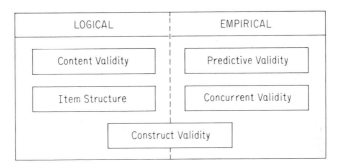

Content validity refers to how well the content of the test samples the subject matter or situation about which conclusions are to be drawn. Content validity is especially important in an achievement test.

> Examples: textbook analysis, description of the universe of items, adequacy of the sample, representatives of test content, inter-correlations of sub-scores, opinions of jury of experts.

Construct validity concerns the psychological qualities a test measures. By both logical and empirical methods, the theory underlying the test is validated.

> Examples: correlations of the test score with other test scores, factor analysis, use of a personality or interest inventory to describe a person, studying the effect of speed on test scores.

Concurrent validity refers to how well test scores match measures of contemporary criterion performance.

> Examples: comparing distribution of scores for men in an occupation with those for men-in-general, correlation of personality test scores with estimates of adjustments made in the counseling interviews, correlation of end-of-course achievement or ability test scores with school marks.

Item structure includes (1) corroborative evidence from *item analysis* supporting the other characteristics of the test; i.e., the interrelationahips between items and scores, and between items and criteria are factors that contribute to the content validity of the test, and (2) item composition. For graphic items, this emphasizes perceptual clarity and related format functions. For verbal items, it emphasizes conceptual clarity in the expression of items. And for both graphic and verbal items it emphasizes the functions of distracters.

Predictive validity relates to how well predictions made from the test are confirmed by data collected at a later time.

> Examples: correlation of intelligence test scores with course grades, correlation of test scores obtained at beginning of the year with marks earned at the end of the year.

Variability   The spread or dispersion of scores, usually indicated by quartile deviations, standard deviations, range of 90–10 percentile scores, etc.

Work-Limit test   A test on which sufficient time is allowed for all or nearly all pupils to complete their work.

Indexes

AUTHOR INDEX

SUBJECT INDEX

DATE			
MAR 1 5 1996			